T0324195

INFORMATION AND COMPLEXITY

World Scientific Series in Information Studies
(ISSN: 1793-7876)

Series Editor: Mark Burgin *(University of California, Los Angeles, USA)*

International Advisory Board:

Søren Brier *(Copenhagen Business School, Copenhagen, Denmark)*
Tony Bryant *(Leeds Metropolitan University, Leeds, United Kingdom)*
Gordana Dodig-Crnkovic *(Mälardalen University, Eskilstuna, Sweden)*
Wolfgang Hofkirchner *(ICT&S Center, University of Salzburg, Salzburg, Austria)*
William R King *(University of Pittsburgh, Pittsburgh, USA)*

World Scientific Series in Information Studies — **Vol. 6**

INFORMATION AND COMPLEXITY

Edited by

Mark Burgin
University of California, Los Angeles, USA

Cristian S Calude
University of Auckland, New Zealand

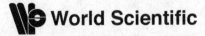

World Scientific

NEW JERSEY · LONDON · SINGAPORE · BEIJING · SHANGHAI · HONG KONG · TAIPEI · CHENNAI · TOKYO

Published by

World Scientific Publishing Co. Pte. Ltd.

5 Toh Tuck Link, Singapore 596224

USA office: 27 Warren Street, Suite 401-402, Hackensack, NJ 07601

UK office: 57 Shelton Street, Covent Garden, London WC2H 9HE

Library of Congress Cataloging-in-Publication Data
Names: Burgin, M. S. (Mark Semenovich) | Calude, Cristian, 1952–
Title: Information and complexity / [edited by] Mark Burgin (UCLA), Cristian S. Calude
    (University of Auckland, New Zealand).
Description: New Jersey : World Scientific, 2016. | Series: World scientific
    series in information studies ; volume 6
Identifiers: LCCN 2016023758 | ISBN 9789813109025 (hc : alk. paper)
Subjects: LCSH: Information theory. | Computational complexity.
Classification: LCC Q360 .I5275 2016 | DDC 003/.54--dc23
LC record available at https://lccn.loc.gov/2016023758

British Library Cataloguing-in-Publication Data
A catalogue record for this book is available from the British Library.

Desk Editors: V. Vishnu Mohan/Tan Rok Ting

Typeset by Stallion Press
Email: enquiries@stallionpress.com

Printed in Singapore

Contents

Contents vii

Preface

The Interplay Between Information and Complexity

Although today information and complexity have become popular and important notions in science and society, experts agree that it is hard (if not impossible, as some think) to define them (Capurro *et al.*, 1999; Capurro and Hjorland, 2003; Gell-Mann and Lloyd, 1996; Burgin, 2010). At the same time, a diversity of definitions have been suggested for both terms. For instance, 130 definitions of data, information and knowledge formulated by 45 scholars are collected in Zins (2007), while a variety of approaches to define information appears in the book of Burgin (2010) and in the encyclopedia article of Bates (2010).

Information is related to everything and everything is related to information. Why is it so difficult to define information? There are many factors contributing, including the diversity of information types, contradictory usages of the term information and the confusion between information and data or knowledge, on the one hand, and information carriers (such as messages) and information measures (such as Shannon's entropy), on the other hand. An endeavor to create a general theory of information based on a system of postulates (principles) is presented in Burgin (2010) and in the mathematical form in Burgin (2010a).

Similarly, there is no general definition of complexity. The "symptom" or "mark" of complexity is generally associated with some action. The complexity of a system or process is related to some ways to describe it, to build it, to control it, and so on. High complexity appears in systems composed of many parts, which interact with each other in multiple ways. However, when the action is, for example, the possibility to give an algorithmic description of a system, the complexity can be low because a simple algorithm can describe the system.

Complexity can be dynamic, like time or space complexity, or descriptive, as size complexity. Complexity studies appear in a multitude of areas and domains including, but not restricted to:

(i) Computer science – computational complexity (Trakhtenbrot, 1956; Rabin, 1959), algorithmic information theory via Kolmogorov complexity (Solomonoff, 1964; Kolmogorov, 1965; Chaitin, 1977) and its generalizations), Boolean circuit complexity (Savage, 1976), structural complexity (Balcazar *et al.*, 1988), communication complexity (Yao, 1979);

(ii) Physics – statistical mechanics entropy (Lavenda, 2010);

(iii) Mathematics – Krohn–Rhodes complexity (Kambites, 2007);

(iv) Complex systems (Grassberger, 1990);

(v) Cognitive sciences (Isaac *et al.*, 2014).

The fact that there are many forms (definitions) of and approaches to complexity is not a weakness nor a sign of lack of maturity. Indeed, neither form of complexity is "better" than the other; they are just targeting different aspects. Studying the algorithmic complexity of the genetic code may help understanding the redundancy of the genetic code, its role in inheritance and evolution and could be used in genetic engineering problems. Studying the computational complexity of the process of translating the genetic code into anatomical details of a living being is different and important for other reasons.

The most popular theory of information is Shannon's theory (Shannon, 1949), which studies the transmission, processing, utilization, and extraction of information by a purely syntactic method, devoid of any meaning. Entropy, a key measure in this theory, quantifies the uncertainty involved in predicting the value of a random variable. The theory has the broadest range of applications, from engineering and data analysis to biology and linguistics.

Algorithmic information theory, based on the concept of Kolmogorov complexity or more generally, on the algorithmic complexity of objects, combines the theory of algorithms with Shannon's information theory by measuring the size of algorithmic descriptions of (finite or infinite) objects (Calude, 2002; Li and Vitanyi, 1997). The theory has been applied to a wide range of areas including theory of computation, physics, biology, economics, combinatorics, inductive reasoning, machine learning and cognitive sciences.

Information is intimately related to energy. According to John Wheeler, every physical quantity derives its ultimate significance and meaning from information. He aptly expressed it by "It from Bit", where It stands for things, while Bit refers to the most popular information unit (Wheeler, 1990). The principles of a general theory of information developed in Burgin (2003; 2010) demonstrate that energy is a kind of information in a broad sense.

There is also a very strong relation between complexity and information. As a simple observation, we note that measuring complexity is a way to understand information, while obtaining information helps to decrease the complexity. The duality between complexity and information plays an important role in impossibility results, which reflect infinite complexity and the inaccessibility of exact information. The impossibility of constructing a *perpetuum mobile* led to the notion of energy and to the development of thermodynamics, the impossibility of traveling faster than light was a starting point of relativity theory, and the impossibility of measuring the speed and position of a particle simultaneously is fundamental in quantum mechanics. The impossibility results regarding complexity and information – for example, the impossibility of solving the Halting Problem for Turing machines or, more generally, the undecidability results in computability theory (Cutland, 1980) – have far reaching consequences. The Halting Problem for Turing machines is the problem of deciding in *finite time* whether an arbitrary Turing machine stops or not on a given input. It is interesting to examine the reason of its undecidability from an informational perspective. The restriction to "finite time" is crucial and the problem can or cannot be solved depending on the tools processing the given information: Turing machine and input. If we use Turing machines to solve the problem, the given information remains inaccessible, hence the Halting Problem for Turing machines is undecidable. However, the more powerful inductive Turing machines can retrieve and "extract" this information to solve the Halting Problem for Turing machines (Burgin 2001). Furthermore, one can also "approximately" solve the Halting Problem with arbitrary precision (Calude and Dumitrescu 2015).

In this volume, leading researchers present recent results in a variety of areas related to information and complexity. The contributions are divided into three groups comprising three parts of the book: (1) classical information and complexity, (2) quantum information and complexity, and (3) complexity and information applications. Inside each group, the authors are ordered alphabetically.

The chapter "The 'Paradox' of Computability and a Recursive Relative Version of the Busy Beaver Function" by Felipe S. Abrahão studies relative properties of computability in the context of metabiology and total Turing machines. Metabiology is a field of theoretical computer science that studies general principles of biological relations at a meta-level using methods from evolutionary biology and algorithmic information theory (Chaitin, 2014). The author proves that a Busy Beaver function introduced by G. Chaitin behaves to total Turing machines in the "same" way as the original Busy Beaver function behaves to all Turing machines. This is termed a "paradox" of computability *a la* Löwenheim-Skolem (Löwenheim, 1915; Skolem, 1920) – a function that is computable when "seen from the outside" the subsystem, but incomputable when "seen from within" the same subsystem. This result is aimed at modeling biological phenomena. From the perspective of information, Abrahão illustrates how information inaccessible within a system becomes accessible in a larger system. From the viewpoint of complexity, this chapter shows how complexity of a problem is decreased from infinity to a finite quantity.

Shannon entropy has become the most popular measure of information. In his chapter "Inductive complexity and Shannon entropy", Mark Burgin studies another measure of information, called inductive complexity. This complexity is similar to Kolmogorov complexity: instead of Turing machines it uses inductive Turing machines, which are super-recursive algorithms because they can compute much more than recursive algorithms (Burgin, 2001). The main goal is to compare inductive complexity as a measure of information with Shannon entropy. It is proved that the average of the prefix inductive complexity $IK(x)$ with respect to an inductively computable probability distribution f is equal to Shannon entropy up to some additive constant that depends on f. A similar inequality was proved for recursively computable probability distributions and the conventional (Kolmogorov) prefix complexity (Grunwald and Vitanyi, 2004; Muchnik and Vereshchagin, 2006). The result proved in this chapter has the following advantages:

1. There are more inductively computable probability distributions than recursively computable probability distributions.
2. For infinitely many functions f, the estimate $IK(f)$ is more exact than the estimate $K(f)$ obtained prefix complexity because the value of $IK(f)$ is smaller than the value of $K(f)$ (Burgin, 2005).

Estimating relations between inductive complexity and Shannon entropy, Burgin uses only inductive Turing machines of the first order. However, there is an advanced hierarchy of inductive Turing machines (Burgin,

2005). Thus, it would be interesting to find relations between Shannon entropy and inductive complexity based on inductive Turing machines of higher orders.

One of the most important ways to understand information and complexity is through the axiomatic method. Axiomatic approach to complexity started with Blum, who defined the size of a machine as a direct complexity measure by two simple axioms (see (Blum, 1967) and the presentation in Calude (1988)). To develop axiomatic foundations for Kolmogorov complexity and algorithmic information theory, Burgin (1982) enhanced and expanded Blum's axioms to a system of five axioms building static dual complexity measures, which encompassed all known forms of algorithmic complexity. In his chapter "Blum's and Burgin's Axioms, Complexity, and Randomness", Cezar Câmpeanu explores relations between complexity, randomness and information in the context of the axiomatic theory of dual static complexity measures. The author uses this framework to reveal the important connections between information and complexity, on the one hand, and algorithmic randomness for infinite sequences, on the other hand.

In his chapter "Planckian Information (I_P): A Measure of the Order in Complex Systems", Sungchul Ji constructs a new information measure called Planckian information. He shows that Planckian information is a better measure of order in organized complex systems than either the Boltzmann-Gibbs entropy S or Shannon entropy H. This statement is supported with examples from atomic physics, protein folding, single-molecule enzymology, whole-cell mRNA metabolism, T-cell receptor variable region diversity, fMRI (Functional Magnetic Resonance Imaging), the quantitative study of words and texts, econophysics, and astrophysics.

In algorithmic information theory, complexity and randomness are studied for relatively simple objects such as sequences of symbols from a given alphabet. In the chapter "On Algorithmically Random Universal Algebras", Bakhadyr Khoussainov extends this approach to mathematical systems with additional structures, such as universal algebras, and develops an abstract mathematical framework for answering the following question: What is an algorithmically random infinite universal algebra? The proposed definition of algorithmic randomness for infinite universal algebras is based on Martin-Löf tests of randomness and its adequacy is justified by explication of some natural properties of random algebras.

In his chapter "Structural and Quantitative Characteristics of Complexity in Terms of Information", Marcin J. Schroeder studies issues related to overcoming or controlling complexity seen in the entire intellectual development of humanity, although, historically, the emphasis was on its opposition – simplicity. First, the author reviews various conceptualizations of complexity in the European philosophical and scientific tradition from Pre-Socratic thinkers of Antiquity to the present time. Special focus is given on the contributions of Aristotle whose works strongly influenced the view on reality of his followers, as well as of his adversaries. Then, this historical perspective is used for a critical summary of the ways complexity is studied today and for an attempt to provide a unified conceptual framework for the various forms of complexity considered in the past. To this purpose, the author uses the general concept of information developed in Schroeder (2005) as an identification of a variety and various concepts characterizing it. Finally, a quantitative description in the form of two related measures of complexity and information integration is presented.

In the chapter "Multiscale Information Theory for Complex Systems: Theory and Applications", Blake Stacey, Benjamin Allen and Yaneer Bar-Yam construct a mathematical formalism based on information theory to make precise the intuition that a complex system exhibits structure at multiple scales. They correctly assume that science in general and the science of complex systems, in particular, require a general way to understand and represent structure. Even in mathematics, the concept of structure is still in the process of development and a comprehensive mathematical representation of this concept is elaborated in the general theory of structures (Burgin, 2012).

This article treats structure as the totality of relationships between a system's components, which is according to the general theory of structures, a first-order inner structure of a system, and uses information theory to quantify these relationships. To this aim Stacey Allen and Bar-Yam create an axiomatic system for characterizing an information measure by developing quantitative indices – the complexity profile (CP) and the marginal utility of information (MUI) – which describe the system structure.

A complex system exhibits structure at many scales and levels of organization. For instance, one can study human beings at any magnification, from the molecular level to the societal. Thus, the concept of a scale becomes crucial and the authors of this chapter use the mathematical formalism developed in their previous work (Allen *et al.*, 2014) to operate with it. Often, *scale* is interpreted in terms of length or of time. However, in the context of system theory developed in this chapter, a scale reflects the number of components in the system. Besides, in the context of multiscale physics and scalable topology, a scale C of a system R is the theoretical (mathematical) structure used to model R (Burgin, 2006). This chapter also demonstrates the applications of the proposed theory to evolutionary biology, economics and finite geometry.

Kolmogorov complexity is one of the most important measures of information and complexity. In his chapter "Bounds on the Kolmogorov complexity function", Ludwig Staiger presents a detailed analysis of the Kolmogorov complexity function examining its bounds for maximally complex infinite sequences. Lower and upper bounds on the Kolmogorov complexity function are closely related to algorithmic randomness, in particular to partial randomness. The performed analysis provides interesting connections between information, complexity, Hausdorff dimension, fractal geometry and randomness.

The main goal of quantum information science is to use quantum phenomena to improve the performance of information processing systems. The current theoretical progress led in some cases to commercial applications. As Marco Lanzagorta and Jeffrey Uhlmann note in their chapter "Quantum Computational Complexity in Curved Spacetime", the "optimism about their potential advantage over classical alternatives is invariably founded on the theoretical analysis that implicitly assumes a flat spacetime operating environment, i.e., that their operations will not be influenced by local gravitation". However, gravity affects quantum information, hence, its role requires a careful analysis. This paper develops a new quantum computational complexity in which gravity is no longer ignored.

In her chapter "A Silk Road from Leibniz to Quantum Information", Rossella Lupacchini brings about interesting relations between the monads of Leibniz and qubits of contemporary quantum information theory exploring the meaning of the principles of continuity and distinguishability as well as of the notions of causality and correlation. From Leibniz's point of view, the ontological separation of *nature* and *thought*, which pervades the Western philosophy, violates the principle of continuity. Lupacchini compares Leibniz's pre-established harmony and the harmony emerging from Chinese "correlative thinking" in order to contrast the *principle of sufficient reason* with the Chinese *principle of connectedness*. According to Leibniz's metaphysics, there must be a reason to cause the harmony of monads, while in the ancient Chinese thought the fundamental harmony of the universe has no reason, it is a harmony of resonant possibilities. In this perspective, the divide between Leibniz's causal determinism and quantum randomness turns into a *coincidentia oppositorum*.

It might be helpful to frame Leibniz's *Monadology* in millennia of philosophical search for a "fundamental principle", unit or essence from which all things originate. Plato, for instance, conjectured that all things are drawn from triangles. Democritus asserted that everything is made from atoms. In his turn, Leibniz conceived monads as elementary constituents for all things. As a simple substance and a unity of perceptions, however, each monad encapsulates all information of the universe. Indeed, monads are viewed as "incorporeal automata". Now, as elements of things, the monads are "the true atoms of nature", but as they have neither extension nor shape, they are unobservable. In mathematical terms, the essential character of monads, which is continuous change, is captured by a unitary transformation demonstrating that it is intrinsically formed as a fundamental triad (Burgin, 2012). Thus, Lupacchini regards Leibniz's monads as remote ancestors of qubits, the building blocks of quantum information theory.

For the classical mind, quantum mechanics is boggling enough. Nevertheless, in the chapter "Generalized Event Structures and Probabilities", Karl Svozil studies an even more sophisticated world where basic structures can transcend the quantum domain. In it, predictions and probabilities are neither classical nor quantum, but are subject to sub-classicality, that is, the additivity of probabilities for mutually exclusive, co-measurable observables, is formalized by admissibility rules and frame functions. Starting with the Specker's oracle, Svozil develops an information-theoretic framework for analyzing a strange, but logically not impossible, universe through a calculus with generalized event structures and their probabilities.

In the chapter "An upper bound on the asymptotic complexity of global optimization of smooth univariate functions", James M. Calvin studies complexity of adaptive optimization algorithms using real-number model of computations. The main characteristic of adaptive algorithms is that to make the next step of computation, they utilize information gained in the previous steps. Efficient utilization of such information allows decreasing complexity of algorithms.

Set theory has no informational tools to distinguish between the "size" of the set of natural numbers and the "size" of the set of all even natural numbers. Intuitively, the size of the later set is one half of the size of the former one. Can this statement be rigorously proved? The answer is affirmative. A formal method introduced by Sergeyev uses the resource-based informational new language of Grossone to deal with infinities and infinitesimals in a computational way (Sergeyev, 2009). Another approach to the rigorous distinction between the "sizes" of the set of all natural numbers and the set of all even natural numbers is based on utilization of hypermeasures. Note that the measure of set is a kind of its complexity, while measuring provides information about this complexity. In their chapter "Cellular Automata and Grossone Computations", Louis D'Alotto and Yaroslav Sergeyev use the language of Grossone to perform computations on cellular automata. This allows measuring the quantity of information that can pass through a central viewing window under a cellular automaton rule.

In the chapter "Cognition and Complexity", Yuri Manin analyses scientific cognition as an information process by means of Kolmogorov complexity. The author shows that many scientific theories, from Ptolemy's epicycles to the Standard Model of elementary particles, consist of two distinct parts: the part with the relatively small Kolmogorov complexity ("laws", "basic equations", "periodic table", "natural selection, genotypes, mutations") and another part, of indefinitely large Kolmogorov complexity ("initial and boundary conditions", "phenotypes", "populations"). The data for the latter part are obtained by planned observations, focused experiments, and are afterwards collected in growing databases (formerly known as "books", "tables", "encyclopedias", etc.). The former part is meant to "make sense" of the latter one.

In his chapter "Informational Perspective on QBism and the Origins of Life", Koichiro Matsuno studies the interpretation of quantum mechanics called Quantum Bayesianism or QBism with the emphasis on the role of information in understanding quantum processes. Then Matsuno uses his approach as a tool for exploration of the origins of life as emergence of an observer of quantum processes considered in quantum mechanics.

Bibliography

Allen, B., Stacey, B. C. and Bar-Yam, Y. (2014) An information-theoretic formalism for multiscale structure in complex systems, arXiv:1409.4708 [cond-mat.stat-mech].

Balcazar, J.L., Diaz, J., and Gabarro, J. (1988) *Structural Complexity*, Springer-Verlag, Berlin/Heidelberg/ New York.

Bates, M. J. (2010) Information, in *Encyclopedia of Library and Information Sciences*, Third Edition, v. 1, pp. 2347-2360.

Blum, M. (1967) On the size of machines, *Information and Control*, v. 11, pp. 257-265.

Burgin, M. (2001) How We Know What Technology Can Do, *Communications of the ACM*, v. 44, No. 11, pp. 82-88.

Burgin, M. (2003) Information theory: a multifaceted model of information, *Entropy*, v. 5, No. 2, pp. 146-160.

Burgin, M. (2005) *Super-recursive Algorithms*, Springer, New York/Heidelberg/Berlin.

Burgin, M. (2006) Scalable Topological Spaces, 5th *Annual International Conference on Statistics, Mathematics and Related Fields, 2006 Conference Proceedings*, Honolulu, Hawaii, pp. 1865-1896.

Burgin, M. (2010) *Theory of Information: Fundamentality, Diversity and Unification*, World Scientific, New York/London/Singapore.

Burgin, M. (2010a) Information operators in categorical information spaces, *Information*, v. 1, No.1, pp. 119-152.

Burgin, M. (2012) *Structural Reality*, Nova Science Publishers, New York.

Calude, C (1988). *Theories of Computational Complexity*, North-Holland, Amsterdam.

Calude, C.S. (2002) *Information and Randomness: An Algorithmic Perspective*, Texts in Theoretical Computer Science. An EATCS Series, Springer-Verlag, Berlin.

Calude, C. S. and Dumitrescu, M. (2015) Two Anytime Algorithms for the Halting Problem, CDMTCS Research Report 493.

Capurro, R., Fleissner, P. and Hofkirchner, W. (1999) Is a Unified Theory of Information Feasible? in *The Quest for a unified theory of information, Proceedings of the 2nd International Conference on the Foundations of Information Science*, pp. 9-30.

Capurro, R. and Hjorland, B. (2003) The concept of information, *Annual Review of Information Science and Technology*, v. 37, No. 8, pp. 343-411.

Chaitin, G.J. (1977) Algorithmic information theory, *IBM Journal of Research and Development*, v. 21, No. 4, pp. 350-359.

Chaitin, G. J. (2014) *Conceptual Complexity and Algorithmic Information*, Federal University of Rio de Janeiro, Rio de Janeiro, Brazil.

Cutland, N. (1980) *Computability: An Introduction to Recursive Function Theory*, Cambridge University Press, Cambridge.

Gell-Mann, M. and Lloyd, S. (1996) Information measures, effective complexity and total information, *Complexity*, v. 2, No. 5, pp. 16-19.

Grassberger, P. (1990) Information and complexity measures in dynamical systems, in *Information Dynamics*, Plenum press, New York.

Grunwald, P. and Vitanyi, P. (2004) *Shannon Information and Kolmogorov Complexity*, preprint in Computer Science, arXiv:cs/0410002.

Isaac A.M.C, Szymanik J. and Verbrugge R. (2014) Logic and complexity in cognitive science, in A. Baltag and S. Smets (Eds.), *Johan van Benthem on Logic and Information Dynamics*, Springer, pp. 787-824.

Kambites, M. (2007) On the Krohn–Rhodes complexity of semigroups of upper triangular matrices, *International Journal of Algebra and Computation*, v. 17, No. 1, pp. 187–201.

Kolmogorov, A.N. (1965) Three approaches to the definition of the quantity of information, *Problems of Information Transmission*, No. 1, pp. 3-11.

Lavenda B. H. (2010) *A New Perspective on Thermodynamics*, Springer, Berlin.

Leibniz, G. W. (1989) *Philosophical Essays* (Ariew, R. and Garber, D. (Eds.)) Hackett Publishing Company, Indianapolis & Cambridge.

Li, M. and Vitanyi, P. (1997) *An Introduction to Kolmogorov Complexity and its Applications*, Springer-Verlag, New York.

Muchnik, An. and Vereshchagin, N. (2006) Shannon entropy vs. Kolmogorov complexity, *Lecture Notes in Computer Science*, v. 3967, pp. 281-291.

Schroeder, M. J. (2005) Philosophical foundations for the concept of information: selective and structural information, in *Proceedings of the Third International Conference on the Foundations of Information Science*, Paris, July 2005, (http://www.mdpi.org/fis2005/proceedings.html).

Sergeyev, Y. (2009) Numerical computations and mathematical modeling within finite and in infinitesimal numbers, *Journal of Applied Mathematics and Computing* 29, pp. 177-195.

Skolem, T. (1920) Logisch-kombinatorische Untersuchungen über die Erfüllbarkeitoder Beweisbarkeit mathematischer Sätze nebst einem Theoreme über dichte Mengen, *Videnskapsselskapet Skrifter*, I. *Matematisk-naturvidenskabelig Klasse*, v. 4, pp. 1–36.

Solomonoff, R.J. (1964) A formal theory of inductive inference, *Information and Control*, v. 7, No. 1, pp. 1-22; No. 2, pp. 224-254.

Trakhtenbrot, B.A. (1956) Signalizing functions and tabular operators. *Uchionnye Zapiski Penzenskogo Pendinstituta (Transactions of the Penza Pedagogical Institute)*, v. 4, pp. 75–87 (in Russian).

Wheeler, J.A. (1990) Information, physics, quantum: the search for links, in *Complexity, Entropy, and the Physics of Information* (Zurek, W., ed.), Redwood City, CA: Addison-Wesley, pp. 3–28.

Zins, C. (2007) Conceptual approaches for defining data, information, and knowledge, *Journal of the American Society for Information Science and Technology*, v. 58, No. 4, pp. 479–493.

M. Burgin
C. Calude

PART I

Classical Information and Complexity

Chapter 1

The "Paradox" of Computability and a Recursive Relative Version of the Busy Beaver Function

Felipe S. Abrahão*

Federal University of Rio de Janeiro, Brazil

Abstract

In this article, we will show that uncomputability is a relative property not only of oracle Turing machines, but also of subrecursive classes. We will define the concept of a Turing submachine, and a recursive relative version for the Busy Beaver function which we will call Busy Beaver Plus function. Therefore, we will prove that the computable Busy Beaver Plus function defined on any Turing submachine is not computable by any program running on this submachine. We will thereby demonstrate the existence of a "paradox" of computability *a la* Skolem: a function is computable when "seen from the outside" the subsystem, but uncomputable when "seen from within" the same subsystem. Finally, we will raise the possibility of defining universal submachines, and a hierarchy of negative Turing degrees.

1.1. Introduction

In first place, we must briefly introduce the ideas behind the definitions, concepts and theorems exposed in the present article. It is true that, following an interdisciplinary course of study, this work focuses on manifold inspirations coming from several different fields of knowledge. However, for present purposes it is essential to mention the two foremost: Skolem's "paradox" and metabiology.

---

*The author was supported by Conselho Nacional de Desenvolvimento Científico e Tecnológico (CNPq).

Skolem's "paradox" derives from Cantor's famous theorem on the un-
countability of infinite sets, for instance of real numbers or of the set of all
subsets of natural numbers, and also from Löwenheim-Skolem's theorem on
the size of models in satisfiable theories. Briefly, the "paradox" is: there is
a countably infinite model for a theory (e.g. ZFC, if we accept it as consistent) that proves there are uncountably infinite sets. Therefore, when we
look at the set of elements in the theorys model which correspond homomor-
phically to the elements in the set that the theory demonstrates contain an
uncountable amount of elements, may however contain a countable amount
of elements. Does this contradiction represent, in fact, a paradox?

That question was answered by Skolem in 1922, being that the property
of countability of real numbers depends on the existence of a function within
the model that makes this bijective enumeration. This function cannot exist
within any ZFC model – if that is the chosen model – because, if it existed,
it would render countable the set of all real numbers. However, it may
exist when seen "from the outside", when this function never belongs to
the model. In other words, the function that "bijects" the natural onto the
real numbers never belongs to any model of any Set Theory[1] – but exists
nevertheless. Thus, it is understood that this does not constitute a true
paradox. It forms what one may call a pseudoparadox: when seen "from
the outside", an object has a certain property, but when seen seem "from
within" it has the opposite property. For this reason, it makes sense to
call the Skolem's "paradox" a pseudoparadox of countability. Therefore,
one may ask the question: just as there is a pseudoparadox of countability,
could there be a pseudoparadox of computability? We will address this
subject in the present paper.

Metabiology is a field of theoretical computer science with a transdisciplinary "heart" that studies general principles of biological relations at a
meta-level focusing on the open-ended evolution of systems and is inspired
by both the theories of biological evolution and by algorithmic information theory (AIT). While the already developed and well-established fields
of population genetics and evolutionary computations are driven towards
simulations of evolutionary populations and statistical properties of those
populations, metabiology is driven towards achieving theorems. It uses all
available tools from theory of computation, algorithmic information and
metamathematics to build and study abstract models – applicable or not.

Unlike the first models made by Chaitin, if we want a "nature" without

---

[1]Of course, provided it is strong enough and satisfiable.

access to oracles – at least, without access to real oracles – it needs to be a system that can be completely simulated on a universal Turing machine, or on a sufficiently powerful computer. This would also allow us to do experimental computer simulations on the evolution of digital organisms in the future.

In attempting to create a metabiological nature which is computable, but that "behaves in the same way" as an oracular one, i.e., in the same way as an uncomputable nature – in other words, as a hypercomputer – we face a series of difficulties. The first, highlighted in the literature, is the absence of a program that will solve the *halting problem*. This is required to determine whether or not an algorithmic mutation will result in a new organism/program (a mutations output given by a prior organism as input) and whether or not the organism/program has a higher fitness (its output) than the previous one. A computable nature would necessarily need to be capable of running a function capable of accomplishing this task, which we know is impossible for any arbitrary program. Note also that solving the halting problem, computing the bits of a Chaitin number Ω, and computing the Busy Beaver function, are equivalently uncomputable problems of Turing degree $0'$. How would evolution, then, occur within a computable simulation of "Nature"?

However, this paper does not intend to present mathematical exercises in metabiology, but to focus on presenting the elements which allow proving a computable metabiological model: "**sub-uncomputability**". The present paper comes from a solution we gave to the question to the above, as shown in [4]. We intend to demonstrate several fruitful properties and raise issues for future study within the mathematics of theoretical computer science.

Basically, we will call a **Turing submachine** any Turing machine that always gives an output for any input, i.e. always halts. The prefix "sub" parallels the term subrecursion. A subrecursive class is one defined by a proper subset of the set of all problems with Turing degree 0. Therefore, a **subcomputable** class of problems will be subrecursive, because it will never contain all recursive/computable problems. The term subrecursion is also used to characterize subrecursive hierarchies, as in Kleene and Grzegorczyk, covering all primitive recursive functions. But for us, the prefix refers more specifically to the concept of subrecursive class.

Note that Turing submachine is just another terminology for **total Turing machines**. However, despite the fact that they are just different names for the same object and can be used interchangeably, the expression "total Turing machine" might not immediately capture its relevant properties related to the present paper.

Every total computable function (or total Turing machine) defines a subrecursive class which is a proper subclass of others subrecursive classes (and of the class of all recursive functions). For example, the total Turing machine will be a subsystem of another total machine which is capable of computing functions that are relatively uncomputable by the former. This very idea of being part of another non-reducibly more powerful machine – that comes from sub-uncomputability, as we will show – is the core notion of the expression "submachine", conveying and bearing the ideas of hierarchies of subrecursive classes together with the powerful concept of Turing machines. Thus, the terminology Turing submachine emphasizes this property of total Turing machines being always able to be part of another proper and bigger machine. For more of this discussion, see item 4.

The central theme is building, or rather proving, a system (a Turing machine) that can "behave" in relation to a subsystem (its Turing submachine) in the same way as a hypercomputer (an oracle Turing machine) would behave in relation to a subsystem (in particular, a universal Turing machine). In fact, we will not emulate all – which might be impossible – the properties of a hypercomputer in relation to a computer, but focus on defining a function $BB^+{}_{P'_T}(N)$ analogous to a Busy Beaver function (in Chaitin's work, function $BB'(N)$), so that this function will behave in relation to the Turing submachine in the "same" way as the original Busy Beaver behaves in relation to a universal Turing machine. In other words, $BB^+{}_{P'_T}(N)$ must be relatively uncomputable by any **subprogram** (a program running on a Turing submachine), the same way the original Busy Beaver is uncomputable by any program running on a universal Turing machine. This phenomenon will be called **recursive relative uncomputability,** or **sub-uncomputability.**

1.2. Language *L*

The first important definition that needs to be established is the very programming, or universal machine, language with which we will work. It is important to us that the submachine $U_{P'_T}$ must be programmable. This language can be used on any usual computer, that is, its properties and rules of well-formation are programmable. Ultimately, this will lead us to the conclusion that the phenomenon of subcomputation may occur "within" computers as we already know them, which are universal Turing machines with limited resources.

Why concatenations? They provide a direct way of symbolizing a program taking any given bit string as input – for example, a program p that is, actually, program p' taking program p'' as input – which makes this program act as a function. Note that this type of program is already used to demonstrate the halting problem, or demonstrate that the Busy Beaver function is uncomputable. But the form it may assume is completely arbitrary, as a universal Turing machine, in any case, will run it. Therefore, it is no wonder we need this condition – this functionalizing special concatenation – in our language. As we are trying to build a computer that can emulate uncomputability, it is necessary that we can "teach" a machine to perform and recognize these "concatenations" within the language it is working in.

Many of the properties of the L language, below, are not required for this study; however, they were required to demonstrate the evolution of metabiological subprograms *a la* Chaitin.

To differentiate from the optimal functionalizing concatenation, which is joining strings in the most compressed way possible, provided it remains well-formulated, this special functionalizing concatenation will be denoted as "$\circ$", while the optimal functionalizing concatenation will be symbolized as "$*$".

1.2.1.   *Definition*

We say a universal programming language l, defined on a universal Turing machine U, is **recursively functionalizable** if there is a program that, given any bit strings P and w as inputs, will return a bit string belonging to l which will be denoted as $P \circ w$, whereby $U(P \circ w)$ equals "the result of the computation (on U) of program P when w is given as input". In addition, there must be a program that will determine whether or not a bit string is in form $P \circ w$ for any P and w, and is capable of returning P and w separately. Analogously, the latter must be true for the successive concatenation $P \circ w_1 \circ \cdots \circ w_k$, with program P receiving $w_1, \ldots, w_k$ as inputs.

Now, the general definition of language L can be defined as: let U be a universal Turing machine running language L, a universal language that is **binary, self-delimiting, recursive,** and **recursively functionalizable** and that there are constants $\in$, C and C', for every $P, w_1, \ldots, w_k$, where:

$$|w_i| < |P \circ w_1 \circ \cdots \circ w_k|, \text{for } i = 1, 2, \ldots, \text{ or } k$$

and

$$|P \circ w_1 \circ \cdots \circ w_k| \leq C \times k + |P| + |w_1| + |w_2| + \cdots + |w_k|$$

and

$$H(N) \leq C' + \log_2 N + (1+\epsilon) \log_2 (\log_2 N).$$

1.3.   Definitions

(a) W is the set of all finite bit strings, where the computable enumeration
of these bit strings has the form $l_1, l_2, l_3, \ldots, l_k, \ldots$
For practical purposes, a language may be adopted where $l_1 = 0$.

(b) Let $w \in W$.
$|w|$ denotes the size or number of bits contained in w.

(c) Let N simply symbolize the corresponding program in language L for
the natural number N. For example, $P \circ N$ denotes program $P \circ w$
where w is the natural number N in the language L.

(d) If function f is computable by program P, then f may also be called
function P.

1.4.   Turing Submachines

A key concept in the present article is the idea that a subsystem can do
almost anything its system can, however, with resources limited by the very
system. We follow the conventional understanding in which a computation
that is a part of another machine may be called a subcomputation, and a
machine that is a part of another machine may be called a submachine. In
our case, a system can be taken as a Turing machine, and a subsystem can
be taken as a Turing submachine. For example, a Turing submachine can
be a program or subroutine that the "bigger" Turing machine runs, always
generating an output, while performing various other tasks. Note that it
is true (a theorem) that for every total Turing machine there is another
Turing machine that completely emulates and contains the former total
Turing machine, in a manner that the computations of the latter contains
the computations of the former.

In fact, we are using a stronger notion of subsystem based upon this
conventional notion: a subsystem must be only able do what the system
knows, determines and delimits. This way, submachines will only be those
machines for which there is another "bigger" machine that can decide what
is the output of the former and whether there is an output at all. Note that
every machine that falls under this definition always defines an equivalent

total Turing machine (with a signed output corresponding to the case where the former does not halt); and every total Turing machine falls under this definition.

We will use another concept of vital importance: **computation time.** Similarly to time complexity, we will call T a program that calculates how many steps or basic operations U performs when running program p. Thus, if $U(p)$ does not halt, then $U(T * p)$ will not halt either, and vice versa.

Let P_f be a program running on U defined in language L, computing a total function (a function defined for all possible input values) f such that $f : L \longrightarrow X \subseteq W$. The language W does not need necessarily to be self-delimiting, and may be comprised of all bit strings of finite size, as long as they may be recursively enumerated in order, as $l_1, l_2, l_3, \ldots$ For practical reasons, we will choose an enumeration where $l_1 = 0$.

A **"Turing submachine"** or total Turing machine U/f is defined as a Turing machine in which, for every bit string w in the language of U, $U/f(w) = U(P_f \circ w)$.

This definition is quite general and transforms any total computable function into a Turing submachine. In fact, as said in the introduction, Turing submachines are just another name for total Turing machines. Anyway, Turing submachines can always be subsystems of either abstract universal Turing machines or of powerful (big) enough everyday computers (which are also some sort of total Turing machine, i.e. a universal Turing machine with limited resources).

Note that the class of all submachines is infinite, but not recursive.

When we talk of **subprograms** we refer to programs run on a Turing submachine. Herein, only submachines of a particular subclass will be dealt with: submachines defined by a computation time limited by a computable function. In fact, both these and the more generic submachines defined above are equivalent in computational power. To demonstrate this, just note that if a program computes a total function, then there is a program that can compute the computation time of this first program. Therefore, for every computable and total function, there is a submachine with limited computation time capable of computing this function – and, possibly, other functions as well. The reverse follows from the definition of submachine.

Let P_T be an arbitrary program that calculates a computation time for a given program w. That is, let P_T be an arbitrary total computable function. Thus, there is a **Turing submachine U_{P_T} defined by the computation-time function P_T.**

We then define submachine $U/P_{SM} \circ P_T$ (which will be a program running on U that computes a total function), where P_{SM} is a program that receives P_T and w as inputs, runs $U(P_T \circ w)$ and returns:

(i) l_1, if $U(w)$ does not halt within computation time $\leq U(P_T \circ w)$;
(ii) l_{k+1}, if $U(w)$ halts within computation time $\leq U(P_T \circ w)$ e $U(w) = l_k$.

This program defines a Turing submachine that returns a known symbol (in this case, zero) when program w does not halt in time $\leq U(P_T \circ w)$ or returns the same output (except for a trivial bijection) as $U(w)$ when the latter halts in time $\leq U(P_T \circ w)$.

To be a Turing submachine, $U/P_{SM} \circ P_T$ must be defined for all inputs. This occurs because P_T is total by definition. In addition, as computation time P_T becomes more increasing, the more submachine $U/P_{SM} \circ P_T$ approaches the universality of U.

Therefore, we will denote only as U_{P_T} a Turing submachine $U/P_{SM} \circ P_T$, so that:

$$\forall w \in L \; (U_{P_T}(w) = U/P_{SM} \circ P_T(w) = U(P_{SM} \circ P_T \circ w)).$$

1.5. Function $BB^+{}_{P'_T}(N)$

Let P'_T be a total function. Let us define function $BB^+{}_{P'_T}(N)$, which we will call Busy Beaver Plus, through the following recursive procedure:

 (i) Generate a list of all outputs of $U_{P'_T}(w)$ such that $|w| \leq N$;
(ii) Take the largest number on that list;
(iii) Add 1;
(iv) Return that value.

The name of this function refers to the Busy Beaver $BB(N)$ function and, consequently, it is no coincidence that the two have almost the same definition. If step (iii) is removed, it becomes exactly the Busy Beaver function for Turing submachines, here denoted as $BB_{P'_T}(N)$. Thus:

$$BB^+(N) = BB(N) + 1$$

and

$$BB^+{}_{P'_T}(N) = BB_{P'_T}(N) + 1.$$

But why use function BB^+ instead of BB? This might be, one supposes, the reader's first and immediate question. As we are dealing with Turing submachines and P'_T is arbitrary, it is possible there is a program on $U_{P'_T}$ with size $\leq N$ such that computes the highest value returned by any other program on $U_{P'_T}$ with size $\leq N$. When dealing with a universal Turing machine U, this cannot occur – except for a constant. However, with submachines, it can. Thus, function $BB^+{}_{P'_T}$ is triggered to assure it, in itself, is not relatively computable – or compressible – by any program on $U_{P'_T}$, although it can be by a program on U. Since P'_T is a program that computes a total function, then $BB^+{}_{P'_T}(N)$ is computable.

The Busy Beaver contains the idea of the greatest output of any $\leq N$ sized program; so the Busy Beaver Plus function contains the idea of increasing, at least by 1, any $\leq N$ sized program. Respectively, the first gives us maximization, and the second, an "almost" minimal increment.

Following this line of thought, to symbolize this new function, the image may be evoked of the proverbial man sitting on a hungry donkey and driving the animal by a carrot hanging from a fishing rod. As the carrot looms in front of the donkey's face, the hungry donkey is driven to walk forward to reach the carrot, which is never reached. Not because it is an infinite distance away, but because with every step it takes the carrot moves forward along with it. The carrot is always "one step" ahead of the donkey. No matter how dutifully the donkey walks toward the carrot, it will always remain at the same distance, just beyond reach, unattainable. No matter how rapidly increasing is the function P'_T, the program on U that computes $BB^+{}_{P'_T}(N)$ simply bases itself on the $U_{P'_T}$ outputs to overcome them by a minimum. No matter how powerful $U_{P'_T}$ may be, $BB^+{}_{P'_T}(N)$ will always be "one step" ahead of the best that any subprogram (i.e., any program $U_{P'_T}$) can do.

It is worthy of note that, analogously to the Busy Beaver, the $BB^+{}_{P'_T}(N)$ may be used to measure the "creativity" or *"sub-algorithmic complexity"* of the subprograms in relation to Turing submachine $U_{P'_T}$. Why? By its very definition, if a subprogram generates an output $\geq BB^+{}_{P'_T}(N)$, it must necessarily be of size $> N$. It needs to have over N bits of relatively incompressible information, i.e. over N bits of relative creativity.

Of course, one may always build a program that will compute function $BB^+{}_{P'_T}(N)$, if function P'_T is computable. This would allow a far smaller program than N there to exist – e.g., of size $\leq C + \log_2 N +$

$(1 + \epsilon)\log_2(\log_2 N)$ – that will compute $BB^+{}_{P'_T}(N)$. But that does not constitute a contradiction, because this program can never be a subprogram of $U_{P'_T}$, in other words, it can never be a program that runs on the computation time determined by P'_T. If it was, it would enter into direct contradiction with the definition of $BB^+{}_{P'_T}$: the program P'_T will become undefined for an input, which by assumption is false. Then, as we will show in item 6, we will immediately get the "paradox" of computability.

1.6. Sub-uncomputability: Recursive Relative Uncomputability

Now we will prove the crucial, yet simple, result that governs this paper.

Let P'_T be a total function and $U_{P'_T}$ a Turing submachine. Then, we can prove that function $BB^+{}_{P'_T}(N)$ is **relatively uncomputable** by any program on $U_{P'_T}$. Or: there is no subprogram that, for every input N, returns an output equal to $BB^+{}_{P'_T}(N)$.

A more intuitive way to understand what is going on is to look for a program and concatenate its input, such as $U_{P'_T}(P*N)$ for instance. Where "$*$" denotes the optimal functionalizing concatenation, and not necessarily the "concatenation" "$\circ$" defined in item 2. In fact, this applies to any way to compress the information of P and N in an arbitrary subprogram. Therefore, it may not be in the form $P \circ N$.

We avail ourselves of the same idea used in the demonstration of Chaitin's incompleteness theorem. Now, however, to demonstrate an uncomputability relative to the submachine $U_{P'_T}$.

When N is given as input to any program P, it comes in its compressed form with size $\cong H(N)$ – in fact, we use the property $|P \circ N| \leq C + |P| + C' + \log_2 N + (1 + \epsilon)\log_2(\log_2 N)$ –, whereby $|P \circ N| \cong C + H(N)$. But, as already known by the AIT, for any constant C there is a big enough N_0 such that $C + H(N_0) < N_0$. Therefore, according to the definition of $BB^+{}_{P'_T}$, the output of $P \circ N_0$ when run on submachine $U_{P'_T}$, will be taken into account when one calculates $BB^+{}_{P'_T}(N_0)$. Thus, necessarily,

$$BB^+{}_{P'_T}(N_0) \geq U_{P'_T}(P \circ N_0) + 1 > U_{P'_T}(P \circ N_0),$$

which will lead to contradiction, if P computes $BB^+{}_{P'_T}$ when running on submachine $U_{P'_T}$. The same holds for "$*$".

Also, following the same argument, it can be shown promptly that $BB^+{}_{P'_T}(N)$ is a **relatively incompressible, or sub-incompressible,** function by any subprogram smaller than or equal to N. That is, no program of size $\leq N$ running on P'_T will result in an output larger than or equal to $BB^+{}_{P'_T}(N)$.

1.7. Conclusion and Final Comments

First, a self-delimiting universal language L was defined for a universal Turing machine U. Then, we defined the Turing submachines (or total Turing machines) $U_{P'_T}$. It has been further demonstrated that the phenomenon of "sub-uncomputability" is ubiquitous: for every Turing submachine $U_{P'_T}$, if there is a program that computes a total function, then the computable function $BB^+{}_{P'_T}(N)$ is relatively uncomputable by any program running on $U_{P'_T}$ in the same manner that the Busy Beaver function $BB'(N)$ is in relation to any program. Also, by the very definition of $BB^+{}_{P'_T}$, there cannot be any program of size $\leqslant N$ running on $U_{P'_T}$ that will generate an output higher than or equal to $BB^+{}_{P'_T}(N)$ – which may be called the sub-incompressibility of the function $BB^+{}_{P'_T}$.

To recreate/relativize the classic uncomputability of the Busy Beaver function, essentially, we had do to Turing and Radó the same as Skolem did to Cantor: we relativized the uncomputability of function $BB'(N)$. It was demonstrated that it depends on "being seen from the outside, or from the inside". Thus, it was proven that there is a "paradox" of computability *a la* Skolem, i.e. there is a function that is computable if "seen from without", that is uncomputable if "seen from within". As both language L and the submachines can be programmed, this phenomenon can occur within our everyday computers.

However, not "all uncomputabilities" of a first-order hypercomputer were relativized in relation to a universal Turing machine. Only what was described above was relativized. However, following this line of mathematical inquiry enabled us to build metabiological evolutionary models that are fully analogous to Chaitins models of Intelligent Design and Cumulative Evolution – as shown in [4]. For this purpose, a Turing submachine $U_{P^{**}{}_T \circ P_T}$ was built and a relative and computable Chaitin Omega number $\Omega_{P^{**}{}_T \circ P_T}$ – in the case, a time-limited halting probability – was defined. Clauses were added to $U_{P^{**}{}_T \circ P_T}$ to allow the existence of finite lower approximations ρ to $\Omega_{P^{**}{}_T \circ P_T}$ that can be used by a program P when running on $U_{P^{**}{}_T \circ P_T}$ to compute values of $BB^+{}_{P^{**}{}_T \circ P_T}(N)$, so that $2N + C \geqslant |P \circ \rho| \geqslant N + 1$, where C is a constant. This was also designed to mimic what a universal Turing machine can do with lower approximations to Ω with the purpose of calculating values of $BB'(N)$. Also, another clauses were added to enable the relative versions of key mutations/programs from Chaitins models to also become subprograms. Thus, the open-ended evolution of subprograms revealed itself as isomorphically fast as the open-ended evolution of programs. It allowed us to recursively relativize more "behaviors" of a first order hypercomputer in relation to a computer, making them happen between machines and submachines.

An upcoming mathematical inquiry this article suggests is proving whether or not there is a way to define – relatively – universal Turing submachines. A universal submachine should be analogous to a universal machine, so there is a class of subcomputable problems, always reducible within a subcomputable time, that are computable by this universal submachine. The questions would be: how to define a computation time P_U so that U_{P_U} is a universal Turing submachine? Is it possible? This mathematical problem also involves studying the greatest amount of first order uncomputable functions that can be relativized to become sub-uncomputable. If this Turing submachine is possible, a negative Turing degree can be defined. Moreover, as for each Turing submachine $U_{P'_T}$ there is always another more powerful and non-reducible submachine $U_{P''_T}$ such that P''_T is sufficient computation time to compute $BB^+{}_{P'_T}$, so it would likewise be possible to create an infinite hierarchy of negative Turing degrees.

To what extent can a computer be made to "behave", in relation to one of its subcomputers, as if it was a hypercomputer?

Bibliography

Abrahao, F. S. (2011). Questoes em metabiologia, *Scientiarum Historia*.

Abrahao, F. S. (2013). Metabiologia cantoriana, *Scientiarum Historia*.

Abrahao, F. S. (2014). "Paradoxo" da computabilidade, *Scientiarum Historia*.

Abrahao, F. S. (2015). *Metabiologia, Subcomputacao e Hipercomputacao: em direo a uma teoria geral de evolucao de sistemas*, Ph.D. thesis, Federal University of Rio de Janeiro.

Barwise, J. (ed.) (1977). *Handbook of Mathematical Logic* (Elsevier Science Publisher B.V.).

Basu, S. (1970). On the structure of subrecursive degrees, *Journal of Computer and System Sciences*.

Burgin, M. (2005). Measuring power of algorithms, programs, and automata, *Artificial Intelligence and Computer Science*, pp. 1–61.

Calude, C. (ed.) (2007). *Randomness and Complexity* (World Scientific).

Chaitin, G. (2012). *A Computable Universe: Understanding and Exploring Nature as Computation*, chap. Life as Evolving Software (World Scientific), pp. 277–302.

Chaitin, G. (2013). *Proving Darwin: Making Biology Mathematical* (Vintage Books).

Chaitin, G., Chaitin, V., and Abrahao, F. S. (2014). Metabiologia: los origenes de la creatividad biologica, *Investigacion y Ciencia*, p. 448.

Enderton, H. (2001). *A Mathematical Introduction to Logic* (Academic Press).

Ewert, W., Dembski, W., and Marks II, R. J. (2013). Active information in metabiology, *Bio-Complexity*.

Lewis, H. R. and Papadimitriou, C. H. (2000). *Elementos de Teoria da Computacao* (Bookman).

Rogers, H. (1992). *Theory of Recursive Functions and Effective Computability* (MIT Press).

Rose, H. (1987). Subrecursion: Functions and hierarchies, *The Journal of Symbolic Logic*.

Zenil, H. (ed.) (2011). *Randomness through Computation* (World Scientific).

Zenil, H. (ed.) (2013). *A Computable Universe* (World Scientific).

Chapter 2

Inductive Complexity and Shannon Entropy

Mark Burgin

University of California, Los Angeles
405 Hilgard Ave. Los Angeles, CA 90095, USA

Abstract

Shannon's approach based on the concept of entropy became the mainstream information theory. Although some think that this direction represents information theory as the whole, there are other directions and fields in the theory of information. One of most prominent is based on Kolmogorov or algorithmic complexity. This approach has found applications in many areas including medicine, biology, neurophysiology, physics, economics, hardware and software engineering. Conventional Kolmogorov/ algorithmic complexity and its modifications are based on application of conventional, i.e., recursive, algorithms, such as Turing machines. In this chapter, we study inductive complexity, which is similar to Kolmogorov complexity but instead of Turing machines it is based on inductive Turing machines, which are super-recursive algorithms as they compute much more than recursive algorithms. The main goal of this work is to compare inductive complexity with Shannon entropy.

2.1. Introduction

Continuing research of Hartley, Shannon published his paper *The Mathematical Theory of Communication* in 1948 introducing a mathematical definition of information and making information a prominent notion. Although the word *information* does not appear in the title, this approach was later called information theory. The approach of Hartley and Shannon is the mainstream of the statistical information theory and to a great extent, of the whole information theory. It became so popular that many even did not know about existence of other directions. The bias towards this approach is very strong even now.

In the 1950s and 1960s, Shannon's theory spread its influence to a variety of disciplines. However, researchers in these disciplines were not satisfied with this purely statistical approach to information and elaborated other definitions of information specific for their disciplines (cf., for example, Neisser (1967), Seiffert (1968), Attneave (1974)).

One of the pivotal approaches to information with a different definition of this concept is based on complexity. Being a scientific reflection of efficiency, complexity has become a buzzword in contemporary science. There are different kinds and types of complexity with a diversity of different complexity measures. One of the most popular and important of them is Kolmogorov, also called algorithmic, complexity, which has turned into an important and popular tool in many areas such as information theory, computer science, software development, probability theory, and statistics. Algorithmic complexity has found applications in medicine, biology, neurophysiology, physics, economics, hardware and software engineering. In biology, algorithmic complexity is used for estimation of protein identification (Dewey, 1996; 1997). In physics, problems of quantum gravity are analyzed based on the algorithmic complexity of a given object. In particular, the algorithmic complexity of the Schwarzschild black hole is estimated (Dzhunushaliev, 1998; Dzhunushaliev and Singleton, 2001). Benci *et al.* (2002) apply algorithmic complexity to chaotic dynamics. Zurek elaborates a formulation of thermodynamics by inclusion of algorithmic complexity and randomness in the definition of physical entropy (Zurek, 1989; 1991). Gurzadyan (2003) uses Kolmogorov complexity as a descriptor of the Cosmic Microwave Background (CMB) radiation maps. Kreinovich, and Kunin (2004) apply Kolmogorov complexity to problems in classical mechanics, while Yurtsever (2000) employs Kolmogorov complexity in quantum mechanics. Tegmark (1996) discusses what can be the algorithmic complexity of the whole universe. The main problem with this discussion is that the author identifies physical universe with physical models of this universe. To get valid results on this issue, it is necessary to define algorithmic complexity for physical systems because conventional algorithmic complexity is defined only for such symbolic objects as words and texts (Li and Vitanyi, 1997). Then it is necessary to show that there is a good correlation between algorithmic complexity of the universe and algorithmic complexity of its model used by Tegmark (1996).

In economics, a new approach to understanding of the complex behavior of financial markets using algorithmic complexity is developed (Mansilla, 2001). In neurophysiology, algorithmic complexity is used to measure characteristics of brain functions (Shaw *et al.*, 1999). Algorithmic complexity has been useful in the development of software metrics and other problems of software engineering (Burgin, and Debnath, 2003; Debnath and Burgin, 2003; Lewis, 2001). Crosby and Wallach (2003) use algorithmic complexity to study low-bandwidth denial of service attacks that exploit algorithmic deficiencies in many common applications' data structures.

Thus, we see that Kolmogorov/algorithmic complexity is a frequent word in present days' scientific literature, in various fields and with diverse meanings, appearing in some contexts as a precise concept of algorithmic complexity, while being a vague idea of complexity in general in other texts. The reason for this is that people study and create more and more complex systems.

However, there is a serious problem: How is algorithmic complexity, as a measure of information, related to its information theoretical interpretation? It is generally assumed that the algorithmic complexity of a binary string x measures the amount of information in the string x. Thus, according to algorithmic information theory, random sequences have maximum complexity as by definition, a random sequence can have no generating algorithm shorter than simply listing the sequence. It means that information content of random sequences is maximal.

Physicists were the first to notice this peculiarity. For instance, Richard Feynman (1999) wrote:

"How can a random string contain *any* information, let alone the maximum amount? Surely we must be using the wrong definition of 'information'?..."

As Gell-Mann (1995) pointed out, this contradicted the popular understanding that random sequences should contain no information. He wrote that this property of algorithmic information content (Kolmogorov complexity) revealed the unsuitability of the quantity as a measure of information, since the works of Shakespeare had less algorithmic information content than random gibberish of the same length that would typically be typed by the proverbial roomful of monkeys.

Raatikainen (1998) thoroughly analyzed this discrepancy and came to the grounded conclusion that the algorithmic complexity and the conventional information content of a linguistic expression had no real connections.

To eliminate these contradictions and discrepancies that are prevalent in algorithmic information theory and to solve the problem of correct understanding the meaning of the Kolmogorov complexity $C(x)$ of an object (text) x, it is more adequate to consider $C(x)$ and all its versions as *measures of information about* x or the *information size of* x with the special goal to build or reconstruct x (Burgin, 2010b). It means that in reality, x is not the *carrier of information* measured by $C(x)$, but the *object of this information*. In this context, it becomes not surprising that people, or a machine, need more information about a random sequence of letters to reconstruct it than about a masterpiece, such as a tragedy by Shakespeare, poem by Dante or novel by Cervantes, because the latter has more regularities.

Algorithmic complexity in its classical form gives an estimate of how many bits of information we need to build or restore a given text by algorithms from a given class. Conventional Kolmogorov/algorithmic complexity and its modifications, such as uniform complexity, prefix complexity, monotone complexity, process complexity, conditional Kolmogorov complexity, time-bounded Kolmogorov complexity, space-bounded Kolmogorov complexity, conditional resource-bounded Kolmogorov complexity, time-bounded prefix complexity, and resource-bounded Kolmogorov complexity, use conventional, i.e., recursive, algorithms, such as Turing machines. Besides, researchers studied quantum Kolmogorov complexity (Vitanyi, 2001). Inductive complexity studied in this chapter is a special type of the generalized Kolmogorov complexity (Burgin, 1990), which is based on inductive Turing machines. Inductive Turing machines formalize inductive reasoning prevalent in science and are super-recursive as they can compute much more than recursive algorithm can. Inductive Turing machines form the next natural step of the development of Turing machines. Thus, it was natural to develop algorithmic theory of complexity and randomness based on inductive Turing machines obtaining inductive complexity (Burgin, 2004). It is possible to apply inductive complexity in all cases where Kolmogorov complexity is used. In particular, inductive complexity has been used in the study of mathematical problem complexity (Calude *et al.*, 2012; Hertel, 2012; Burgin *et al.*, 2013).

The main goal of this work is to compare inductive complexity with Shannon entropy. In Section 2.2, we recall the necessary definitions and results from coding theory and probability. In Section 2.3, we evoke the necessary definitions and results from the theory of simple inductive Turing machines, computability of functions by means of these machines and inductive complexity (Burgin, 2005). Note that throughout this chapter inductive computability means computability by means of simple inductive Turing machines although there are inductive Turing machines of higher orders. In Section 2.4, we establish relations between inductive complexity and Shannon entropy. Although these relations are similar to relations between Kolmogorov complexity and Shannon entropy, the new relations essentially extend the application domain of these relations, as there are much more inductively computable functions than recursively computable functions. In addition, utilization of inductive complexity makes these relations more exact as for infinitely many objects, inductive complexity is essentially smaller than Kolmogorov complexity (Burgin, 2004).

The reason for this is the higher level modeling mental activity achieved by inductive Turing machines in comparison with Turing machines. While a Turing machine formalizes the work of an accountant or a human computer, an inductive Turing machine formalizes the work of a scientist.

Denotations

If X is an alphabet, then X^* is the set of all words (finite sequences) in the alphabet X.

$l(x)$ is the length of a word x.

$\log n = \log_2 n$.

N is the set of all natural numbers.

R is the set of all real numbers.

$IK(x)$ is the prefix inductive complexity of an object (word) x.

$K(x)$ is the prefix Kolmogorov complexity of an object (word) x.

A relation $R \subseteq X \times Y$ is *cofunctional* if there are no elements from Y that are assigned to more than one element from X.

2.2. Coding, probability and entropy

Let us consider the set B of all words in the alphabet $\{0, 1\}$, i.e., $B = \{0, 1\}^*$, and an arbitrary countable set Z.

A cofunctional relation $E \subseteq Z \times B$ is called an *encoding* of the set Z. It is fully characterized by the *decoding function* $E^{-1} = D : B \to Z$. If $Z \subseteq B$, then the domain Dom D of D is called the set of *source words* and the range Rg D of D is called the set of *code words*. Usually, D is called a *binary code*.

It is possible to associate the length function L_D with any decoding function D by the following formula

$$L_D(x) = \min\{l(y); D(y) = x\}.$$

A set $Z \subseteq B$ is called *prefix-free* if for any pair of distinct elements from Z neither is a prefix of the other.

If the set of its source words is prefix-free, then D is called a prefix code.

The following useful result is well-known (cf., for example, Grunwald and Vitanyi (2004)).

Lemma 2.1. *It is possible to convert any code into a prefix code by a one-to-one recursively computable function.*

Indeed, changing each word w from Dom D into the word $1^{l(w)}0w$, we obtain a prefix code.

Kraft found conditions when there is a prefix code with the given lengths of its elements.

Theorem 2.2 (Kraft, 1949). *If $L = \{l_1, l_2, l_3, ...\}$ is a sequence of natural numbers, then there is a binary prefix code with this sequence as lengths of its elements if and only if*

$$\sum_{n \in N} 2^{-l_n} \leq 1.$$

If X is a countable set, then a function $f: X \to [0, 1]$ is called a probability distribution (probability mass function) on a set X if

$$\sum_{n \in X} f(x) = 1$$

and is called a sub-probability distribution (sub-probability mass function) on a set X if

$$\sum_{n \in X} f(x) \leq 1.$$

Naturally, any sub-probability distribution is a probability distribution.

Taking a prefix code $D: B \to N$ and a probability distribution f on the set B, we find the expected value of the length of the code word by the formula

$$L_D = \sum_{n \in B} f(x) \cdot l_x,$$

where l_x is the length of the code word of the source word x.

This expected value is related to the entropy introduced by Shannon in his studies of communication and described by the famous formula

$$H(f) = \sum_{n \in X} p_x \cdot \log_2 (1/p_x),$$

where p_x is the probability for a random variable X to be equal to x and p_x is equal to $f(x)$ for a given probability distribution f.

The Noiseless Coding Theorem (Shannon, 1948) implies the following result.

Proposition 2.3. *For any prefix code $D: B \to N$,*

$$0 \leq H(f) \leq L_D.$$

2.3. Inductive Turing machines

Here we consider only simple inductive Turing machines (Burgin, 2005) and for simplicity call them inductive Turing machines although there are other kinds of inductive Turing machines. A simple inductive Turing machine M works with words in some alphabet and has the same structure and functioning rules as a Turing machine with three heads and three linear tapes (registers) – the input tape (input register), output tape (output register) and working tape (working register). Any inductive Turing machine of the first order is functionally equivalent to a simple inductive Turing machine (Burgin, 2005).

The machine M works in the following fashion. At the beginning, an input word w is written in the input tape, which is a read-only tape. Then the machine M rewrites the word w from the input tape to the working tape and starts working with it. From time to time in this process, the machine M rewrites the word from the working tape to the output tape erasing what was before written in the output tape. In particular, when the machine M comes to a final state, it rewrites the word from the working tape to the output tape and stops without changing the state.

The machine M gives the result when M halts in a final state, or when M never stops but at some step of the computation, the content of the output tape (register) stops changing. The computed result of M is the word that is written in the output tape of M. In all other cases, M does not give the result.

This means that a simple inductive Turing machine can do what a Turing machine can do but in some cases, it produces its results without stopping. Namely, it is possible that in the sequence of computations after some step, the word (say, w) on the output tape (in the output register) is not changing, while the inductive Turing machine continues working. Then this word w is the final result of the inductive Turing machine. Note that if an inductive Turing machine gives the final result, it is produced after a finite number of steps, that is, in finite time, even when the machine does not stop. So contrary to confusing claims of some researchers, an inductive Turing machine does not need infinite time to produce a result.

If an inductive Turing machine M transforms words from Σ^* into words from Σ^*. Then Σ^* is called the *domain* and *codomain* of M.

If an inductive Turing machine M transforms numbers from N into numbers from N, Then N is called the *domain* and *codomain* of M.

The set of words (numbers) for which the machine M is defined (gives the result) is called the *definability domain* of M.

The set of words (numbers) computed (generated) by the machine M is called the *range* of M.

A *prefix inductive Turing machine* gives results only for elements from a prefix-free set of words.

Note that a universal inductive Turing machine that works with a prefix code of inductive Turing machines is a prefix inductive Turing machine.

We call a function $f : B \to N$ ($g : N \to N$ or $h : B \to B$) *inductively computable* if there is a simple inductive Turing machine that computes f (g or h, respectively).

Note that any recursively computable function is inductively computable but the converse is not true (Burgin, 2005).

A function $f : B \to R$ is *inductively computable* if there is a simple inductive Turing machine K such that for any pair (x, n) with $x \in B$ and $n \in N$ the computes $f(x)$ with the precision $1/n$.

A function $f : B \to R$ is *lower* (*upper*) *inductively semi-computable* if there is a simple inductive Turing machine K computing a total function $g(x, y)$ such that $g(x, y) \le g(x, y + 1)$ ($g(x, y) \ge g(x, y + 1)$) and $f(x) = \lim_{n \to \infty} g(x, n)$.

Note that inductively semi-computable functions are computable by limit Turing machines (Burgin, 1992).

2.4. Inductive complexity

Here we define and study prefix inductive complexity for finite objects such as natural numbers or words in a finite alphabet. Usually, it is the binary alphabet $\{0, 1\}$. Besides, we define prefix inductive complexity of inductively computable functions, which are infinite objects but have a finite representation when they are enumerated.

Definition 2.4. The *inductive complexity* $IC_M(x)$ of an object (word) x with respect to an inductive Turing machine M is defined as

$$IC_M(x) = \begin{cases} \min\{l(p);\ M(p) = x\} & \text{when there is } p \text{ such that } M(p) = x, \\ \text{undefined} & \text{when there is no } p \text{ such} \\ & \text{that } M(p) = x. \end{cases}$$

Note that if M is a Turing machine, then inductive complexity $IC_M(x)$ with respect to M coincides with Kolmogorov complexity $C_M(x)$ with respect to M.

If M is a prefix simple inductive Turing machine, then the inductive complexity $IC_M(x)$ is the prefix inductive complexity $IK_M(x)$.

However, as in the case of conventional Kolmogorov complexity and prefix Kolmogorov complexity, we need an invariant complexity of objects. This is achieved by using a universal prefix simple inductive Turing machine (Burgin, 2004; 2005).

Definition 2.5. The *prefix inductive complexity* IK(x) of an object (word) x is defined as

$$IK(x) = \begin{cases} \min \{l(p); \ U(p) = x\} & \text{when there is } p \text{ such that } U(p) = x, \\ \text{undefined} & \text{when there is no } p \text{ such that } U(p) = x, \end{cases}$$

where $l(p)$ is the length of the word p and U is a universal prefix simple inductive Turing machine.

Note that prefix inductive complexity is a special case of generalized Kolmogorov complexity (Burgin, 1990), which in turn, is a kind of axiomatic dual complexity measures (Burgin, 2005).

The prefix inductive complexity IK(x) is optimal in the class of prefix inductive complexities $IK_T(x)$. Optimality is based on the relation $\preccurlyeq$ defined for functions $f(n)$ and $g(n)$, which take values in natural numbers:

$$f(n) \preccurlyeq g(n) \text{ if there is a real number } c$$
$$\text{such that } f(n) \leq g(n) + c \text{ for almost all } n \in N$$

Let us consider a class **H** of functions that take values in natural numbers. Then a function $f(n)$ is called *optimal* for **H** if $f(n) \preccurlyeq g(n)$ for any function $g(n)$ from **H**.

Results from the axiomatic theory of dual complexities (Burgin, 1990; 2010a) imply the following theorem.

Theorem 2.6. *The function IK(x) is optimal in the class of all prefix inductive complexities $IK_T(x)$ with respect to a prefix simple inductive Turing machine T.*

As there is a simple inductive Turing machine M such that $M(x) = x$ for all words x in the alphabet $\{1, 0\}$, we have the following result.

Proposition 2.7. *IK(x) is a total function.*

It is proved that for infinitely many objects, inductive complexity is essentially less than Kolmogorov complexity (Burgin, 2004; 2005). Consequently, for infinitely many objects, prefix inductive complexity is essentially less than prefix Kolmogorov complexity.

Lemma 2.8. $\sum_{x \in B} 2^{-\text{IK}(x)} \leq 1.$

Indeed, as prefix inductive Turing machines determine prefix coding, by Kraft inequality, we have

$$\sum_{x \in B} 2^{-\text{IK}(x)} \leq 1.$$

It is also possible to define inductive complexity and prefix inductive complexity of inductively computable functions. Let f be an inductively computable function and consider an invertible recursive enumeration of simple inductive Turing machines $\{M_1, M_2, M_3, \ldots, M_i, \ldots\}$.

Definition 2.9. The *prefix inductive complexity* IK(f) of the function f is defined as

$$\text{IK}(f) = \min\{\text{IK}(i); \text{ the simple inductive Turing machine } M_i \text{ computes } f\}$$

Let us consider the set B of all words in the alphabet $\{0, 1\}$ and denote by *IPD* the set of all inductively computable sub-probability distributions on the sample space B defining the function in(x) by the formula

$$\text{in}(x) = \sum_{f \in IPD} 2^{-IK(f)} \cdot f(x).$$

It is called the *universal inductive sub-probability distribution*.

Note that the universal inductive sub-probability distribution is larger than the universal recursive sub-probability distribution studied in the theory of Kolmogorov complexity and algorithmic information theory (Li and Vitanyi, 1997).

Lemma 2.10. *in(x) is a sub-probability distribution on the sample space B.*

Proof. As $\sum_{x \in B} f(x) = 1$, by Lemma 2.8, we have

$$\sum_{x \in B} \text{in}(x) = \sum_{x \in B} \sum_{f \in IPD} 2^{-IK(f)} \cdot f(x)$$

$$= \sum_{f \in IPD} \left(\sum_{x \in B} f(x) \right) \cdot 2^{-IK(f)} \leq \sum_{f \in IPD} 2^{-IK(f)} \leq 1.$$

Definitions imply the following result.

Lemma 2.11. $in(x) \geq 2^{-IK(f)} \cdot f(x)$ *for any sub-probability distribution from IPD.*

Theorem 2.12. $\log in(x) = IK(x) + O(1)$.

The proof is similar to the proof of Theorem 2.12 from Li and Vitanyi (1997).

Obtained properties of inductive complexity allow us to compare the expected value of the prefix inductive complexity with Shannon entropy.

2.5. Relations between Inductive Complexity and Shannon Entropy

The Shannon entropy $H(X)$ may be interpreted as the minimal expected length of the description of the random variable X. Therefore, it is interesting to compare $H(X)$ with the expected value (probabilistic average) of the prefix inductive complexity $IK(x)$.

Let us consider the set B of all words in the alphabet $\{0, 1\}$ and a random variable X with the probability $f(x) = P(X = x)$ for the event $X = x$. It is possible to express the average of the prefix inductive complexity $IK(x)$ with respect to the probability distribution f by the following formula

$$\sum_{x \in B} f(x) \cdot IK(x).$$

In the case of an inductively computable probability distribution f, this average is equal to Shannon's entropy up to some constant as the following result demonstrates.

Theorem 2.13. *If $f(x) = P(X = x)$ is an inductively computable probability distribution on the sample space B associated with a random source X, then*

$$0 \leq \sum_{x \in B} f(x) \cdot IK(x) - H(X) \leq IK(f) + O(1).$$

Proof. By Lemma 2.11, we have

$$in(x) \geq 2^{-IK(f)} \cdot f(x).$$

Consequently,

$$\log in(x) \geq \log f(x) - IK(f).$$

Thus,

$$-\log \text{in}(x) \leq - \log f(x) + \text{IK}(f) = \log (1/f(x)) + \text{IK}(f).$$

By Theorem 2.12,

$$\log \text{in}(x) = \text{IK}(x) + O(1).$$

Consequently,

$$- IK(x) + O(1) \leq \log (1/f(x)) + \text{IK}(f)$$

and

$$\text{IK}(x) \leq \log (1/f(x)) + \text{IK}(f) + O(1)$$

and

$$\text{IK}(x) - \log (1/f(x)) \leq \text{IK}(f) + O(1).$$

Applying all these inequalities, we obtain the necessary result:

$$\sum_{x \in B} f(x) \cdot \text{IK}(x) - \sum_{x \in B} f(x) \cdot \log (1/f(x))$$

$$\leq \sum_{x \in B} f(x) \cdot (\text{IK}(f) + O(1)) = \text{IK}(f) + O(1).$$

Besides, as $\text{IK}(x)$ is the code word length of a prefix code for x, Proposition 2.3 implies the inequality

$$0 \leq \sum_x f(x) \cdot \text{IK}(x) - H(X).$$

Theorem is proved.

2.6. Conclusion

We have demonstrated that the average of the prefix inductive complexity $\text{IK}(x)$ with respect to an inductively computable probability distribution f is equal to Shannon entropy up to some additive constant that depends on f. A similar inequality is proved for recursively computable probability distributions and the conventional (Kolmogorov) prefix complexity (Grunwald and Vitanyi, 2004; Muchnik and Vereshchagin, 2006). The result proved in this chapter has the following advantages:

1. There are more inductively computable probability distributions than recursively computable probability distributions.

2. For infinitely many functions f, the estimate $IK(f)$ in the result of this paper is more exact than the estimate $K(f)$ in the result for prefix complexity because the value of $IK(f)$ is smaller than the value of $K(f)$ according to the results from (Burgin, 2004).

Here we studied prefix inductive complexity using simple inductive Turing machines. However, these machines form only the lowest level in the constructive hierarchy of inductive Turing machines. Thus, it would be appealing to study prefix inductive complexity based on inductive Turing machines of higher orders and compare the expected value of such a complexity with Shannon entropy.

As we know, Shannon entropy has a complete axiomatic characterization (Shannon, 1948). At the same time, Kolmogorov complexity has only a constructive definition. It would be interesting to obtain a complete axiomatic characterization of Kolmogorov complexity. One of the possible approaches to this problem is to use the axiomatic theory of dual algorithmic complexity measures because Kolmogorov complexity is a special case of these measures (Burgin, 2010a).

Another interesting problem is to compare the inductive algorithmic mutual information, which is defined similar to recursive algorithmic mutual information (Li and Vitanyi, 1997), with the mutual probabilistic (Shannon's) information.

Acknowledgments

The author wants to thank the unknown reviewer for useful remarks.

Bibliography

1. Attneave, F. (1974) Informations theorie in der Psychologie: Grundbegriffe, in *Techniken Ergebnisse*, Verlag Hans Huber, Bern/Stuttgart/Wien.

2. Benci, V., Bonanno, C., Galatolo, S., Menconi, G. and Virgilio, M. (2002) *Dynamical Systems and Computable Information*, Preprint in Physics cond-mat/0210654, (electronic edition: http://arXiv.org).

3. Burgin, M. S. (1990) Generalized Kolmogorov complexity and other dual complexity measures, *Cybernetics and System Analysis*, 26(4), pp. 481-490.

4. Burgin, M. (1992) Universal limit Turing machines, *Notices of the Russian Academy of Sciences*, 325(4), pp. 654-658.

5.   Burgin, M. (2004) Algorithmic complexity of recursive and inductive algorithms, *Theoretical Computer Science*, 317(1/3), pp. 31-60.

6.   Burgin, M. (2005) *Superrecursive Algorithms*, Springer, New York.

7.   Burgin, M. (2010a) Algorithmic complexity of computational problems, *International Journal of Computing & Information Technology*, 2(1), pp. 149-187.

8.   Burgin, M. (2010b) *Theory of Information: Fundamentality, Diversity and Unification*, World Scientific, New York/London/Singapore.

9.   Burgin, M., Calude, C.S., Calude, E. (2011) Inductive complexity measures for mathematical problems, *International Journal of Foundations of Computer Science*, 24(4), 2013, pp. 487-500.

10. Burgin, M. and Debnath, N.C. (2003) Complexity of algorithms and software metrics, in *Proceedings of the ISCA 18th International Conference "Computers and their Applications"*, International Society for Computers and their Applications, Honolulu, Hawaii, pp. 259-262.

11. Calude, C.S., Calude, E. and Queen, M.S. (2012) Inductive complexity of P versus NP problem, in *Unconventional Computation and Natural Computation*, Lecture Notes in Computer Science, vol. 7445, pp. 2-9.

12. Crosby, S. A. and Wallach, D. S. (2003) *Denial of Service via Algorithmic Complexity Attacks*, Technical Report TR-03-416, Department of Computer Science, Rice University.

13. Debnath, N.C. and Burgin, M. (2003) Software metrics from the algorithmic perspective, in *Proc. ISCA 18th Int. Conf. "Computers and their Applications"*, Honolulu, Hawaii, pp. 279-282.

14. Dewey, T .G. (1996) The algorithmic complexity of a protein, *Physical Review E*, 54, R39-R41.

15. Dewey, T .G. (1997) Algorithmic Complexity and Thermodynamics of Sequence: Structure Relationships in Proteins, *Physical Review E* 56, pp. 4545-4552.

16. Dzhunushaliev, V. D. (1998) Kolmogorov's algorithmic complexity and its probability interpretation in quantum gravity, *Classical and Quantum Gravity*, 15, pp. 603-612.

17. Dzhunushaliev, V. D. and Singleton, D. (2001) *Algorithmic Complexity in Cosmology and Quantum Gravity*, Preprint in Physics gr-qc/0108038 (electronic edition: http://arXiv.org).

18. Feynman Lectures on Computation, (1999) (Hey, A.J.G. and Allen, R.W., Eds.) Addison-Wesley, Reading, MA.

19. Gell-Mann, M. (1995) Remarks on Simplicity and Complexity, *Complexity*, 1, pp. 16-19.

20. Grunwald, P. and Vitanyi, P. (2004) *Shannon Information and Kolmogorov Complexity*, Preprint in Computer Science, arXiv:cs/0410002.

21. Gurzadyan, V. G. (2003) Kolmogorov complexity, cosmic background radiation and irreversibility, in *Proceedings of XXII Solvay Conference on Physics*, World Scientific, pp. 204-218.

22. Hertel, J. (2012) Inductive complexity of Goodstein's theorem, in *Unconventional Computation and Natural Computation*, Lecture Notes in Computer Science, vol. 7445, pp. 141-151.

23. Kolmogorov, A.N. (1965) Three approaches to the definition of the quantity of information, *Problems of Information Transmission*, 1, pp. 3-11.

24. Kraft, L.G. (1949) *A device for quantizing, grouping and coding amplitude modulated pulses*, Master's thesis, Department of Electrical Engineering, MIT, Cambridge, MA.

25. Kreinovich, V. and Kunin, I. A. (2004) *Application of Kolmogorov Complexity to Advanced Problems in Mechanics*, University of Texas at El Paso, Computer Science Department Reports, UTEP-CS-04-14.

26. Lewis, J. P. (2001) Limits to software estimation, *Software Engineering Notes*, 26, pp. 54-59.

27. Li, M. and Vitanyi, P. (1997) *An Introduction to Kolmogorov Complexity and its Applications,* Springer-Verlag, New York.

28. Mansilla, R. (2001) *Algorithmic Complexity in Real Financial Markets*, Preprint in Physics cond-mat/0104472 (electronic edition: http://arXiv.org).

29. Muchnik, An. and Vereshchagin, N. (2006) *Shannon Entropy vs. Kolmogorov Complexity*, Lecture Notes in Computer Science, vol. 3967, pp. 281-291.

30. Neisser, U. (1967) *Cognitive Psychology*, Appleton-Crofts, New York.

31. Raatikainen, P. (1998) *Complexity and Information — A Critical Evaluation of Algorithmic Information Theory*, Reports from the Department of Philosophy, University of Helsinki, No 2 (http://www.mv.helsinki.fi/home/praatika/information. pdf).

32. Seiffert, H. (1968) *Information über die Information, Verständigung im Alltag, Nachrichtentechnik, wissenschaftliches Verstehen, Informationssoziologie, das Wissen des Gelehrten*, Verlag C. H. Beck, München.

33. Shannon, C. E. (1948) The mathematical theory of communication, *Bell System Technical Journal*, 27(1), pp. 379-423; 27(3), pp. 623-656.

34. Shaw, F. Z., Chen, R.F., Tsao, H. W. and Yen, C. T. (1999) Algorithmic complexity as an index of cortical function in awake and pentobarbital-anesthetized rats, *Journal of Neuroscience Methods*, 93(2), 101-110.

35. Tegmark, M. (1996) Does the universe in fact contain almost no information? *Found. Phys. Lett.*, 9, pp. 25-42.

36. Vitanyi, P. M. B. (2001) Quantum Kolmogorov complexity based on classical descriptions, *IEEE Transactions on Information Theory*, 47(6), pp. 2464-2479.

37. Yurtsever, U. (2000) Quantum mechanics and algorithmic randomness, *Complexity*, 6(1), pp.27–34.

38. Zurek, W. H. (1989) Algorithmic randomness and physical entropy, *Physical Review A* (3), 40(8), pp. 4731-4751.

39. Zurek, W. H. (1991) Algorithmic information content, Church-Turing thesis, physical entropy, and Maxwell's demon, in *Information Dynamics* (*Irsee*, 1990), NATO Adv. Sci. Inst. Ser. B Phys., vol. 256, Plenum, New York, pp. 245-259.

Chapter 3

Blum's and Burgin's Axioms, Complexity, and Randomness

Cezar Câmpeanu

Department of Computer Science, University of Prince Edward Island
Canada

Abstract

In this chapter we give sufficient condition to prove that Muchnik Theorem is valid in the general case of Blum-Burgin Static Complexity spaces. We also show that the randomness defined in Encoded Blum-Burgin Universal Static Complexity spaces is equivalent to the extended Martin-Löf randomness.

3.1. Introduction

Static complexity was defined in the 1960s in terms of minimal description length (MDL), more precisely, the complexity of an object was defined as the length of the minimal program that will produce that object as its output. As programs, we can use Turing Machines (TM), and we can encode all objects as binary strings. This approach was initiated by Solomonoff [1, 2], Kolmogorov in [3], also by Chaitin in [4] in the mid 1960s. Using it, a string is declared random if its length is greater than the size of the minimal program that will produce that string as its output.

In 1966, Martin-Löf [5] defined randomness of infinite sequences using sequential statistical tests, i.e., if they contain a word x, it will also contain any word y having x as a prefix. The reason for this approach is that the infinite sequences are assimilated with real numbers represented in base p, thus the sequential Martin-Löf[1]-tests will use measurable open sets, with respect to the topology induced by the prefix order, over an alphabet with p letters. A random object should be rejected by all ML statistical tests,

---

[1]Shortly, ML.

therefore an ML test W will reject an object x at level m if $x \notin W_m$. The critical level of x is the level where we first reject x and a string is declared random by an ML test if it is rejected by a test, in other words, if the critical level of the string is low.

Chaitin considered that only prefix-free TM should be used, because legal code in many programming languages, most notably the functional ones such as LISP, must be prefix-free. He proved that almost all initial segments of an ML-random sequence have prefix complexity greater than their length, and the difference between their complexity and their length approaches infinity. He established a link between ML statistical tests and complexity, based on randomness.

In 1967, Blum in [6] observed that we can use two axioms to describe the properties of the size of machines, saying that "These axioms are so fantastically weak that any reasonable model of a computer and any reasonable definition of size and step satisfies them."

In spite of the fact that almost every time it was mentioned the idea of static complexity, by citing Blum's paper, nobody was really using the power of axioms to prove results, but almost always the specifics of the particular model involved. Some relevant papers for this "tied to the model" approach are [7] and [8], where plain and prefix complexity are compared with each other. This approach of Blum is classified by Burgin in [9] as a semi-axiomatic approach, and we can now say that Blum's axioms are fundamental for the idea of static complexity in relation with algorithmic information theory. As explained in [9], algorithmic information complexity in the sense of Kolmogorov can be expressed as a dual static complexity measure. It was first observed by Burgin in 1982 [10, 11] by expanding the approach of Blum; if Blum used only two axioms to define complexity as a size of a machine, Burgin used five axioms to express algorithmic complexity and many other static complexities as dual static complexities. We must note that two of the axioms used by Burgin are Blum's axioms, and Blum assumed a third axiom of Burgin without explicitly mentioning it. For this reason, we can consider that the axiomatic approach of Burgin is an extension of the approach of Blum. Moreover, "the size of machines" used by Blum was introduced by Burgin as "a direct complexity measure", in a more general context than the one used by Blum. We must emphasize that the axioms used by Burgin, which extend the measure of "the size of machines", can be used to produce a generalized theory of dual static complexity in a uniform way, where algorithmic complexity, as defined by Kolmogorov, is a particular case.

Burgin's original approach [11], extended in [12, 13], did not include provisions to study randomness, as he considered that "... an attempt to define in this setting an appropriate concept of randomness was unsuccessful. It turned out that the original definition of Kolmogorov complexity was not relevant for that goal. To get a correct definition of a random infinite sequence, it was necessary to restrict the class of utilized algorithms." In [14–16], are considered only four of Burgin's axioms and this allows us to prove that we can expand the axiomatic approach of complexity and define randomness in a uniform way in a Blum-Burgin (Universal) Static Complexity[2] space,[3] or even in a more general framework: in an Encoded Measured Blum-Burgin (Universal) Static Complexity[4] space [17].

It is now imperative necessary to establish the new relation between randomness defined in a BSC/BUSC and ML randomness, which is dependent on the probability measure we consider. Several efforts were dedicated to study of how the computability, non-computability, or other properties of outer measures considered, including changing the exterior measure of tests, could influence the definition of ML randomness [18–20].

To keep the paper self-contained, we start by revising the notations and definitions for a BUSC space in Section 3.2, then we prove that in different BUSC spaces, two objects can have significantly different values for their complexities, therefore we generalize Muchnik theorems [8, 21] in Section 3.3.

In Section 3.4 we establish a strong connection between the randomness generated by ML tests and the randomness defined in a BUSC space. We use a similar approach to the one in [18–20], to modify the measures used in the definition of ML tests, their representability, and their relation with complexity, to prove that all universal computers will generate universal representable ML tests for a certain subclass. Using the results obtained in [15] for random sequences and ML tests, we can now interpret these new results in a different light and explain in a different way the old results concerning relations between random strings, random sequences, and complexity. The new interpretation generates several directions of research and open problems, presented in Section 3.5.

---

[2]Shortly, BUSC/BSC.
[3]Called Blum (Universal) Static Complexity space in previous papers [14–17].
[4]Shortly, EBSC/EBUSC.

3.2.   Notations and Definitions

For a set A, $\#A$ is its cardinal; we use the set of natural numbers $\mathbb{N} = \{0, 1, \ldots, \}$, and following the terminology used in [22], an algorithm for computing a partial function $f : \mathbb{N} \xrightarrow{\circ} \mathbb{N}$ is a finite set of instructions which on any given input $x \in \text{dom}(f)$, outputs $y = f(x)$ after a finite number of steps. The algorithm must specify how to obtain each step in the computation from previous steps and from the input. In case f is computed by an algorithm, we call it *partial computable function*; if f is also total, then is called a *computable function* (the old terminology referred to these as partial recursive and recursive functions [22]). A set is computable enumerable (c.e.) if it can be enumerated by a partially computable function, and it is computable if it can be enumerated by a computable function.

A function $\langle \cdot, \cdot \rangle : \mathbb{N} \times \mathbb{N} \longrightarrow \mathbb{N}$ is called a pairing function if it is injective, and its inverses $(\cdot)_1, (\cdot)_2 : \mathbb{N} \xrightarrow{\circ} \mathbb{N}$ satisfy the following properties:

(1) $\langle (z)_1, (z)_2 \rangle = z$;
(2) $(\langle x, y \rangle)_1 = x, (\langle x, y \rangle)_2 = y$.

In case $\langle \cdot, \cdot \rangle$ is bijective, the inverses $(\cdot)_1, (\cdot)_2$ are total functions.

In what follows we will use only computable pairing functions. Using pairing functions, we can extend unary functions to functions having more than one argument by defining $\phi_i^{(2)}(x, y) = \phi_i^{(1)}(\langle x, y \rangle)$, and to consider that indexes of algorithms are encodings of algorithms over a standard finite alphabet $A_p = \{0, \ldots, p - 1\}$. In case $p = 2$, the encoding is over the binary alphabet $A_2 = \{0, 1\}$. Examples of pairing functions over A_p can be found in [15, 17, 22]. We also mention the fact that, in general, we can have multiple encodings of algorithms in a space possessing its own measure [16, 17, 23], and we don't necessarily need to use the alphabet A_p and the length measure over A_p^*, but most examples will use an encoding over a finite alphabet A_p.

We reiterate the convention that a function $f : \mathbb{N} \longrightarrow \mathbb{N}$, when applied to a string $w \in A_p^*$, is in fact the function f applied to $\text{string}_p^{-1}(w)$, and when the result is in A_p^*, we apply the function string_p to the result of f. In case the function f has k arguments, i.e., $f : \mathbb{N}^k \longrightarrow \mathbb{N}$ and some arguments are strings, the function f is applied to string_p^{-1} for those strings. Thus, we do not distinguish between a number $n \in \mathbb{N}$ and its representation $\text{string}_p(n) \in A_p^*$.

We refer the reader to [24–26] for more on computability, computable functions, and recursive function theory.

3.2.1. *Blum-Burgin universal static complexity*

We consider an acceptable enumeration of the set of all partial computable functions over $\mathbb{N}$, $\mathcal{F} = (\phi_i^{(n)})_{i \in \mathbb{N}}$, i.e., an enumeration satisfying the Wagner-Strong axioms [25, 26].[5]

In [11, 12], the definitions of direct and dual complexity measures are stated in a formalism similar with the one that follows.

Let $\mathcal{G} \subseteq \mathcal{F}$, $\mathcal{G} = (\psi_i^{(n)})_{i \in I}$ be a class of algorithms. A function $m : I \longrightarrow \mathbb{N}$ is called a (direct) complexity measure [12][6] if it satisfies:

(1) (Computational axiom) m is computable;
(2) (Re-computational Axiom) for every $n \in \mathbb{N}$, the set $\{j \mid m(j) = n\}$ is computable;
(3) (Cofiniteness Axiom) for every $n \in \mathbb{N}$, we have $\#\{j \mid m(j) = n\} < \infty$.

In [12], additional axioms are considered for defining axiomatic complexity measures:

(4) (Re-constructability Axiom) For any number n, it is possible to build all algorithms A from $\mathcal{G}$ for which $m(A) = n$, or using our notations, it will imply that the set $\{j \mid m(j) = n\}$ is computable.[7]
(5) (Compositional Axiom) If $A \subseteq B$, then $m(A) \leq m(B)$.

Since the semantics of the relation "$\subseteq$" between algorithms is usually defined depending on some encoding of the algorithm, in this paper we will only consider the axioms 1–4.

Definition 3.1 ([14]). A space $(\mathcal{G}, m)$ satisfying the axioms (1)–(4) is called *Blum-Burgin Static Complexity (BSC) space*.

Definition 3.2 ([11, 12]). Let $d : \mathbb{N} \longrightarrow \mathbb{N}$ be a function. An algorithm $U : \mathbb{N} \times \mathbb{N} \overset{\circ}{\longrightarrow} \mathbb{N}$ is called d-universal for the set $\mathcal{G} = (\psi_i)_{i \in I}$, if $\psi_i(n) =$

---

[5]In $\phi_i^{(n)}$, the exponent (n) represents the number of arguments of the function with index i.

[6]See also [27].

[7]Not all the finite sets are computable. For example, the set of the first 10 indexes of the programs for which the halting program is undecidable is finite, as it has 10 elements, but it is not computable. Please see also [12] for a complete explanation of the difference between axiom 2 and axiom 4.

$U(d(i), n)$, for all $i \in I$ and $n \in \mathbb{N}$.

If U is a two argument universal algorithm for the algorithms with one argument, i.e., $U(i, x) = \psi_i(x)$, then U is $1_\mathbb{N}$-universal for $\mathcal{G}$.

Given a complexity measure $m : I \longrightarrow \mathbb{N}$ and $\psi \in \mathcal{G}$, *the dual to m* measure with respect to ψ is[8]

$$m_\psi^0(x) = \min\{m(y) \mid y \in I, \psi(y) = x\}.[9]$$

If I is the encoding of algorithms over A_p, then $m(I)$ is usually the length of the encoding; in this case, m_ψ^0 is called dual to length complexity of x, with respect to the algorithm ψ.

Since the measure m satisfies the Cofiniteness Axiom (3), we can define the maximum complexity of objects having a certain measure as:

$$\Sigma_\phi^\mathcal{G}(n) = \max\{m_\phi^0(x) \mid m(x) = n\}.$$

Using the notation $C_\phi^\mathcal{G} = m_\phi^0$, for dual to length complexity measures, we get:

$$\Sigma_\phi^\mathcal{G}(n) = \max\{C_\phi^\mathcal{G}(x) \mid m(x) = n\}.$$

If there exists i_0 such that for all $i \in I$, there is a $c \in \mathbb{N}$ satisfying the inequality:

$$C_{\psi_{i_0}}^\mathcal{G}(x) \leq C_{\psi_i}^\mathcal{G}(x) + c \tag{3.1}$$

for all $x \in \mathbb{N}$, then the algorithm ψ_{i_0} is a universal algorithm for the family $\mathcal{G}$.[10]

Using the notation $C_{\phi_{i_0}}^\mathcal{G} = C^\mathcal{G}$, we get:

$$\Sigma^\mathcal{G}(n) = \Sigma_{\phi_{i_0}}^\mathcal{G}(n) = \max\{C^\mathcal{G}(x) \mid |x| = n\}.$$

Throughout the rest of the paper we consider that m is the length complexity measure, $|\cdot|$, and we denote the dual to m complexity measure by $C_\psi^\mathcal{G} = m_\psi^0$. When the space $\mathcal{G}$ is understood, we may omit the superscript $\mathcal{G}$.

In [14] we propose such a set of properties for the encoding, and for keeping the paper self-contained, we include them here:

---

[8]We use $\min \emptyset = \infty$.

[9]We can consider that I is embedded in $\mathbb{N}$.

[10]The constant c depends on i and i_0, but does not depend on x.

Definition 3.3 ([14]). Let e and E be two computable functions satisfying the following properties:

(1) E is injective and is a length increasing function in the second argument, i.e., there exists c_e, such that if $|x| \leq |y|$, then $|E(i, x)| \leq |E(i, y)| + c_e$.

(2) $|E(i, x)| \leq |E(i', x)| + \eta(i, i')$, for some function $\eta : \mathbb{N}^2 \longrightarrow \mathbb{N}$.

Then we say that the pair (e, E) is an encoding.[11]

Definition 3.4 ([14]). We say that the family $\mathcal{G} = (\psi_j)_{j \in J}$ is an (e, E)-encoding of the family $\mathcal{H} = (\mu_i)_{i \in I}$, if we have that:

(1) $\mu_i(x) = \psi_{e(i)}(E(i, x))$, for all $i \in I$ and $x \in \mathbb{N}$,

(2) if $\psi_j(z) = y$, then $e(i) = j$ and $E(i, x) = z$, for some $i \in I$ and $x \in \mathbb{N}$.

Theorem 3.5 ([14]). *If $\mathcal{H}$ has a universal algorithm in $\mathcal{H}$, and $\mathcal{G}$ is an encoding of $\mathcal{H}$, then $\mathcal{G}$ has a universal algorithm in $\mathcal{G}$.*

In case $\mathcal{G}$ encodes $\mathcal{F}$, then $\mathcal{G}$ is called *Blum-Burgin universal static complexity space* (BUSC). One can check that (Prefix-free) Turing Machines, together with their sizes, form a BUSC space, more details being presented in [11, 14].

If $\mathcal{G}$ is a BUSC space, with the universal function ψ_{i_0}, then the canonical program of x is $x^* = \min\{y \in \mathbb{N} \mid \psi_{i_0}(y) = x\}$. Since we work with complexities that are dual to length measures, and because $x < y$ implies $|\text{string}(x)| \leq |\text{string}(y)|$, it follows that we can also write $x < y$ implies $|x| \leq |y|$. Thus, if $\mathcal{G}$ is an (e, E)-encoding of $\mathcal{F}$, then:

$$\text{if } x < y, \text{ it follows that } |E(i, x)| \leq |E(i, y)| + c_e. \tag{3.2}$$

We say that a number x is t-compressible in $\mathcal{G}$, if $C^{\mathcal{G}}(x) < \Sigma^{\mathcal{G}}(|x|) - t$, and that it is t-incompressible, if $C^{\mathcal{G}}(x) \geq \Sigma^{\mathcal{G}}(|x|) - t$. A t-incompressible element is also called t-random in $\mathcal{G}$, and the set of all these elements is denoted by $\text{Rand}_t^{\mathcal{G}}$. We denote by non-$\text{Rand}_t^{\mathcal{G}} = \mathbb{N} \setminus \text{Rand}_t^{\mathcal{G}}$.

The following results have already been proved in [14] for a BUSC $\mathcal{G}$:

(1) The set of canonical programs is immune.

(2) The function $f(x) = x^*$ is not computable.

(3) The function $C^{\mathcal{G}}$ is not computable.

(4) The set $\text{Rand}_t^{\mathcal{G}}$ is immune.

---

[11]Please note that the constant c_e depends on the function e, but does not depend on i or y.

3.2.2.   *Martin-Löf tests*

For a partially computable set $V \subseteq \mathbb{N} \times N$, we define $V_t = \{x \in \mathbb{N} \mid (x,t) \in V\}$, the m section of V (see [5, 22]).

A statistical test should consist of an enumerable sequence of sets $(V_t)_{t \geq 0}$ such that their probability decreases, or in terms of measure theory, their measure tends to 0 when t goes to ∞. The condition that $V_{t+1} \subseteq V_t$ is necessary, because for each level we should not accept strings already rejected at a previous level.

For discrete measures, the usual condition is that the probability of elements to be in V_t should be less than $\frac{1}{p^t}$, and for elements of length n, we must have that $\#(A_p^n \cap V_t) < p^{n-t}$. This is the original condition used by Martin-Löf in [5]. In Section 3.4 we analyze the conditions that can be used to test the sets V_t such that the randomness induced by the tests is the same as the randomness in a BUSC $\mathcal{G}$.

We start our results by analyzing a theorem by Muchnik [21].

3.3.   Muchnik Theorem in BUSC Spaces

Muchnik proved in [21] that for every threshold M we can find two words u and v such that the difference between the plain complexity of u and v is above the threshold, and the difference between the prefix complexity of v and u is also above the threshold.

Using the BUSC terminology, if $\mathcal{G}$ is the BUSC for the prefix complexity, and $\mathcal{F}$ is the BUSC for plain complexity, then we have the following.

Theorem 3.6 ([8, Theorem 4.1; 21, Theorem 2.8]). *For every* $M \in \mathbb{N}$ *we can find* $u, v \in \mathbb{N}$ *such that*

$$C^{\mathcal{F}}(u) + M < C^{\mathcal{F}}(v)$$

and

$$C^{\mathcal{G}}(v) + M < C^{\mathcal{G}}(u).$$

In what follows we check the conditions that will allow us to obtain a similar result for any two arbitrary BUSC spaces $\mathcal{G}$ and $\mathcal{H}$. We use the following definitions from [15].

Definition 3.7 ([15]). We say that the encoding (e, E) is a normal encoding if for any $T \in \mathbb{N}$, there exists $t \in \mathbb{N}$ such that, if $|x| \leq |y| - t$, then $|E(i,x)| \leq |E(i,y)| - T$.

We can see that the proof of Theorem 8 in [15] works for $\mathcal{G}$ as a normal encoding of $\mathcal{H}$, where both $\mathcal{G}$ and $\mathcal{H}$ are BUSC spaces. Therefore, we can state the following.

Theorem 3.8 ([15]). *Let $\mathcal{G}$ be a normal encoding of $\mathcal{H}$. Then, for every $m \in \mathbb{N}$, there is a $t \in \mathbb{N}$ such that for each $x \in N$, $C^{\mathcal{H}}(x) < \Sigma^{\mathcal{H}}(|x|) - t$, implies $C^{\mathcal{G}}(x) < \Sigma^{\mathcal{G}}(|x|) - m$.*

In other words, the last result shows that if x is $\mathcal{G}$-m-random, then it must be $\mathcal{H}$-t-random.

Now we prove two technical results, showing that in order to have complexities defining different random sets, the difference between the size of encodings must be also as big as possible. Assume $\mathcal{G} = (\psi_i^{(n)})_{i \in \mathbb{N}}$ and $\mathcal{H} = (\gamma_i^{(n)})_{i \in \mathbb{N}}$, and i_0 is the index for a universal computer in $\mathcal{H}$. Using [14], $\psi_{e(i_0)}$ is a universal computer in $\mathcal{G}$.

Theorem 3.9. *Let $\mathcal{G}$ and $\mathcal{H}$ be two BUSC spaces such that $\mathcal{G}$ is an encoding of $\mathcal{H}$. If for all $T \in \mathbb{N}$, there is $t \in \mathbb{N}$ such that:*

$$\forall x, y \in \mathbb{N} \text{ such that } |x| - |y| \leq t \text{ implies } |E(i,x)| - |E(i,y)| \leq T, \quad (3.3)$$

then for every $T \in \mathbb{N}$, we can find $t \in \mathbb{N}$ such that $C^{\mathcal{G}}(x) < \Sigma^{\mathcal{G}}(|x|) - T$ implies $C^{\mathcal{H}}(x) < \Sigma^{\mathcal{H}}(|x|) - t$.

Proof. Because $\mathcal{G}$ is an encoding of $\mathcal{H}$, if $\psi_{e(i)}(E(i,y)) = x$, then $\gamma_i(y) = x$.

Let $x \in \mathbb{N}$ be such that $C^{\mathcal{G}}(x) < \Sigma^{\mathcal{G}}(|x|) - T$. There must be some $z_1 \in \mathbb{N}$ with $\gamma_{i_0}(z_1) = x$, $C^{\mathcal{G}}(x) = |E(i_0, z_1)|$, and some $v_1 \in \mathbb{N}$ with $\gamma_{i_0}(v_1) = w_1$, $\Sigma^{\mathcal{G}}(|x|) = C^{\mathcal{G}}(w_1) = |E(i_0, v_1)|$ such that

$$|E(i_0, z_1)| < |E(i_0, v_1)| - T. \quad (3.4)$$

Let $z \in \mathbb{N}$ be such that $z = E(i_0, z_1)$, $|z| = C^{\mathcal{G}}(x)$ and let v be such that $v = E(i_0, v_1)$, $|v| = C^{\mathcal{G}}(w_1) = \Sigma^{\mathcal{G}}(|x|)$, then $|z| \leq |z_1|$, $|v_1| \leq |v|$, $|E(i_0, z_1)| \leq |E(i_0, z)|$, and $|E(i_0, v)| \leq |E(i_0, v_1)|$. In case $C^{\mathcal{H}}(x) \geq \Sigma^{\mathcal{H}}(|x|) - t$, we have $|z_1| \geq |z| > |v| - t \geq |v_1| - t$, therefore $t > |v_1| - |z_1|$. Using our hypothesis, we have that $|E(i_0, v_1)| - |E(i_0, z_1)| \leq T$, which contradicts Eq. (3.4). $\square$

It is clear that if we can prove that for every $T \in \mathbb{N}$ we can find $t \in \mathbb{N}$ such that $C^{\mathcal{H}}(x) \geq \Sigma^{\mathcal{H}}(|x|) - t$, implies $C^{\mathcal{G}}(x) \geq \Sigma^{\mathcal{G}}(|x|) - T$, then (3.3) cannot be satisfied.

Theorem 3.10. *Let $\mathcal{G}$ and $\mathcal{H}$ be two BUSC spaces such that $\mathcal{G}$ is an encoding of $\mathcal{H}$. If for all $x \in \mathbb{N}$, $||E(i,x)| - |x|| < M$, then for every $t \in \mathbb{N}$ we can find $m \in \mathbb{N}$ such that $C^{\mathcal{G}}(x) < \Sigma^{\mathcal{G}}(|x|) - m$ implies $C^{\mathcal{H}}(x) < \Sigma^{\mathcal{H}}(|x|) - t$.*

Proof. Because $\mathcal{G}$ is an encoding of $\mathcal{H}$, if $\psi_{e(i)}(E(i,y)) = x$, then $\gamma_i(y) = x$ and we make the observation that is enough to prove the theorem in the case when the complexity is computed in $\mathcal{G}$ with respect to ψ_{i_0} and in $\mathcal{H}$ with respect to $\gamma_{e(i_0)}$.

In this case we prove that for every t there is $m = t + 2M$ such that $C^{\mathcal{G}}(x) < \Sigma^{\mathcal{G}}(|x|) - (t + 2M)$ implies $C^{\mathcal{H}}(x) < \Sigma^{\mathcal{H}}(|x|) - t$.

First, we use the assumption about M to show that

$$|C^{\mathcal{H}}(x) - C^{\mathcal{G}}(x)| < M, \text{ for all } x \in \mathbb{N}.$$

For the case $C^{\mathcal{G}}(x) \geq C^{\mathcal{H}}(x)$, let y be such that $\gamma_{i_0}(y) = x$. Because $\mathcal{G}$ is an encoding of $\mathcal{H}$, if $\psi_{e(i_0)}(E(i,y)) = x$, it follows that $|y| = C^{\mathcal{H}}(x)$, thus $C^{\mathcal{G}}(x) \leq |E(i_0, y)|$. Then $C^{\mathcal{G}}(x) - C^{\mathcal{H}}(x) \leq |E(i_0, y)| - |y| < M$. The case $C^{\mathcal{G}}(x) < C^{\mathcal{H}}(x)$ can be handled analogously. We show that

$$|\Sigma^{\mathcal{H}}(n) - \Sigma^{\mathcal{G}}(n)| < M, \text{ for all } n \in \mathbb{N}.$$

Let $v_1, v_2 \in \mathbb{N}$ with $|v_1| = |v_2| = n$ be such that $\Sigma^{\mathcal{H}}(n) = C^{\mathcal{H}}(v_1)$ and $\Sigma^{\mathcal{G}}(n) = C^{\mathcal{G}}(v_2)$.

If $\Sigma^{\mathcal{H}}(n) > \Sigma^{\mathcal{G}}(n)$, then $\Sigma^{\mathcal{H}}(n) - \Sigma^{\mathcal{G}}(n) = C^{\mathcal{H}}(v_1) - C^{\mathcal{G}}(v_2) \leq C^{\mathcal{H}}(v_1) - C^{\mathcal{G}}(v_1) < M$. The case $\Sigma^{\mathcal{G}}(n) > \Sigma^{\mathcal{H}}(n)$ is similar.

Now, let $t \in \mathbb{N}$, choose $m = t + 2M$, and assume $C^{\mathcal{G}}(x) < \Sigma^{\mathcal{G}}(|x|) - m$. We have that $C^{\mathcal{H}}(x) < C^{\mathcal{G}}(x) + M$, which implies

$$\begin{aligned}
C^{\mathcal{H}}(x) &< C^{\mathcal{G}}(x) + M < \Sigma^{\mathcal{G}}(|x|) - m + M \\
&< \Sigma^{\mathcal{H}}(|x|) + M - m + M = \Sigma^{\mathcal{H}}(|x|) + 2M - 2M - t \\
&= \Sigma^{\mathcal{H}}(|x|) - t. \qquad \square
\end{aligned}$$

Using Theorem 3.8 and Theorem 3.10, it follows that if $\mathcal{G}$ is an encoding of $\mathcal{H}$ and their encodings do not differ too much, then they have the same power in defining randomness. Again, if $\mathrm{Rand}_t^{\mathcal{H}} \subseteq \mathrm{Rand}_T^{\mathcal{G}}$, then we must have that $\limsup_{x \to \infty} ||E(i,x)| - |x|| = \infty$.

One can check that in case we take $\mathcal{H} = \mathcal{F}$, where $C^{\mathcal{F}}$ is plain Kolmogorov complexity, and $\mathcal{G}$ is the BUSC for prefix complexity, then[12]: $\lim_{x \to \infty} ||E(i,x)| - |x|| = \lim_{x \to \infty} (H(x) - |x|) = \lim_{x \to \infty} |x| + \log(|x|) - |x| = \infty$, and the condition 3.3 is not satisfied.

Indeed, the statement: if for all $T \in \mathbb{N}$, there exists $t \in \mathbb{N}$ such that

$$\forall x, y \in \mathbb{N} \text{ such that } |x| - |y| \leq t \text{ implies } |E(i,x)| - |E(i,y)| < T,$$

does not hold.

---

[12] Here H denotes prefix complexity.

Let us take x, y such that $|x|+t = |y|$, and $\psi_{i_0}(E(i_0, x)) = u$, $u \in \text{Rand}_T^{\mathcal{G}}$ $\psi_{i_0}(E(i_0, y)) = v$, $u \in \text{non-Rand}_T^{\mathcal{G}}$, $H(v) = \log|v| + O(1)$. We have that $|E(i_0, x)| - |E(i_0, y)| = H(u) - H(v) = |u| + \log(|u|) + O(1) - \log|v| - O(1) > |u| > T$, regardless of the value of t.

Thus, we conjecture the following theorem, although we believe that we need an additional condition beside the two enumerated here.

Theorem 3.11. *Let $\mathcal{G}$ and $\mathcal{H}$ be two BUSC spaces such that $\mathcal{G}$ is a normal encoding of $\mathcal{H}$. If*

(1) $\lim\limits_{x \to \infty} |E(i, x)| - |x|| = \infty$ *and*
(2) *(3.3) is not satisfied,*

then for every $T \in \mathbb{N}$, we can find $t \in \mathbb{N}$ such that $\text{Rand}_t^{\mathcal{H}} \not\subseteq \text{Rand}_T^{\mathcal{G}}$.

Theorem 3.11 is essential in proving a result by Muchnik [21], that shows that we can have two strings for which two different complexities disagree as much as we want. Thus, finding the minimal conditions for two BUSC spaces $\mathcal{H}$ and $\mathcal{G}$ to have strict inclusion of their random numbers is essential, and it remains an open problem.

When the BUSC $\mathcal{G}$ uses the dual to length measure on a free monoid A_p^*, we have that $\# \bigcup_{i=0}^{n-1}\{x \mid |x| = i\} = \frac{p^n - 1}{p - 1} < p^n = \#\{x \mid |x| = n\}$, thus $\Sigma^{\mathcal{G}}(n) \geq n$ and there is at least one element $x \in \text{Rand}_t^{\mathcal{G}}$, $|x| = n$.

Hence, it makes sense to use only BUSC spaces with $\Sigma^{\mathcal{G}}(n) \geq n$ and we implicitly assume it for next results; moreover, we may also assume that $\Sigma^{\mathcal{G}}$ is a non-decreasing function[13] and that $\{x \in \text{Rand}_t^{\mathcal{G}} \mid |x| = n\} \neq \emptyset$, for all $n \in \mathbb{N}$.

Lemma 3.12. *For a BUSC space $\mathcal{G}$ we have:*

(1) $\lim\limits_{n \to \infty} \Sigma^{\mathcal{G}}(n) = \infty$.
(2) *If $f : \mathbb{N} \longrightarrow \mathbb{N}$ is such that $\lim\limits_{n \to \infty} (n - f(n)) = \infty$, then*

$$\lim\limits_{n \to \infty} (\Sigma^{\mathcal{G}}(n) - \Sigma^{\mathcal{G}}(f(n))) = \infty.$$

Proof. The first one is a direct consequence of Axiom 3, as there are a finite number of numbers of a fixed complexity. For the second one, we first observe that for every $K \in \mathbb{N}$ there is $M \in \mathbb{N}$ and $n_{0,1} \in \mathbb{N}$ such that $\Sigma^{\mathcal{G}}(n) - \Sigma^{\mathcal{G}}(n - M) > K$, for all $n \geq n_{0,1}$.

---

[13]All known complexities have this property, thus this assumption is reasonable.

For every M, there is $n_{0,2}$ such that $n - f(n) > M$, for all $n \geq n_{0,2}$, which means that $n - M > f(n)$, for all $n \geq n_{0,2}$. Hence, for every $K \in \mathbb{N}$, $\Sigma^{\mathcal{G}}(n) - \Sigma^{\mathcal{G}}(f(n)) \geq \Sigma^{\mathcal{G}}(n) - \Sigma^{\mathcal{G}}(n - M) > K$, for all $n \geq n_0 = \max\{n_{0,1}, n_{0,2}\}$, which implies that

$$\lim_{n \to \infty} (\Sigma^{\mathcal{G}}(n) - \Sigma^{\mathcal{G}}(f(n))) = \infty.$$

$\square$

We observe that for all $x \in \mathrm{Rand}^{\mathcal{H}}$, then $x \in \mathrm{Rand}_t^{\mathcal{H}}$, thus $x \in \mathrm{Rand}^{\mathcal{H}} \setminus \mathrm{Rand}_T^{\mathcal{G}}$ implies $x \in \mathrm{Rand}_t^{\mathcal{H}} \setminus \mathrm{Rand}_T^{\mathcal{G}}$.

Now, let $f : \mathbb{N} \longrightarrow \mathbb{N}$ be a non-decreasing function such as, for every $M \in \mathbb{N}$, there is $n_M \in \mathbb{N}$ such that

$$\Sigma^{\mathcal{G}}(n - t) - \Sigma^{\mathcal{G}}(n) + f(t) > M, \tag{3.5}$$

for every $t \geq n_M$ and $n > t$.

We say that $\mathcal{G}$ is $\Sigma - f$-bounded if (3.5) is true. It must be noted that both plain and prefix complexity are Σ-f-bounded, for $f(t) = 2t$. Indeed, in case of plain complexity $\Sigma^{\mathcal{F}}(n) = n + O(1)$, thus

$\Sigma^{\mathcal{F}}(n-t) - \Sigma^{\mathcal{F}}(n) + f(t) = n - t + O(1) - n - O(1) + f(t) = f(t) - t + O(1) = t + O(1) > M$, if $n > t$ and $t > M$.

For prefix complexity $\Sigma^{\mathcal{G}}(n) = n + \log n + O(1)$, therefore

$\Sigma^{\mathcal{G}}(n-t) - \Sigma^{\mathcal{G}}(n) + f(t) = n - t + \log(n - t) + O(1) - n - \log n - O(1) + f(t) = t + \log \frac{n-t}{n} + O(1) > \frac{t}{2} + O(1) > M$,

if $t > 2M$ and $n > 2t$.

We use Σ-f-bounded property to prove Muchnik theorem for BUSC spaces:

Theorem 3.13. *Let $\mathcal{G}$ and $\mathcal{H}$ be two BUSC spaces such that $\mathcal{G}$ is a normal encoding of $\mathcal{H}$ and $n_0 \in \mathbb{N}$, such that for every $k \in \mathbb{N}$ and for every $n \geq n_0$, we can find x with $|x| = n$ and $x \in \mathrm{Rand}^{\mathcal{H}} \setminus \mathrm{Rand}_k^{\mathcal{G}}$.*

If $\mathcal{G}$ is Σ-f-bounded, then for every $M \in \mathbb{N}$, we can find $v, w \in \mathbb{N}$ such that:

(1)

$$C^{\mathcal{H}}(w) - C^{\mathcal{H}}(v) > M$$

and

(2)

$$C^{\mathcal{G}}(v) - C^{\mathcal{G}}(w) > M.$$

Proof. Let $g, v : \mathbb{N} \longrightarrow \mathbb{N}$ be any functions such that

(1) v is non-decreasing, $2v(t) < t$, and $\lim_{t \to \infty} v(t) = \infty$,
(2) $g(t) > \max\{f(t), n_0\}$,
(3) $\lim_{t \to \infty}(g(t) - v(t)) = \infty$, and
(4) $\lim_{t \to \infty}(g(t) - f(t)) = \infty$.

For every $k \in \mathbb{N}$, choose a number $x_k \in \mathrm{Rand}_0^{\mathcal{H}} \setminus \mathrm{Rand}_k^{\mathcal{G}}$ of length $g(k)$ and for every t such that $g(k) - v(t) > 0$, $y_{k,t} \in \mathrm{Rand}_t^{\mathcal{G}}$ having the measure $|y_{k,t}| = g(k) - v(t)$. We have that:

$$C^{\mathcal{H}}(x_k) - C^{\mathcal{H}}(y_{k,t}) \geq \Sigma^{\mathcal{H}}(g(k)) - \Sigma^{\mathcal{H}}(g(k) - v(t)).$$

Now, using Lemma 3.12(2) for $\mathcal{H}$ applied for $n = g(k)$, $f(n)$ as $n - v(t)$, and M, we obtain that

$$C^{\mathcal{H}}(x_k) - C^{\mathcal{H}}(y_{k,t}) > M$$

if t and k are large enough.

We also have that:

$$
\begin{aligned}
C^{\mathcal{G}}(y_{k,t}) - C^{\mathcal{G}}(x_k) &> \Sigma^{\mathcal{G}}(g(k) - v(t)) - t - \Sigma^{\mathcal{G}}(g(k)) + k \\
&\geq \Sigma^{\mathcal{G}}(g(k) - v(t)) - \Sigma^{\mathcal{G}}(g(k)) + k - t \\
&= \Sigma^{\mathcal{G}}(g(k) - v(t)) - \Sigma^{\mathcal{G}}(g(k)) + f(v(t)) \\
&\quad + k - t - f(v(t)).
\end{aligned}
$$

It follows that for t and k large enough, i.e., $g(k) - v(t) > 0$, k such that $k > t + f(v(t))$, and $v(t) > n_M$

$$C^{\mathcal{G}}(y_{k,t}) - C^{\mathcal{G}}(x_k) > M.$$

Hence, we have at the same time: $C^{\mathcal{G}}(y_{k,t}) - C^{\mathcal{G}}(x_k) > M$, and $C^{\mathcal{H}}(x_k) - C^{\mathcal{H}}(y_{k,t}) > M$, which is exactly what we need to prove. $\qquad\square$

This result proves that Theorem 3.6 is a particular case of Theorem 3.13.

We can see that the only essential condition for two complexities to disagree is to have numbers of any length in $\mathrm{Rand}_t^{\mathcal{H}} \setminus \mathrm{Rand}_T^{\mathcal{G}}$, which is only true for complexities that do not have the same "growth"; such complexities will be called incompatible. It must be noted that all the proofs of Muchnik theorems for plain and prefix-free complexity use similar constructions, but the effectively build the functions similar to the ones present in the proof of the theorem.

3.4.   Blum-Burgin Static Complexity and Martin-Löf Tests

In this section we establish the connection between randomness defined
by BUSC spaces and Martin-Löf randomness.   First of all, we need to
use Martin-Löf tests that have the same measures as the one used in the
corresponding BUSC. Thus, if the BUSC $\mathcal{G}$ has measure m, then the same
one must be used for ML tests. If we consider the probability of i, $m(i) = n$
in space $S_n = \{x \mid m(x) = n\}$, we get it as $\frac{1}{\#S_n}$. A statistical test V at
level n containing k elements will have the probability less than $\frac{k}{\#S_n}$.

If $m : \mathbb{N} \longrightarrow \mathbb{N}$ is a direct measure on N, we can define $h(i) = \sum_{j=0}^{i-1} \#\{x \in \mathbb{N} \mid m(x) = j\}$.

For most BUSC spaces studied so far we always had that $h(n) < \#\{x \mid m(x) = n\}$, and we can ask the probability of an element of $x \in V_t$ to be
less than $\frac{1}{h(t)}$.

Definition 3.14. Let m be a direct measure on $\mathbb{N}$.   A Martin-Löf test
$V \subseteq \mathbb{N} \times \mathbb{N}$ is a partially computable set such that:

(1) $V_{n+1} \subseteq V_n$;
(2) $\#\{x \in V_m \mid m(x) = n\} < \frac{h(n+1)}{h(t+1)-h(t)}$.

We denote by $\mathcal{M}$ the set of all ML tests.

Checking Definition 3.14 for A_p^* and the usual length, we get

$$\#\{x \in V_m \mid m(x) = n\} < \frac{h(n+1)}{h(t+1)-h(t)} = \frac{\frac{p^n-1}{p-1}}{p^t} = \frac{p^{n-t}-\frac{1}{p^t}}{p-1}.$$

Because the number of elements is an integer, we find that this condition
matches the condition considered in [22]: $\#\{x \in V_m \mid m(x) = n\} < \frac{p^{n-t}}{p-1}$.

The critical level of an element $x \in \mathbb{N}$ is the index of the first section of
a test rejecting it, $m_V(x) = \min\{t \mid x \notin V_t\}$.

Definition 3.15. Let $\mathcal{T} \subseteq \mathcal{M}$ be a family of ML tests. An ML test $U \in \mathcal{T}$
is universal for $\mathcal{T}$ if for every $V \in \mathcal{T}$, there is a constant c such that:

$$V_{t+c} \subseteq U_t,$$

for all $t \in \mathbb{N}$. In case the test is universal, $m_V(x) \leq m_U(x) + c$, for all
$x \in \mathbb{N}$.

It is known that universal ML tests for $\mathcal{M}$ exist [22].

For a BUSC $\mathcal{G}$, consider the function $\sigma^{\mathcal{G}}(n) = \min\{k \mid \Sigma^{\mathcal{G}}(k+1) > n\}$.
It is clear that $\Sigma^{\mathcal{G}}(\sigma^{\mathcal{G}}(n)) \leq n$ and $\sigma^{\mathcal{G}}(\Sigma^{\mathcal{G}}(n)) = n$.

Now, let us take a function $F \in \mathcal{G}$, and another function $f : \mathbb{N} \longrightarrow \mathbb{N}$,
and we analyze the set $V(F) = \{(x,t) \mid C_F^{\mathcal{G}}(x) < f(|x|) - t\}$. If $V(F)$ is

an ML test, then $\#\{x \mid x \in V(F), |x| = n\} < \frac{h(n+1)}{h(t+1)-h(t)}$. This means that $\#\{x \mid C_F^{\mathcal{G}}(x) < f(n) - t\} < \frac{h(n+1)}{h(t+1)-h(t)}$. It follows that $h(f(n) - t) < \frac{h(n+1)}{h(t+1)-h(t)}$, i.e.,

$$h(f(n) - t)(h(t+1) - h(t)) < h(n+1). \tag{3.6}$$

In case we work on A_p^*, the (3.6) becomes

$$\frac{p^{(f(n)-t)} - 1}{p - 1} p^t < \frac{p^n - 1}{p - 1},$$

which is equivalent to

$$(p^{(f(n)-t)} - 1)p^t \leq p^n$$

and

$$(p^{(f(n)-t)} - 1) \leq p^{n-t}.$$

For n large enough, $f(n) - t \leq n - t$, which means

$$f(n) \leq n. \tag{3.7}$$

We must note that $\sigma^{\mathcal{G}}$ satisfies (3.7), if $\mathcal{G}$ uses the dual to length measure on A_p^*, as $\Sigma^{\mathcal{G}}(n) \geq n$. Hence, we can state the following result.

Lemma 3.16. *Let $\mathcal{G}$ be a BUSC and $F \in \mathcal{G}$, and $f : \mathbb{N} \longrightarrow \mathbb{N}$ be a function satisfying (3.6). Then $V(F) = \{(x,t) \mid C_F^{\mathcal{G}}(x) < f(|x|) - t\}$ is an ML-test.*

Proof. Because the set $V(f)_t = \{C_f^{\mathcal{G}}(x) < \Sigma^{\mathcal{G}}(|x|) - t\}$ is c.e. for every $t \in \mathbb{N}$, [15], the set $V(f)$ is c.e. The inclusion $V(f)_{m+1} \subseteq V(f)$ is obvious. The last condition is true because f satisfies (3.6). $\square$

Corollary 3.17. *If $\mathcal{G}$ uses the dual to length measure on A_p^*, the set $V(F) = \{(x,t) \mid C_F^{\mathcal{G}}(x) < \sigma^{\mathcal{G}}(|x|) - t\}$ is an ML test.*

These last results suggest our next definition.

Definition 3.18. Let f be a function satisfying (3.6). A ML test is f representable if we can find $F \in \mathcal{G}$ such that $W = V(F)$.

We must note that the Definition 3.18 is an extension of representability of ML tests presented in [22], and it will only coincide when the BUSC space is $\mathcal{F}$. In that case, because there is a $d \in \mathbb{N}$ such that $C^{\mathcal{F}}(x) < |x| + d$, for all $x \in \mathbb{N}$, we have that $V_{t+d} = \{x \mid (x, t+d) \in V\} \subseteq \{x \mid t + d \leq |x| - C^{\mathcal{F}}(x) + d\} = \{(x,t) \mid C_F^{\mathcal{G}}(x) < \sigma_f^{\mathcal{F}}(|x|) - t\} = V(\psi_{i_0})$, and this means that $V(\psi_{i_0})$ is universal for all ML tests, not only for representable ML tests.[14,15]

The following theorem established the link between universal computers, and universal ML tests. It must be noted that in case we use the old definition of representability, the following theorem is only valid for plain complexity, but using the new Definition 3.18 of representability, it is valid for all complexities.

Theorem 3.19. *If $\psi_{i_0} \in \mathcal{G}$ is a universal computer in $\mathcal{G}$, then $V(\psi_{i_0})$ is universal for all $\sigma^{\mathcal{G}}$ representable ML tests.*

Proof. Let $V = V(\psi)$ be a representable ML test. This means that $V(\psi) = \{(x,t) \mid C_\psi^{\mathcal{G}}(x) < \sigma^{\mathcal{G}}(|x|) - t\}$. Hence, $V(\psi)_{t+c} = \{(x, t+c) \mid C_\psi^{\mathcal{G}}(x) < \sigma^{\mathcal{G}}(|x|) - t + c\} = \{(x, t+c) \mid C_\psi^{\mathcal{G}}(x) < \sigma^{\mathcal{G}}(|x|) - t + c, C_\psi^{\mathcal{G}}(x) \leq C^{\mathcal{G}}(x) + c\} \subseteq \{(x, t+c) \mid C^{\mathcal{G}}(x) < \sigma^{\mathcal{G}}(|x|) - t\} = V(\psi_{i_0})_t$, which proves our theorem. $\square$

Now we are ready to establish the link between ML randomness and randomness defined by a BUSC. It would be nice to prove that a number is declared random by an ML test, iff it is also declared random by a BUSC $\mathcal{G}$.

Because various BUSCs define different type of randomness, we need to change the definition for randomness for ML tests.

We already know that a string is declared random by a BUSC $\mathcal{G}$ if $C^{\mathcal{G}}(x) \geq \Sigma^{\mathcal{G}}(|x|) - t$, thus, the corresponding f-representable ML test is $V(\phi_{i_0}) = \{(x,t) \mid C^{\mathcal{G}}(x) < f(|x|) - t\}$. Hence, a number x is declared t-random by $V(\phi_{i_0})$ if x is rejected at level m, where $m < \Sigma^{\mathcal{G}}(|x|)$. This means that for the function f, we must have $f(n) \leq \sigma^{\mathcal{G}}(n)$, for all $n \in \mathbb{N}$.

Therefore, by introducing a stronger form of randomness, we can establish the equivalence between randomness in the sense of ML, and randomness defined in BUSC spaces.

Definition 3.20. Let $\mathcal{T}$ be a family of ML tests, and U a universal ML test for $\mathcal{T}$. For a function σ, we call x σ-ML t-random if $m_U(x) < \sigma(|x|) - t$.

---

[14] Please note that not every ML test is f representable, as we can use Example 5.15 in [22].

[15] The number i_0 is the index of the universal algorithm in $\mathcal{G}$.

One can easily check that for plain complexity, we obtain the family $\mathcal{M}_{\mathcal{F}}$ equal with all representable ML tests, and for prefix-complexity, only the ML tests that are $\sigma^{\mathcal{G}}$ representable. As we could see, it just happens that the universal test for $\mathcal{M}_{\mathcal{F}}$ is also universal for the whole set $\mathcal{M}$.

This result confirms the results obtained by Miller and Nies [28, 29], but in a more general context.

Hence, we can conclude the canonical link between ML tests and BUSC spaces:

Theorem 3.21. *If $\mathcal{T}$ is a set of $\mathcal{G}$-representable ML tests, then $x \in \mathbb{N}$ is $\sigma^{\mathcal{G}}$-ML-random iff x is $\mathcal{G}$-random.*

Corollary 3.22. *The weakest form of randomness is the one induced by the set of all ML tests.*

The latest result confirms the result obtained in [15], where plain complexity induces the weakest form of randomness, because this one corresponds to the randomness induced by all ML tests.

3.5. Conclusions

We proved that, in case the encodings of two BUSC spaces are not within a constant of each other, a significant difference could appear for both complexities of two distinct objects, making the two BUSC spaces incompatible. We conjecture that the conditions in Theorem 3.11 may not be strong enough to determine the incompatibility of the BUSC spaces involved, and we think that some additional condition may be necessary.

We have established a canonical connection between a BUSC space and a corresponding subset of ML tests in such a way that randomness defined by any of the models is the same. We reinforced the fact that randomness defined by either plain complexity or all ML tests is the weakest.

When we restrict the test to $\mathcal{T} \subseteq \mathcal{M}$, we do not necessarily get a weaker form of randomness, as we need to define it for a universal test W, and in case W is representable and corresponds to a universal function in BUSC $\mathcal{G}$, then W must be stronger than any universal test for $\mathcal{M}$. Please note that the rejecting level in a subfamily $\mathcal{T} \subseteq \mathcal{M}$ is $f(|x|)$, where f is a function, and not the length of x, $|x|$. This is the main reason why universal test W is stronger, and ML randomness for $\mathcal{M}$ is the weakest form of randomness and not the strongest, as one might think, influenced by the old definition.

For every ML test V, the set $\{V\}$ contains V, and V is universal for $\{V\}$, therefore there is a maximal set $\mathcal{V} \subseteq \mathcal{M}$ containing V, and V is universal for $\mathcal{V}$. Thus, for every BUSC $\mathcal{G}$ we can find a corresponding subset of $\mathcal{M}$ defining the same random set Rand_t, $t \geq 0$, as the BUSC $\mathcal{G}$. We proved that the maximal set should include all σ-representable tests, in the extended sense, but it remains open the problem of finding the maximal set. We only know that in case $\mathcal{G} = \mathcal{F}$, the maximal set is $\mathcal{M}$.

A sequence is random if it contains infinitely many random prefixes, thus prefix complexity of a prefix (of a random sequence) is higher than its length, and apparently, because prefix complexity is stronger than plain complexity we have, yet, another contradiction. However, this is exactly the confirmation of what we proved in Section 3.3, where we choose a number with high complexity with respect to the first space and non-random in the second space. These numbers would have a very high variance in their relative complexity, and that's another reason why infinite sequences cannot have all prefixes but a finite set, random. From time to time, their complexity will drop, regardless of BUSC space, thus confirming once more the result obtained in [15].

We can also formulate a few other open questions:

Can we find an infinite hierarchy $(\mathcal{G}_i)_{i \in \mathbb{N}}$ such that $\mathcal{G}_{i+1}$ is an encoding of $\mathcal{G}_i$ and $\mathcal{G}_{i+1}$ is incompatible with $\mathcal{G}_i$? Is it possible that random sequences defined by $\mathcal{G}_i$, $i \geq 0$, would be all different? Is it possible that these spaces will generate a finite hierarchy? What would be the corresponding ML tests and what would be their properties? For Definition 3.18: find conditions for f such that if $F \in \mathcal{G}$, $V(F)$ is f-representable.

There are several other problems to solve for relating random sequences defined by a BUSC $\mathcal{G}$ and sequential ML tests, because no sequential ML test is representable in the restrictive sense defined in [22]. We plan to address some of these questions in a future paper.

Bibliography

[1] R. J. Solomonoff, A Formal Theory of Inductive Inference, Part I, *Information and Control* **7**, 1, pp. 1–22 (1964).

[2] R. J. Solomonoff, A Formal Theory of Inductive Inference, Part II, *Information and Control* **7**, 2, pp. 224–254 (1964).

[3] A. N. Kolmogorov, Three approaches to the quantitative definition of information, *Problems of Information Transmission* **1** (1965).

[4] G. J. Chaitin, On the length of programs for computing finite binary sequences, *Journal of the ACM* **13**, 4, pp. 547–569 (1966).

[5] P. Martin-Löf, The Definition of Random Sequences, *Information and Control* **9**, pp. 602–619 (1966).

[6] M. Blum, A machine-independent theory of the complexity of recursive functions, *Journal of the ACM* **14**, 2, pp. 322–336 (1967).

[7] R. M. Solovay, Draft of paper (or series of papers) on Chaitin's work. Unpublished notes, (1975).

[8] J. S. Miller, Contrasting plain and prefix-free Kolmogorov complexity, Research Note, University of Connecticut (2000), http://www.math.wisc.edu/~jmiller/Notes/contrasting.pdf.

[9] M. Burgin, *Super-Recursive Algorithms*. Springer, New York/Heidelberg/Berlin (2005).

[10] M. Burgin, Generalized Kolmogorov complexity and duality in theory of computations, *Notices Academy of Sciences of USSR* **264**, pp. 19–23 (1982).

[11] M. Burgin, Generalized Kolmogorov complexity and other dual complexity measures, *Kibernetica* **4**, pp. 21–29 (1990).

[12] M. Burgin, Algorithmic complexity of recursive and inductive algorithms, *Theoretical Computer Science* **317**, pp. 31–60 (2004).

[13] M. Burgin, Algorithmic complexity as a criterion of unsolvability, *Theoretical Computer Science* **383**, pp. 244–259 (2007).

[14] C. Câmpeanu, A note on Blum static complexity measures, *Lecture Notes in Computer Science* **7160**, pp. 71–80 (2012a).

[15] C. Câmpeanu, Randomness in Blum universal static complexity spaces, *Journal of Automata, Languages and Combinatorics* **17**, 2–4, pp. 107–122 (2012b).

[16] C. Câmpeanu, Blum static complexity and encoded spaces, *Lecture Notes in Computer Science* **8031**, pp. 1–13 (2013).

[17] C. Câmpeanu, Descriptional Complexity in encoded Blum Static Complexity Spaces, *International Journal of Foundations of Computer Science* **25**, 7, pp. 917–932 (2014).

[18] J. S. Miller and L. Yu, On initial segment complexity and degrees of randomness, *Transactions of the American Mathematical Society* **6**, 360, pp. 3193–3210 (2008).

[19] J. Miller and A. Day, Randomness for non-computable measures, *Transactions of the American Mathematical Society* **7**, 365, pp. 3575–3591 (2013).

[20] J. S. Miller and L. Yu, Oscillation in the initial segment complexity of random reals, *Advances in Mathematics* **6**, 226, pp. 4816–4840 (2011).

[21] A. A. Muchnik, and S. Ye. Positselsky, Kolmogorov entropy in the context of computability theory, *Theoretical Computer Science* **271**, pp. 15–35 (2002).

[22] C. S. Calude, *Information and Randomness – An Algorithmic Perspective*. Springer-Verlag (1994).

[23] H. Jürgensen, Invariance and Universality of Complexity, *Lecture Notes in Computer Science* **7160/201**, pp. 140–158 (2012).

[24] C. S. Calude, *Theories of Computational Complexity*. Elsevier (1988).

[25] M. Davis, R. Sigal and E. Weyuker, *Computability, Complexity, and Languages*, second ed. Academic Press, New York (1994).

[26] H. R. Lewis and C. Papadimitriou, *Elements of the theory of computation*, second ed. Prentice-Hall (1998).

[27] M. Blum, On the size of machines, *Information and Control* **11**, pp. 257–265 (1967).

[28] A. Nies, *Computability and Randomness.* Oxford University Press (2009).

[29] G. Barmpalias, J. S. Miller and A. Nies, Randomness notions and partial relativization, *Israel Journal of Mathematics* **191**, pp. 791–816 (2012).

Chapter 4

Planckian Information (I_P): A Measure of the Order in Complex Systems

Sungchul Ji

Department of Pharmacology and Toxicology,
Ernest Mario School of Pharmacy
Rutgers University, Piscataway, NJ 08854, USA

Abstract

A new mathematical formula referred to as the *Planckian distribution equation* (PDE) was derived by S. Ji in 2008 from the blackbody radiation formula discovered by M. Planck in 1900 and has been found to fit long-tailed histograms generated in various fields, including i) atomic physics, ii) protein folding, iii) single-molecule enzymology, iv) whole-cell mRNA metabolism, v) T-cell receptor variable region diversity, vi) fMRI (Functional Magnetic Resonance Imaging), vii) glottometrics (quantitative study of words and texts), viii) econophysics, and ix) Big Bang astrophysics. PDE can be derived from the Gaussian-like distribution equation (GLE) (which replaces the pre-exponential factor of the Gaussian distribution with a free parameter) by transforming the random variable, x, into a non-linear function, while keeping the Gaussian y coordinates invariant. Assuming that GLE represents a random distribution, it is possible to define a binary logarithm of the ratio between the areas under the curves of PDE and GLE as a measure of the non-randomness (i.e., order). This new function has been named the *Planckian information*, I_P, which appears to be a better measure of *order* in 'organized complex systems' of Weaver (1948) than either the Boltzmann-Gibbs entropy, S, or Shannon entropy, H, both of which being measures of *disorder*. It is postulated that, underlying all Planckian processes (defined as those *physicochemical, biomedical, socioeconomic* and *cosmological* processes that generate numerical data fitting PDE), there exists a common mechanism referred to as the **SID-TEM-TOF** mechanism, the acronym for *Signal-Induced Deactivation of Thermally Excited Metastable state leading TO Functions*. The universal applicability of PDE to many right or left long-tailed histograms is attributed to (i) the role of Planckian processes in generating functions and organizations in complex systems through *goal-directed selection* of subsets of random processes, and (ii) the *wave-particle duality* that is postulated to operate in living and non-living systems alike, ranging in size from atoms to the Universe.

4.1. Introduction

The American chemist, logician and philosopher, Charles S. Peirce (1839-1914) (2015), believed that there existed simple concepts applicable to every subject:

> *"The undertaking which this volume inaugurates is to make a philosophy like that of Aristotle, that is to say, to outline a theory so comprehensive that, for long time to come, the entire work of human reason, in philosophy of every school and kind, in mathematics, in psychology, in physical science, in history, in sociology, and in whatever other department there may be, shall appear as the filling up of its details. The first step toward this is to find **simple concepts applicable to every subject**. "* (Hartshorne and Weiss, 1931; emphases were added)."

$$(4.1)$$

For convenience, we may refer to the "simple concepts" described above as "Peirce's simple concepts" (PSC). There are three main objectives of this chapter: **(i)** to demonstrate the possibility that the Planckian distribution equation (PDE) discovered at Rutgers in 2008 (Ji, 2012a) qualifies as an example of PSC; **(ii)** to suggest that the Planckian information (I$_P$) that can be derived from PDE and a Gaussian-like equation (GLE) is a new measure of *order* in organized complex systems of Weaver (1948); and **(iii)** to formulate possible mechanisms capable of generating Planckian information in physicochemical, biomedical, socioeconomic, and cosmological processes.

4.1.1. Complexity

In his book, "Complexity, Multi-Disciplinarily, and Beyond", Finkenthal (2008) quotes S. Y. Auyang's definition of complexity:

> "*I use complex and complexity intuitively to describe self-organizing systems that have many components and many characteristic aspects, exhibit many structures in various scales, undergo many processes in various rates, and have the capabilities to change abruptly and adapt to external environment.*"

$$(4.2)$$

Although Auyang's definition accurately captures many of the salient features of complex systems, it seems incomplete because it deals only with *self-organized systems*, excluding the complexity inherent in *other-organized systems* such as Bernard convection cells (Ji, 2012a, p. 17). The distinction between *self-* and *other-organizations* is based on whether the organization is driven by internal or external forces, respectively. In addition, Auyang's definition does not distinguish between *organized* and *disorganized* complexities described by Weaver (1948) and between active and passive complexities described in (Ji, 2012a, pp. 127-129).

4.1.2. Disorganized vs. organized complexity

Weaver (1948) divides complexity into "disorganized" and "organized" complexities as follows:

> "... it is clear what is meant by a problem of **disorganized complexity**. It is a problem in which the number of variables is very large, and one in which each of the many variables has a behavior which is individually erratic, or perhaps totally unknown. However, in spite of this helter-skelter, or unknown, behavior of all the individual variables, the system as a whole possesses certain orderly and analyzable **average** properties. . . . . . .

(4.3)

> This new (i.e., **the statistical**) method of dealing with disorganized complexity, so powerful an advance over the earlier two-variable methods (of **classical mechanics**), leaves a great field untouched. One is tempted to oversimplify, and say that scientific methodology went from one extreme to the other – from two variables to an astronomical number – and left untouched a great middle region. The importance of this middle region, moreover, does not depend primarily on the fact that the number of variables involved is moderate – large compared to two, but small compared to the number of atoms in a pinch of salt. The problems in this middle

region, in fact, will often involve a considerable number of variables. The really important characteristic of the problems of this middle region, which science has as yet little explored or conquered, lies in the fact that these problems, as contrasted with the **disorganized** *situations with which statistics can cope, show the essential feature of* **organization**. *In fact, one can refer to this group of problems as those of* **organized complexity** (**bold** emphases are my additions)."

$$(4.4)$$

4.1.3. Passive vs. active complexity

In (Ji, 2012a, pp. 127-129), two kinds of complexities were distinguished, depending on whether the complexification process involved is active or passive:

> *"We can recognize two kinds of 'complexities' in nature – active and passive, in analogy to active and passive transport. For example, snowflakes . . . exhibit passive complexity or complexification, while living cells . . . exhibit active complexity in addition to passive complexity. Unlike passive complexity, active complexity is exhibited by living systems utilizing free energy, and organisms with such a capability is thought to be more likely to survive complex environment than those with passive complexity only. According to the Law of Requisite Variety (LRV) . . . no simple machines can perform complex tasks. Applying LRV to cells, it can be inferred that*
>
> *"No simple cells can survive complex environment."*
>
> *If this conjecture is true, it is not only to the advantage of cells (both as individuals and as a lineage) but also*

essential for their survival to complexify (i.e., increase the complexity of) their internal states."

(4.5)

4.1.4. A parametric definition of complexity

Mark Burgin (2005) provides the following very comprehensive definition of complexity, which is based on the actions or work performances involved:

"...if we analyze what does it mean when we say that some system or process is complex, we come to conclusion that it is complex to do something with this system or process: to study it, to describe it, to build it, to control it, and so on. Thus, complexity is always complexity of doing something. Being related to activity and functioning, complexity allows one to represent efficiency in a natural way: when a process .has high efficiency, it is simple and when a process has low efficiency, it is complex. For example, we can take time as a measure of efficiency: what is possible to do in one hour is efficient, while what is impossible to do even in a year is inefficient. There is a corresponding measure of computational complexity that estimates time of computation or any other algorithmic process.

Definition 5.1.5. *Complexity of a system R is the amount of resources necessary for (used by) a process P involving R.*

There are different kinds of involvement.

P may be a process in the system R. For example, R is a computer, P is an electrical process in R, and the resource is energy.

P may be a process that is realized by the system R. For example,   R is a computer, P is a computational process in R, and the resource is memory.

P may be a process controlled by the system R. For example, R is a program, P is a computational process controlled by R, and the resource is time.

P may be a process that builds the system R. For example, R is a software system, P is the process of its design, and the resource is programmers.

P may be a process that transforms, utilizes, models, and/or predicts behavior of the system R.

In cognitive processes complexity is closely related to information, representing specific kind of information measures."

Evidently, this definition includes all three intuitive, non-parametric definitions of complexity given in Sections 4.1.1–4.1.3.

4.2. The Planckian Distribution Equation (PDE)

The Planckian distribution equation (PDE) (i.e., Eq. (4.7) or (4.8)) was derived from the blackbody radiation equation discovered by Planck in 1900 (See Planck's Law at http://en.wikipedia.org/ wiki/Planck's_law; http://hyperphysics.phy-str.gsu.edu/hbase/ mod6.html). Blackbody radiation refers to the emission of photons by material objects that completely absorb photons impinging on them (hence appearing black). When the light intensity of a blackbody is measured at a fixed temperature, the so-called "blackbody radiation spectrum" is obtained (http://en.wikipedia. org/wiki/Black-body_radiation).

In 1900, M. Planck (1858-1947) derived Eq. (4.6) that quantitatively accounted for the blackbody radiation spectra. The key to his successful derivation of the so-called *Planck radiation equation* was his assumption that light is emitted or absorbed by matter in discrete quantities called "quanta of action," which led to the birth of *quantum mechanics* revolutionizing physics in the 20th century.

In 2008 (Ji, 2012a), I noticed that the histogram of the single-molecule enzyme-turnover times shown in Figure 4.1 a) reported by Lu *et al.* (1998) resembled the blackbody radiation spectrum at 5000 °K. This observation led me to generalize the Planck radiation equation, Eq. (4.6), to Eq. (4.7) by replacing the universal constants and temperature by free parameters, a and b. In 2009, one of my students at Rutgers, Kenneth So, found that Eq. (4.7) could fit a more diverse set of long-tailed histograms if x was replaced with (Ax + B), leading to a 4-parameter equation (not shown). This 4-parameter equation could be reduced to the 3-parameter equation, Eq. (4.8) (Ji, 2015a) which fitted the single-molecule enzyme kinetic data reasonably well (Figure 4.1 b).

Equation (4.7) was originally referred to as the "blackbody radiation-like equation" (BRE) (Ji, 2012a), but as the equation was found to apply to more and more data sets, it was thought appropriate to refer to it as either the "generalized Planck equation" (GPE), or the "Planckian distribution equation" (PDE) in analogy to the Gaussian distribution equation.

$$E(\lambda, T) = \frac{2\pi h c^2}{\lambda^5 (e^{\frac{hc}{\lambda k T}} - 1)}, \tag{4.6}$$

where
  E = Energy,
  λ = Wavelength,
  c = Speed of light,
  k = Boltzmann constant,
  h = Planck's constant,
  e = 2.71828182,

[T] = Kelvin (temperature),
[λ] = Meters,
$h = 6.626.10^{34}$ J.s,
$c = 2.998.10^8$ m/s,
$k = 1.381 \times 10^{-23}$ J/K.

Number of vibrational modes per unit frequency per unit volume

Average energy per mode

$$y = \frac{a}{x^5} \cdot \frac{1}{e^{b/x} - 1}, \tag{4.7}$$

$$y = \frac{A}{(x + B)^5} \cdot \frac{1}{e^{C/(x + B)} - 1}, \tag{4.8}$$

where y is the y coordinate or the frequency of a long tailed histogram under consideration, x is the x coordinate or the bin number to which each event or object belongs, and A, B and C are free parameters.

a)

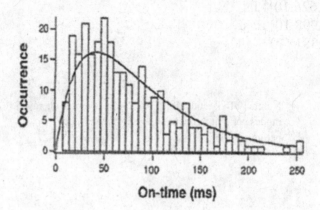

b)

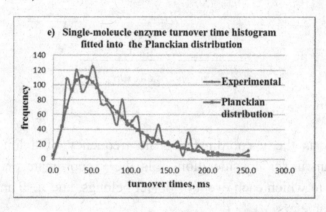

Figure 4.1. a) Single molecules of cholesterol oxidase embedded in gel can be observed to undergo "blinking" due to its coenzyme FAD which fluoresces when in its oxidized state and is non-fluorescent when it is reduced by its substrate, cholesterol (Lu *et al.*, 1998). One cycle of blinking of the coenzyme constitutes one turnover time of the enzyme. The turnover times of the enzyme were not constant, but varied widely, generating a histogram as shown here. Lu *et al.* (1998) fitted the histogram with a double exponential function (see the solid curve). b) The same data as in a) were simulated using the Planckian distribution equation, Eq. (4.8). The fitting of the experimental data to the theoretical curve was carried out using the *Solver* software available in *Excel*.

The Planckian distribution equation (PDE) has been found to fit not only the single-molecule enzyme kinetic data as shown in Figure 4.1 b) but also numerous other long-tailed histograms generated by processes ranging from protein folding to cell metabolism, decision-making, word-length frequency distribution in human speech, economic activities in the human Society, and the polarization of the cosmological microwave background radiation. The histograms that do not fit PDE are also presented (Figure 4.2 e), h) and r)). Typical examples of the numerical values of the parameters of PDE are collected in Table 4.1, and brief descriptions of some of the histograms in Figure 4.2 are given in Sections 4.2.1–4.2.11. The remainder of Figure 4.2, i.e., Figures 4.2 a), b), c), k), l), m), p), q), and r) are explained elsewhere (Ji, 2015a, b).

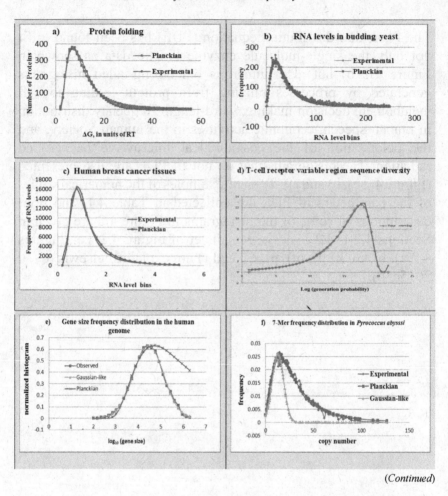

(*Continued*)

Figure 4.2. (*Continued*)

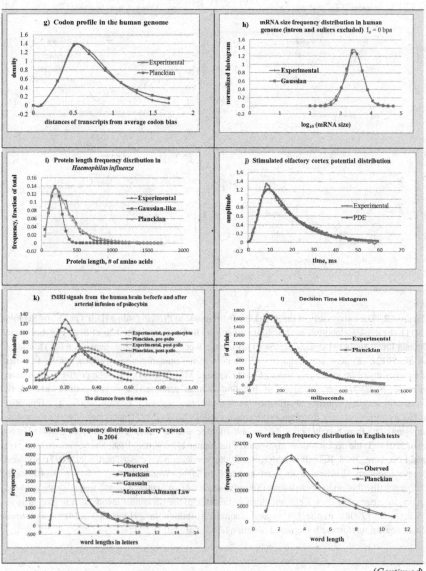

(*Continued*)

Figure 4.2. (*Continued*)

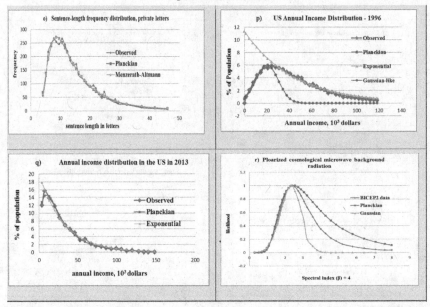

Figure 4.2. The universality of the Planckian distribution. a) Protein folding (Dill, Ghosh and Schmit, 2011); b) RNA metabolism in unicellular organism (Ji, 2012a, Chapter 12); c) RNA metabolism in human breast tissues (Perou *et al.*, 2000); d) human T-cell variable region gene diversity (Murugan *et al.*, 2012); e) gene size frequency distribution in the human genome (Insana, 2003); f) 7-mer frequency distribution in *Pyrococcus abyssi* (Zhou and Mishra, 2004); g) codon profile in the human genome; h) mRNA size frequency distribution in huan genome (intron and outlieers excluded); i) protein length frequency distribution in *Haemophilus influenze* (Zhang, 2000); j) Stimulated olfactory cortex potential distribution (Freeman, 1960, 1972); k) fMRI (functional magnetic resonance imaging) data from human brains before and after the arterial infusion of psilocybin Carhart-Harris *et al.*, 2014); l) the decision-time histogram of the human brain (Luce, 1986; Deco *et al.*, 2013; Roxin and Lederberg, 2008; Ratcliff and McKoon, 2006; Vandekerckhove and Tuerlinckx, 2007); m) word length frequency distribution in Kerry's speech in 2004 (Words/phrases, 2004); n) word-length frequency distribution in English texts (Sigurd *et al.*, 2004); o) Sentence-length frequency distribution in private letters (Grzybek, Kelih and Stadlober, 2008); p) the US annual income distribution in 1996 (Yakovenko, 2008); q) the US annual income distribution in 2013 (Cho, 2014); r) Polarized cosmological microwave background radiation (Ade *et al.*, 2014).

Table 4.1. The numerical values of the parameters of the Planckian distribution, Eq. (4.7) or (4.8), that fit the histograms shown in Figure 4.2. The italicized numbers in Row **k)** are the parameter values measured after administering psilocybin.

From Figure 4.2	a	b	A	B	C	b/A	I_P*
a) Protein folding	1.24×10^{14}	368.3	9.45	6.82	–	38.97	877
b) RNA levels (yeast)	–	–	1.11×10^{12}	13.962	159.30		989
c) RNA levels (breast tissues)	8×10^{10}	40	8	1.7	–	5.00	855
d) T-Cell receptor	–	–	7.02×10^{6}	0.063	25.00	–	–
f) 7-Mer frequency	–	–	5.05×10^{7}	12.123	123.78		0.873
i) Protein chain length	–	–	2.04×10^{13}	5.655	1257.4	–	0.846
	5.0×10^{11}	601.7	0.478	30.29	–	1257.7	–
k) fMRI signals	7.6×10^{10}	107.67	115.9	0	–	0.928	
	4.4×10^{10}	43.17	26.7	0	–	1.617	
l) Decision times	8.5×10^{11}	101.49	0.1077	6.345	–	942.34	3.57
m) Word length in speech	–	–	1.80×10^{7}	–0.001	12	–	0.557
o) Sentence length in letters	–	–	3.11×10^{9}	0.861	47.57	–	0.664
r) Cosmos	3.6×10^{2}	6.00	1.140	–0.14	–	4.65	–

*Planckian information, in mbits (millibits), i.e., 10^{-3} bits.

4.2.1. T-cell receptor structure diversity

This histogram is left long-tailed, whereas the corresponding histogram explained in (Ji, 2015a, Figure 7 d)) is right long-tailed, but the same explanation applies. This indicates that PDE can fit both the left and right long-tailed histograms that are mirror images to each other.

4.2.2. Gene size frequency distribution

Figure 4.2 e) shows that the distribution of the gene sizes in the human genome does not fit PDE but rather fits the so-called Gaussian-like equation (GLE), Eq. (4.9) (Ji, 2015a, b). GLE is symmetric with respect to its mode, μ, with the width of its base being approximately 4 σ:

$$y = Ae^{-(x-\mu)^2/2x\sigma^2}. \tag{4.9}$$

The difference between GLE, (4.9), and the Gaussian distribution equation (GDE), (4.10), is that the pre-exponential factor A of the former is equal to the height of the peak distribution of PDE, whereas that of the latter is the function of σ, i.e., $A = (2\pi\sigma^2)^{-0.5}$:

$$y = ((2\pi\sigma^2)^{-0.5})e^{-(x-\mu)^2/2\sigma^2}. \tag{4.10}$$

Since any data fitting GDE are likely to be generated by some random process, it would be logical to infer that any data fitting PDE would be generated by non-random process, or "ordered" or "organized" processes. For this reason, it will be suggested in Section 4.4.1 that the deviation of PDE from GDE can be utilized to construct a novel method for measuring the degree of organization underlying many, if not all, long-tailed histograms of certain kind.

4.2.3. 7-Mer frequency distribution

In contrast to the gene size distribution in the human genome, Figure 4.2 e), that fits the Gaussian-like equation, Eq. (4.9), the 7-mer (i.e., DNA words consisting of 7 nucleotides (Zhou and Mishra, 2004) frequency distribution in *Pyrococcus abyssi* fits PDE (Figure 4.2 f)). This indicates that the nucleotide sequences of the 7-mers are non-random and hence are likely the results of some selection processes which may be identified with the biological evolution.

4.2.4. Codon profile in the human genome

There are 64 codons in all organisms, of which 61 code for 20 amino acids (e.g., for the Standard Code). Hence, on average, about 3 codons encode one amino acid, although the actual numbers vary from 1 to 6. In addition, not all the codons encoding an amino acid are utilized with an equal probability — some are utilized more frequently than others, thus giving rise to the phenomenon of the "codon usage bias". A codon profile is a record of the preferred use of the four bases at the three positions inside the codon (Insana, 2003). As shown in Figure 4.2 g), the codon profile distances of transcripts from the average codon bias is distributed non-randomly (Insana, 2003) and fits PDE. This indicates that the codon profile is determined by some as-yet-unidentified selection mechanisms in the living cell.

4.2.5. mRNA size frequency distribution

It is not surprising that the mRNA size frequency is distributed symmetrically (see Figure 4.2 h)), obeying the Gaussian-like equation, Eq. (4.9), just as the gene size frequency is similarly distributed, since the size (but not copy number) of mRNA would be determined by the size of corresponding genes, which act as their template.

4.2.6. Protein-length frequency distribution

Unlike the *gene* and *mRNA size* frequency distributions, which are both Gaussian (Figure 4.2 e) and h)), the *protein size* (or length) frequency distribution is Planckian as shown in Figure 4.2 i). If we can assume that gene and mRNA size distributions are relatively stable (or static) while protein size distribution is dynamic (probably because of the rapid turnover of protein synthesis and degradation), we may identify the former as a "equilibrium structure" and the latter as a "dissipative structure" of Prigogine (1977; Ji, 2012a, Section 3.1). This same thermodynamic dichotomy may be applicable to linguistics, namely, to the difference between the word-length frequency distribution in a *dictionary,* related to the so-called second articulation in linguistics (Culler, 1991) and to equilibrium structure of Prigogine, and word-length frequency distribution in a *speech,* related to the so-called first articulation in linguistics and to dissipative structure of Prigogine. If these analogies are valid, it would be logical to conclude that *glottometrics* and *genomics* are symmetric in the sense that Prigogine's thermodynamic dichotomy of "equilibrium" and "dissipative" structures apply to both. In other words, word-length and gene-size may be viewed as *equilibrium structures,* while word-length frequency and protein-length frequency distributions may be treated as *dissipative structures,* since the letter, but not the former, will disappear if free energy dissipation is disrupted or stopped.

4.2.7. Stimulated olfactory cortex potentials

Figure 4.2 j) shows that the EEG signals from stimulated olfactory cortex are distributed non-randomly, obeying PDE, indicating the possibility that these signals resulted from some selection processes imposed on a more or less randomly generated set of the EEG signals intrinsic to the olfactory cortex (Freeman, 1960, 1972).

4.2.8. fMRI signals from the human brain before and after psilocybin

The functional magnetic resonance imaging (fMRI) technique, when applied to the human brain, allows neuroscientists to monitor neuronal firing activities in different regions of the brain noninvasively within seconds of infusing a psychedelic drug such as psilocybin. Carhart-Harris *et al.* (2014) measured the fMRI signals from the brains of 15 healthy volunteers before and after the intravenous infusion of psilocybin lasting for 60 seconds. The subject's consciousness, cerebral blood flow (CBF), and fMRI signals responded within seconds. CBF values decreased in all regions of the brain and the subject reported that their "thoughts wandered freely". Out of the 9 brains regions examined (2° visual, 1° visual, motor, DAN, auditory, DMN, R-FP, L-FP, salience), four regions exhibited significant changes in their fMRI signals characterized by increases in the deviations of the local signals from their mean, i.e., an increase in variance. By "local" is meant to indicate brain tissue volume elements (voxels) measuring a few mm in linear dimensions. When the distances of the signals from individual voxels from the group-mean fMRI signal are calculated and grouped into bins and their frequencies are counted, histograms are obtained such as shown in Figure 4.2 f), which could be fitted reasonably well to the Planckian distribution equation (see Planckian). The numerical values of the Planckian distribution equation fitting these two histograms differed, especially the b/A ratios which increased from 0.93 to 1.62 by the psilocybin infusion (see Table 4.1).

4.2.9. Human decision-time histograms

The drift-diffusion model (DDM) of decision-making is a widely utilized in behavioral neurobiology (Carhart-Harris *et al.*, 2014; Deco *et al.*, 2013; Ratcliff and McKoon, 2006; Vandercckhove and Tuerlinckx, 2007). DDM accurately reproduces the decision-time histograms (see Experimental in Figure 4.2 l), reflecting the well-known phenomena (Luce, 1986) that it takes the brain longer to process more difficult tasks than easier ones.

4.2.10. Word-length frequency distribution in English texts

The word-length frequency distribution in English texts shown in Figure 4.2 n) can be almost exactly reproduced by PDE, indicating that the writers of the letters selected their words non-randomly, since random selection of words would have resulted in a Gaussian-like distribution.

4.2.11. Sentence-length frequency distribution in private letters

The sentence-length frequency distribution in private letters also fits PDE as shown in Figure 4.2 o), indicating that the sentence lengths were selected by letter writers non-randomly under the control of the writers' mind.

4.2.12. US Annual income distributions in 1996 and 2013

The Rayleigh-Jeans law (Wikipedia, 2016) predicts that the power of radiation emitted by a heated body increases with the frequency raised to a fourth power. This exponential law works fine at long wavelengths but fails dramatically at short wavelengths, leading to the so-called the 'ultraviolet catastrophe' (Wikipedia, 2016).

Some physicists (Yakovenko, 2008) have suggested that the distribution of incomes in a society may be modeled using the Boltzmann-Gibbs equation making the analogy that money can be treated as energy. This statistical mechanical approach works fine for high income levels but fails badly at low income levels (see Figure 4.2 p)). However, PDE, Eq. (4.8), fits both the 1996 and 2013 US annual income distributions almost exactly.

If we assume that the exponential distribution shown in Figures 4.2 p) and q) are analogous to the Rayleigh-Jeans law and the Planckian distribution is analogous to the Planck radiation law, Eq. (4.6), we can reasonably conclude that the deviation of the exponential distributions from the observed income distributions are analogous to the 'ultraviolet catastrophe' in physics of about a century ago (Ultraviolet catastrophe, Wikipedia, 2016).

The resolution of the ultraviolet catastrophe in physics in the early decades of the 20th century with the discovery of Planck's radiation law introduced a new concept into physics, i.e., quantum of action, as the unit of organizing matter and energy in abiotic systems. Similarly, the resolution of the "econophysics" version of the ultraviolet catastrophe with the Planckian distribution equation demonstrated in Figures 4.2 p) and r) may introduce yet another novel concept into natural and human sciences – the quantization of organization in terms of what may be called the Planckian information, IP, defined in Section 4.4.1.

4.2.13. Big Bang Cosmology

Although PDE has been found to fit almost exactly most fat-tailed histograms generated in various disciplines that we have examined so far (over 50), the polarized CMB (Cosmic Microwave Background) data as shown in Figure 4.2 r) is an exception in that the data could not be made to fit PDE exactly using the Solver program in Excel. The falling phase of the CMB polarization curve is thinner than PDE curve and considerably fatter than the Gaussian-like curve.

As can be seen in Figures 4.2 a-d), and f-p), if PDE fits the rising phase of the histogram, it fits the falling phase of the histogram as well, except the polarized CMB data in Figure 4.2 r). The areas under the curves (AUC) of the Gaussian-like distribution (GLE), the CMB data, and PDE were found to be, respectively, 10.3, 13.97, and 16.98 units. From these numbers, we can calculate the Planckian information, IP, defined in Section 4.4.1

$$IP = \log 2 \, (AUC(PDE)/AUC(GLE))$$
$$= \log 2 \, (16.98/10.3) = 0.721 \text{ bits}$$

which is equivalent to selecting 70 out of 100, i.e., the information needed to select or generated by selecting 70 out of 100 possibilities.

Our current interpretation of the Planckian information is that it represents the degree of organization of a physical system (in contrast to the Boltzmann-Gibbs entropy which represents the disorder/disorganization of a physical system), whether the system involved is atoms, enzymes, cells, brains, human societies, or the Universe.

Based on Figure 4.2 r), the Planckian information associated with the polarized CMB data is found to be 0.44 bits which contrasts with the IP associated with the Planckian distributions (and hence with the blackbody radiation) of 0.72 bits, the difference being almost 2 fold. One possible explanation of this difference may be that the polarized CMB radiation 'lost' some of its original information about the order or the organization of the Big Bang due to the randomizing effects of the galactic dust. It is hoped that this idea can be experimentally tested by experts in the field.

4.3. Mechanisms Underlying the Planckian Processes

It is convenient to define *Planckian processes* as those i) *physic-chemical,* ii) *biomedical,* iii) neurophysiological, iv) *psychological,* v) *linguistic,* vi) *socioeconomic,* and vii) *cosmological* processes that generate numerical data fitting the *Planckian distribution equation* (PDE), Eq. (4.8).

4.3.1. Quantization of the free energy content of enzymes

Since single-molecule enzyme kinetic data fit PDE (see Figure 4.1. b)), *enzyme catalysis* can be considered as one of the simplest Planckian processes on the physicochemobiological level of organization. Just as the fitting of the blackbody radiation spectra to Planck's radiation equation, Eq. (4.6), implies the *quantization of the energy levels* of electrons in an atom, so it may be postulated that the fitting of the single-molecule enzyme-turnover time histogram to the Planckian distribution equation, Eq. (4.7) or (4.8), as demonstrated in Figure 4.1 b), implies that the conformational states (and hence conformational energy) of an enzyme molecule are discrete and *quantized,* consistent with the concept of "conformational substates" of Frauenfelder *et al.* (2001) and the quantization of the Gibbs free energy levels of an enzyme postulated in (Ji, 2012a, Section 12.14). Gibbs free energy, G, rather than energy, E, must be considered here because, under the conditions of constant temperature and pressure, it is G, not E, that drives all spontaneous processes in living systems (Callen, 1985; Lauffer, 1983). The quantization of *Gibbs free energy* (hereafter called *energy* for brevity) in enzymes is schematically represented in Figure 4.3 b) in analogy to the energy quantization in atoms shown in Figure 4.3 a).

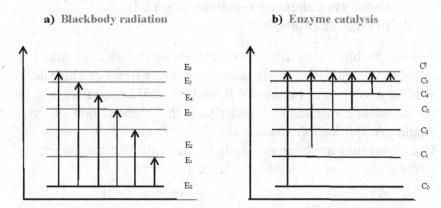

a) Blackbody radiation

E_6
E_5
E_4
E_3

E_2
E_1

E_0

b) Enzyme catalysis

$C^\ddagger$
C_5
C_4
C_3

C_2

C_1

C_0

Figure 4.3. The postulated isomorphism between *energy quantization* in atoms and the quantization of the conformational states (and hence of Gibbs free energy levels) in enzymes. a) The quantization of the energy levels of electrons in an atom, suggested by the fitting of the blackbody radiation spectra with the Planck radiation equation discovered in 1900. b) It is postulated that the fitting of the single-molecule turnover time histogram of cholesterol oxidase by the Planckian distribution equation, Eq. (4.7) or (4.8), implies quantization of energy levels of enzymes, most likely due to the existence of discrete conformational states in enzymes (Frauenfelder *et al.*, 2001), denoted as C_i above, where the index i running from 1 to n, the number of conformational states of an enzymes (Frauenfelder *et al.*, 2001). *Reproduced from (Ji, 2012a, Section 11.3.3).*

A single molecule of cholesterol oxidase is postulated to exist in n different conformational states (i.e., conformational substates of Frauenfelder *et al.* (2001)). Each conformational state (also called a *conformer,* or *conformational isomer*) is thought to exist in a unique Gibbs free energy level and carries a set of sequence-specific conformational strains (called *conformons*) (Ji, 2000, 2012a, Chapters 8 and 11) and can be excited to a common transition state (denoted as $C^\ddagger$ in Figure 4.3 b)) by thermal fluctuations (or Brownian motions), leading to catalysis (Ji, 1974b, 2012a, Section 11.3.3).

In other words, the reason that both blackbody radiation and single-molecule enzyme catalysis fit PDE is suggested to be due to the similarity (or the isomorphism) between their microscopic processes as schematically depicted in Figures 4.3 a) and b).

4.3.2. RASER (rate amplification through the substrate-enhanced reaction): a model of enzyme catalysis

Just as the blackbody radiation equation of Planck was found to apply to the single-molecule enzyme turnover times of cholesterol oxidase as shown in Figure 4.4 b) and (Ji, 2012a, Chapter 11), so the subatomic mechanisms underlying the phenomenon of *laser* (Light Amplification based on the Stimulated Emission of Radiation) may apply analogically to the molecular mechanism of enzyme action, as suggested in Figure 4.4:

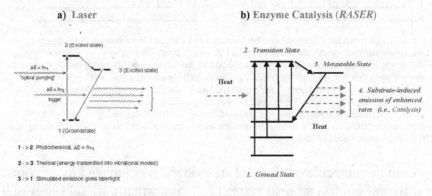

Figure 4.4.   a) Mechanism underlying laser (Light Amplification based on the Stimulated Emission of Radiation). b) RASER (Rate Amplification through the Substrate-Enhanced Reaction) model of enzyme catalysis.

In the mechanism of laser, the input of "pumping" photons, $h\nu_1$, causes the electrons of the atoms of the laser medium (e.g., ruby crystal) to undergo a transition from the ground-state energy level to the excited-state energy level (see the 1 to 2 arrow in Figure 4.4 a)). The excited state is short-lived (lasting for about 10^{-12} seconds) and loses some of its energy as heat, undergoing a transition to a lower energy level called "metastable" state (see the 2 to 3 arrow, Figure 4.4 a)). State 3 is more stable than State 2 but still much more unstable than the ground state (see 1). When there are enough number of electrons in the metastable/excited state (thereby creating the so-called "population inversion"), the arrival of triggering photons, hv_2, induces the de-excitation of electrons from the metastable excited state back to the ground state (see the 3 to 1 arrow), accompanied by the emission of photons identical to the triggering photons, hv_2, but larger in number than the original triggering photons, leading to amplification. The emitted photons are "coherent" in that they are identical with respect to (i) amplitude, (ii) frequency, and (ii) phase.

Unlike electrons in atoms that are all in the lowest electronic energy (i.e., ground) state before absorbing photons, *enzymes appear to exist in different ground states to begin with*, before thermal excitation (i.e., before absorbing thermal energy), as indicated by the four solid bars in Figure 4.4 b), which is enabled by the quantization of the Gibbs free energy postulated in Figure 4.3 b).

When an enzyme molecule absorbs enough thermal energies through Brownian motions, it is excited to the transition state lasting for a short period of time, probably about 10^{-12} seconds, the periods of chemical bond vibrations, or less. The thermally excited enzyme is thought to undergo a transition to a more stable state called the "metastable" or "activated" state lasting probably for about 10^{-9} seconds. It appears that the metastable/activated state can be deactivated in two ways: (i) spontaneously (as in "spontaneous emission" in laser), and (ii) induced by substrate binding (as in "induced emission" in laser). During spontaneous deactivation of the active/metastable state of an enzyme, the excess energy of the metastable state may be released as uncoordinated random infrared photons, whereas, during the substrate-induced deactivation, the excess energy of the enzyme-substrate complex may be released in a coordinated manner, resulting in catalysis, just as the triggering photon-induced de-activation of population-inverted electrons in atoms results in the amplification of emitted photons in laser.

4.3.3. The SID-TEM-TOF mechanism and Planckian processes

The enzyme catalytic mechanism postulated in Figure 4.4 b) is referred to as the **SID-TEM-TOF** mechanism, because it embodies the following three key steps:

(i) Substrate- or Stimuli-Induced Deactivation in Step 4,
(ii) Thermally Excited Metastable state in the 1 to 2 and 2 to 3 steps
(iii) leading TO Function, i.e., catalysis, in the 3 to 1 Step.

It is here postulated that the SID-TEM-TOF mechanism underlies all of the living processes listed in Figure 4.2, and these living processes include linguistics (Figures 4.2 m), n) and o)), neurophysiology (Figure 4.2 k)), psychology (Figure 4.2 l)), and economics (Figures 4.2 p) and q)).

4.3.4. Fourier theorem-based fitting of the long tailed histograms

According to the Fourier theorem (https://en.wikipedia.org/wiki/Fourier_series), any wave-like functions (including long tailed histograms) can be constructed as sums of a series of sine waves (Herbert, 1987). In Figure 4.5, the long tailed histogram of the stimulated olfactory cortex potentials (Freeman, 1960, 1972) (Figure 4.5 a)) was simulated by series of 4 (Figure 4.5 b)), 8 (Figure 4.5 c)), or 12 (Figure 4.5 d)) sine functions. As can be seen in Figure 4.5 c), eight sine functions are sufficient to accurately simulate the olfactory cortex potential distributions accurately. Although we have not yet carried out the simulation, it is likely to be the case that those long tailed histograms that cannot fit PDE (e.g., Figures 4.2 e) and r)) will be able to be simulated by series of N sine waves, where N may vary from 10 to 20.

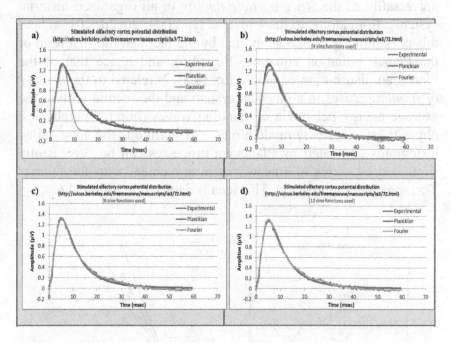

Figure 4.5. Simulating long tailed histograms with linear combinations of sine waves based on the Fourier theorem (Herbert, 1987).

4.3.5. Wave-particle duality: the common mechanism of Planckian processes

As demonstrated in Figure 4.2 and Table 4.1, the Planckian distribution equation (4.7) or (4.8) has been found to fit the long tailed histograms generated in a surprisingly wide range of disciplines, from atomic physics (i.e., blackbody radiation itself; see Figure 5 in Ji, 2015b) to enzymology, to cell metabolism, to brain neurophysiology, to psychology, to economics, and to cosmology. These findings may indicate that, underlying all the varied phenomena obeying the Planckian distribution equation, there exist common mechanisms (just as all the phenomena obeying the Gaussian distribution law implicate common mechanisms, namely,

random processes).   One possible *common mechanism* responsible
for the Planckian distribution may be sought in the postulated
universality of the *wave-particle duality* in all organized material
systems, from atoms to the Universe (Ji, 2004, 2012d, 2015a), and
this possibility is in part supported by the fact that the first term of
the Planck radiation equation, Eq. (4.6), and hence that of the
Planckian distribution equation, Eq. (4.8), is related to the *number
of standing waves* in a physical system and the second term to the
average energy per mode of standing waves (http://hyperphysics.
phy-astr.gsu.edu/hbase/mod6.html).   In addition, the long tailed
histograms generated by Planckian processes can be successfully
simulated by series of sine waves in agreement with the Fourier
Theorem (see Figure 4.5). This idea is depicted in Figure 4.6.

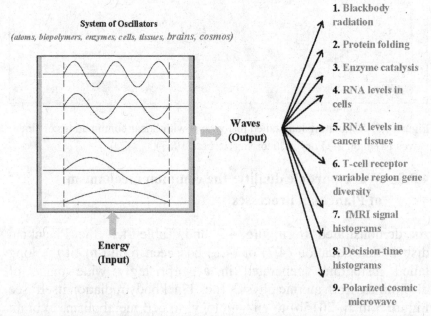

Figure 4.6. The postulate that the universality of the Planckian distribution equation in nature is the
result of the operation of the principle of the *wave-particle duality* in the Universe at all scales of
material systems, from atoms to the living cell, to the human brain, to human societies, and to the
Universe (Ji, 2004, 2012d, 2015a), i.e., from ***Matter to Mind*** (Ji, 2016).

4.3.6. Living systems as musical instruments: the '*Petoukhov Hypothesis*'

Through an entirely different approach than here described, the Russian biophysicist, Sergey Petoukhov (2015a, b, c), reached the conclusion that the properties of living systems can be modeled as systems of *resonance waves*, in agreement with the conclusions summarized in Figure 4.6. To obtain a glimpse of his thoughts, I reproduce below some of his statements from (Petoukhov, 2015b, c):

> "*Any living organism is a great chorus of coordinated oscillatory (also called vibrational; my addition) processes (mechanical, electrical, piezoelectric, biochemical, etc.), which are connected with their genetic inheritance along chains of generations.*" (4.11)

> "*From a formal point of view, a living organism is an oscillatory system with a large number of degrees of freedom, Resonances in such a system can serve as mechanisms for harmonization and ordering of its set of oscillatory processes.*" (4.12)

> "*A new slogan can be proposed: **any living body is a musical instrument** (a synthesizer with an abundance of rearrangements of resonant modes).*" (4.13)

These statements are reminiscent of my own writing published 4 decades earlier wherein I wrote (Ji, 1974b):

> "*An ordinary enzyme possesses 10^3 to 10^4 vibrational degrees of freedom. It is therefore reasonable to assume that the vibrational motions of individual bonds in the enzyme will be far more important in enzyme catalysis than the translational or rotational motions of the enzyme as a whole. Given all the vibrational frequencies of the individual bonds in an enzyme, as well as their three–dimensional arrangements, we can in principle deduce the thermodynamic and catalytic properties of the enzyme under any conditions.*"   (4.14)

All the above statements appear to support the conclusion drawn in (Ji, 2015a) that

> "The universal applicability of PDE (Planckian Distribution Equation) to many long tailed histograms is attributed to
>
> (i)   its role in generating functions and organizations through goal-directed selection of subsets of Gaussian processes, and
> (ii)   *the wave-particle duality operating in living systems.*"   (4.15)

4.4. Planckian Information (I_P) as a Measure of Order

It is generally accepted that there are at least three distinct aspects to information – *amount*, *meaning*, and *value* (Volkenstein, 2009), although Burgin (2010, p. 130) lists additionally cost, entropy, uncertainty, effectiveness, completeness, relevance, reliability, and authenticity, etc.

Planckian information is primarily concerned with the *amount* (and hence the *quantitative* aspect) of information. There are numerous ways that have been suggested in the literature for *quantifying information* besides the well-known Hartley information, Shannon entropy, algorithmic information, etc. There are at least 35 such methods listed in (Burgin, 2010, pp. 131-133), each method applicable to different aspects of information determined by the generalized parameter called "infological (i.e., informational-ontological) systems (Burgin, 2010, pp. 104, 113, 114, 499, 509; Brenner, 2012). The Planckian information defined below is a new measure of information that applies to specific processes called the *Planckian process* (defined in Section 4.3) which may be viewed as the *infological parameter* of I$_P$.

4.4.1. Definition

As illustrated in Figures 4.2 f), i), m), p), and r), the Planckian distribution equation (PDE), Equation (4.7), overlaps with GLE, (4.9) in its rising phase. Using the areas under the curves (AUC) of PDE and GLE, a new function was defined called the Planckian information, I$_P$ (Ji, 2015a, b):

$$I_P = \log_2 (AUC(PDE)/AUC(GLE)) \qquad (4.16)$$

My current interpretation of the Planckian information defined in Eq. (4.16) is that it represents the degree of organization (and hence the order) of a physical system resulting from symmetry-breaking selection processes applied to some randomly accessible (and hence symmetrically distributed) processes, whether the system involved is atoms, enzymes, cells, brains, languages, human societies, or the Universe (Ji, 2015a, b; see Figure 4.2).

4.4.2. Possible relations among Planckian information, quanta, and entropy

One way to better understand the possible meaning of I_P may be to compare it with the concept of Boltzmann-Gibbs and Shannon entropies which are well-known measures of disorder.   The meanings of the terms 'entropy' (and its derivative 'negentropy') and 'information' are controversial (Wicken, 1987). But this is fortunately not the case for the word 'quantum of action' or 'quanta of action'. Hence, if 'entropy' and 'information' can be shown to be related to 'quanta' mathematically, such a triadic relation may help to clarify the true meanings of 'entropy' and 'information'.

The concepts of entropy, quanta, and information all share the common property of being characterizable in three distinct ways: (i) experimentally, (ii) statistical mechanically, and (iii) mathematically or category-theoretically (Spivak, 2013; Brown and Porter, 2006), as summarized in Table 4.2.

Table 4.2 A possible relation among entropy, quanta, and information.

1. Concept	**Entropy** (1)	**Quanta** (2)	**Information** (3)
2. Field of study	Thermodynamics	Quantum mechanics	Informatics
3. Experiment/ Measurement	$S = \Delta Q/T$	Blackbody radiation spectra	Selecting m out of n possibilities or choices
4. Statistical mechanical formulations	$S = -k\, \Sigma\, p_i \log p_i$	$U(\lambda,T) = (2\pi hc^2/\lambda^5)/ (e^{hcl\,\lambda kT} - 1)$	$I_P = \log_2(\text{AUC}(P)/ \text{AUC}(G))$
	Boltzmann-Gibbs entropy (1866)*	Planck radiation equation (PRE) (1900)	where I_P = Planckian information, AUC = area under curve; P = PDE, and G = Gaussian-like equation, i.e., $y = Ae^{-(x-\mu)^2/(2\sigma^2)}$

(Continued)

Table 4.2 *(Continued)*

5. Mathematical formulation	$H = -K\Sigma\, p_i \log p_i$	$y = (A/(x + B)^5)/(e^{C/(x + B)} - 1)$	$I = \log_2 (n/m)$
	Shannon entropy (1948)	Planckian distribution equation (PDE) (2008)	A unified theory of the amount of information
6. Emerging Concept	A measure of **DISORDER**	Quantization of action essential for **ORGANIZATION**	A measure of the **ORDER** of an organized system

*Which reduces to $S = k \ln W$ when all p_i values are equal and W stands for the number of the microstates consistent with the macrostate of the system.

There is a close formal similarity between the mathematical equations for H and S (see Rows 4 and 5, Column 1). But this provides only a shallow reason for giving both functions the same name, 'entropy', without first checking that both mathematical functions share some common principles or mechanisms. Since the meaning of 'entropy' in thermodynamics is well established (e.g., a measure of disorder, obeying the Second Law), giving this same name to the H function may lead to unwittingly attributing the same thermodynamic meaning of entropy to H. In fact many scientists have taken this road, thereby creating confusions (see (Wicken, 1987) for a review).

A somewhat similar events have transpired during the past 7 years at Rutgers. We derived a new equation, the Planckian distribution equation (PDE), (see Row 5, Column 3), by replacing the universal constants and temperature in the Planck radiation equation (PRE) (see Row 4, Column 3) with free parameters, A, B and C (see Section 4.2). As already indicated, we defined "Planckian processes" as those physicochemobiological, biomedical, psychological, socio-economic and cosmological processes that generate numerical data fitting PDE, and there are many such processes found in natural and human sciences (as shown in Figure 4.2). In a certain sense, H function of Shannon can be thought of being related to the S function of Boltzmann and Gibbs as PDE is related to PRE. Therefore, if there are functors (Spivak, 2013; Brown and Porter,

2006) connecting PDE and PRE (e.g., energy quantization, wave-particle duality) as I believe, it is likely that there can be at least one functor connecting H and S which I do not believe is the Second Law as some physicists and mathematicians claim. The functor connecting H and S can well be "variety" as suggested by Wicken (1987, p. 186) or 'disorganized complexity' of Weaver (1948).

In addition to the "mathematical functors" described above, there may be "non-mathematical" or "qualitative" functors connecting H and S on the one hand and PDE and PBRE on the other, and I am inclined to think that these "qualitative functors" can be identified with the Peircean sign triad or ITR (Irreducible Triadic Relation (Ji, 2015b, Figure 27) (see Appendix I for a related discussion).

If the contents of Table 4.2 turn out to be true in principle, we may be justified to recognize two kinds of functors in 'generalized' (?) category theory: "quantitative" and "qualitative" functors, the former belonging to the domain of mathematics and the latter to that of the *non-mathematical branch of semiotics.*

There may be an irreducibly triadic relation (ITR) among THERMODYNAMICS, QUANTUM MECHANICS, and INFORMATICS (see Row 2, Table 4.2), thus forming a mathematical category (the TQI category ?). This idea is represented diagrammatically in Figure 4.7.

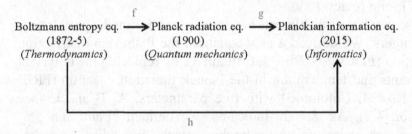

Figure 4.7. The hypothesis that the TQI (Thermodynamics, Quantum mechanics, and Informatics) category is essential for communication or semiosis. f = quantization or organization; g = selection; h = grounding, or realization. (Naming of these arrows are of the secondary importance, because there may be more than one ways of naming them, depending on the context of discourse or the infological parameters (Burgin, 2010). The commutative condition is thought to be satisfied: f x g = h, i.e., *f followed by g leads to the same result as h.*

The derivation of PRE (see Row 4-Column 3) by M. Planck in 1900 utilized the concept of thermodynamic entropy (Row 4, Column 1) (W. Vlasak, "Plancks' theory and thermodynamics", http://pubs.acs.org/subscribe/archive/ci/31/102/html/02learning.ht ml; M. Fowler, "Plancks' Route to the Black Body Radiation Formula and Quantization", http://galileo.phys.virginia.edu/ classes/252/PlanckStory.htm) which establishes a *paradigmatic* (to borrow the concept from linguistics (Culler, 1991) relation between *Entropy* and *Quanta*. Therefore, Quanta seem paradigmatically related to both *Entropy* and *Information*, which indicates that Quantum mechanics mediates the interaction between Thermodynamics and Informatics (e.g., energy dissipation underlying all communication of information), thus leading to the following possible irreducible triad (ITR) or a 'generalized' category:

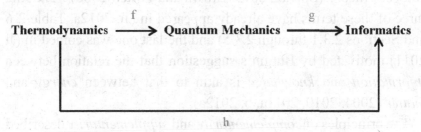

Figure 4.8. A possible irreducibly triadic relation (ITR) among *thermodynamics*, *quantum mechanics*, and *informatics*. In other words, f followed by g leads to the same result h. f = cosmogenesis (?); g = cognogenesis (?); and h = information flow or grounding.

4.4.3. The energy-information relation

Burgin's suggestion that the relation between *information* and *knowledge* (or *structure* more generally) is akin to that between *energy* and *matter* (Burgin, 2010, 2012a) is depicted at the center of Figure 4.9 (see Arrows 1 and 4 in this figure and Table 21-2 in (Ji, 2012e)). Since *energy* and *matter* are quantitatively related through $E = mc^2$, which can be viewed as a *supplementary relation*, and, since the combination of *energy* and *matter* is conserved according to the First Law of thermodynamics, it would be natural to combine these two terms into one word, *matter-energy* or *mattergy,* as is often done. Analogously, it may be convenient to coin a new word to represent the combination of *information* and *knowledge*, namely, 'information-knowledge' or 'infoknowledge', more briefly (see Arrows 4/5 relative to Arrows 1/8).

Figure 4.9 is a diagrammatic representation of the theory of everything (TOE) proposed in (Ji, 2012e) that seems consistent with similar theories proposed by Popper (1978), Rosen (1991), Penrose (2007), and Burgin (2010, 2011a, b). The TOE depicted in Figure 4.9 is an attempt to correlate and integrate the following four hybrid words, i.e., *mattergy*, *gnergy*, *liformation*, and *infoknowledge,* using *category theory* (Spivak, 2013; Brown and Porter, 2006). The first three of these terms have already appeared in (Ji, 2012a, Table 2-6 and Sections 2.3.1 through 2.3.5) and the last one was coined in (Ji 2011) motivated by Burgin's suggestion that the relation between *information* and *knowledge* is akin to that between *energy* and *matter* (2004, 2010, 2011a, b, 2012a).

The principles of *complementarity* and *supplementarity* described in (Ji, 2012a, Section 2.3.1) may play key roles in integrating the four hybrid terms and their associated theories and philosophies. Supplementarity is an additive relation, i.e., $A + B = C$, and complementarity is non-additive, i.e., $A^{\wedge}B = C$, where the symbol $^{\wedge}$ indicates that A and B are complementary aspects of a third entity C. These principles led to the coining of the terms, *gnergy* and *liformation*, respectively, as described in (Ji, 2012a, Table 2-6).

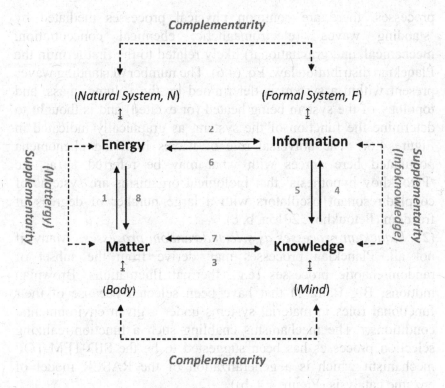

Figure 4.9. The suggested qualitative (or *complementary*) and quantitative (or *supplementary*) relations among *energy, matter, information,* and *knowledge*. The meanings of the numbered arrows are explained in Table 21-2 in (Ji, 2012e). *Mattergy* = the combination of matter and energy that is conserved in the Universe, according to the First Law of thermodynamics. '*Infoknowledge*' = a new term coined by combining *information* and *knowledge* in analogy to mattergy. Unlike mattergy which is conserved, *infoknowledge* may increase with time. *Reproduced from (Ji, 2012e).*

4.5. Conclusion

(1) *The universality of the Planckian distribution.* We have demonstrated that the Planckian distribution, Eq. (4.7) or (4.8), is a new distribution law, comparable to the Gaussian distribution equation, that applies to a wide range of long tailed histograms measured from atoms, biopolymers, living cells, languages, brains, human societies, and the cosmos (Figure 4.6). One plausible explanation for these findings is that, underlying all Planckian processes, there are common physical processes mediated by 'standing waves' (electromagnetic, chemical concentration, mechanical, and gravitational) likely related to the first term in the Planckian distribution law, Eq. (4.6). The number of standing waves present within a system is determined by the volume, mass, and topology of the system being heated (or excited) and is thought to determine the function of the system, as graphically indicated in Figure 4.6. The universal role of waves in living phenomena postulated here agrees with what may be referred to as the 'Petoukhov hypothesis' that biological organisms are systems of coupled/resonant oscillators with a large number of degrees of freedom (Petoukhov, 2015a, b, c).

(2) *Planckian processes as selected random processes.* Many, if not all, Planckian processes may derive from the subset of random/chaotic processes (e.g., thermal fluctuations, Brownian motions, Big Bang ?) that have been selected because of their functional roles in material systems under a given environmental conditions. The mechanisms enabling such a function-realizing selection processes has been suggested to be the SID-TEM-TOF mechanism which is a generalization of the RASER model of enzyme catalysis (Figure 4.4 b)).

(3) *The wave-particle duality in biomedical sciences.* Since **(i)** the Planckian distribution equation (4.7) or (4.8), in analogy to the Planck radiation equation (4.6), consists of two components – one likely related to the number of standing waves per volume and the other to the average energy of the standing waves, **(ii)** the wave aspect of the Planck radiation equation is fundamental in accounting for not only blackbody radiation spectra but also subatomic organization of atoms in terms of atomic orbitals, and **(iii)** the Planck distribution equation applies to both atoms (since PDE reproduces the blackbody radiation spectra; see Figure 2 in (Ji, 2015a)) and living systems (Figures 4.2 a), b), c), d), f), g), h), i), j), k), l), m), n), o), p), and q)), it appears logical to infer that the wave aspect of the wave-particle duality may play a fundamental role in the behavior of living structures and processes in biology and medicine, in agreement with the 'Petoukhov hypothesis' described in **1)** above.

If this inference turns out to be true upon further research, it may be predicted that biomedical scientists will find it impossible to completely account for living processes, both in the normal and diseased states, without taking into account their *wave aspect* along with their *particle aspect.*

4) The Petoukhov (2015a, c) hypothesis states that living organisms are akin to musical instruments. Ji postulated that enzymes (Ji, 1974b) and genes (Ji, 2012a, pp. 428-433) are *molecular machines* most likely obeying the principle of wave-particle duality (Ji, 2012d). Based on these findings and others summarized in Figure 4.6, it seems reasonable to infer that the Universe is a *self-organizing system of oscillators* or, metaphorically speaking, *a musical instrument,* in agreement with the concept of *Musica Universalis* (https://en.wikipedia.org/wiki/Musica_universalis) advocated by Pythagoras and Plato more than two millennia ago.

Acknowledgment

I thank my students for their help in performing some of the computations presented in this paper. My special thanks go to Kenneth So, Seungkee Kim, Vinay Valadi, and Woo H. Park. I am also thankful to M. Burgin and S. Petoukhov for their thoughtful comments and valuable suggestions, to the members of the [biosemiotics] and PEIRCE_L lists for stimulating discussions and constructive criticisms over the years, to K. A. Dill and K. Ghosh for kindly providing the protein folding free energy data underlying Figure 4.2 a), and to E. T. Rolls for introducing me to the literature on the drift-diffusion model of decision making.

Appendix A: The Peircean Sign as Mathematical Category, or *vice versa*

Re: [PEIRCE-L] Re: Teridentity & Triadic Sign Relation   9/16/14

Sungchul Ji <sji@rci.rutgers.edu>
to Jon, Peirce, biosemiotics, me

(For undistorted figures, see the attached.)

Hi,

While preparing for my interdisciplinary lecture on complementarity to
first-year students at Rutgers, called a Byrne seminar, the following
thoughts occurred to me today that may help apply abstract mathematical
concepts to Peirces' triadic sign relation which is based on his triadic
metaphysics:

The Essentiality of Threeness:

(**1**) One has NO RELATION.
   Two has only ONE RELATION.
   Three is the minimum to give rise to a RELATION between RELATIONS.

The Essentiality of the Threeness for Semiosis or Communication:

(**2**) What characterizes the Peircean sign relation is the transfer of
information from the object to the interpretant mediated by the sign:

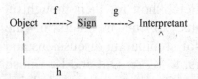

Figure A.1. The triadic sign relation of Peirce. f = sign generation; g =
information transfer from the utterer to the hearer; h = coincidence of
the original and the received information. Thus the composition condition
of the category theory in mathematics holds, i.e., $f \times g = h$.

(**3**) What mathematicians call "a category" can be viewed as the
generalization of Peirce's triadic sign relation. Both are the mechanisms
or the devices for transferring information from the source to the destination
through an intermediate.

(**4**) Both Pericean sign relation and mathematical category can be represented as a diagram called the "ur-category":

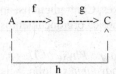

Figure A.2. The ur-category to which all categories and triadic relations belong. f = information preserving mapping (e.g., sign generation); g = information-preserving mapping (e.g., Fourier transform, transcription of DNA information to mRNA information, etc.); h = coincidence of the information between its source and receiver or target.

(**5**) Words alone are insufficient to convey the basic ideas behind the sign relations. The diagrams must be combined with words to adequately represent the subtle ideas behind the sign relation and the mathematical category and their mutual relations.

(6) (Added during the proof stage on 12/23/2015)
It should be pointed out that the Peirce's triadic relation of signs described here is related not only to the concept **category** in mathematics but also to the more recent concept of the **fundamental triad**, which is claimed by M. Burgin to be the most basic structure both in the physical and structural worlds (Burgin, 2010, 2011a, b, 2012a, b).

Bibliography

Ade, P. A. R *et al.* (2014) BICEP2 I: Detection of B-mode polarization at degree angular scales. arXiv:1403.3985v2 [astro-ph.CO] 18 Mar 2014. Figure 8 was manually digitized using *Paint.NET v 3.5.11* available in *Excel.*

Brenner, J. E. (2012) Mark Burgin's theory of information. *Information* 3:224-228.

Brown, R. and Porter, T. (2006) *Category Theory: an abstract setting for analogy and comparison,* PDF at http://citeseerx.ist.psu.edu/viewdoc/download?doi=10.1.1.65.2083&rep=rep1&type=pdf.\

Burgin, M. (2004). Data, information, and knowledge, *Information,* 7: 47-57.

Burgin, M. (2005). *Super-recursive Algorithms,* Springer, New York/Heidelberg/Berlin.

Burgin, M. (2010). *Theory of Information: Fundamentality, Diversity and Unification.* World Scientific, New Jersey.

Burgin, M. (2011a). Information in the structure of the world. *Information: Theories & Applications* **18** (1): 16–32.

Burgin, M. (2011b). *Theory of Named Sets*, Mathematics Research Developments, Nova Science Pub Inc.

Burgin, M. (2012a). *Structural Reality*, Nova Science Publishers, New York.

Burgin, M. (2012b). The Essence of Information: Paradoxes, Contradictions, and Solutions. Downloaded from http://www.infoamerica.org/documentos_pdf/wiener05.pdf

Callen, H. B. (1985) *Thermodynamics: An Introduction to the Physical Theories of Equilibrium Thermostatics and Irreversible Thermodynamics.* John Wiley & Son, Inc., New York, pp. 90-101.

Carhart-Harris RL, *et al.* (2014) The entropic brain: a theory of consciousness informed by neuroimaging research with psychedelic drugs. *Front Human Neurosci* **8**: 1-22.

Cho, A. (2014) Physicists say it's simple. Science **344**: 828.

Cowen, R. (2015) Gravitational waves discovery now officially dead. *Nature*, Jan 30, 2015.

Culler, J. (1991) *Ferdinand de Saussure,* Revised Edition, Cornell University Press, Ithaca. Dill, K. A., Ghosh, K. and Schmit, J. D. (2011) Physical limits of cells and proteomes. *Proc. Natl. Acad. Sci. USA* **108** (44): 17876-17582.

Deco G., Rolls E. T., Albantakis L. and Romo R. (2013) Brain mechanisms for perceptual and reward-related decision-making. *Progr Neurobiol* **103**: 194–213.

Dill, K. A., Ghosh, K. and Schmit, J. D. (2011) Physical limits of cells and proteomes. *Proc. Nat. Acad. Sci. (U.S.A.)* **108**(44): 17876-82.

Eroglu, S. (2014) Menzerath-Altmann Law: Statistical Mechanical Interpretation as Applied to a Linguistic Organization. *J. Stat. Phys.* **175**: 392-405.

Finkenthal, M. (2008) *Complexity, Multi-Disciplinarily, and Beyond,* Peter ang, New York, p. 12.

Frauenfelder, H., McMahon, B. H., Austin, R. H., Chu, K. and Groves, J. T. (2001) The role of structure, energy landscape, dynamics, and allostery in the enzymatic function of myoglobin. *Proc. Natl. Acad. Sci. (U.S.A.)* **98**(5): 2370-74.

Freeman, W. J. (1960) Repetitive electrical stimulation of prepyriform cortex in Cat. *J. Neurophysiol.* **23**: 383–396. PDF at http://sulcus.berkeley.edu/free manwww/manuscripts/iia3/60.html

Freeman, W. J. (1972) Linear analysis of the dynamics of neural masses. *Ann. Rev. Biophys. Bioengineering* **1**: 225-256.

Grzybek, P., Kelih, E. and Stadlober, E. (2008). The relation between word length and sentence length: an intra-systemic perspective in the core data structure. *Glottometrics* **16**: 111-121.

Hartshorne, C. and Weiss, P. (1931) Collected Papers of Charles Sanders Peirce, Volumes I: Principles of Philosophy. Harvard University Press, Boston, p. vii.

Herbert, N. (1987) *Quantum Reality: Beyond the New Physics and the Meaning of Reality.* Anchor Books, New York.

Hockett, C. F. (1960) The origin of speech. *Sci. Am.* **203** (3): 89-96.

Insana, G. (2003) *DNA Phonology: Investigating the Codon Space.* A dissertation submitted to the University of Cambridge for the degree of Doctor of Philosophy, November, 2003.

Ji, S. (1974a) A General Theory of ATP Synthesis and Utilization. *Ann. N. Y. Acad. Sci.* **227**: 211-226.

Ji S (1974b) Energy and negentropy in enzymic catalysis. *Ann. N. Y. Acad. Sci.* **227:** 419-437.

Ji, S. (1991) Biocybernetics: A Machine Theory of Biology, *in Molecular Theories of Cell Life and Death,* S. Ji (ed.), Rutgers University Press, New Brunswick, pp. 1-237.

Ji, S. (1997). Isomorphism between cell and human languages: molecular biological, bioinformatics and linguistic implications. *Biosystems* **44:** 17-39.

Ji, S. (1999). The linguistics of DNA: words, sentences, grammar, phonetics, and semantics. *Ann. N. Y. Acad. Sci.* **870**: 411-417.

Ji, S. (2000). Free energy and information contents of conformons in proteins and DNA. *BioSystems* **54:**107-130.

Ji, S. (2001). Isomorphism between cell and human languages: micro- and macrosemiotics. In: *Semiotics 2000: "Sebeok's Century"* (S. Simpkins, J. Deely, eds.), Legas, Ottawa, pp. 357-374.

Ji, S. (2004) Semiotics of life: A unified theory of molecular machines, cells, the mind, Peircean signs, and the universe based on the principle of information-energy complementarity, in *Reports, Research Group on Mathematical Linguistics, XVII Tarragona Seminar on Formal Syntax and Semantics,* Rovira i Virgili University, Tarragona, Spain, April 23-27, 2003. Available at - http://grammars.grlmc.com/GRLMC/reports/ or at http://www.conformon. net under Publications > Proceedings and Abstracts.

Ji, S. (2011). A category-theoretical framework to integrate physics, biology and informatics based on complementarity and supplementarity principles, in *A short talk presented at the 106th Statistical Mechanics Conference*, Rutgers University, Piscataway, NJ, December 18-29, 2011.

Ji, S. (2012a) Isomorphism between blackbody radiation and enzymic catalysis, in *Molecular Theory of the Living Cell: Concepts, Molecular Mechanisms, and Biomedical Applications,* New York: Springer, 2012, pp. 343-368.

Ji, S. (2012b) Complementarity. in *Molecular Theory of the Living Cell: Concepts, Molecular Mechanisms, and Biomedical Applications.* Springer, New York, pp. 24-50. PDF at http://www.conformon.net

Ji, S. (2012c) *Two Kinds of Complexities in Nature – Passive* and *Active*, in *Molecular Theory of the Living Cell: Concepts, Molecular Mechanisms, and Biomedical Applications, Springer,* New York. pp. 127-129.

Ji, S. (2012d). The Wave-particle complementarity in physics, biology, and philosophy. *ibid.* pp. 43-50. Available online at http://www.conformn.net under Publications > Book Chapters.

Ji, S. (2012e). Towards a Category Theory of Everything (cTOE). *ibid.* pp. 633-642. Available online at http://www.conformn.net under Publications > Book Chapters.

Ji, S. (2012f) Synchronic Versus Diachronic Information. *ibid.,* pp. 92-95.

Ji, S. (2014) The Unreasonable Arbitrariness of Mathematics (UAM): Evidence. Posted at biosemioitc@lists.ut.ee on June 29, 2014. *Attached as Appendix II.*

Ji, S. (2015a) Planckian distributions in molecular machines, living cells, and brains: The wave- particle duality in biomedical sciences, *Proceedings of the International Conference on Biology and Biomedical Engineering.* Vienna, March 15-17, 2015. Pp. 115-137.

Ji, S. (2015b) Planckian information (I$_P$): A new measure of order in atoms, enzymes, cells, brains, human societies, and the cosmos. in *Unified Field Mechanics: Natural Science beyond the Veil of Spacetime* (R. Amoroso, P. Rowlands, and L. Kauffman, eds.) World Scientific, New Jersey, pp. 579-589.

Ji, S. (2016) *The Cell Language Theory: Connecting Matter to Mind.* Imperial College Press, London (to appear).

Lauffer, M. A. (1983) The Significance of entropy-driven processes in biological systems. *Comments Mol. Cell. Biophys.* **2** (2): 99-109.

Lu, H. P., Xun, L. and Xie, X. S. (1998) Single-molecule enzymatic dynamics, *Science* **282**, 1877-1882.

Luce R D (1986) Response Times: Their Role in Inferring Elementary Mental Organization. New York: Oxford University Press. Figure 11.4.

Marty, R. (2014) "76 Definitions of The Sign by C. S. Peirce," 2014, http://www.cspeirce.com/rsources/76defs/76defs.htm. Retrieved in November, 2015.

Murugan, A. Mora, T., Walczak, A. M. and Callan, C. G., Jr. (2012). Statistical inference of the generation probability of T-cell receptors from sequence repertoires. *arXiv:* 1208.3925v1 [q-bio.QM], 20 Aug 2012.

Peirce, C. S. (2015) at http://en.wikipedia.org/wiki/Charles_Sanders_Peirce.

Penrose, R. (2007) *The Large, the Small and the Human Mind.* Cambridge University Press, Cambridge.

Perou, C. M., Sorlie, T. *et al.* (2000). Molecular portraits of human breast tumors. *Nature* **406** (67970): 747-52.

Petoukhov, S. V. (2015a) The genetic code, algebra of projection operators and problems of inherited biological ensembles. *http://arxiv.org/abs/1307.7882*

Petoukhov, S. V. (2015b) Music and the Modeling approach to genetic systems of biological resonances. *Extended Abstract, The 4th ISIS Summit*, Vienna, Austria, 2015.

Petoukhov, S. V. (2015c) The system-resonance approach in modeling genetic structures. *BioSystems* **139**: 1-11.

Popper, K. (1978) Three Worlds, The Tanner Lecture On Human Values Delivered at The University of Michigan April 7, 1978. http://tannerlectures. utah.edu/_documents/a-to-z/p/ popper80.pdf

Prigogine, I. (1977) Dissipative structures and biological order, *Adv. Biol. Med. Phys.***16**: 99-113.

Raleigh-Jeans law. http:// en.wikipedia.org/ wiki / Rayleigh%E2%80%93Jeans_ law. Retrieved in 2016.

Ratcliff, R. and McKoon, G. (2006) The diffusion decision model. http://digital union.osu.edu/r2/summer06/webb/index.html.

Rosen, R. (1991). *Life Itself.* Columbia University Press, New York.

Roxin, A. and Lederberg, A. (2008) Neurobiological models of twochoice decision making can be reduced to a one-dimensional nonlinear diffusion equation. *PLoS Computat. Biol.* **4**(3): 1-13.

Sigurd, B., Eeg-Olofsson, M., van der Weijer, J. (2004) Word Length, Sentence Length and Frequency.- Zipf Revisited. *Studia Linguistica.* **58**(1): 37-52.

Spivak, D. I. (2013) *Category Theory for the Sciences.* The MIT Press, Cambridge, Massachusetts. Open Access HTML Version at *http://category-theory.mitpress.mit.edu/*

Ultraviolet catastrophe. http://en.wikipedia.org/wiki/Ultraviolet_catastrophe. Retrieved in 2016.

Vandekerckhove, J. and Tuerlinckx, F. (2007) Fitting the Ratcliff diffusion model to experimental data. *Psychonomic Bull. Rev.* **14**(6):1011-1026.

Volkenstein, M. V. (2009) *Entropy and Information*, Birkhäuser, Basel.

Weaver, W. (1948) Science and Complexity, *American Scientist* **36**: 536-544.

Wicken, J. S. (1987). Entropy and Information: suggestions for Common Language. *Phil. Sci.* **54**: 176-193.

Wigner, E. (1960) The Unreasonable Effectiveness of Mathematics in Natural Sciences. *Commun. Pure Appl. Math.* **13**: 1-14.

Words/phrases spoken by Kerry during the 2004-09-30 Deabte (2004) Retrieved from file:///J:/Glottometrics/Words%20phrases%20spoken%20by%20Kerry %20during%20the%202004-09-30%20Debate.htm

Yakovenko, V. M. (2008) Econophysics, Statistical Mechanics Approach to. arXiv:0709.36624v4 [q-fin.ST] 3 Aug 2008.

Zhang, J. (2000) Protein-length distributions for the three domains of life. *TIG* **16**(3): 107-109.

Zhou, Y. and Mishra, B. (2004) Models of genomic evolution. in *Modelling in Molecular Biology* (G. Ciobanu and G. Rozenberg, eds.), Springer, Berlin, pp. 287-305.

Chapter 5

Algorithmically Random
Universal Algebras

Bakhadyr Khoussainov

Department of Computer Science, University of Auckland
Auckland, New Zealand

Abstract

This paper introduces the concept of algorithmically random universal algebra.
This is done through introducing a natural measure into the class of finitely
generated algebras. We prove that algorithmically random universal algebras
exist. We also show that such algebras can not be computable. Finally, we
construct an algorithmically random universal algebra computable in the halting set.

5.1. Introduction

5.1.1. *Motivation*

Consider one of the simplest infinite algebraic structures, known as the successor structure on the set ω of natural numbers, $(\omega; S)$ where $S(n) = n+1$
for all $n \in \omega$. Intuitively, this algebraic structure has no randomness in
it. We can simply describe this structure, in the class of all infinite structures, as follows: (1) the structure is generated by 0, (2) for all distinct x,
y we have $S(x) \neq S(y)$. Consider another simple example $(\mathcal{Z}; +)$, where
$\mathcal{Z}$ is the set of all integers. Again this is an algebraic structure that, intuitively, has no randomness in it. We can describe this structure, also in
the class of all infinite structures, as follows: (1) The operation $+$ satisfies
axioms of abelian groups, (2) The structure is generated by 1, and (3) the
operation $+1$ is injective. These two structures are examples of universal
algebras, and the class of universal algebras is the focus of this paper. Our
goal is to attack the following question of fundamental mathematical and

98

philosophical interest. What is an algorithmically random infinite universal algebra? For this, we develop algebraic and computability-theoretic tools that allow us to solve this fundamentally important question. We employ basics of universal algebra and the theory of algorithmic randomness.

Algorithmic randomness investigates random individual elements in various spaces equipped with a natural measure. The emphasis is mostly given to the study of algorithmic randomness for infinite binary strings. Recently, there have been significant advances in the investigation of algorithmic randomness of infinite strings. Monographs by [Downey and Hirschfeldt (2010)] and by [Nies (2009)], and the textbooks by [Calude (2002)] and [Li and Vitani (2008)] on the topic of randomness and computability give an account of the most recent research activities in the area. The history of this subject goes back to the work of [Kolmogorov (1965)], [Martin-Löf (1966)], [Chaitin (1969)], and later [Schnorr (1971)], [Schnorr (1972)] and [Zvonkin and Levin (1970)]. There are many notions of algorithmic randomness defined through the concepts of Martin Löf tests, Schnorr tests, prefix free complexity, K-triviality, and martingales. The most common and arguably central of these is the notion of Martin-Löf randomness.

We briefly recall the definition of Martin-Löf randomness in the case of infinite binary strings. The set of all infinite binary sequences is denoted by $\{0,1\}^\omega$. This is the Cantor space and is viewed as the complete infinite binary tree. This set is equipped with the canonical topology generated by the cones $C(w)$ consisting of all binary infinite strings extending the finite string w. Lebesgue measure on Cantor space is induced by the function $\lambda(C(w)) = 2^{|w|}$, where $|w|$ denotes the length of w. A *Martin-Löf test*, or ML-test for short, is a computably enumerable set $W \subseteq \omega \times 2^{<\omega}$ such that, with $W_n = \{w \in 2^{<\omega} \mid (n,w) \in W\}$, for all n we have:

$$\lambda(W_n) = \sum_{w \in W_n} 2^{-|w|} \leq 2^{-n}.$$

The sets W_n describe a shrinking sequence of open sets. Their intersection is a set of measure zero; the set W is an effective null-set.

A sequence $\alpha \in 2^\omega$ passes the ML-test W if

$$\alpha \notin \bigcap_n \bigcup_{w \in W_n} C(w).$$

In other words, α is not contained in the null-set generated by W. It is said that α is *Martin-Löf random* if it passes all Martin-Löf tests. There are only countably many ML-tests, hence the union of all null-sets given by tests is a set of measure zero. Therefore, the set of all ML-random sequences has Lebesgue measure one. In particular, ML-random sequences exist.

Thus, an important ingredient for defining the concept of algorithmic randomness in the Cantor space $\{0,1\}^\omega$ is the natural Lebesgue measure present in the space. Our definition of algorithmic randomness for infinite universal algebras will also be based on Martin-Löf tests considered on appropriate measurable spaces.

We can view every infinite binary string α as the following universal algebra together with one unary predicate

$$(\omega; S, P),$$

where ω is the domain of the universal algebra, S is the successor function defined as $S(i) = i + 1$ for all $i \in \omega$, and P is a unary predicate on ω such that P is true at n if and only if $\alpha(n) = 1$. In this respect, algorithmic randomness of strings can be identified with algorithmic randomness of specific infinite universal algebras of the type $(\omega; S, P)$. However, this view does not provide a satisfactory answer to the following question:

What is an algorithmically random infinite universal algebra?

In spite of much work, research on randomness of infinite strings has excluded the investigation of algorithmic randomness for infinite algebraic structures such as universal algebras. The main obstacle in introducing algorithmic randomness for the classes of infinite universal algebras is that these classes of structures lack measure. More precisely, it is unclear how one would define a meaningful measure through which it would be possible to introduce algorithmic randomness for infinite structures. In this paper, we overcome this obstacle by proposing a limited amount of finiteness conditions. Namely, we show how one can introduce algorithmic randomness into the class of infinite finitely generated universal algebras. Through our framework, we believe, one can investigate algorithmic randomness for traditional mathematical structures such as finitely generated groups and rings.

5.1.2. *What do we expect from random universal algebras?*

Algebraic objects of this paper are infinite universal algebras. Our goal is to present a reasonable definition to the intuitive notion of algorithmically random universal algebras. The algebraic objects of our study are defined as follows:

Definition 5.1. A *universal algebra* is a tuple $(A; f_1, \ldots, f_n, c_1, \ldots, c_m)$, where A is a nonempty set called the *domain* of $\mathcal{A}$, each f_i is a *total* function

$A^{k_i} \to A$ called a *atomic operation* of arity k_i, and each c_j is a *distinguished element* (or a *constant*) of $\mathcal{A}$.

For universal algebra $\mathcal{A} = (A; f_1, \ldots, f_n, c_1, \ldots, c_m)$, the sequence of symbols $f_1, \ldots, f_n, c_1, \ldots, c_m$ is called the signature of the algebra $\mathcal{A}$. For instance, the signature of the universal algebra $\omega; S, +, 0)$ consists of one unary operation symbol and one binary operation symbol, and a constant.

What algebraic, computability-theoretic and logical properties should we expect from an algorithmically random infinite structure? We now list some of those properties that should necessarily be implied from the definition.

Absoluteness property. We would like algorithmic randomness to be a property of the isomorphism type of the universal algebras rather than a property of some of their isomorphic copies. This is a natural requirement as structures are typically identified up to isomorphisms. Theorem 5.24 addresses this property.

Largeness Property. We would like random structures to be in abundance, the continuum, just like in the case of random infinite binary strings. This represents randomness as a property of collective, the idea that goes back to [Mises (1919)]. Corollary 5.22 exhibits this largeness property.

Non-computability property. We would like no computable universal algebra to be counted random. In computable algebras all the atomic operations, including the equality relation, are effectively calculable. Thus, by the absoluteness property no random universal algebra can be isomorphic to a computable universal algebra. Non algorithmic randomness of computable algebras is confirmed in Theorem 5.26.

There are many other questions that can be investigated for algorithmically random universal algebras. For instance, algorithmically random infinite strings possess immunity property. The property states that any effective attempt to list an effective infinite subsequence in an algorithmically random string fails. It is natural to ask if algorithmically random universal algebras possess immunity like properties. Other questions could be related to model-theoretic or algebraic descriptions of algorithmically random universal algebras. For instance, one can ask if any (infinite) finitely presented universal algebras in the class of all algebras can be algorithmically random. We discuss some of these questions in this paper. In particular, we show that our definition of algorithmic randomness for universal algebras imply all the three properties that we outlined above.

5.2.   Basics of Universal Algebras

Let $\mathcal{A} = (A; f_1, \ldots, f_n, c_1, \ldots, c_m)$ be a universal algebra. Recall that the *signature* of $\mathcal{A}$ is the sequence $f_1, \ldots, f_n, c_1, \ldots, c_m$ of symbols representing the operations and constants. Denote this signature by Γ_m, where m indicates the number of constants. The signature also specifies the arity k_i for each f_i. Note that we used the sequence $f_1, \ldots, f_n, c_1, \ldots, c_m$ in two ways: one as representing operations and elements of the algebra and the other as a sequence of symbols. Which of these meanings is used in any particular context will be clear from the context. In this paper, we always assume that the signature Γ_m contains at least two unary operation symbols or a function symbol of arity greater than 1. For a background on universal algebras, see [Gratzer (2008)] but below we will mention some of the basic definitions.

5.2.1.   *The heights of universal algebras*

Let V be a set of variables. The *terms* of the signature Γ_m are defined inductively as follows.

Definition 5.2 (Terms). Each constant symbol and each variable is a term. If $t_1, \ldots, t_{k_i}$ are terms, then so is the expression $f_i(t_1, \ldots, t_{k_i})$. We call a term a *ground term* if it contains no variables. The set of all ground terms is denoted by T_G.

The set T_G of ground terms can be turned into the following universal algebra of signature Γ_m as follows. The interpretation of each c_i is just the constant c_i. For each function symbol f_i and tuple of ground terms $(t_1, \ldots, t_{k_i})$, set the value of f_i on this tuple be the ground term $f_i(t_1, \ldots, t_{k_i})$. The resulting algebra is called a *term algebra* and we denote it by $\mathcal{T}_G$. Sometimes the universal algebra $\mathcal{T}_G$ is also called *absolutely free* universal algebra. The term algebra $\mathcal{T}_G$ has the following properties [Gratzer (2008)]:

(1) The algebra $\mathcal{T}_G$ is generated by its constants.
(2) Each universal algebra of signature Γ_m generated by its constants is a homomorphic image of $\mathcal{T}_G$.
(3) Let $\mathcal{A}$ be a universal algebra (over signature Γ_m) generated by the constants. If each universal algebra of signature Γ_m generated by its constants is a homomorphic image of $\mathcal{T}_G$, then $\mathcal{A}$ is isomorphic to $\mathcal{T}_G$.

Let $\mathcal{A}$ be a universal algebra of signature Γ_m. We extend a function $s : V \to A$ which we think of as an interpretation of the variables in A. The *interpretation* $i(t)$ of terms t in $\mathcal{A}$ is defined by induction as follows. First, for each a variable x, let $i(x) = s(x)$, and for each constant symbol c_j, let $i(c_j) = c_j$ (where c_j on the right is the value of the constant in $\mathcal{A}$). In the inductive step, for each basic operation f_j, let $i(f_j(t_1, \ldots, t_{k_j})) = f_j(i(t_1), \ldots, i(t_{k_j}))$. Note that f_j on the left side of this equality is the symbol f_j from the signature, while f_j on the right side represents the algebra operation (that we also denoted by f_j). The value of $i(t)$ depends on the s-values of variables occurring in t. Therefore, if $t \in T_G$ then $i(t)$ does not depend on s. So, we use the notation $t_{\mathcal{A}}$ for the values of the ground terms t in the algebra $\mathcal{A}$ without specifying the functions s. Note that if $\mathcal{A}$ is the term algebra T_G, then for this algebra we clearly have $i(t) = t$ for all $t \in T_G$.

Definition 5.3 (c-generated universal algebra). We say that the algebra $\mathcal{A}$ is *c-generated* if every element of $\mathcal{A}$ is the interpretation of some ground term.

Thus, if every element of $\mathcal{A}$ can be obtained from its constants by some chain of basic operations of $\mathcal{A}$ then the universal algebra $\mathcal{A}$ is *c-generated*. In other words, c-generated universal algebras $\mathcal{A}$ are such that for every element $a \in A$ there is a ground term t for which $t_{\mathcal{A}} = a$. We call t a *representation* of a in the universal algebra $\mathcal{A}$. Note that the element a might have more than one representations (or in fact, infinitely many) ground terms t representing it. Every c-generated universal algebra is finitely generated. However, there are finitely generated algebras of signature Γ_m that are not c-generated.

Let t be a ground term of the signature Γ_m. The *height* $h(t)$ of a ground term t is defined by induction as follows.

Definition 5.4. If $t = c_i$ is a constant symbol then $h(t) = 0$. If t is of the form $f_i(t_1, \ldots, t_{k_i})$, then $h(t) = \max\{h(t_1), \ldots, h(t_{k_i})\} + 1$.

If a universal algebra $\mathcal{A}$ is c-generated then for every element a there is a ground term t such that $t_{\mathcal{A}} = a$. Hence, with the element a of $\mathcal{A}$ we can associate its height defined as follows.

Definition 5.5. For a c-generated universal algebra $\mathcal{A}$ and an element a of $\mathcal{A}$, the *height* $h(a)$ of the element a is the minimal height among the heights of all the ground terms representing a. The *height* of the universal algebra $\mathcal{A}$ is the supremum of all the heights of its elements.

We note that for any ground term t of height n and any $i \leq n$ there exists a universal algebra $\mathcal{A}$ such that the height of the element $t_{\mathcal{A}}$ is i. If $\mathcal{A}$ is c-generated algebra, then every element a of it has a height. The following is an easy observation:

Proposition 5.6. *A c-generated universal algebra is finite if and only if there exists an n such that all elements of $\mathcal{A}$ have height at most n.*

So, infinite c-generated algebras are exactly those with infinite height ω. From now on we use the following notation borrowed from the theory of formal languages. Given signature Γ_m, denote the class of all c-generated finite universal algebras by $\Gamma_m^{\star}$, and the class of c-generated infinite universal algebras by Γ_m^{ω}.

5.2.2.　*Proper partial algebras*

Let $\mathcal{A}$ be a c-generated universal algebra of the signature Γ_m. For each $n \in \omega$, define the following subset of $\mathcal{A}$:

$$A[n] = \{a \in A \mid h(a) \leq n\}.$$

Each k_i-ary basic operation f_i of $\mathcal{A}$ gives rise to a *partial operation* $f_{i,n}$ on $A[n]$ defined as follows. For all $a_1, \ldots, a_{k_i}$ from $A[n]$

(1) if $h(a_i) < n$ for all $i = 1, \ldots, k_i$, then the value of $f_{i,n}(a_1, \ldots, a_{k_i})$ is equal to $f_i(a_1, \ldots, a_{k_i})$, and
(2) If there is an a_i among $a_1, \ldots, a_{k_i}$ such that $h(a_i) = n$, then the value of $f_{i,n}$ on $(a_1, \ldots, a_{k_i})$ is undefined.

Thus, we have the *partial universal algebra* $\mathcal{A}[n]$ obtained by restricting $\mathcal{A}$ to all elements of height at most n in $\mathcal{A}$. For instance, the domain of $\mathcal{A}[0]$ is the set $\{c_1, \ldots, c_m\}$ of all (values of) constants. We call the partial universal algebra $\mathcal{A}[n]$, the *n-th slice* of $\mathcal{A}$.

Definition 5.7. We say that two c-generated universal algebras $\mathcal{A}$ and $\mathcal{B}$ *agree at n*, if the partial universal algebras $\mathcal{A}[n]$ and $\mathcal{B}[n]$ are isomorphic.

For instance, two c-generated universal algebras $\mathcal{A}$ and $\mathcal{B}$ agree at level 0 if and only if for all constants c_i and c_j we have $c_i = c_j$ in $\mathcal{A}$ if and only if $c_i = c_j$ in $\mathcal{B}$. The following is an easy lemma that characterizes isomorphic c-generated universal algebras in terms of n-th slices of algebras. The lemma states that the isomorphism between c-generated universal algebras is a Π_1^0-condition.

Lemma 5.8. *Two c-generated universal algebras $\mathcal{A}$ and $\mathcal{B}$ are isomorphic if and only if they agree at n for all n.*

Proof. If $\mathcal{A}$ and $\mathcal{B}$ are isomorphic then any isomorphism between them induces the isomorphisms between the n-th slices $\mathcal{A}[n]$ and $\mathcal{B}[n]$ of these universal algebras. If $\mathcal{A}[n]$ is isomorphic to $\mathcal{B}[n]$ for each n then $t_{\mathcal{A}} \to t_{\mathcal{B}}$ must induce an isomorphism from $\mathcal{A}$ into $\mathcal{B}$. ☐

The next two lemmas show that the class Γ_m^* of all finite c-generated algebras is dense in the class Γ_m^ω.

Lemma 5.9. *Let $\mathcal{A}$ be an infinite c-generated universal algebra. For each $n \geq 0$ there exists a finite universal algebra $\mathcal{B}$ such that $\mathcal{A}$ and $\mathcal{B}$ agree at level n.*

Proof. Consider the partial universal algebra $\mathcal{A}[n]$. We define a finite c-generated universal algebra $\mathcal{B}$ as follows. The domain of $\mathcal{B}$ is $A[n] \cup \{s\}$, where s is a new element not present in $A[n]$. For each tuple $(a_1, \ldots, a_{k_i})$ of $A[n]$ and each basic (partial) operation $f_{i,n}$ such that $f_{i,n}(a_1, \ldots, a_{k_i})$ is not defined in $\mathcal{A}[n]$, declare the value of $f_{i,n}$ on the tuple $(a_1, \ldots, a_{k_i})$ be s. Also, declare the value of $f_{i,n}$ on any tuple that contains the new element s to be equal to s. In all other tuples $(a_1, \ldots, a_{k_i})$ keep the value $f_{i,n}(a_1, \ldots, a_{k_i})$ unchanged. It is easy to see that $\mathcal{B}$ defined above is a finite c-generated universal algebra that agrees with $\mathcal{A}$ at level n. ☐

Lemma 5.10. *If $\mathcal{B}$ is a finite c-generated universal algebra of height n, then there is an infinite c-generated universal algebra $\mathcal{A}$ such that $\mathcal{A}$ and $\mathcal{B}$ agree at level n.*

Proof. We fix an element b from the universal algebra $\mathcal{B}$ such that the height of b is n. With each ground term $t \in T_G$, we associate a *b-reduced term* $r_b(t)$ defined as follows:

(1) Each (value of the) constant c of $\mathcal{B}$ is b-reduced term $r_b(c)$.
(2) Consider a ground term $t = f(t_1, \ldots, t_k)$. Assume that we have defined $r_b(t_1), \ldots, r_b(t_k)$. Then

 (a) If each of the b-reduced terms $r_b(t_1), \ldots, r_b(t_k)$ belongs to $\mathcal{B}$ and b does not belong to $\{r_b(t_1), \ldots, r_b(t_k)\}$ then declare the b-reduced term $r_b(t)$ be the value of $f(r_b(t_1), \ldots, r_b(t_k))$ in the universal algebra $\mathcal{B}$.
 (b) Otherwise, $r_b(t)$ is just the expression $f(r_b(t_1), \ldots, r_b(t_k))$.

Clearly, the set of all b-reduced terms is infinite. The definition of the b-terms above also determines the interpretations of the basic operation symbols f (from the signature Γ_m) on all b-reduced terms. This defines the universal algebra $\mathcal{A}$ on the set of all b-reduced terms. It is not hard to see that the algebra $\mathcal{A}$ is c-generated and agrees with $\mathcal{B}$ at level n. $\quad\square$

We single out the n-slices of c-generated algebras in the following definition.

Definition 5.11. We call a finite universal partial algebra $\mathcal{B}$ *proper algebra* if it is an n-th slice of some universal algebra $\mathcal{A}$ from Γ_m^ω. We call n the *height* of the proper algebra $\mathcal{B}$.

Note that for any proper partial algebra $\mathcal{B}$ of height n and a ground term t with $h(t) \le n$, the value $t_\mathcal{B}$ of the ground term t in $\mathcal{B}$ exists. A syntactic characterization of proper partial algebras is given in the next lemma whose proof follows from the definitions.

Lemma 5.12. *A universal partial algebra $\mathcal{B}$ is proper if and only if there exists an n such that $\mathcal{B}$ satisfies the following properties:*

(1) For all $t \in T_G$ with $h(t) \le n$, the value $t_\mathcal{B}$ is defined.
(2) For all atomic operations f_i (of arity k_i) and all tuples $b_1, \ldots, b_{k_i}$ from $\mathcal{B}$ if $h(b_1) < n, \ldots, h(b_{k_i}) < n$ then $f_i(b_1, \ldots, b_{k_i})$ is defined, and if there is a b_i such that $h(b_i) = n$ then $f(b_1, \ldots, b_{k_i})$ is undefined. $\quad\square$

For instance, a proper algebra of height 0 has its domain $\{c_1, \ldots, c_m\}$, where some of the constants c_i might be equal to c_j, such that the functions f_i are undefined on any k_i tuple from the domain.

5.3.　A Measure for Universal Algebra Class

In this section we introduce a measure into the class Γ_m^ω, all infinite c-generated universal algebras. The measure will be akin to Lebesgue measure on Cantor space $\{0,1\}^\omega$. Through the measure, we then define ML-random infinite algebras.

5.3.1.　*Viewing Γ_m^ω as paths in a tree*

We fix signature Γ_m. There are finitely many non-isomorphic proper algebras of height n. Let $r_m(n)$ be the number of non-isomorphic proper partial algebras of height n. For instance, it is not too hard to see that $r_m(0)$ is the number of equivalence relations on the set $\{c_1, \ldots, c_m\}$.

Based on the assumption put on the signature, we have $r_m(n) < r_m(n+1)$ for all $n \in \omega$. Note that the function $n \to r_m(n)$ is computable. Based on the previous section, below we show that the class Γ_m^ω of all infinite c-generated algebras of the signature Γ_m can be viewed as paths through a finitely branching tree $\mathcal{T}_m$. Using the tree $\mathcal{T}_m$, we then introduce topology, measure and metric into the set Γ_m^ω.

We formally define the tree $\mathcal{T}_m$ as follows.

(1) The root of $\mathcal{T}_m$ is the empty set. This is level -1 of $\mathcal{T}_m$.
(2) The nodes of the tree $\mathcal{T}_m$ at level $n \geq 0$ are proper partial algebras of height n. There are exactly $r_m(n)$ of them.
(3) $\mathcal{B}$ be a proper partial algebra of height n. Its successor on the tree $\mathcal{T}_m$ is any proper partial algebra $\mathcal{C}$ of height $n+1$ such that $\mathcal{B}$ and $\mathcal{C}$ agree at level n.

Lemma 5.13 (Computable Tree Lemma). *The tree $\mathcal{T}_m$ satisfies the following properties:*

(1) Given any node x of $\mathcal{T}_m$, we can effectively compute the proper partial algebra $\mathcal{B}_x$ associated with the node x. We identify the nodes x of $\mathcal{T}_m$ and the proper partial algebras $\mathcal{B}_x$.
(2) For each x in $\mathcal{T}_m$, the partial algebra $\mathcal{B}_x$ has an immediate successor. Moreover, we can compute the number of immediate successors of x.
(3) For each path $\eta = \mathcal{B}_0, \mathcal{B}_1, \ldots$ in $\mathcal{T}_m$ we have: $\mathcal{B}_0 \subset \mathcal{B}_1 \subset \cdots$. The union of this chain is the universal algebra $\mathcal{B}_\eta = \bigcup_i \mathcal{B}_i$ from Γ_m^ω.
(4) The mapping $\eta \to \mathcal{B}_\eta$ is a bijection between all the infinite paths of $\mathcal{T}_m$ and the class Γ_m^ω.

Proof. Parts (1), (2) and (3) are clear. The part that requires the proof is part (4). But the proof of part (4) follows from Lemma 5.8. $\square$

5.3.2. *Topology, measure and metric*

Using the tree $\mathcal{T}_m$ we can introduce the topology, measure, and metric into the class Γ_m^ω.

Definition 5.14 (Topology). Let $\mathcal{B}$ be a proper partial algebra of height n. The **cone** of $\mathcal{B}$ is:

$$\text{Cone}(\mathcal{B}) = \{\mathcal{A} \mid \mathcal{A} \in \Gamma_m^\omega, \text{ and } \mathcal{A} \text{ and } \mathcal{B} \text{ agree at } n\}.$$

Declare the cones $\text{Cone}(\mathcal{B})$ to be the *base open sets* of the topology on Γ_m^ω. We refer to the proper partial algebra $\mathcal{B}$ as the *base of the cone*.

The measure μ_m of the cone $\text{Cone}(\mathcal{B}_x)$, where $x \in \mathcal{T}_m$, is defined by induction as follows.

Definition 5.15 (Measure). The measure of the cone at the root is 1. Assume that the measure $\mu_m(\text{Cone}(\mathcal{B}_x))$, where $\mathcal{B}_x$ is a proper partial algebra of height n, has been defined. Let e_x be the number of proper partial algebras of height $n + 1$ that agree with $\mathcal{B}_x$ at level n. Then for any immediate successor y of x the measure of $\text{Cone}(\mathcal{B}_y)$ is $\mu_m(\text{Cone}(\mathcal{B}_y)) = \mu_m(\text{Cone}(\mathcal{B}_x))/e_x$.

For this definition we note that $e_x \geq 2$ because the signature contains at least two unary function symbols or at least one operation symbol of arity at least 1.

Example 5.16. Assume that the signature consists of two unary symbols f and g and a constant symbol c. Let $\mathcal{B}_x$ be a proper partial algebra of height n of the signature such that $\mathcal{B}$ has exactly one element of height n and the cardinality of $\mathcal{B}_x$ is t. Then the number of immediate successors y of x equals $2 \cdot t + 1$. Hence the measure of the cone $C(\mathcal{B}_y)$ is $\mu(\mathcal{B}_x)/(2 \cdot t + 1)$.

As expected, we can also introduce metric into the set $\Gamma_m^\star \cup \Gamma_m^\omega$ as follows.

Definition 5.17 (Metric). For two c-generated universal algebras $\mathcal{A}$ and $\mathcal{B}$, let n be the maximal level at which $\mathcal{A}$ and $\mathcal{B}$ agree, that is $\mathcal{A}[n] = \mathcal{B}[n]$. Let $\mathcal{C}$ be the n-th slice of $\mathcal{A}$ (hence of $\mathcal{B}$). The distance $d(\mathcal{A}, \mathcal{B})$ between the algebras is then defined as follows: $d(\mathcal{A}, \mathcal{B}) = \mu_m(\text{Cone}(\mathcal{C}))$.

The next lemma shows that the distance d determines a metric in Γ_m^ω. Note, we identify universal algebras up to isomorphism. So, an isomorphism maps values of constants c in one universal algebra to the values of the same constants c in the other.

Lemma 5.18. *The function d is a metric in the space $\Gamma_m^\star \cup \Gamma_m^\omega$.*

Proof. Lemma 5.8 shows that a universal algebra $\mathcal{A}$ is isomorphic to $\mathcal{B}$ if and only if $d(\mathcal{A}, \mathcal{B}) = 0$. It is obvious that $d(\mathcal{A}, \mathcal{B}) = d(\mathcal{B}, \mathcal{A})$. So, we need to show that the triangle inequality $d(\mathcal{A}, \mathcal{B}) \leq d(\mathcal{A}, \mathcal{C}) + d(\mathcal{C}, \mathcal{B})$ holds for all universal algebras $\mathcal{A}$, $\mathcal{B}$ and $\mathcal{C}$.

If two of these three universal algebras are isomorphic then the triangle inequality obviously holds. So, assume that the universal algebras $\mathcal{A}$, $\mathcal{B}$ and $\mathcal{C}$ are pairwise not isomorphic. Let $n(\mathcal{A}, \mathcal{B})$ be the maximal level at which $\mathcal{A}$ and $\mathcal{B}$ agree. Similarly, consider $n(\mathcal{A}, \mathcal{C})$ and $n(\mathcal{C}, \mathcal{B})$.

If $n(\mathcal{A}, \mathcal{B}) > n(\mathcal{A}, \mathcal{C})$ then clearly the triangle inequality holds. If $n(\mathcal{A}, \mathcal{B}) \leq n(\mathcal{A}, \mathcal{C})$ then the $n(\mathcal{A}, \mathcal{B})$-th slice of $\mathcal{A}$ is isomorphic to the $n(\mathcal{A}, \mathcal{B})$-th slice of the universal algebra $\mathcal{C}$. This implies that $n(\mathcal{C}, \mathcal{B}) = n(\mathcal{A}, \mathcal{B})$. Therefore, $d(\mathcal{A}, \mathcal{B}) \leq d(\mathcal{A}, \mathcal{C}) + d(\mathcal{C}, \mathcal{B})$. $\qquad\square$

The following proposition follows from the lemmas and definitions above.

Proposition 5.19. *The space $\mathcal{M} = (\Gamma_m^\star \cup \Gamma_m^\omega, d)$ has the following properties:*

(1) $\mathcal{M}$ is compact.
(2) The countable set $\Gamma_m^\star$ is countable and dense in $\mathcal{M}$.
(3) Finite unions of cones form clo-open sets in the topology.
(4) The set of all μ_m-measurable sets is a σ-algebra. $\qquad\square$

5.4. ML-randomness for universal algebras

The set-up above allows us to formally define ML-random universal algebras. We start with the following definitions from algorithmic randomness applied to our setting.

Definition 5.20. A class $C \subseteq \Gamma_m^\omega$ of universal algebras is a Σ_1^0-*class* if there is computably enumerable (c.e.) sequence $\mathcal{B}_0, \mathcal{B}_1, \ldots$ of proper partial algebras such that the following two properties are satisfied:

(1) $C = \bigcup_{i \geq 1} \text{Cone}(\mathcal{B}_i)$.
(2) The function that associates i with the open diagram of $\mathcal{B}_i$ is computable. In particular, we can compute the cardinality and the atomic partial operations of $\mathcal{B}_i$.

For the next definition, we use the measure μ_m given in Definition 5.15.

Definition 5.21. Consider the class Γ_m^ω.

(1) A *Martin-Löf test* is a uniformly c.e. sequence $\{G_n\}_{n \geq 1}$ of Σ_1^0-classes in Γ_m^ω such that $G_{n+1} \subset G_n$ and $\mu_m(G_n) < 1/2^{-n}$ for all $n \geq 1$.
(2) A c-generated universal algebra $\mathcal{A}$ *fails* the *Martin-Löf test* $\{G_n\}_{n \geq 1}$ if $\mathcal{A}$ belongs to $\bigcap_n G_n$. Otherwise, we say that $\mathcal{A}$ *passes* the test.
(3) A c-generated universal algebra $\mathcal{A}$ is ML-*random* if it passes every Martin-Löf test.

We refer to Martin-Löf tests as ML-tests. It turns out that there exists a *universal ML-test* in the sense that passing that test is equivalent to passing all ML-tests. Formally, an ML-test $\{U_n\}_{n \geq 1}$ is *universal* if for any

ML-test $\{G_m\}_{m\geq 1}$ it is the case that $\cap_m G_m \subseteq \bigcap_n U_n$. A construction of a universal ML-test is easy. Indeed, enumerate all ML-tests $\{G_k^e\}_{k\geq 1}$, where $e \geq 1$, uniformly on e and k, and set $U_n = \bigcup_e G_{n+e+1}^e$. It is not hard to see that $\{U_n\}_{n\geq 1}$ is an ML-test and for any ML-test $\{G_m\}_{m\geq 1}$ we have $\bigcap_m G_m \subseteq \bigcap_n U_n$. Therefore, to prove that a c-generated algebra $\mathcal{A}$ is ML-random it suffices to show that $\mathcal{A}$ passes the universal ML-test $\{U_n\}_{n\geq 1}$. Thus, we have the following simple corollary.

Corollary 5.22. *The number of ML-random algebras is continuum.*

Proof. The class of all c-generated algebras $\mathcal{A}$ that are not ML-random is a class of μ_m-measure 0. Hence, the number of ML-random algebras is continuum. $\qquad\square$

5.5.   Generator Independence Theorem

We prove that randomness in c-generated universal algebras does *not* depend on the generators. This resembles the fact that randomness of reals is independent on the base of representations [Calude (2002)]. This will prove that ML-randomness is an isomorphism invariant property. More formally, we prove that $\mathcal{A}$ is ML-random with respect to one set of generators if and only if $\mathcal{A}$ is ML-random with respect to any other set of generators in the class of all finitely generated algebras. The theorem also shows that the definition of ML-randomness for universal algebras is robust.

We start with a simple definition of inessential expansion used in model theory. Let $\mathcal{A}$ be a universal algebra of the signature Γ_m. An *inessential expansion* of $\mathcal{A}$ in signature Γ_m is a universal algebra of the form $(\mathcal{A}, b_1, \ldots, b_k)$, where b_1, $\ldots$, b_k are arbitrary chosen elements of $\mathcal{A}$. Thus, inessential expansions are thus just universal algebras over an extended signature Γ_{m+k}.

Definition 5.23. A universal algebra $\mathcal{A}$ of signature Γ_m is *finitely generated* if some inessential expansion $(\mathcal{A}, b_1, \ldots, b_k)$ of $\mathcal{A}$ is c-generated.

Of course there are universal algebras over Γ_m not generated by the constants of the signature, but that have inessential expansions that make them c-generated over the extended (by constants) signature. Thus, a universal algebra $\mathcal{A}$ of signature Γ_m is finitely generated if and only if there are finitely many elements $b_1, \ldots, b_k$ such that the following holds. For each $a \in A$ there is a ground term t over the signature Γ_{m+k}, where the new constants $c_{m+1}, \ldots, c_{m+k}$ are interpreted as $b_1, \ldots, b_m$ respectively, such that the value of t in the expanded universal algebra equals a.

Theorem 5.24 (Generator independence).
Martin-Löf randomness for universal algebras is independent of the generators.

Proof. The proof idea is simple but some care should be taken with calculations. Let $\bar{b} = b_1, \ldots, b_m$ and $\bar{c} = c_1, \ldots, c_k$ be two sets of generators of a universal algebra $\mathcal{A}$. We can assume that the signature of $\mathcal{A}$ contains no constant symbols. Thus, we have $(\mathcal{A}, \bar{b}) \in \Gamma_m^\omega$ and $(\mathcal{A}, \bar{c}) \in \Gamma_k^\omega$. Our goal is to show that $(\mathcal{A}, \bar{b})$ is ML-random if and only if $(\mathcal{A}, \bar{c})$ is ML-random.

There exist ground terms $t_1, \ldots, t_k$ and $q_1, \ldots, q_m$ over Γ_m and Γ_k, respectively, such that $t_i(\bar{b}) = c_i$ and $q_j(\bar{c}) = b_j$, where $i = 1, \ldots, k$, and $j = 1, \ldots, m$. Call these equalities the *base equalities*. These equalities depend on $\mathcal{A}$ and we fix them. We set

$$j_0 = 2 \cdot \max\{h(t_i) + h(q_j) \mid i = \overline{1,k}, \; j = \overline{1,m},$$
$$k_0 = \max\{h(t_i) \mid i = \overline{1,k}\} \text{ and } m_0 = \max\{h(q_j) \mid j = j = \overline{1,m}\},$$

where h is the height function. If $(\mathcal{D}, c_1, \ldots, c_k)$ from Γ_k^ω satisfies the base equalities then $(\mathcal{D}, q_1(\bar{c}), \ldots, q_m(\bar{c}))$ belongs to Γ_m^ω. Denote this mapping $(\mathcal{D}, c_1, \ldots, c_k) \to (\mathcal{D}, q_1(\bar{c}), \ldots, q_m(\bar{c}))$ by α. This is a partial map from the set Γ_k^ω into the set Γ_m^ω. On the domain of α this map is an injective map.

Let S_k be the class of all proper partial algebras of signature Γ_k in which the base equalities hold. This set is decidable, that is, there is an algorithm that given a partial universal algebra over the signature Γ_k decides if the universal algebra belongs to S_k. Set

$$[S_k] = \bigcup_{\mathcal{B} \in S_k} C(\mathcal{B}).$$

Similarly, consider the set $[S_m]$ of universal algebras of signature Γ_m in which the base equalities hold. Both $[S_k]$ and $[S_m]$ are open Σ_1^0-sets and have non-zero measure with measures x_k and x_m, respectively. The function α defined above is a bijection from $[S_k]$ to $[S_m]$. Below we identify the universal algebras from the class $[S_k]$ with the algebras from $[S_m]$ via α.

Let $\mathcal{B} = (B; \bar{c}) \in S_k$ and let t be the height of $\mathcal{B}$ such that $t > j_0$. With $\mathcal{B}$, associate a proper partial algebra $\mathcal{B}'$ of signature Γ_m such that

$$B' = \{x \in B \mid h(x) \leq t - k_0\} \text{ and } b_1 = q_1(\bar{c}), \ldots, b_m = q_m(\bar{c}).$$

Clearly, if $\mathcal{B}$ and $\mathcal{C}$ are isomorphic then $\mathcal{B}'$ and $\mathcal{C}'$ are also isomorphic. Similarly, we map proper partial algebras $\mathcal{B}'$ of height $t - k_0$ in signature

Γ_m into proper partial algebras $\mathcal{B}''$ of height $t - k_0 - m_0$ in signature Γ_k. Note that $\mathcal{B}''$ satisfies the base equalities due to the choice of constants j_0, k_0 and m_0. The mappings $\mathcal{B} \to \mathcal{B}'$ and $\mathcal{B}' \to \mathcal{B}''$ satisfy the following properties:

(1) If $\mathcal{B}'$ is a proper partial algebra of height $t - k_0$ in Γ_m satisfying the base equalities then there is a proper partial algebra $\mathcal{B}$ in the class S_k such that $\mathcal{B} \to \mathcal{B}'$.
(2) $r'_k(t - k_0 - m_0) \leq r'_m(t - k_0) \leq r'_k(t)$, where $r'_k(i)$ and $r'_m(j)$ are the numbers of proper partial algebras of height i in signatures Γ_k and Γ_m, respectively, satisfying the base equalities.
(3) $C(\mathcal{B}) \subseteq C(\mathcal{B}') \subseteq C(\mathcal{B}'')$.

Parts (1) and (2) are clear. Part (3) uses the map α.

Let $\{G_n\}_{n \geq 1}$ be an ML-test that fails $(\mathcal{A}, c_1, \ldots, c_k)$, that is the universal algebra $(\mathcal{A}, c_1, \ldots, c_k)$ belongs to G_n for every n. We transform this test into an ML-test that fails $(\mathcal{A}, b_1, \ldots, b_m)$. This will prove the theorem.

We can assume that the base of every cone in G_n satisfies the base equalities for all n. Hence, $C(\mathcal{B}) \subseteq [S_k]$ for all cones $C(\mathcal{B})$ in G_n. Therefore, we will assume that

$$\bigcup_{\mathcal{B} \in G_n} C(\mathcal{B}) \subseteq [S_k].$$

For each cone $C(\mathcal{B}) \subseteq G_n$, the measure $\mu_{[S_k]}(C(\mathcal{B}))$ of $C(\mathcal{B})$ in the set $[S_k]$ is $\mu_{[S_k]}(C(\mathcal{B})) = (1/x_k) \cdot \mu_k(C(\mathcal{B}))$. Hence, we can bound the measure $\mu_{[S_k]}(G_n)$ of G_n in $[S_k]$ as follows:

$$\mu_{[s_k]}(G_n) = (1/x_k) \cdot \mu_k(G_n) \leq (1/x_k) \cdot (1/2^n).$$

Thus, for the ML-test $\{G_n\}_{n \geq 1}$ we have:

(1) $G_n \subseteq [S_k]$.
(2) $\mu_{[S_k]}(G_n) \leq (1/x_k) \cdot (1/2^n)$.
(3) $G_n \supseteq G_{n+1}$.

For a given $\epsilon > 0$ proceed as follows with the note that all proper partial algebras $\mathcal{B}$ below are from the set S_k.

(1) Find a level $n(\epsilon)$ in the tree $\mathcal{T}_k$ such that $\mu_k(\mathcal{B}'') < \epsilon$ for all proper partial algebras $\mathcal{B}$ of height $n(\epsilon)$.
(2) Let $\delta(\epsilon)$ be the minimal measure of all the cones $C(\mathcal{B})$ among all proper partial algebras $\mathcal{B}$ of height $n(\epsilon)$.

(3) Compute $k(\epsilon)$, the number of proper partial algebras of height $n(\epsilon)$.
(4) Finally, find the first $t(\epsilon)$ such that $\mu(G_{t(\epsilon)}) < \delta(\epsilon)/k(\epsilon)$.

Note that $n(\epsilon)$, $\delta(\epsilon)$ and $k(\epsilon)$ can all be effectively calculated. Choosing $G_{t(\epsilon)}$ in this way guarantees that for all cones $C(\mathcal{B})$ in $G_{t(\epsilon)}$ we have the height of $\mathcal{B}$ is at least $n(\epsilon)$ and also $\mu(\mathcal{B}'') < \epsilon/t(\epsilon)$.

Set $V_n = G_{t(1/2^n)}$ for $n \geq 1$. This sequence $\{V_n\}_{n\geq1}$ is a ML-test that fails $(\mathcal{A}, c_1, \ldots, c_k)$. Since the sequence $\{V_n\}_{n\geq1}$ is a Σ_1^0-sequence, we can effectively write each V_n is a union of pairwise disjoint cones, that is,

$$V_n = \bigcup C(\mathcal{B}),$$

where the cones in the union are pairwise disjoint. Now for each n set

$$V_n' = \bigcup C(\mathcal{B}') \quad \text{and} \quad V_n'' = \bigcup C(\mathcal{B}'').$$

From the construction, it is not too hard to see that the sequence $\{V_n''\}_{n\geq1}$ is a ML-test in the space Γ_k^ω such that $\mu(V_n'') < 1/2^n$ for all n and the universal algebra $(\mathcal{A}, c_1, \ldots, c_k)$ fails this test.

The sequence $\{V_n'\}_{n\geq1}$ is a Σ_1^0-sequence in the space Γ_m^ω. Recall that we have the inclusion as we have indicated above:

$$C(\mathcal{B}) \supseteq C(\mathcal{B}') \supseteq C(\mathcal{B}'').$$

Moreover, $V_n' \supseteq V_{n+1}'$ for all n. Due to the inequality (2)

$$r_k'(t - k_0 - m_0) \leq r_m'(t - k_0) \leq r_k'(t)$$

above, we also have: $\mu_k(V_n) \leq \mu_m(V_n') \leq \mu_k(V_n'')$. All these imply that the sequence $\{V_n'\}_{n\geq1}$ is a ML-test that fails the universal algebra $(\mathcal{A}, b_1, \ldots, b_m)$ from Γ_m^ω. This is what was required to be proved. $\square$

5.6. Randomness in the Halting Set

An infinite universal algebra $\mathcal{A}$ is *computable* if it is isomorphic to a structure with domain ω and whose all atomic operations are computable. Thus, computability is an isomorphism property of universal algebras. Let $\mathcal{A}$ be a c-generated infinite universal algebra and $h : \mathcal{T}_G \to \mathcal{A}$ be the homomorphism from the term algebra $\mathcal{T}_G$ onto $\mathcal{A}$. The *word problem* of $\mathcal{A}$ is the set:

$$WP(\mathcal{A}) = \{(t, q) \mid t, q \in \mathcal{T}_G \ \& \ h(t) = h(q)\}.$$

The following proposition is an easy exercise.

Proposition 5.25. *The universal algebra* $\mathcal{A} \in \Gamma_m^\omega$ *is computable if and only if the word problem* $WP(\mathcal{A})$ *for* $\mathcal{A}$ *is decidable.* $\square$

As expected we have the following fact.

Theorem 5.26. *If $\mathcal{A}$ is a computable infinite universal c-generated algebra then the algebra $\mathcal{A}$ is not ML-random.*

Proof. There exists an effective procedure that given $n \in \omega$, computes the proper partial algebra $\mathcal{A}[n]$, nth-slice of the universal algebra $\mathcal{A}$. Indeed, this follows from the fact that given an element $a \in A$, we can effectively find a ground term t such that $t_{\mathcal{A}} = a$. This allows us to compute the height of the element a. Hence, the sequence of cones

$$\text{Cone}(\mathcal{A}[0]), \ \text{Cone}(\mathcal{A}[1]), \ \text{Cone}(\mathcal{A}[2]), \ \ldots$$

forms a Martin-Löf test that the universal algebra $\mathcal{A}$ fails. $\qquad\square$

A natural and wider class that contains the class of all computable algebras is the class of algebras computable in the Halting set. This class contains, for instance, all finitely presented algebras in finitely based verities (e.g. finitely presented groups). We denote the halting set by $\mathcal{H}$. Here is a definition.

Definition 5.27. A universal algebra $\mathcal{A} \in \Gamma_m^\omega$ is $\mathcal{H}$-*computable* if the word problem $WP(\mathcal{A})$ of $\mathcal{A}$ is computable in $\mathcal{H}$.

Every computable universal algebra is $\mathcal{H}$-computable. The next theorem shows that there are ML-random $\mathcal{H}$-computable universal algebras. Thus, the theorem above cannot be extended to $\mathcal{H}$-computable universal algebras.

Theorem 5.28. *Martin-Löf random $\mathcal{H}$-computable universal algebras exist.*

Proof. We build an $\mathcal{H}$-computable random universal algebra $\mathcal{A}$ of signature $\Gamma_1 = (f, g, c)$ where f and g are unary functions and c is a constant. The signature is not too important as the reasoning below can easily be adapted to other signatures. The universal algebra will thus be generated by the (value of the) constant c. Let $\{U_n\}_{n \geq 1}$ be the universal ML-test in the class Γ_1^ω for the class of finitely generated universal algebras of the signature Γ_1. So, $\mu_1(U_n) < 1/2^n$ for all $n \geq 1$. We want construct $\mathcal{A}$ such that $\mathcal{A} \notin \cap_n U_n$. For this it suffices to build $\mathcal{A}$ such that $\mathcal{A} \notin U_1$. Since

$$U_1 = C(\mathcal{B}_1) \cup C(\mathcal{B}_2) \cup \cdots$$

is the union of uniformly c.e. set of cones we will build $\mathcal{A}$ so that $\mathcal{A}$ avoids all the cones $C(\mathcal{B}_i)$ for all $i \geq 1$. Using the oracle $\mathcal{H}$, we assume that the union $C(\mathcal{B}_0) \cup C(\mathcal{B}_1) \cup \cdots$ satisfies the following properties:

(1) For all $i \neq j$ we have $C(\mathcal{B}_i) \cap C(\mathcal{B}_j) = \emptyset$.
(2) For all i, $\text{height}(C(\mathcal{B}_i)) \leq \text{height}(C(\mathcal{B}_{i+1}))$.

The universal algebra $\mathcal{A}$ is built by stages. At stage n, we define a proper partial algebra $\mathcal{A}_n$ so that $\mathcal{A}_n$ avoids the cone $C(\mathcal{B}_n)$ and $\mathcal{A}_{n-1} \subseteq \mathcal{A}_n$.

Stage 1. Let t_1 be the last number m so that $\mathcal{B}_1, \ldots, \mathcal{B}_m$ all have the same height h_1. Let $\mathcal{A}_1$ be a proper partial algebra of height h_1 such that

$$\mathcal{A}_1 \notin \{\mathcal{B}_1, \ldots, \mathcal{B}_{t_1}\} \text{ and } \mu_m(C(\mathcal{A}_1)) > \mu_m\left(C(\mathcal{A}_1) \bigcap \left(\bigcup_{i > t_1} C(\mathcal{B}_i)\right)\right).$$

Such partial algebra $\mathcal{A}_1$ exists as otherwise, we would have $\mu_1(U_1) \geq 1/2$.

Stage $s + 1$. Let t_{s+1} be the first m such that $\mathcal{B}_{t_s+1}, \ldots, \mathcal{B}_m$ all have the same height, say h_{s+1}. Set $\mathcal{A}_{s+1}$ to be a proper partial algebra such that $\mathcal{A}_{s+1}$ has height h_{s+1}, $\mathcal{A}_{s+1} \notin \{\mathcal{B}_{t_s+1}, \ldots, \mathcal{B}_{t_{s+1}}\}$, $\mathcal{A}_s \subset \mathcal{A}_{s+1}$, and $\mu_m(C(\mathcal{A}_{s+1})) > \mu_m(C(\mathcal{A}_s) \cap (\bigcup_{i > t_{s+1}} C(\mathcal{B}_i)))$. Such proper partial algebra $\mathcal{A}_{s+1}$ exists. Otherwise, we have a contradiction with the choice of $\mathcal{A}_s$.

Thus, the universal algebra $\mathcal{A} = \bigcup_{s \geq 1} \mathcal{A}_s$ does not belong to U_1. Hence, it passes the universal ML-test $\{U_n\}_{n \geq 1}$. So, $\mathcal{A}$ is ML-random. Note that at each stage we can select the partial algebra $\mathcal{A}_s$ computably. Hence, the universal algebra $\mathcal{A}$ is $\mathcal{H}$-computable as stipulated by the condition put on the sequence $C(\mathcal{B}_1), C(\mathcal{B}_2), \ldots$ at the start of the construction. □

An important class of algebras between the class of computable and the class of $\mathcal{H}$-computable algebras is the class of computably enumerable algebras. Here is a definition:

Definition 5.29. A universal algebra $\mathcal{A} \in \Gamma_m^\omega$ is *computably enumerable* if the word problem $WP(\mathcal{A})$ for it is a computably enumerable set.

Every computable universal algebra is computably enumerable and every computably enumerable universal algebra is $\mathcal{H}$-computable. We do not know if a ML-random computably enumerable universal algebras exist.

Bibliography

[Calude (2002)]C. S. Calude. *Information and Randomness — An Algorithmic Perspective.* 2nd Edition, Revised and Extended, Springer-Verlag, Berlin, 2002.
[Chaitin (1969)]G. J. Chaitin. On the length of programs for computing finite binary sequences, *Journal of the ACM*, 16:145–159, 1969.

[Downey and Hirschfeldt (2010)]R. Downey and D. Hirschfeldt. *Algorithmic Randomness and Complexity, Theory and Applications of Computability*, Springer, New York, 2010.

[Gratzer (2008)]G. Grätzer, *Universal Algebra*, revised reprint of the second edition, Springer, New York, 2008.

[Kolmogorov (1965)]A. Kolmogorov. Three approaches to the quantitative definition of information, *Problems of Information Transmission* 1:1–7, 1965.

[Li and Vitani (2008)]M. Li and P. Vitanyi. *An Introduction to Kolmogorov Complexity and Its Applications*, 3rd Edition, Springer-Verlag, 2008.

[Martin-Löf (1966)]P. Martin-Löf. The definition of random sequences, *Information and Control* 9(6):602–619, 1966.

[Mises (1919)]R. von Mises. Grundlagen der Wahrscheinlichkeitsrechnung, *Mathematische Zeitschrift* 5(191):52–99, 1919.

[Nies (2009)]A. Nies. *Computability and Randomness*, Oxford University Press, 2009.

[Schnorr (1971)]C.P. Schnorr. A unified approach to the definition of random sequences, *Mathematical Systems Theory* 5(3):246–258 (1971).

[Schnorr (1972)]C. P. Schnorr. The process complexity and effective random tests, *Proceedings of the Fourth ACM Symposium of Theory of Computing*, 1972.

[Zvonkin and Levin (1970)]A.K. Zvonkin and L. A. Levin. The complexity of finite objects and the development of the concepts of information and randomness by means of the theory of algorithms, *Russian Mathematical Surveys*, 25(6):83-124, 1970.

Chapter 6

Structural and Quantitative Characteristics of Complexity in Terms of Information

Marcin J. Schroeder

Akita International University, Akita, Japan

Abstract

Issues related to overcoming or controlling complexity accompanied entire intellectual development of humanity, although originally stress was on its opposition – simplicity. This paper reviews various conceptualizations of complexity in the European philosophical and scientific tradition from Pre-Socratic thinkers of Antiquity to the present time. Special focus is on the contributions of Aristotle whose works shaped the view of reality of his followers, as well as of his adversaries. However, many, if not majority of significant developments in the studies of complexity and simplicity are at least briefly described. This historical perspective is used for a critical summary of the ways complexity is studied today and for an attempt to provide a unified conceptual framework for the various modes of complexity considered in the past. For this purpose, the author uses his earlier developed general concept of information as an identification of a variety and concepts characterizing it. Finally, a quantitative description in the form of two related to each other measures of complexity and of information integration is presented.

6.1. Introduction

There is a curious disparity between two cognitive human capacities of being able to discern differences in the perception of sensory inputs and of being able to grasp in one act of comprehension a number of perceived differences. Thus, we can easily distinguish the differences in intensity of stimuli in the range of the strongest being at least billion times more intensive than the weakest ones. In our experience of color we can distinguish hundreds of hues and when differences in saturation (purity of the color) are considered, the ability to make distinctions between colors is equally impressive.

Curiously, we are able to assess without counting the number of objects presented to our attention only up to the "magical seven, plus or minus two" (Miller, 1952) and in this capacity we are not better than many other animals, such as for instance crows. Also, humans are already born with the capacity to assess the differences in the numbers of objects, although the span of the simultaneous object recognition may be reduced up to three objects (Izard *et al.*, 2009). Thus, the ability to comprehend the number of objects in a single act does not develop much beyond that with which we are born. The limitation applies equally well to the assessment of the number of physically defined objects, as to the assessment of the number of more general objects presented to human attention, not necessarily in the form of the difference between being present and absent.

The disparity between these two capacities, to discern differences in stimuli (in kind and in degree) and to assess the number of sources of these stimuli has a natural consequence for the comprehension of reality as complex. This complexity has reflection in the intuitive fundamental opposition between one and many. In the absence of the disparity between the two capacities, we could expect that the human comprehension would have been simply organized into the number of categories corresponding to the maximum number of possible distinctions, with the category of "one" not much different from other accessible to simultaneous comprehension categories and without need for the indefinite category of "many" and corresponding to it sense of complexity escaping comprehension. Recognition of the number of discernible differences well beyond the number of perceived objects made "many" and corresponding to it "complexity" major obstacles to human exploration and understanding of reality and possibly the most important reason for the development of intelligent behavior. Intelligence can be understood as the ability to overcome obstacles of complexity.

The most basic solution to the bottleneck caused by the very limited ability to comprehend in one cognitive act multiple objects of perception is so called "chunking", i.e. grouping of items and dealing with such constructed aggregates as though they were united into a higher order whole (Lindley, 1966). Of course, "chunking" is a reduction of the number, transition from "many" towards 'one', or at least towards the number within the "magical seven" range. But what is actually a subject of chunking? How is chunking related to the characteristics of environment? What is the outcome of chunking? Isn't it what we call an object?

Further discussion of these matters, as well as the issues of complexity of human experience, actions, artifacts, and of reality requires more precise conceptual framework. "Complexity" is an abstraction derived from the qualification described with the adjective "complex". But what is that which is complex? Typically, it is assumed that it is a "system" or "process". But what in turn is the meaning of these terms? They are sometimes left undefined, or defined in terms related to complexity (sometimes in a hidden way) as collections of elements or changes exhibiting some form of organization or interdependence, i.e. complexity.

6.2. Complexity and Information

Since complexity and its negation — simplicity definitely involve some relationship to multiplicity and unity, these are natural candidates for fundamental concepts for the study, although we do not have to oversimplify complexity by reducing it to multiplicity. Obviously, multiple does not necessarily mean complex. On the other hand, it is difficult to imagine an instance of complexity in the complete absence of multiplicity.

The reduction of many to one was associated by the present author with information (Schroeder, 2005). Thus, in this article information will be understood in terms of the categorical opposition of one and many. Many philosophers, from Pythagoras to Kant and beyond, recognized this opposition as categorical, not reducible to more general concepts. This means that both these concepts and their opposition have to be left undefined, but possibly characterized by some axioms. Then information may be understood as that which makes one out of many, either by selection of one out of many (selective manifestation of information) or by a structure which makes one out of many (structural manifestation of information).

It has to be emphasized that the expressions "selection" or "making one" do not mean an act of selection or construction by an agent, but rather should be considered in terms of an abstract realization of the fundamental opposition. One of possible interpretations of selection can be found in the transition from potentiality, which requires multiplicity, to actuality, which requires unity, however "transition" does not have to be understood in the diachronic way. Instead of construction, we can think about composition understood in the synchronic manner. For this reason information was defined as identification of a variety (Schroeder, 2005).

Identity of one of the elements of a variety realizing its opposition to predetermined plurality is a selective manifestation, while the fact that the variety is distinguished as a whole by its structure is a structural manifestation. Information in this sense makes selection or construction possible for an agent of some type, but is independent from the actual existence or action of such agent. This has obvious ontological consequences that information is an independent entity, which may, but does not have to determine the outcome of actual actions.

We can say that the variety in question is a carrier of information which becomes an information system with appropriate identifying mechanism (selective or structural). It should be noticed that the term "system" has here, within the concept of information system, a very clearly defined meaning. Information system could have been called simply "system", if not a possible confusion with the earlier uses of this word. The nebulous concepts of a system or process in common use become synchronic or diachronic descriptions of information systems.

The distinction of the identifying mechanism as selective or structural is described as difference in manifestation, not type, as one manifestation necessarily coexists with the other, however for different, although related carriers of information. Two elements of a variety can be distinct only through their own structural differences, which dictate the method of selection. On the other hand, a structure binding many into one is always one selected out of many possible structures. Thus, we can consider that we have two dual, coexisting manifestations of the same concept of information. Which of the two we consider depends on our choice of information carrier.

One of surprising consequences of these dual characteristics of information is that the process of differentiation of a whole into its components, directly opposed to unification of many into one, involves information too. Differentiation can be associated with analysis as opposed to synthesis in which we start from components and "construct" some whole in agreement with our understanding of information. Then, how is analysis related to information? When we differentiate some whole into components, we have to give each of them some form of identity, i.e. we have to give them some structural characteristics. We cannot predicate about something "many", if there is nothing that gives these components unity. Therefore, "many" implies "one" in the plural form ("many of one's"), while "one" implies "many" ("unity of many").

The use of the term "information" here is a matter of convention. Someone who prefers to conceptualize information in a different way, for instance at a lower level of abstraction, can substitute different name for the concept defined as identification of a variety. Since complexity is naturally associated with multiplicity and its opposition to unity or simplicity, the content of the present paper will not be influenced much by such nominal dissociation from the study of information when what here is called "information" is called in some alternative way. However, it should be clear that the concept of information used here has as special instances the majority of concepts of information as known from literature. For instance, if we consider that information carrier is a set (alphabet) equipped with a probability distribution (probability of selection), the resulting selective manifestation can be associated with information considered in the spirit of Shannon (1948). On the other hand, structural manifestation can be associated with information as understood by Thom (1975).

The concept of information understood in the sense explained above can be formalized with the use of general algebra (Schroeder, 2011a; 2014). The variety is then a set S and the informational structure is defined as a closure space, i.e. a set with a general closure operator f (i.e. function

$f: 2^S \rightarrow 2^S$, *such that for all* $A, B \subseteq S$ & $A \subseteq f(A)$ & $A \subseteq B \Rightarrow f(A) \subseteq f(B)$, *and* $f(f(A)) = f(A)$).

There is a distinguished family $\mathcal{J}$ of subsets of S which are closed under operation of f (i.e. such that $f(A) = A$). The inclusion of sets orders this family into a complete lattice L_f.

More on this and other mathematical concepts used in this paper can be found in any text on general algebra, but the monograph by Garret Birkhoff on lattice theory (1967) gives a very comprehensive, classic overview of the subject.

This complete lattice L_f of closed subsets can be understood as a generalization of the concept of logic from the linguistic context to an arbitrary information system (Schroeder, 2012a). On the other hand any family of subsets $\mathcal{J}$ of some set S is sufficient to describe informational system, if entire S belongs to it and if it is closed with respect to arbitrary intersections. Then $f(A)$ can be introduced simply as the intersection of all subsets of $\mathcal{J}$, which have A as a subset.

The association of this mathematical structure with information becomes easier to understand when we search for the place in which linguistic information enters mathematical formalisms. We can observe that in the set theory we associate information understood in the linguistic way with subsets of elements which have some property expressed in the language of predicate logic. Informational aspect of the set theory can be identified in the separation axiom schema, which allows interpretation of $x \in A$, as a statement of some formula $\varphi(x)$ formulated in the language of predicate logic, such that $\varphi(x)$ is true whenever $x \in A$. Then the set A consists of all elements which possess the property expressed by $\varphi(x)$. Of course, the formula is a linguistic form of information about the elements of the distinguished set A. Since relations can be understood as subsets of an appropriate direct product of sets, we can extend this interpretation from unary predicates associated with sets, to higher level relational predication.

If we are interested in a more general concept of information, not necessarily in the context of a language (i.e. with an information system not necessarily defined with the use of some natural or artificial language), we can consider more general relationship than $x \in A$ described by a binary relation R between the set S and its power set 2^S: *xRA if* $x \in f(A)$.

When this closure operator f is trivial (i.e. for every subset A its closure $f(A) = A$) we get the usual set-theoretical relation of belonging to a set xRA *if* $x \in A$. In a more general case, risking some oversimplifica-tion, we could say that only closed subsets correspond to properties carrying information.

Our concept of information does not have representational character. The operation of the closure operator f does not have to be defined by formulas $\varphi(x)$ involving exclusively variables with values in set S, but of course nothing prevents us from considering this as a special case. The closure operator f can be defined not in terms of properties of elements of S, but in terms of mathematical structures defined at the level of collectives (e.g. geometric or topological). In this we can see an essential extension of the concept of information.

The dualism of selective and structural manifestations of information allows an extension of the methods to characterize information. The natural association of selective manifestation with the orthodox study of information initiated by Shannon (1948) gives the quantitative description of information in terms of entropy, or other magnitudes based on the probability distribution of a selection. In the present context, more appropriate would be one of magnitudes which gives value 0 in absence of distinction of elements (uniform distribution) and maximum value (for instance the value of $\log_2 n$ for the information carrier with n elements) when the selection of one particular element is determined with probability 1 (Schroeder, 2004). Such alternative will be outlined in the last, more mathematical section of this paper.

The dualism of selective and structural manifestations gives another characteristic of information referring to its structure. It was defined by the author as a level of integration (Schroeder, 2009). The level of information integration refers to the reducibility of the complete lattice L_f, which plays the role of the logic for given information system, into a product of component lattices. If the lattice is completely irreducible into a product of components (as it is in the case of quantum mechanical systems with unlimited superposition principle or in other words without super-selection rules), then we have completely integrated information. If the logic is an atomic Boolean lattice, then it can be reduced completely to the product of trivial two-element lattices (independent yes-no systems) and the information is completely disintegrated. Otherwise we have a large range of intermediate possibilities for different levels of integration.

This characteristic will be used in the last section of this paper for to introduce measures of complexity and of information integration.

Finally, it should be emphasized that the formalization of information in terms of the set theory and closure spaces is a matter of choice independent from the definition of the concept of information. For instance, it is possible to consider some form of mereology instead of set theory as a framework for formalization. However, there are some compelling reasons to use set-theoretic based formalism, at least in the context of complexity. As it will be shown in this paper, foundations for the structural conceptualization of complexity can be traced at least to the works of Aristotle, where it appears in two different modes. One of them was formulated in terms of the structure defined by predication, the other in terms of the structure built by the part-whole (mereologic) relation. The former initiated a sequence of conceptual, logical developments with set theory as its ultimate product. The latter found some representation (possibly not universally satisfactory) within set theory in terms of substructure systems.

Mereology was a subject of some early philosophical discussions in the Antiquity and of many discussions among Scholastics. Later, in the first half of the 20th Century mereology was formalized and studied as an alternative for set theory. However, while part-whole relationship can be described in terms of set theory in a way giving some insight into its nature, mereology thus far did not give any non-trivial description of set theory within itself. Since both alternatives (that focusing on predication and that focusing on part-whole relation) were involved in studies of complexity, set theoretical formalism is more suitable for our purpose.

Now we can go back to the issue of human cognitive capacities and their limitations. We could see that the ability to discern multiple differences between sensory stimuli perceived in separation is in the strong contrast with the limitation in simultaneous perception and comprehension of coexisting differences (many objects of perception means simply many differences distinguishing objects). We can easily formulate this issue in terms of information. Cognitive mechanisms in humans (and other animals) exhibit very extensive capacity to process unimodal selective manifestation of information. However, our environment is an information system with the high volume of information manifested in selective way, but also with the high level of integration. Our cognitive mechanisms have to overcome the barriers of both types.

In the present work, complexity will be analyzed as a combined qualification of information systems involving their selective and structural aspects. The first step will be to review the earlier attempts to study complexity and to demonstrate that the approach involving our concept of information is relevant for this purpose. Then the methods of information analysis will be applied to analysis of complexity.

The motif of unification (or making one out of many) will be present in all parts of the paper. It is important for the way information is understood here, but also whatever is the specific understanding of the concept of complexity, its origin is in the Latin "*complexus*" which literally means "braided or entwined together", but can be translated as "composition" (Gell-Mann, 1996). Therefore, it is natural to ask about the mechanism of this composition. It turns out that even if the issues related to complexity always attracted attention of philosophers from the very beginning of human inquiry, such mechanisms were absent in philosophical reflection until very recently.

6.3.   Foundations for Study of Complexity of Substance

Although the issues of complexity were present in all philosophical traditions from the beginnings of humanity, more often the question actually asked was "What is simple?" Complexity was considered as given and the problem was whether we can find a way to eliminate it or to overcome it by some type of reduction to that which is simple. In the present paper the focus will be on the Western philosophical tradition, but obviously the problem how to deal with complexity was and is present in all cultures.

It is not a surprise that already in Pre-Socratic Greek philosophy the concepts of unity and simplicity were compared and either identified or contrasted. Entire Greek philosophical tradition was optimistic in the sense of common belief that in spite of apparent complexity, reality is simple, or at least is comprehensible through rational thought. The word "cosmos" was the opposite to the word "chaos" and the association of cosmos with entire reality was an expression of the belief that in spite of the apparent complexity of the world it is a harmonious, highly ordered system.

Pythagoreans for instance used the term "cosmos" directly as the order of the world.

There were differences in the interpretations of observed complexity of our experience. Heraclitus believed that the most fundamental characteristic of reality is that it is changing (temporal diversity), but the ways objects of our inquiry change are constrained, and therefore we can find unity, and therefore reduce complexity, studying uniformity or patterns of transformations. For Parmenides and other members of Eleatic school of philosophy, reality was one (uniform) and variety, change, complexity were illusionary. Thus, the task is to eliminate that which is illusionary, primarily through demonstration of inconsistencies and contradictories resulting from the admission of variety. One of continuing subjects of inquiry already in Pre-Socratic stage was the search for the fundamental simple component of all objects. For instance Heraclitus believed that all variety comes from the rarefication or solidification of fire. Democritus introduced the opposition of matter and void, and searched for the source of diversity among the objects of our experience in the differences of relatively few geometric shapes of atoms, indivisible material micro-components of objects.

The views of Pre-Socratic philosophers, although very different in details, had a common motif of the belief that the reality is essentially simple and that the diversity and complexity of human experience is either illusionary or is a result of the composition of only few basic ingredients in diverse proportions or densities. Thus, in the latter case, the secret of the large diversity in our experience of reality is in the large multiplicity of possible choices of proportions or densities of very few substances or even singular primary substance. The rules of composition (structural aspect) were overshadowed by quantitative rules of proportions (selective aspect). Composition was not much more than the result of mixing or diluting ingredients.

The edifice of Aristotelian philosophy is too large to discuss in detail all its concepts, ideas and claims related to the issues of complexity, although Aristotle did not consider complexity as a separate philosophical theme, but rather as his predecessors as the context for unity and simplicity. Thus, instead of searching for his views on complexity it is more relevant to identify what in his philosophy influenced the way complexity was understood and studied through the centuries of its role as a foundation for intellectual inquiry in Western civilization. The task is not easy as there are many instances when some later views (e.g. of the Scholastic thinkers) are projected back on the legacy of Aristotle. Also, his views in different works not always are consistent. For this reason, in the following his statements of will be carefully traced to his works.

The special attention to the work of Aristotle in the present paper has two different reasons. One of them is its fundamental role in the formation of the conceptual framework for Western philosophy. Even those, who as for instance Francis Bacon believed to revolt against Aristotelian tradition, formulated their views using its concepts. In the past and also today philosophers and scientists frequently mix concepts of Aristotle with concepts explicitly rejected by him. Probably the most typical example would be the modern common sense understanding of matter and form, in which form is the shape of the body constituting the border between matter and void. Thus, no matter what philosophical systems of the Western tradition are considered, Aristotelian philosophy gives the best reference frame to compare them or to differentiate them from the views of Aristotle.

The second reason for the special attention is that the concepts used by the present author in the study of complexity and of information, although more general than concepts of Aristotle have some affinity with them. In some sense, the approach proposed by the author is an attempt to purge Aristotelian philosophy from its dependence on language, or rather on the linguistic form of information. Of course Aristotle, the present author, or whoever carries out inquiry has to use one language or another, but Aristotle derived his tools for the analysis of reality from the tools to analyze language. Because of that, he could not avoid some confusion between language and reality. This should and can be avoided when more general than linguistic types of information are introduced.

Thus, we have to start from the observation that the methodology of Aristotelian philosophy is founded on the analysis of the linguistic methods to describe reality, although he frequently declares the distinction between language and reality. Aristotle believed that the ultimate source of knowledge is in experience, but considered language as repository of experience accumulated through generations. For him a long-term, continuing, Greek as well as barbarian, use of some linguistic forms or terminology belongs to the criteria for the truth of a statement or the validity of a reasoning. For instance, he writes in *On the Heavens*, 286^a9- 286^b9: "For all men have some conception of the nature of the gods, and all who believe in the existence of the gods at all, whether barbarian or Greek, agree in allotting the highest place to the deity, (...) The common name, too, which has been handed down from our distant ancestors even to our own day, seems to show that they conceived of it in the fashion which we have been expressing. The same ideas, one must believe, recur in men's mind not once or twice but again and again. And so, implying that the primary body is something else beyond earth, fire, air, and water, they gave the highest place a name of its own, *aether*, derived from the fact that it 'runs always' for an eternity of time" (Aristotle, 1955).

Even more direct evidence for the fundamental role of language in Aristotelian philosophy is in his constant use of the concept of predication in philosophical argumentation. He is aware of the difference between predicability and other modes of relating objects in a closer association with existence, and therefore reality. For instance, he writes in *Categories*, 1^a21-2^b21: "Of things themselves some are predicable of a subject, and are never present in a subject. Thus 'man' is predicable of the individual man, and is never present in a subject. By being 'present in a subject' I do not mean present as parts are present in a whole, but being incapable of existence apart from the said subject. Some things, again, are present in a subject, but are never predicable of a subject. (...) Other things, again, are both predicable of a subject and present in in a subject. (...) There is, lastly, a class of things which are neither present in a subject nor predicable of a subject, such as the individual man or the individual horse. But, to speak more generally, that which is individual and has the character of a unit is never predicable of a subject. Yet, in some cases there is nothing to prevent such being present in a subject" (Aristotle, 1955).

The primary role of the linguistic analysis in the works of Aristotle without doubt influenced the way of thinking of many generations of philosophers reflected in the continuing until 17th Century common belief that the language itself, or rather linguistic realm, to include products of the use of language, is a sufficiently faithful model of reality to be an exclusive subject of study. Aristotle did not make this claim of sufficiency and clearly sought the ultimate source of knowledge in experience writing explicitly in *Metaphysics*, 980^{a}21-983^{a}32: "Experience is almost identified with science and art, but really science and art come to men *through* experience; (...) And art arises, when from many notions gained by experience one universal judgment about a class of objects is produced. (...) The reason is that experience is knowledge of individuals, art of universals, and actions and productions are all concerned with the individual" (Aristotle, 1955).

This does not contradict preoccupation of Aristotle with language and its analysis, as he trusted in the experience accumulated in language. More important for our study is that his methods of reducing complexity observed in reality through experience (for obvious reason of very limited technological advancement mainly sensory perception) made essential use of the conceptual framework built for linguistic analysis. Even when his studies (for instance related to the issue of reducing the large variety of perceptible bodies into composition of simple ones) started from investigation of the relationships between observations (classification of the bodies according to their heaviness or lightness and correlated with it classification of their "natural" motions), they ended up in the explanation in terms of essences and universals qualifying matter.

Aristotle made the distinction between universals and substance very clear, for instance in *Metaphysics*, 1037^{b}8-1038^{a}8: "For it seems impossible that any universal term should be the name of a substance. For primary substance is that kind of substance which is peculiar to an individual, which does not belong to anything else; but the universal is common, since that is called universal which naturally belongs to more than one thing. Of which individual then will this be the substance? Either of all or of none. But it cannot be the substance of all; and if it is to be the substance of one, this one will be the others also; for things whose substance is one and whose essence is one are themselves also one. Further, substance means that which is not predicable of a subject, but the universal is predicable of some subject always. (...) If, then, we view the matter from these standpoints, it is plain that no universal attribute is a substance, and this is plain also from the fact that no common predicate indicates a 'this', but rather a 'such'" (Aristotle, 1955).

While universal is what can be predicated of a subject, and therefore can be identified as a linguistic concept (Aristotle sometimes, for instance in the quotation above, uses the expression "universal term"), substance is placed directly in reality. We can find in in *Metaphysics*, 1028^a10-1030^b6: "There are several senses in which a thing may be said to 'be', as we pointed out previously (...) While 'being' has all these senses, obviously that which 'is' primarily the 'what', which indicates the substance of the thing. (...) Therefore, that which is primarily and is simply (not 'is something') must be substance. (...) We have now outlined the nature of substance, showing that it is that which is not predicated of a subject, but of which all else is predicated" (Aristotle, 1955). Now, substance is described by Aristotle as the compound of substratum and essence, and alternatively as the compound of matter and form. However, in both cases the notion of composition is obscure. For instance we can find in *Metaphysics*, 1045^a7-1045^b23: "(...) an essence is by its very nature a kind of unity as it is a kind of being.(...) people look for a unifying formula, and a difference, between potency and complete reality. But, as has been said, the proximate matter and the form are one and the same thing, the one potentially, the other actually. Therefore to ask the cause of their being one is like asking the cause of unity in general; for each thing is a unity, and the potential and the actual are somehow one. Therefore there is no other cause here unless there is something which caused the movement from potency into actuality" (Aristotle, 1955).

Although the concept of "essence" was used by Aristotle as the actual mode of substance in *Metaphysics*, as it was seen above, it was used in *Topics,* 100^a18-102^b26 in the context of universals, i.e. for the purpose of linguistic analysis. Here "essence" is that which is expressed in the definition of a thing, "property" is a predicate which does not indicate the essence of a thing, but yet belongs to that thing alone, and "accident" can be predicated of a thing, or not, or can be predicated sometimes. The distinction between "essence" and "property" is an expression of the belief that the linguistic model of reality is sufficiently faithful to reflect all aspects of reality. Therefore, there should be some form of necessity in essence lacking in properties. However, Aristotle did not provide any criterion how to make such distinction beyond human intention.

Moreover, he maintained in *Posterior Analytics*, 92^{b}35: "It appears (...) that definition neither demonstrates nor proves anything, and that knowledge of essential nature is not to be obtained either by definition or by demonstration" (McKeon, 1941).

Aristotelian concept of substance was much more general than those of his predecessors in Pre-Socratic philosophy who focused on the objects of sensory experience. Substance was for Aristotle a relatively simple object combining essence and matter, which could be diversified by properties or accidents, but this diversity seemed of secondary importance. However, the diversity of sensory experience expressed in terms of multiple qualities of individual bodies as well as diverse configuration of bodies required some explanation, i.e. reduction of their complexity to simple rules.

In *On the Heavens,* 268^{b}11-269^{a}32 Aristotle classified bodies according to their natural capacity to move either in circular motion around the center, straight up from, or straight down to the center. Each of five types of simple bodies have a particular type of natural motion (fire or air upward, water or earth downward, aether circular), compound bodies follow the motion of the prevailing simple element. Now, the natural motion is a result of the natural place for each of types of simple bodies. Thus, the structure of the universe is a result of the individual predispositions (natures) of the bodies within it. However, these predispositions are not explained by any structural characteristics of the bodies. The same applies to simple bodies and compound ones and the latter are simply mixtures in which one of simple bodies prevail. Aristotle in *On the Heavens,* 308^{a}34-311^{a}11 explains movement up of fire and down of earth by the conformity with their nature dictating the direction of change the same way the nature of other things is dictated by their respective natures ("healable attains health and not whiteness"). He observes some distinction in this case: "The only difference is that in the last case, viz. that of the heavy and the light, the bodies are thought to have a spring of change within themselves, while the subjects of healing and increase are thought to be moved purely from without. (...) But the reason why the heavy and the light appear more than these things to contain within themselves the source of their movements is that their matter is nearest to being" (Aristotle, 1955). The last sentence refers to the view that matter itself does not have capacity of actualization without essence, i.e. form. Its potentiality however admits different levels approaching actualization.

Aristotle made further distinction in *On Generation and Corruption*, 329^a24-331^a6 between the bodies exemplifying contrary qualities and the contrary qualities of matter themselves: "A more precise account of these presuppositions has been given in another work: we must however, give a detailed explanation of the primary bodies as well, since they too are similarly derived from the matter" (Aristotle, 1955).

Thus, his analysis of perceptible bodies is secondary with respect to more general considerations of substance, especially that his understanding of perceptibility was narrowed in his analysis to the human sense of touch: "For it is in accordance with a contrariety – a contrariety, moreover, of *tangible* qualities – that the primary bodies are differentiated. (...) Accordingly, we must segregate tangible differences and contrarieties, and distinguish which amongst them are primary. Contrarieties correlative to touch are following: hot-cold, dry-moist, heavy light, hard-soft, viscous-brittle, rough-smooth, coarse-fine. (...) It is clear, then, that all the other differences reduce to the first four, but that these admit no further reduction. (...) Hence it is evident that the 'couplings' of the elementary qualities will be four: hot with dry and moist with hot, and again cold with dry and cold with moist. And these four couples have attached themselves to *apparently* 'simple' bodies (Fire, Air, Water, and Earth) in a manner consonant with theory" (Aristotle, 1955). It is quite clear that the reduction of the complexity experienced in tactile experience was achieved by Aristotle not by the discovery of simple bodies (elementary substances), but by identification of elementary qualities, i.e. universals (or rather their couplings) whose association with actual bodies was only apparent.

We can go even further. As it was stated before, Aristotle in his general works did not address matters of complexity directly being more interested in what is simple and assuming that the rules of composition for the compounds are within natures of the simple components, as we could see in his analysis of the structure of the universe. Simplicity in turn was a quality which can be predicated of a subject that is simple. For this reason, simplicity as well as complexity should be studied in terms of universals, i.e. things that can be predicated of substance, not in terms of substance itself. We can find in *Metaphysics*, 1071^b3-1075^a19: "The one and the simple are not the same; for 'one' means a measure, but 'simple' means that the thing itself has a certain nature" (Aristotle, 1955).

Aristotle gave as the reason for his preoccupation with universals and their relations (such as predicability) rather than substances and their relations (i.e. linguistic forms rather than actual entities) the necessity to transcend what is accessible to perception and to employ demonstration in search for scientific knowledge. He wrote in *Posterior Analytics*, 87^b27: "Scientific knowledge is not possible through the act of perception. Even if perception as a faculty is of 'the such' and not merely of 'this somewhat', yet one must at any rate actually perceive a 'this somewhat', and at a definite present place and time: but that which is commensurately universal and true in all cases one cannot perceive, since it is not 'this' and it is not 'now'; if it were, it would not be commensurately universal – the term we apply to what is always and everywhere. Seeing, therefore, that demonstrations are commensurately universal and universals imperceptible, we clearly cannot obtain scientific knowledge by the act of perception" (McKeon, 1941).

In the preceding quotation, Aristotle is referring to the limitations of perception to now and here, but of course the same applies to other limitations of human perception implied by "many", even if we are not concerned with the transcending "now and here".

We can observe using our modern perspective that Aristotle did not have conceptual tools to study structural characteristics of substances. Substance, or more precisely primary substance (the word "substance" Aristotle used in many different meanings) as a combination, whatever is the meaning of this word, of matter and form, more specifically essence, did not have any structure understood as components bound by some interactions or rules of configuration. We can find an explicit statement of this in *Metaphysics*, 1037^b8-1038^a8: "(...) a substance cannot consist of substances present in it actually (...)" (Aristotle, 1955). He considered only three forms of relationship between "things" (the most general term which he never clearly defined): they could be predicated of each other, they could be present in each other and finally they could belong to each other. The last relationship is simply reverse of the first, so basically we have only two independent relations.

To be "present in a subject" has for Aristotle different meaning from the common understanding as indicated in *Categories*, 1ª22: "By being 'present in a subject' I do not mean present as parts are present in a whole, but being incapable of existence apart from the said subject" (Aristotle, 1955).

Thus, the only tool for his analysis was embedded in the language of discourse concept of predication. This concept was sufficient for giving the collection of universals a rich structure, which today we can identify as a partial order, although Aristotle is writing explicitly only on *transitivity* and *antisymmetry*, considering reflexivity obvious. Thus, for instance he writes in *Categories*, 1ᵇ10-11: "When one thing is predicated of another, all that which is predicable of the predicate will be predicable also of the subject" and in the context of the distinction between genus and species, 2ᵇ20: "the genus is predicated of the species, whereas the species cannot be predicated of the genus" (McKeon, 1941).

Predication of universals in turn was defined by Aristotle with use of primary substances or individuals, as seen in *Categories*, 2ª34-3ᵇ21: "Everything except primary substances is either predicable of a primary substance or present in a primary substance. (...) Moreover, primary substances are most properly called substances in virtue of the fact that they are the entities which underlie everything else, and that everything else is either predicated of them or present in them. Now the same relation which subsists between primary substance and everything else subsists also between the species and genus: for the species is to the genus as subject to predicate, since the genus is predicated of the species, whereas the species cannot be predicated of the genus. Thus we have a second ground for asserting that the species is more truly substance than the genus. (...) All substance appears to signify that which is individual. In the case of primary substance this is indisputably true, for the thing is a unit. In the case of secondary substances, when we speak, for instance 'man' or 'animal', our form of speech gives impression that we are here also indicating that which is individual, but the impression is not strictly true; for a secondary substance is not an individual, but a class with certain qualification; for it is not one and single as a primary substance is; the words 'man', 'animal', are predicable of more than one subject. (...) species and genus determine the quality with reference to substance: they signify substance qualitatively differentiated. The determinate qualification covers a larger field in the case of the genus than in that of the species: he who uses word 'animal' is herein using a word of wider extension than he who uses the word 'man'" (McKeon, 1941).

The concepts of genus and species refer to the study of essential attributes, as they were introduced for the purpose to explain definition. However, most of that which referred to genera and species can be applied to the wider class of attributes, not necessarily essential. This more general concept of universal coming out of linguistic considerations was defined in *On Interpretation*, 17ᵃ38: "Some things are universal, others individual. By the term 'universal' I mean that which is of such nature as to be predicated of many subjects, by 'individual' that which is not thus predicated" (McKeon, 1941).

The collective understanding of predication in the case of universals becomes even more clear when Aristotle considers the rules of demonstration in which there are differences of the modes of predication. He writes in *Prior Analytics*, 24ᵃ15-20 "A premise then is a sentence affirming or denying one thing of another. This is either universal or particular or indefinite. By universal I mean the statement that something belongs to all or none of something else; by particular that it belongs to some or not to some or not at all; by indefinite that it does or does not belong, without any mark to show whether it is universal or particular" (McKeon, 1941).

The study of demonstration is of special interest for us as in this context Aristotle writes more extensively on the issue of unifying function of predication, and therefore on the relationship between the linguistic and real structures reflected in complexity.

For instance, Aristotle writes in *Posterior Analytics*, 77ᵃ5-10: "So demonstration does not necessarily imply the being of Forms nor a One beside a Many, but it does necessarily imply the possibility of truly predicating one of many; (...) We conclude, then, that there must be a single identical term unequivocally predicable of a number of individuals" (McKeon, 1941).

Aristotle makes distinction between linguistic unity and real unity in *On Interpretation*, 20ᵇ13-21ᵃ20: "There is no unity about an affirmation or denial which, either positively or negatively, predicates one thing of many subjects, or many things of the same subject, unless that which is indicated by the many is really some one thing. I do not apply this word 'one' to those things which, though they have a single recognized name, yet do not combine to form a unity. Thus, man may be an animal, and biped, and domesticated, but these three predicates combine to form a unity. On the other hand, the predicates 'white', 'man', and 'walking' do not thus combine. Neither, therefore, if these three form the subject of an affirmation, nor if they form its predicate, is there any unity about that affirmation. In both cases the unity is linguistic, but not real. (...) Some combinations of predicates are such that the separate predicates unite to form a single predicate. Let us consider under what conditions this is and is not possible. We may either state in two separate propositions that man is an animal and that man is biped, or we can combine the two, and state that man is an animal with two feet. Similarly we may use 'man' and 'white' as separate predicates, or unite them into one. Yet if a man is shoemaker and is also good, we cannot construct a composite proposition and say that he is a good shoemaker. (...) Thus it is manifest that if a man states unconditionally that predicates can always be combined, many absurd consequences ensue. (...) Those predicates, and terms forming the subject of predication, which are accidental either to the same subject or to another, do not combine to form a unity. (...) Those predicates, again, cannot form a unity, of which the one is implicit in the other" (McKeon, 1941).

Aristotle wrote about the unity of predicates in many contexts, for instance in *Metaphysics,* 1037ᵇ20-28: "And even if the genus does share in them, the same argument applies, since the differentiae present in man are many, e.g. endowed with feet, two-footed, featherless. Why are these one and not many? Not because they are present in one thing; for on this principle a unity can be made out of *all* the attributes of a thing. But surely all the attributes in the definition *must* be one; for the definition is a single formula and a formula of substance, so that it must be a formula of some one thing; for substance means 'one' and a 'this', as we maintain" (McKeon, 1941).

Although the homogeneity of the views of Aristotle scattered over several of his writings may be questioned, we can attempt to summarize his views on the relationship between complex and simple into a unified picture. First, we can observe that his main tool for analysis is language and its structure in particular these aspects of language which have long tradition. Aristotle derives scientific knowledge ultimately from experience, but language is for him a repository of the collective experience. Virtually all concepts used in his studies are derived from language, but he makes a very clear distinction of that which is real and that which is linguistic.

Although Aristotle tries to be very careful in defining all his concepts, he is constantly using one term "thing" without definition. All what we know about "thing" is that it has some form of unity, can have a name (language counterpart), can have attributes, and sometimes can be predicated of other "things" (therefore it does not have to be a primary substance). This variable hidden concept is important, since its main characteristic unity (*Categories*, 2^a34-3^b21: "for the thing is a unit) is introducing through the back door the category of "one".

The traditional account of complexity of the objects of sensory perception (perceptible bodies) in terms of mixtures or alternations of simple bodies are by Aristotle considered as results of the confusion caused by mistaking simple qualities for simple bodies. Complexity according to Aristotle arises from the structure of attributes, not of material substratum which is simple. He indirectly makes distinction of complexity resulting from the variety of haphazard accidental attributes and from the structured variety of essential attributes. The former is beyond the scientific study and knowledge, the latter, due to its unity within the nature of the object of study, is the actual subject of scientific knowledge.

The tool for discovery of the structure of essential attributes is in the relationship between multiplicity and unity. Although Aristotle never uses the concept of structure, we can interpret this way his "predication one of many". However, Aristotle neglects entirely the relationship between a whole and its parts in his theoretical works delegating it to natural philosophy (*Parts of Animals*), and even his concept of participation of one thing in another plays a marginal role in his analysis. Thus, his study is almost entirely focused on "predication", or the inverse relation of "belonging to" as explained in *Prior Analytics*, 24^b26: "That one term is included in another as in a whole is the same as for the other to be predicated of all of the first" (McKeon, 1941). We can learn about the nature of substances by discovering which of their attributes can be united into a whole. It is clear that not all. First, they have to be essential, but it is only a necessary condition. For instance, Aristotle writes in *Parts of Animals*, 643^a27: "Further, the differentiae must be elements of essence, and not merely essential attributes" (McKeon, 1941). For this reason we have to consider entire structure involving genera and species together with some restrictions which determine unification into essences, which in modern terminology can be associated with a partial order which definitely is not a Boolean algebra of all subsets.

The particular relations giving the roles of a genus and species depend on the subject of study. This is why Aristotle felt compelled to write books on so many subjects. He believed in very strict divisions between genera not sharing species dividing knowledge into separate domains. For instance, we can find an expression of his, today obviously anachronistic, belief in *Posterior Analytics*, 75^a39: "We cannot, for instance, prove geometrical truth by arithmetic" (McKeon, 1941).

Complexity of a nature of the object of study could be reduced using demonstration. Perfect syllogisms are reducing more obscure statements regarding predication to simpler ones with absolute necessity. Thus, we need only "immediate premises" which can be easily known as true and through the application of perfect syllogisms we can get multiplicity of necessarily true conclusions.

We can find in *Posterior Analytics*, 71^b27-72^a9: "The premises must be primary and indemonstrable; (...) The premises must be causes of the conclusion, better known than it, and prior to it; (...) Now 'prior' and 'better known' are ambiguous terms, for there is a difference between what is prior and better known in the order of being and what is prior and better known to man. I mean that objects nearer to sense are prior and better known to man; objects without qualification prior and better known are those further from sense. (...) In saying that the premises of demonstrated knowledge must be primary, I mean that they must be 'appropriate' basic truth, for I identify primary premise and basic truth. A 'basic truth' in a demonstration is an immediate proposition. An immediate proposition is one which has no other proposition prior to it. A proposition is either part of an enunciation, i.e. it predicates a single attribute of a single subject" (McKeon, 1941).

Thus, we can see that demonstration with perfect syllogisms is a tool for the reduction of complexity. Reduction is not through elementary substances (all primary substances are according to Aristotle equally primary, no matter how complex are their attributes), but through the reduction of human knowledge to the immediate propositions. Moreover, Aristotle assessed demonstrations with fewer premises as superior in *Posterior Analytics*, 86^a33: "We may assume the superiority *ceteris paribus* of the demonstration which derives from fewer postulates or hypotheses – in short from fewer premises" (McKeon, 1941).

It is rarely recognized that Aristotle provided also a tool for a meta-level reduction of complexity reducing the complexity of demonstration tools – syllogisms in *Prior Analytics*, 29^b1-25: "It is possible also to reduce all syllogisms to the *universal* syllogisms in the first figure." His proof reduces fourteen perfect syllogisms to two.

Finally, we can observe that the concept of information presented in the introduction to this paper has its conceptual framework apparently similar to that of Aristotelian philosophy, but is more general and does not refer to the indefinite term of "thing". On the other hand, concepts of Aristotle can be interpreted there easily.

Aristotle did not consider the opposition of one and many fundamental. 'Many' was just a negation of 'one' as described in *Metaphysics*, 1017^a3: "Evidently 'many' will have meanings opposite to those of 'one'; some things are many because they are not continuous, others because their matter – either the proximate matter or the ultimate – is divisible in kind, others because the definitions which state their essence are more than one" (McKeon, 1941).

The fact that Aristotle disregards importance of the "one-many" opposition is of secondary importance with respect to the problem of his presentation of the concept of "one". His explanation is clearly based on a "vicious circle". Whenever he defines 'one' (he considers more than one way of its understanding), he refers to 'oneness' of something else. For instance, in the glossary of *Metaphysics* 1015^b16-1016^b18 devoted to 'one', he writes: "Those things also are called one whose genus is one though distinguished by opposite differentiae – these too are called one because the genus which underlies the differentiae is one (e.g. horse, man, and dog form a unity, because all are animals), an indeed in a way similar to that in which the matter is one. (...) Two things are called one, when the definition which states the essence of one is indivisible from another definition which shows us the other (though *in itself* every definition is divisible). (...) In general those things the thought of whose essence is indivisible, and cannot separate them either in time or in place or in definition, are most of all one, and of these especially those which are substances" (McKeon, 1941).

When we recall that the concepts of genus, essence, and even the undefined term "thing" were characterized by unity, but without any clear criteria for what is that which makes them one, the vicious circle of the explanation becomes complete.

In contrast to that, in the study of information outlined in the introduction the opposition of one and many is primary and all other concepts are derived from it. Aristotle is the closest to this way of thinking in his exceptionally general explanation of causes in the glossary of *Metaphysics*, 1013^b16-23: "All the causes now mentioned fall under four senses which are the most obvious. For the letters are the cause of syllables, and the material is the cause of manufactured things, and fire and earth and all such things are the causes of bodies, and the parts are causes of the whole, and the hypotheses are causes of the conclusion, in the sense that they are that out of which these respectively are made; but of these some are cause as the *substratum* (e.g. the parts), others as the essence (the whole, the synthesis, and the form)" (McKeon, 1941).

6.4. Foundations for Study of Mereologic and Functional Complexities

As it was earlier stated, Aristotle did not consider the relationship of the part and whole important for his study of substance and its complexity expressed through predication and participation. This type of knowledge he associated with the first two of the four causes as presented in

Posterior Analytics, 94^{a}20: "We think we have scientific knowledge when we know the cause, and there are four causes: (1) the definable form, (2) an antecedent which necessitates a consequent, (3) the efficient cause, (4) the final cause" (McKeon, 1941). The second of the four causes apparently is the material cause, although defined in a different way from that in Metaphysics (1013^{a}25) which gives the name "material cause". However, the difference does not mean inconsistency, as matter is a potential aspect of substance (that of which anything potentially can be predicated) and in turn a demonstration, as it was stated in the quotation from *Posterior Analytics*, 77^{a}5 above "necessarily imply the possibility of truly predicating one of many", i.e. makes antecedent a potential of consequent.

The other two causes, efficient and final are prominent in the works of Aristotle on animal world, in particular in *Parts of Animals,* where he writes on the multi-level part-whole relation in animal organism. Here, the main concepts are of the function and generation, not of substance with its material and formal components. Aristotle writes in *Parts of Animals*, 641^{b}10: "Moreover, it is impossible that any abstraction can form a subject of natural science, seeing that everything that Nature makes is means to an end" (McKeon, 1941) and earlier, 639^{b}13: "The causes concerned in the generation of the works of nature are, as we see, more than one. There is the final cause and there is the motor cause. (...) Plainly, however, that cause is the first which we call the final one" (McKeon, 1941). Little bit further in *Parts of Animals*, 642^{a}1-14 his explanation changes: "There are then two causes, namely, necessity and the final end. For many things are produced, simply as the results of necessity. It may, however, be asked, of what mode of necessity are we speaking when we say this. For it can be of neither of those two modes which are set forth in the philosophical treatises. There is, however, the third mode, in such things at any rate as are generated. For instance, we say that food is necessary; because an animal cannot possibly do without it. This third mode is what may be called hypothetical necessity. (...) Now, exactly in the same way the body, which like the axe is an instrument – for both the body as a whole and its several parts individually have definite operations for which they are made – just in the same way, I say, the body, if it is to do its work, must of necessity be of such and such a character, and made of such and such materials" (McKeon, 1941). This leads us to the concept of a function and the structure of functions as in *Parts of Animals*, 645^{b}18-33: "Similarly, the body too must somehow or other be made for the soul, and each part of it for some subordinate function, to which it is adapted. (...) When a function is ancillary to another, a like relation manifestly obtains between the organs which discharge these functions; and similarly, if one function is prior to and the end of another, their respective organs will stand to each other in the same relation. Thirdly, the existence of these parts involves that of other things as their necessary consequents" (McKeon, 1941).

We can see that *mereologic* (part-whole) relationship correlated with functions assumes the primary role in *Parts of Animals*, 640^{b}17: "But if men and animals and their several parts are natural phenomena, then the natural philosopher must take into consideration not merely the ultimate substances of which they are made, but also flesh, bone, blood, and all the other homogeneous parts; not only these, but also the heterogeneous parts, such as face, hand, foot; and must examine how each of these comes to be what it is, and in virtue of what force" (McKeon, 1941).

Aristotle does not detach his natural philosophy from his theoretical studies, but builds one over the foundations of the other. He writes in *Parts of Animals*, 640^{b}17: "Animals, then, are composed of homogeneous parts, and are also composed of heterogeneous parts. The former, however, exist for the sake of the latter. For the active functions and operations of the body are carried on by these; that is, by heterogeneous parts, such as the eye, the nostril, the whole face, the fingers, the hand and the whole arm. Bur inasmuch as there is a great variety in the functions and motions not only of aggregate animals but also of the individual organs, it is necessary that the substances out of which these are composed shall present a diversity of properties" (McKeon, 1941).

Thus, the study of organic world led Aristotle to the issues of two additional related types of complexity, that of *mereologic* (part-whole) type and that of functional type. In some sense, similar duality can be found in a very simple form in *On the Heavens*, when the structure of the world was associated with the natural types of motions. Aristotle did not refer there to the final cause, but the explanation was based for instance on the natural place of earth (at the center of the world) to which it will necessarily be moving.

Much more direct association of the *mereologic* structures of the living organisms and of the entire world found its expression in a variety of macrocosm-microcosm schemas influenced by Neoplatonism and

Hermetism. The common theme in these sometimes very different conceptions of reality is in the search for unifying forces. Since the most familiar model of unity for everyone is in human organism and our own experience related to it.

This experience of unity in human perception can be found already in Pre-Socratic philosophy. For instance, one of very few fragments of the works of Xenophanes refers to it "If the divine exists, it is a living thing; if it is a living thing, it sees – for he sees as a whole, he thinks as a whole, he hears as a whole" (Barnes, 2001).

Plato's *Timaeus* popularized for the centuries to come the motif of the creation of the world on the pattern of life: "Plato's *Timaeus* became a breviary for astrologers and magicians; the myth of the Demiurge, creating the world as a living organism, every part of which is intimately related to every other, came to be used as the great justification of ideas of the macrocosm and the microcosm and of the influence of the heavenly bodies on the lives of men" (Artz, 1980: 241).

The extensive corpus of the work of Aristotle left the issue of the mechanism of unification unresolved in all contexts from unification of the essence to that which makes animal a whole. This vacuum tempted many post-Aristotelian thinkers. Since Plato devoted to the relationship one-many much more attention (for instance in his dialog *Parmenides*), the search for solutions was frequently in the framework of Platonic philosophical tradition. But the affiliation of philosophers did not restrict the interest in these matters.

For instance, according to Posidonius of Rhodes, Stoic philosopher of the 2nd Century B.C. who tried to incorporate into his view of the world elements of Platonic and Aristotelian thought, claimed that the whole world is united by internal connections of "sympathy" (*sumpatheia*), but living organisms have a special uniting and generating type of the vital force which emanates from the sun and radiates to earth. Here too, we have the relation between the two different scales, that of life and that of cosmos.

Neoplatonic thought placed man in the middle between microcosm and macrocosm. Later in the Middle Ages, more typical was the dualistic view. Christian mystics of the 12th Century, such as Bernard Sylvester of

Tours or Hildegard of Bingen envisioned the universe (macrocosm) in analogy to human organism (microcosm) (Singer, 1958). Of course, this analogy resonated well with astrological beliefs that configurations of astronomical bodies can serve for explanation or prediction of the events in human life.

The role of *mereologic* and functional complexity in the inquiry of reality increased with the interest in practical applications of knowledge, in particular in medicine. The limited scope of this article does not allow a review of all twists and turns of the study of complexity in historical perspective. Only few of most relevant developments are examined or mentioned in post-Aristotelian philosophy and mainly those which indicate arrival of new methods of study or understanding of complexity. In particular, the influence of the eclectic attempts to merge Aristotelian views with those of Plato (Neoplatonism) and with materialistic tradition of Democritus (Epicureanism) on the conceptualization of complexity and simplicity will not be given attention commeasurable with their engagement with these issues. Scholastic philosophy with its variety of interpretations of Aristotle requires a separate study regarding the views on complexity in the contexts of the development of the disciplines such as logic or mereology; After all the original concept of information was born in this philosophical tradition. However, in the present paper this particular contribution of Scholasticism is not examined. It did not owe much to Aristotle being more a common sense interpretation of his views, and it did not influence much the concept of information in modern studies, except for its role as a reminder that probabilistic description of information neglects its structural aspects.

The concept of information presented in the introduction to this paper is sufficiently general to include as its special instances all relations considered by Aristotle. Therefore, the shift of attention in post-Aristotelian philosophy to *mereologic* (part-whole) study of complexity and the inclusion of accidentals into the scope of scientific interests can be considered internal with respect to the subject of so generally defined information. Moreover, in this conceptual framework, the relationship between *mereologic* and functional description of animals explained by Aristotle with the use of effective and final causes can be analyzed in terms of the dynamics of information (Schroeder, 2013b).

The issue is of great importance, as we can find the dialectics between structure and form being one of the main motivations for the philosophy of life in the works of Humberto Maturana and Francisco Varela

(Maturana & Varela, 1980), as well as for entire contemporary discussion of life (Rashevsky, 1965, 1972; Rosen, 1958, 1987, 1991). The relationship is, in the perspective used in this paper, a reflection of the dualism of the selective and structural manifestations of information.

In short, function is a selection of one of possible time-related transformations of the information system, while structure is understood as structural manifestation of information within this system. The selection is governed by the rules of information dynamics which assumes that we have at least two information systems with at least two different levels of its organization built by the selective-structure duality. Since the dynamics of information is beyond the scope of the present paper, its more detailed exposition can be found elsewhere (Schroeder, 2013b, c, 2014, 2015b).

6.5. Foundations for Study of Descriptive Complexity

One of most important mediaeval contributions to the subject of reducing complexity from the methodological point of view, Ockham's razor, became popular already before William Ockham in reaction to frequent abuses of the weak points of Aristotelian philosophy in scholastic discourses. One of them was insufficient distinction of the concepts of "belonging" and of "participation". This confusion was compounded with the quite elaborately explained by Aristotle, but frequently ignored distinction of these two relations from the part-whole relationship. Moreover, explanation of the phenomena was referring usually to the nature (essence) of entities without clear criteria for the qualification of the attributes for being essential and without explanation how these essential attributes can be united, which generated the temptation to multiply the essences and to populate the world with spurious entities. The directive to eliminate unnecessary entities was the reaction to the deficiencies of contemporary philosophical discourse, although it might derive its popularity from the directive of Aristotle to use demonstrations with fewer premises in *Posterior Analytics*, 86ª33 quoted above.

The most important early application of this Aristotelian directive, as well as of his concept of demonstration was Euclid's presentation of geometry in the *Elements*. All geometric knowledge accumulated in the works of earlier Greek mathematicians such as Pythagoras and his followers, Hippocrates of Chios, Theatetus of Athens, or Eudoxus of Cnides together with some original contributions of Euclid were derived from the five domain specific axioms – "postulates", five general "common notions" (axioms not referring to the domain specific objects), and twenty three definitions.

Euclid's work produced very sophisticated tool for the reduction of complexity, but its application from the point of view of Aristotelian philosophy should be for the analysis of form only, not substance. After all, Aristotle envisioned this partial role of mathematics in *Metaphysics*, 1003^a21-25: "There is a science which investigates being as being and the attributes which belong to this in virtue of its own nature. Now this is not the same as any of the so-called special sciences; for none of these others treats universally of being as being. They cut off a part of being and investigate the attribute of this part; this is what the mathematical sciences for instance do" (McKeon, 1941). Euclid formulated his geometry in terms of the *mereologic*, part-whole terminology. This makes it even more difficult to position his work with respect to Aristotelian tradition.

The discipline that made use of geometry as a fundamental method was astronomy and in the context of geometric description of the universe appeared the new methodological concept of "saving the appearances". Duhem (1969) ascribed the expression "saving the phenomena" to Plato based on the report in *Commentary on Aristotle's On the Haevens* by Simplicius of Cilicia, but more accurate seems the ascription to Plutarch, since "the oldest extant text in which the expression 'save the phenomena' is only of the first century A.D. namely Plutarch's *On the Face in the Orb of the Moon*" (Evans & Berggren, 2006: 49). However, Bernard Goldstein (1997) provides arguments that it was Geminus of Rhodes who first used the expression in the context of the relationship between mathematics and physics.

Astronomers (who were considered mathematicians) developed models of heavenly phenomena contradicting the views of Aristotle. The most revolutionary was heliocentric model of Aristarchus of Samos in the 3rd Century B.C. The idea of placing Sun in the center was already used by Pythagoreans, but Aristarchus not only hypothesized about the place of the center of universe and the order of planets revolving around the Sun, but made also calculations of relative distances of the Sun, Earth and Moon. Main objection to this model was the lack of the parallax of stars, which Aristarchus explained by the much greater size of the universe than expected.

More than three hundred years later Claudius Ptolemy built his model in agreement with Aristotelian orthodoxy and due to complicated arrangement of geometric objects (spheres) involved in its construction achieved satisfactory agreement with observations. The fact that different mathematical models can give explanation of observed phenomena and help in the prediction of the future ones established the role of mathematics as a tool "saving the phenomena", but also brought into attention of philosophers the issue of the criteria for "real" explanation. Mathematical models were of course tools for dealing with complexity, but simplicity of description lost its association with the assessment of the complexity of reality.

The next revolutionary development had place in the 14th Century. Nicole Oresme in *Tractatus de configurationi bus qualitatu metmotuum* merged qualitative description with geometric modeling (Clagett, 1968). He associated the accidental attributes which admit variation in degree with two characteristics of intensity (*intensio*) and extension (*extensio*). These characteristics of the quality were associated in turn with geometric representations in the form of appropriate segments – vertical called *latitudo*, and horizontal called *longitudo*, respectively. The geometric form of such two dimensional figure would correspond to the quality in question. Oresme called the qualities corresponding to rectangular forms uniform and otherwise difform. In the latter class he distinguished uniformly varying qualities as those with the straight, but inclined upper side. In the case of mechanical motion of an object, *longitudo* was associated with time, *latitudo* with speed, and the area of the figure the distance travelled. By comparing the area of the figure to the area of rectangular figure he concluded that the distance covered in *uniformly difform* motion is the same as in uniform motion with the mean speed (The Mean Speed Theorem).

The revolution initiated by Oresme was not so much in being a precedent to the celebrated result of Galileo, but in the departure from Aristotelian principles. While Aristotle considered accidental attributes outside of the scope of interest of scientific inquiry and focused on essence, Oresme made them the subject of his study. Also, Aristotle maintained a very strict division between genera without common species, Oresme made his method very clearly trans-generic. Every quality admitting variation could be characterized by its intensity and extensity and associated with geometric latitude and longitude.

Galileo Galilei went further adding to these above rediscovered by himself methodological tools the separation of factors influencing phenomena. This separation was achieved either by ingenious design of actual experiments, or by "thought experiments" in which he discussed the outcomes of fictional experiments based on logical consequences of what already was known. For instance in the study of motion, he argued that the vertical and horizontal motions can be considered separately based on common experience. This helped him to refute the objections to the heliocentric model of the universe such as the absence of the wind caused by the diurnal rotation of the Earth. His more conclusive thought experiments were showing that some claims are producing logical contradictions. For example, he demonstrated that the claim of Aristotle that heavier objects fall faster, in the absence of the air resistance leads to contradiction.

The most important consequence of the separation of phenomena into components governed by separate rules was what today is usually called "idealization". For instance, he designed his experiments to minimize the presence of factors distorting the results of observation, such as friction or air resistance. For Galileo, mathematical models were not just instruments for saving the appearances, but accurate descriptions of reality in separation from each other. Thus their simplifying power was in the reduction to fundamental rules governing reality. Complexity of phenomena was the result not of the complex rules, but of the multiplicity of the factors engaged in them.

6.6. Foundations for Modern Methods of Complexity Reduction

While politics surrounding 17th Century philosophy was focused on the issue of the heliocentric system, the actual philosophical revolution was in completely different issues. First of them was the return of the atomistic concept of matter as a side in the opposition matter – void. Galileo in his explanations of phenomena frequently referred to the concept of void (for instance considering the forces which hold thin sheets of metal and the equal speed of fall of objects). He also speculated on the minuscule parts of matter. Rene Descartes was more conservative and did not want to admit the existence of void, but considered entire reality consisting of corpuscles, which were so tightly packed that they filled out the space completely. Mechanics of Isaac Newton established the definitive paradigm of matter organized in the atomic way and finally in 1704, Newton proposed corpuscular theory of light against the views of some of his contemporaries such as Christiaan Huygens, establishing another paradigm lasting to 1801 when Thomas Young vindicated Huygens's wave theory.

Descartes and his followers (including Huygens in his earlier years) believed that only direct contact of extended particles can be responsible for transmission of motion. Mechanics presented in Descartes's *Treatise on the World and the Light* written at the end of the third decade of 17th Century, but published posthumously much later, had the two first principles consistent with the views of Galileo:

- "Bodies at rest remain at rest, those in motion remain in motion unless acted upon some other body.
- Inertial motion is straight line motion with constant velocity.

The third principle was more specific for his approach:

- In the collision of two bodies:
- if first body has smaller force to continue motion than resistance of the second body, first one changes its direction, but does not lose any of its motion,
- otherwise, the first body carries up the second in the original direction losing as much of its motion, as it gives up to the second" (Losee, 1972).

Thus the structure of the physical world consisting of *res extensa* in the framework of his famous division into the two realms of extension and thought was governed by simple rules. The realm of *res cogitans* could remain Aristotelian. While Cartesian mechanics opened the possibility to explain many natural phenomena, the division into two realms created a precipice, which made busy philosophers and scientists of the next centuries in their attempts to bridge it. The division can be understood as a consequence of Aristotelian separation of the subject of philosophical studies of substance with the dominating theme of predication as a human rational capacity (after all, genera and species even for Aristotle have been "res cogitans", not substance) and the subject of natural philosophy dealing with the *mereologic* (part-whole) relations studied with the use of effective and final causes.

In his conservatism, Descartes inherited from Aristotelian philosophy the problem what holds the corpuscles or bodies together. Their unity could not be explained any better than unity of essences.

This is why the greatest revolution of the 17th Century and one of the greatest of all time was in the published in 1687 by Isaac Newton *Principia Mathematica Philosophia Naturalis*. First we have to observe that *Principia* present not an independent study of reality, but an extension of Euclid's *Elements*. Not only because Newton applied consequently the same logical structure in writing them, but because we have here an extension of the geometric studies of Euclid by adding some additional characteristics of points. In geometry points have position in space while in mechanics we have an additional dimension of time.

The recognition of the fact that mechanics can be considered an extension of geometry to four dimensions was not obvious at that time and came about one hundred years after publication of *Principia*. Joseph Louis Lagrange wrote about it in his *Theory of Analytic Functions* in 1797 (Archibald, 1914). However, if we recognize it, we are not much further than Oresme. Mechanics is not just geometry of four dimensional space, because Newton introduced some additional new concepts. Some points are characterized by mass. Moreover, we have a very different type of objects – forces. This was a very puzzling idea, as forces were relating distant points without engagement of the points between.

Newton did not claim that the objects of mechanics are literarily points devoid of extension, but that they can be considered in the analysis of motion as points. Spherical objects could be considered as if their quantity of matter (mass equal to the product of density of matter and volume) was concentrated in their center. If several objects are considered, they can be concentrated at the point of their center of mass. As a consequence of these observations, not in *Principia*, but in further development of mechanics, every extended material object was reduced to a "mass point", whose motion could be described as a composition of linear motion of the center of mass in the Euclidean space in terms of the three position coordinates and rotational motion around the center described in terms of angles.

In *Principia* mass was involved in consideration of the quantity of motion (since 18th Century called momentum and understood as the product of mass and velocity, in agreement with the concept of impetus introduced by Jean Buridan three hundred years earlier) and in the relationship between force and change of velocity, where it plays the role of a coefficient of their proportion. Newton's concept of mass was a universal and essential, not accidental characteristic of matter, dependent only on its distribution in space.

One of most revolutionary, if not the most revolutionary, although too frequently overlooked, of the contributions of Newton was his Third

Principle. The first two Newton himself attributed to Galileo, but the third was never stated before. The principle was stated in a twofold way. First as a statement that to every force acting between two objects "acting from one body towards the other" corresponds equal but opposite force "acting from the other towards the first one". Here we still have "action" as directional process of something on something else. The second, alternative formulation is phrasing it explicitly as "mutual action", i.e. interaction.

The concept of interaction through forces was of great importance, as it was first time when the unification of parts into a whole found some explanation. Newton was aware of the great conceptual difficulty arising with the introduction of "centripetal forces" acting on distance, such as gravitational forces (repulsive forces acting on contact were easy to accept), but this did not stopped him in making the concept of interaction fundamental for mechanics. We can recognized how fundamental was this revolution, when we realize that Cartesian precipice between mind and body can be interpreted in terms of the division between two realms with the former governed by the rules of action or efficient cause, and the latter by the rules of interaction.

Rules of interaction in the form of physical forces such as gravitational force between masses or electric force between electric charges described by the quantitative formula making force inversely proportional to the square of the distance provided well defined mechanism unifying matter into a whole. This made the realm of *res extensa*, or more exactly the realm of bodies represented as mass points, simple. Whenever we know the positions and momenta of n mass points at some initial moment of time and forces acting between these points, we can formulate differential equations whose solutions describe positions of these mass points at any time.

At this point we get to the point of divergence of two different ways in which complexity can be understood. Mechanics gives us simple view of the mechanical reality governed by only few rules. Pierre-Simone Laplace in his 1814 work *A Philosophical Essay on Probabilities* conceived a hypothetical intellect (now called Laplace's demon) capable of learning all positions and momenta of material items present in reality at some moment of time and all forces acting between them, and in addition capable to perform mechanical analysis of them (basically solving all necessary differential equations). This hypothetical intellect would have direct knowledge of all phenomena of the past and future. The claim of Laplace was that the actual existence of such intellect is irrelevant. This potential existence entails mechanical determinism of reality, or at least of the realm of *res extensa*.

The divergence of the ways to understand complexity is in the difference in interpretations of the hypothetical status of the demon. We still cannot provide exact solutions for 3 bodies (there is no analytical general solution involving integrals, but almost always the solution for any given time can be given as a slowly converging series that requires so big number of terms to be calculated that the method is completely impractical). We can conclude that we have the conceptual simplicity of the deterministic character of mechanical world requiring only positions, momenta, and forces to be established in order to fix all future events, and extreme complexity in actual prediction what actually will happen. This form of mechanical "non-computable" complexity will be later followed by other forms of the limits of computation.

Now, we can compare the situation of the other side of the precipice – the realm of *res cogitans*. Here situation was and still is much more difficult. There was no progress at all for long time. The distinction between primary and secondary properties discussed by John Locke can be found already in Scholastic thought. His "associations of ideas" is as passive and simply accumulative process as it was in Aristotelian study of memory and habit. Most importantly, there is nothing about the mechanisms of associations in Locke's works, nor even question about unification.

The only philosopher of that time who addressed this matter explicitly was George Berkeley, and although he did not elaborate on the mechanism or specifics of his claim, the fact that he discussed the issue makes his contribution very important. He claimed that "it is the mind that maketh each thing to be one" (Berkeley, 1948-1957) and referred to the authority of Aristotle who in *On the Soul*, 430^b5: "In each and every case that which unifies is mind" (McKeon, 1941). This passage from *On the Soul* is interesting, as it is in the context of the *mereologic* (part-whole) relation, but in the work of Aristotle it is more about capacity of human mind to gain knowledge of the whole, not just of parts. Berkley interprets it in his idealistic way that without mind there would be no thing as a unity.

The revolution of Newtonian mechanics was followed by its long evolution with many important consequences. For Newton, both space and time were concepts representing objects of reality, even though he followed Galileo in the recognition that all observers moving on straight lines with constant velocities with respect to this real space (i.e. using inertial reference frames) will have their descriptions different in numerical sense and there is no possibility to detect whose description is in the static reference frame. This was not a big problem, as in geometry the distinction between congruent figures was ignored, so differences between descriptions in different inertial reference frames could be ignored as well.

The use of space-time as a descriptive tool (not as a concept describing some type of reality introduced as a consequence of Special Relativity) was implicitly present already in the work of Newton. However in its evolution, mechanics acquired several abstract concepts which deviated from the simple intuition of 17th Century. Mechanical systems started to be described in terms of generalized coordinates which not necessarily coincided with positions in space. Mechanical system of n particles can be described as a point in a $3n$-dimensional space. Then the motions of n points become a single motion of one point.

The next step was the introduction in the second half of the 19th Century of the concept of a phase space of a mechanical system (Nolte, 2010). Coordinates here consist of positions of all mass points and of momenta of these mass points. Since the state of a mechanical system consists of these positions and momenta, each point of the system corresponds to one mechanical state and dynamics of the system is described by a curve in this $6n$-dimensional space. This conceptual framework successfully applied by Henri Poincare in mechanics was adapted outside of mechanics to describe evolution of a very wide range of systems which can be described in a quantitative way and the discipline of dynamical systems (with the name popularized by the very influential book of George David Birkhoff) was born.

The development of the dynamic system theory is important for us, as it involved methods of classification of various types of complexity and methods of the reduction of complexity of the great importance for modern science outside of mechanics. The only difference for the general case is that instead of forces, the derivatives of the functions of time variable describing the state of the system are considered. The state variables can be associated with the quantitative description of objects within multiple contexts. The problem of the prediction of the future values of the state variables based on their initial values and initial values of some of their derivatives is being solved in the manner similar to mechanics. More general approach does not refer to any specific value of the time variable, but the restriction is more distributed into the boundary values of system variables.

In this case, the complexity of a dynamical system is characterized by the configurations of possible trajectories of the system (it is a line parametrized by the time variable, as the state of the system in given time is a point in its phase space). For instance, systems which have their possible trajectories strongly sensitive with respect to the choice of initial values are considered chaotic. Since the measurement of the initial values has always limited precision, chaotic systems, even when they are deterministic, may not have predictable future values. The study of dynamical systems can achieve goals of the reduction of complexity, when it is possible to establish steady states to which systems tend for a wide range of initial values.

In the theory of dynamic systems special role is played by so called linear systems, i.e. systems in which equations describing the system exhibit superposition principle. This means that the sum of solutions is a solution and the solution multiplied by a constant is a solution. It was one of the earliest achievements of the theory that the linear systems cannot be chaotic. Linearity became a condition for the simplicity of dynamic systems. However, with this distinction came the recognition of the fact that many important instances of dynamic systems are non-linear.

The theory of dynamic systems does not have to assume parametrization by the continuous time variable. For discrete dynamical systems differential equations are replaced by difference equations and a parallel, although impoverished theory is available.

The latest of the major studies of complexity appeared with the concepts of algorithms and computation. Computation theory developed from the earlier topics of the finitistic methods of mathematics and of the problems of the relationship between logic and mathematics. Not surprisingly, the original source was in the foundations for set theory. This was a return of the problems which can be traced to Aristotle. Set theory is basically nothing but a theory of predication in terms of the extensional relation $x \in A$, with two primitive (undefined) concepts of a "set" and "belongs".

George Cantor, whose work set the foundations for set theory as a separate mathematical theory believed that a set as "(…) any multiplicity which can be thought as one, i.e. any aggregate of determinate elements which can be united into a whole by some law" (Cantor, 1883). This general view generated strong criticism from the side of mathematicians who, as for instance Leopold Kronecker, believed that for the existence of a set it is necessary to establish a definite construction in a finite number of steps which incorporates elements one by one into a whole.

Edmund Husserl participated in the discussion writing from the philosophical perspective: "Any talk of sets or multiplicities necessarily involves the combination of the individual elements into a whole, a unity containing the individual objects as parts. And though the combination involved may be very loose, there is a particular sort of unification there which would also have to have been noticed as such since the concept of set could never have arisen otherwise.(...) if our view is correct, the concept of set arises through reflection on the particular (...) way in which the contents are unified together (...) in a way analogous to the manner in which the concept of any other kind of whole arises through reflection upon the mode of combination peculiar to it" (Husserl, 1891).

According to historians studying his intellectual biography Husserl has become convinced that the process of integration is of psychological character: "The concept of collection in Brentano's sense, Husserl explained, was to arise through reflection on the concept of collecting. Sets, he thus reasoned, arose out of collective combination, in being conceived as one. This combining process involved when objects are brought together to make a whole only consists in that one thinks of them 'together' and was obviously not grounded in the content of the disparate items collected into the set. It could not be physical, so it must be psychological, a unique kind of mental act connecting the contents of a whole" (Ortiz Hill & Rosado Haddock, 2000). Husserl's view regarding the set theoretical relationship became similar to that of Berkeley regarding the *mereologic* relationship.

Thus the old problem discussed, but nor resolved by Aristotle, about how the one can be predicated of many was back. Set theories did not resolve this issue. After Bertrand Russell in his paradox of a collection of sets which are not elements of themselves showed that the assumption that every definable collection is a set must be false, authors of different axiomatic formulations for set theories simply ensured that the paradox can be avoided. But the main question of the unification of the many into one was simply pushed away from the concerns of mathematicians.

Instead, philosophically inclined mathematicians focused on the issue of the programmatic question of David Hilbert regarding the proof of consistency of mathematics. This could prevent questions of the type of unification, as mathematics could be considered un-interpreted symbolic system validated by its internal consistency and completeness rather than its relationship to any type of reality. Kurt Gödel's work from 1931 ruined the hope and program of Hilbert. The method of the proof had its own value for further development. Gödel in his proof represented statements from mathematics as natural numbers and proofs as functions defined by operations on natural numbers combined in a recursive way. When Alan Turing (1936) presented a simple model of a-machines (today Turing machines) performing arithmetical operations it became clear that such machines can model whatever is done in mathematics (or any symbol manipulation) in a finite number of steps. Turing's celebrated paper contributed even more important achievement – the construction of a universal machine (UTM), which can do what any Turing machine designed for a specific purpose can do, based on the program entered to it with the data for processing.

Both Turing machine and Gödel's methodology are based on reductionist assumption that every process can be decomposed into atomic steps. It obviously works very well with operations on natural numbers, which can be represented as sequences of digits (for instance of 0's and 1's in the binary positional system) and the operations on such sequences can be distributed into operations on their elements. Thus, every algorithm (sequential description of these atomic steps leading to the result of the entire process) can be evaluated for its complexity. Extensive and comprehensive studies of this and other types of complexity analysis related to computation can be found in the literature of the subject (Balcazar *et al.*, 1998; Burgin, 2005, 2012).

Typical approach is through the assessment based on necessary resources to complete the process, i.e. computation. This type of description of computational complexity can be directly identified with a measure of the amount of temporal or spatial resources, such as the actual time of executing an algorithm, related to this time number of elementary operations constituting the algorithm, or the amount of memory used in execution understood as a necessary space for storing information in the process, etc. Since computation in every actual implementation involves the same elementary operations corresponding to the steps of a Turing machine, these measures of computational complexity are sufficiently universal to be considered without reference to particular technological solutions.

Computational complexity tells us about the algorithm in the dynamic perspective of achieving some result with a particular entry of data. Although the same result of the process with the same data entry can be achieved in many different ways and algorithms implementing the process may differ in their complexity measures based on resources, we can apply the concept of computational complexity to computational problems consisting in questions that can be answered by computing device after appropriate data are provided. Computational complexity for a problem is the minimum computational complexity for algorithms leading to the solution of a problem.

Formulation of computational problems in many cases involves human intention and conceptual framework. However, before the question is processed by a computing device, it has to be reduced to more specific form of the input and output data that requires appropriate interface. Once we have input and output in the form of a sequence of component symbols (typically sequence of 0's and 1's) we can proceed to another type of complexity analysis, this time in the static form.

Thus, we can analyze algorithmic complexity of a given sequence of symbols considering it as an output of a universal Turing machine and asking about the shortest input for the machine that can produce it. This way we can go beyond the complexity of a process to the complexity of the structure of the sequence of symbols. This was the basis of algorithmic measure of information in its symbolic format proposed independently by Ray Solomonoff (1964), Andrei Kolmogorov (1965) and Gregory Chaitin (1966).

The measures of complexity in each of its formulations referring to computation by Turing machines are based on the reduction of processes described by an algorithm to its simple units (steps in the algorithm) or of compound symbols to meaningful component symbols. Does it mean that the problems of unification of the many into one have been overcome? The present author presented arguments for the view that they are only hidden within the assumptions which are not explicitly stated in the analysis of computation with Turing machines (Schroeder, 2013b, c).

The hidden part of computation, when understood as a process from natural numbers to natural numbers or more generally as a process of transformation within some linguistic system, is in the encoding of information. The assumption is that a sequence of component symbols (for instance digits such as 0's and 1's) is a natural number, or is an object of discourse in some language. Of course, all symbols, with which a Turing machine works (usually 0 and 1), are meaningful for this machine However, the Turing machine does not have any component synthesizing separate symbols into meaningful compound symbols. This part of the operation of Turing machine is performed by human mind. Therefore the actual complexity cannot be analyzed exclusively in terms of computational or algorithmic complexity, especially that, as it will be discussed later in this paper, complexity is related to integration of information.

There is also a significant feature of the algorithmic complexity, which reflects one of the aspects of inability to integrate information distributed into component symbols within a Turing machine. Although the measure of algorithmic complexity is inductively computable, it is not recursively computable. This means that there is no recursive function, which for any given string of symbols has as the value this string's algorithmic complexity measure. It is related to the fact that a universal Turing machine cannot perform task of producing for any input sequence an output consisting of the shortest sequence of symbols, which when used as input produces original sequence.

6.7.　Plectics and Other Studies of Complexity

Murrey Gell-Mann (1996) proposed a name *Plectics* for the discipline studying complexity. This name did not become popular, possibly because too large variety of competing methodologies of study makes inquiry inherently interdisciplinary. The earlier attempt by Ludwig von Bertalanffy (1950) to set foundations for the General System Theory (GST) was not much more successful. In the latter case the problem was in the lack of clearly defined key concepts and definite methodology.

Bertalanffy followed Jan C. Smuts (1926) in propagating the idea of holism as an alternative to reductionist methodology of science necessary to overcome complexity in the study of life. Smuts' concept of holism and the multiple philosophical attempts to give it more definite form did not go beyond the same intuitions which guided Aristotle, his Neoplatonic successors, Scholastics, mediaeval Mystics, Berkeley and many others. But thus far there were only questions about irreducible to simple components wholes, but not answers. And even the questions were formulated in such a way that they did not guide well the work towards answers (Schroeder, 2012b, 2013a).

Although complexity studies had similar sources as system theories and in the opinion of the present author there are no essential differences between them, they did not start from the negation of existing methodology of science. This more positive approach made complexity easier accepted within the research community.

The initial studies did not bring much beyond rather obvious statements expressed with the use of common sense or common use concepts. In the classical article on complexity Warren Weaver (1948) distinguished its three levels. *Simple systems* devoid of complexity involve small number of variables easily separable in analysis. Systems of *disorganized complexity* involve numerically intimidating number of variables, but because of limited interaction of the components, they may be successfully analyzed using statistical methods. Finally, systems of *organized complexity* reflect "the essential feature of organization" of the big number of components, and escape statistical analysis. In systems of this type components are interacting in an organized way making statistical analysis ineffective.

The present author (2013a) questioned the tendency to put exclusive emphasis on the number of components in the study of complex systems and presented the view that complexity is itself too complex to be described exclusively in terms of numerical characteristics. Quantitative characteristics of complexity have to be complemented by the structural ones.

Complexity does not have to require involvement of many components, but it is a combination of the plurality of any number of components, big or small, with their involvement in a sufficiently tightly knit structure of some whole. If the structure is intricate, number of components can be small. However, lower complication of the structure with the big number of components can constitute equally difficult challenge.

It could be said, using terminology of Waver, that even if the complex system has a small number of components, to be complex it has to have big number of degrees of freedom or big number of possible states. However, the terms "degrees of freedom" or "state" used by Weaver are inherited from very specific instance of complexity in dynamic systems. Moreover, we have many examples of dynamic or mechanical systems which have large number of components, large number of states and large number of degrees of freedom, but which are not complex. It is enough to recall examples from thermodynamics. Complexity enters in such a way that the concepts suitable for reductionist methodology are not sufficient anymore. There is no way to avoid a new, comprehensive conceptual framework, which in the opinion of the present author can be provided by a sufficiently general study of information (Schroeder, 2012b, 2013a).

The study of complexity in terms of specific disciplines, such as dynamic systems or algorithmic analysis, frequently inherits problems of these disciplines. It happens very often that transmission of the concepts or methods from one context to another generates inconsistencies. Classical example is of the use of entropy, the measure of information transmitted in communication defined by Shannon (1948), to the context when the amount of information contained in some information system is considered. Schrödinger (1945) in his famous little book *What is Life?* recognized that not high entropy physical systems, but those of low entropy carry large amount of information. For the purpose of his book only differences between entropies of light was important, so it was sufficient to use the concept of "negative entropy", although the literally understood negation of always positive entropy could not be a positive measure of information. The danger of such simplifying expressions could be seen in their consequences. Brillouin (1956) gave this nonsensical "measure" name *negentropy*, and even seventy years later we can find it currently published papers, while suitable alternative measure suffices (Schroeder, 2004).

The consequences of the confusion between the maximum amount of information that can be transmitted under the constraints of the particular language of the message and the actual amount of information in the message inhibited the development of semantic information theory and caused that Shannon gave up any relationship between information and meaning (Schroeder, 2012a). Within his framework, the message generated by a monkey randomly typing letters had more information than any actual message generated by humans.

Murray Gell-Mann proposed a modification of algorithmic complexity measure to define a descriptive measure of complexity. As in the case of Shannon's measure of information in the message, algorithmic complexity of a random sequence of symbols is the largest, as the sequence cannot be compressed into any shorter program which could generate it with the use of a universal Turing machine. Instead Gell-Mann proposed to use effective complexity: "A measure that corresponds much better to what is usually meant by complexity in ordinary conversation, as well as in scientific discourse, refers not to the length of the most concise description the entity (which is roughly what AIC is), but to the length of a concise description of a set of the entity's regularities. Thus something almost entirely random, with practically no regularities, would have effective complexity near zero. So would something completely regular, such as a bit string consisting entirely of zeros. Effective complexity can be high only in a region intermediate between total order and total disorder" (Gell-Mann, 1995). Gell-Mann himself noticed that this concept is questionable "Since it is impossible to find all regularities of an entity, the question arises as to who or what determines the class of regularities to be identified" (Gell-Mann, 1995). However, he seems not to recognize that his definition is circular. If we can establish appropriate set of regularities, it is just a matter of convenience to express complexity in the quantitative form of the size of their concise description. It is not much more than saying that if we know what is complexity of some entity, then we can measure it by (rather arbitrarily chosen) the length of its description.

Complexity became a commonly invoked concept in so many contexts that as a natural consequence of this variety some authors attempted to develop typologies of complexity. Nicholas Rescher in *Complexity: A Philosophical Overview* (1998) proposed one of probably most extensive classifications. He classified complexity according to three main groups of Epistemic, Ontological, and Functional Modes. The first group included Descriptive Complexity, Generative Complexity and Computational Complexity (each characterized well by its name). The second consisted of Constitutional Complexity (related to the number of components),

Taxonomical Complexity (related to the variety of components) and Structural Complexity divided into two Organizational Complexity (different ways in arranging components, but without any distinction of the levels of composition) and Hierarchical Complexity (in which the distinction of the levels of sub and supra components is prominent). The third included Operational Complexity (related to the variety of modes of operation or types of functions) and Nomic Complexity (related to elaborateness and intricacy of the laws governing phenomena).

Rescher's classification is definitely sufficiently extensive to take into consideration virtually all uses of the term "complexity". However, for the purpose of the study of complexity it can raise some objections, especially regarding the distinctions which are questionable, or at least of questionable importance. For instance, elaborateness and intricacy of the laws governing phenomena is definitely epistemic qualification strongly dependent on the status of human knowledge. We already could see that the number of components does not have to be a good criterion of complexity. Descriptive Complexity is not independent from Computational Complexity.

Another objection can be made to oversimplification of Organizational Complexity characterized in a very general way by the different ways in arranging components. One of the main challenges in the study of complexity is to classify or characterize these ways.

Finally, the classification, because of the lack of clear formulation of its criteria in terms of some uniform conceptual framework, does not give us any tools for further study. Only first step of the division into three groups of modes – Epistemic, Ontological, and Functional – is relatively clear due to the tradition of the use of the terms in philosophy. But even here we can ask for additional clarification. Is the distinction between Ontological and Functional groups of modes actually the distinction between inherent characteristics of instances of complexity, or just a different way of describing the same, but in synchronic and diachronic perspectives respectively. Of course, the answer depends on the way the relationship between structure and function is understood. Without specification of the position on this matter, the classification is superficial.

For the present author a resolution of these problems can be found in the right choice of a sufficiently general and sufficiently elaborate conceptual framework to define complexity and to formulate the criteria for classification. Moreover, the author believes that the concept of information introduced at the beginning of the paper and the framework of concepts derived from it, such as information integration, is the best candidate for this purpose. In the following arguments will be provided that if it is not the best, it is sufficient to provide a significant insight into the nature of complexity.

Before entering more detailed presentation, it suffices to notice that the information concept is fundamental for the study of any language (natural, formal, or computational). On the other hand, information became one of key concepts in science from physics, to biology, to economics, or even to the humanities. Every theory of information which bring together its linguistic forms and its natural or real (i.e. non-artefactual) instances and which provides a framework for the study of complexity eliminates the necessity to separate descriptive and ontological modes of complexity.

6.8. Complexity in Terms of Information

As it was already mentioned in the introduction, when we talk about complexity, we have to answer the question: Complexity of what? Aristotle, if he considered the concept of complexity, would have probably answered "complexity of a thing". More recent contributors to the discussion of complexity as transdisciplinary subject would have answered "complexity of a system". But neither "thing", nor "system" is a clearly defined concept. The attempts to define the concept of a system are not going beyond statements more or less explicitly presenting it as a complex collective. Thus, we are falling into a vicious circle.

To avoid it, in this paper we can say that complexity is a characterization of a variety (a set) which through the selection of an information structure (consisting, as in it was in Introduction to this paper explained, either of the selection of a Moore family of subsets, or selection of a closure operator). Thus, complexity characterizes varieties which are information systems. Now, such information system can have high or low level of complexity. The generic expression "complex" corresponds here to the expression "complex at a high level". Later a measure of complexity will be presented which clearly defines what it means a "level of complexity".

First, we have to ask whether the association of complexity with information is justified. Aristotelian study of substance is dominated by the consideration of predication. Of course, the study of predication in the framework of the predicate logic is leading to set theory and of the study of the relation $x \in A$. Introduction to this paper presented an interpretation of the theory of information defined as identification of a variety as a generalization to a binary relation xRA. Thus, Aristotelian study of that which is simple (and by extension what is complex) in the context of predication is a special instance of information systems.

The same will be when we consider mereologic (part-whole) relationship. When we recall that a Moore family is defined by having as an element entire set and by being closed with respect to arbitrary intersections, we can associate parts as closed subsets. Of course, when we have two (or more) parts which intersect in terms of set intersection, but the intersection is not a part, then they are not separate parts. There is nothing to prevent us from considering a whole set as an improper part of itself. Therefore, information systems can be used for the description and study of *mereologic* part-whole relationship.

We get here even more. Our information theory gives us analysis of selective and structural manifestations of information. The latter is characterized in terms of information integration defined by irreducibility into a direct product of the logic of information (the lattice of closed subsets). It turns out (more details will follow in the next section) we can separate completely integrated (coherent) components of the system and a substructure (so-called center) which corresponds to totally disintegrated information on the variety of the coherent components.

When we discuss predication, the coherent components can be associated with Aristotelean essences and therefore also with substance. In the part-whole relationship, the coherent components are atoms (parts, which themselves do not have parts).

If we go ahead with historical time, we can describe in terms of information systems a variety of geometries (we can utilize the extensive knowledge of lattice theoretical formulations of geometry). We can consider topological information systems. Actually, the terminology of the theory of information systems in terms of closure spaces comes from a generalization of topological closure operations.

Berkley's idea of the role of the mind in creating objects out of separate sensory perceptions is quite close to the theoretical model of consciousness as integrated information (Schroeder, 2009, 2011b). However, the author made his approach neutral with respect to the question whether there is something external, independent from the mechanism of integration information constituting mind.

The role of products involved in the mechanistic description of reality (configuration space and phase space for mechanical systems) can be associated with the reducibility of the classical mechanical systems into components. Reducible mechanical systems correspond to disintegrated information. On the other hand quantum mechanical systems (through irreducible quantum logics) correspond to the complete information integration (Schroeder, 2009).

6.9. Structure and Measure of Complexity

The study of complexity in this work will be concluded with a mathematical description of quantitative measures of information, its integration and of complexity. For the purpose of consistency it will be necessary reintroduce the alternative measure of information presented by the author in the past (Schroeder, 2004). The measures of complexity and of information integration the author introduced very recently.

Whatever guided Shannon in his epoch making paper (1948), his entropy became the orthodox measure of what started to be commonly considered information:

$$H(p_1, p_2, ..., p_n) = -\sum_{i=1}^{n} p_i \log_2 p_i \quad \text{where} \quad \sum_{i=1}^{n} p_i = 1 \ \& \ \forall i: p_i \geq 0.$$

The indices $i = 1, 2, ..., n$ represent the elements of the information carrier S, or what Shannon would rather call elements of the alphabet. We can see that every transformation T of the set S (bijective function $T : S \rightarrow S$) preserves the value of H, as long as $p^S_i = p^{T(S)}_{T(i)}$. Since we have no restriction on the choice of T, we get suspiciously high level of symmetry.

Entropy is an invariant of all transformations of S, and therefore it cannot reflect any structural characteristics of the carrier of information.

Entropy is a functional which assigns a nonnegative real number to each class of equivalent probability distributions. Thus, there is nothing in entropy that cannot be directly derived from the probability distribution. Since entropy cannot be calculated without some pre-determined probability distribution, it is simply a partial characterization of whatever the distribution characterizes or describes. It is only a partial characterization, because two different distributions may give rise to the same entropy. If we believe that entropy is a measure of information, then we have to accept that actual description of information, more complete than entropy, is given by one of probability distributions producing given value of this magnitude.

This brings us to unacceptable consequences. Every geometric structure definitely carries out some information. For instance we can think about the geometric structures of the alphabet letters or numerals. Is it possible to describe geometric structures in terms of probability theory? The answer is obviously not, although of course we can define probability measures within geometric structures. Thus, we cannot expect that probability distributions are sufficient to describe or characterize information. If information cannot be characterized exclusively in terms of probability distributions, entropy is not sufficient characteristic of information.

The puzzle can be easily solved when we observe that Shannon was interested exclusively in measuring of the transfer of information in the process of communication. Thus, he was using as his reference frame the relationship between information source and destination. His entropy can be easily interpreted as a measure of the increase of information within destination, from the original one based on the probability distribution of possible messages, to the final, which is given by the 0-1 distribution probability, which characterizes full information. Of course, if the destination contains full information (one outcome has probability 1, all other 0), there is no increase of information, which corresponds to the fact that entropy is 0. This means an alternative measure of information is more appropriate, and the need for *negentropy* is eliminated (Schroeder, 2004):

$$\text{Inf}(n,p) = \sum_{i=1}^{n} p_i \log_2 (np_i), \qquad \sum_{i=1}^{n} p_i = 1 \; \forall i: p_i \geq 0.$$

Obviously $\text{Inf}(n, p) = H_{\max} - H(n, p)$, where $p = (p_1, p_2, ..., p_n)$.

Then we have a characteristic of the degree of determination of information or relative measure of information:

$$\text{Inf}^*(n, p) = \sum_{i=1}^{n} p_i \log_n (np_i), \quad \sum_{i=1}^{n} p_i = 1 \ \forall i: p_i \geq 0.$$

Or simpler $\text{Inf}^*(n, p) = \text{Inf}(n, p)/\text{Inf}_{\max}$, giving the range $0 \leq \text{Inf}^*(n, p) \leq 1$.

The alternative measure has many useful features of entropy, but also is superior in other respects as it is an invariant of linear transformations and is giving a smooth transition from the finite, discrete probability distributions to the case of infinite, continues probability distributions (Schroeder, 2004).

For our purpose the two most important features are as follows (Schroeder, 2004).

Let S be a disjoint union of the family of probability spaces $\{A_i: i = 1,...,m; A_i \cap A_k = \emptyset, \text{ if } I \neq k\}$, each with probability distribution $p(i)$. Let n indicates the number of elements in S, and n_i of elements in A_i. We can define a probability distribution $p(x)$ on S the following way.

For every x in S, $p(x) = a_i p(i)(x)$, where i is selected by the fact that x belongs to A_i and $a_1 + \cdots + a_m = 1$. Of course, $a_i = p(A_i)$ and we can write $p(x) = p(A_i) p(i)(x)$.

Then,

$$\text{Inf}(n, p) = \sum_{i=1}^{m} p(A_i) \text{Inf}(n_i, p(i)) + \sum_{i=1}^{m} p(A_i) \log_2((n/n_i) p(A_i)).$$

If all sets A_i have the same size k, then the formula for $\text{Inf}(n, p)$ becomes much simpler:

$$\text{Inf}(n, p) = \sum_{i=1}^{n} p(A_i) \text{Inf}(k, p(i)) + \sum_{i=1}^{m} p(A_i) \log_2(m \, p(A_i)).$$

We can interpret this as an assertion that the total information amount $\text{Inf}(n, p)$ can be separated into information identifying the element of the partition A_i, plus the average information identifying an element within subsets of the partition.

Let $S = S_1 \times S_2$ with the probability distribution given by $(p \times q)_{ik} = p_i p_k$. Let S_1 consists of n elements, S_2 consists of m elements. Then Inf $(nm, p \times q) = $ Inf $(n, p) + $ Inf (m, q).

It has to be emphasized that this approach is a purely probabilistic study of information as in the work of Shannon. Thus, the alternative measure can be interpreted as a measure of information provided we can define the concept of information and develop its structural theory justifying the formula.

The attempts related to the quantitative methods initiated by Shannon in his study of communication ignored the structural (qualitative) aspects of information. No wonder that he had to give up the study of semantics for information, if in such perspective information is an amorphous aggregate with the description exclusively in terms of the probability of meaningless components.

In order to combine both aspects of information and to place this concept in the context of non-trivial philosophical conceptual framework, the present author introduced his definition of information in terms of the one – many categorical opposition with a very long and rich philosophical tradition.

The most important characteristic of the structural manifestation of information is its level of information integration describing the specific type of the structure imposed on the variety. This structure may have different levels of integration related to its decomposability into component structures. Decomposability of the structure can be described in terms of irreducibility of the logic L_f of information system into a direct product of component lattices. Quantum mechanics provides examples of completely integrated information systems, but there are many other examples, for instance geometric information systems (Schroeder, 2009).

Analysis of the level of information integration can utilize extensive mathematical knowledge of irreducibility (or reducibility) of partially ordered sets. We will need only fundamentals whose details can be found in the classic monograph on lattice theory written by Garret Birkhoff (1967). In the following text frequent quotations will be made to this monograph, including the numbering of theorems in its *Chapter III*,

Section 8. Simple consequences of the theorems from Birkhoff's monograph for the purpose of this work will be called theorems, but without any risk of confusion they will be presented here without numbering or proofs, which can be found elsewhere (Schroeder, 2015a).

Our goal is to find a quantitative description of the structural characteristics of information.

The main tool for reducibility/irreducibility of partially ordered sets (*posets*) is the concept of a center:

Definition 1. The center of a poset P with 0 and 1 is the set C of elements (called "central elements") which have one component 0 and the other 1 under some direct factorization of P.

Theorem 10. *The center C of a poset P with 0 and 1 is a Boolean lattice in which joins and meets represent joins and meets in P.*

Definition 2. An element a of a lattice L with 0 and 1 is neutral iff (a, x, y) D for all x, y in L, i.e. the triple, x, y generates a distributive sublattice of L.

Theorem 12. *The center of a lattice with 0 and 1 consists of its complemented, neutral elements.*

Corollary. 0 *and* 1 *are central elements in every poset with* 0 *and* 1.

It follows from **Theorem 12** above that the lattices M_5 and N_5 are irreducible and that every Boolean lattice is identical with its center.

We can observe that although the Exchange Property of Steinitz

$$(wE) \ \forall A \subseteq S \ \forall x, y \in S: x \notin f(A) \ \& \ x \in f(A \cup \{y\}) \Rightarrow y \in f(A \cup \{x\})$$

itself does not imply complete irreducibility of the corresponding logic L_f, but it does if every two element set has closure with at least three elements.

From now on, it will be assumed that the logic of information L_f (i.e. the complete lattice of f-closed subsets) is finite.

Lemma 1. *If lattices L_1 and L_2 have their centers C_1 and C_2 respectively, then the direct product $L_1 \times L_2$ has $C_1 \times C_2$ as its center.*

It is a simple corollary of **Theorem 12**.

We will write $|L|$ for the number of elements in set L.

Now we can show using **Theorem 10** and **Theorem 12** that the number of irreducible components of the logic L_f is $\log_2(|C|)$. This number is giving us some indication regarding reducibility of the logic (complete irreducibility is for value 1, the increase indicates that the number of irreducible components is increasing). But as long as we do not know the size of the logic, the value of such measure is limited. It is better to consider first a measure of complexity $m(L)$.

Definition 3. *Measure of complexity $m(L)$ of logic L is given by*
$$m(L) = \log_2(|L|/|C|) = \log_2(|L|) - \log_2(|C|).$$

Theorem 13. *If L is a Boolean lattice (i.e. is completely reducible), then $m(L) = 0$, but when L is completely irreducible, then $m(L) = \log_2(|L|) - 1$.*

Since the center is preserved by all lattice automorphisms, so is $m(L)$.

Also, m is "semi-additive" in the sense that: $m(L_1 \times L_2) = m(L_1) + m(L_2)$.

In particular for a logic $L = L_1 \times L_2 \times L_3 \times \cdots \times L_k$ where all L_i are irreducible, in agreement with the definition we have $m(L) = \log_2(|L|) - k = \log_2(|L|) - \log_2(|C|)$.

The function $m(L)$ was called a measure of complexity, not of irreducibility, as it is increasing to infinity with the size of the logic L. We have simple irreducible two-element logic with $m(L) = 0$, as it is a Boolean lattice. Also, for the completely irreducible logics with lattices M_5 and N_5 we have: $m(M_5) = m(N_5) = \log_2(5/2) \approx 1.32$ while there are many reducible (although not completely) logics with higher values of $m(L)$. So, in order to have a measure of irreducibility we can introduce a relative measure m^* which is an invariant of transformations preserving information structure.

Definition 4. For lattices with at least two elements: $m^*(L) = m(L)/(m_{max} + 1) = m(L)/\log_2(|L|) = \log_2(|L|/|C|)/\log_2(|L|)$, where m_{max} is the maximum complexity $m(L)$ for a logic of size $|L|$.

From the definition it follows directly that
$$m^*(L) = \log_2(|L|/|C|)/\log_2(|L|) = 1 - (\log_2(|C|)/\log_2(|L|)).$$

Then it is easy to see the range of values for $m^*(L)$.

Theorem 14. *If L is a Boolean lattice, $m^*(L) = 0$, but when L is completely irreducible, then: $m^*(L) = 1 - (1/\log_2(|L|))$.*

So $0 \leq m^*(L) < 1$ and m^* is an increasing function of the size of L with limit 1 at infinity.

$$m^*(M_5) = m^*(N_5) = 1 - 1/\log_2(5) \approx 0.57; \ m^*(D_{10}) \approx ca. \ 0.70$$

It is not a surprise that m^* is not semi-additive (in the sense in which m is), because m^* measures irreducibility. When we have a product of logics, we cannot expect increase of irreducibility. Instead we have a logarithmic weighted mean.

Theorem 15.

$m^*(L_1 \times L_2) = \alpha\, m^*(L_1) + \beta\, m^*(L_2)$, *where* $\alpha + \beta = 1$ *and*

$\alpha = \log_1(|L_1|) \,/\, (\log_2(|L_1|) + \log_2(|L_2|))$

$\beta = \log_1(|L_2|) \,/\, (\log_2(|L_1|) + \log_2(|L_2|))$.

Both measures, measure of complexity *m(L)* and measure of information integration $m^*(L)$ are invariants of all transformations which preserve the logic of information (*isomorphisms* of L_f).

There are many cases, when there is a high level of information integration (information logic is not Boolean), but still we can define a generalized form of probabilistic measure. For those cases, we can consider both types of the measure of information. An example can be found in quantum mechanical information systems.

Further question is how to measure selective manifestation for information system whose logic does not admit an *orthocomplementation*, and therefore, when the concept of probabilistic measure does not make sense.

6.10. Conclusion

This paper did not present any explanation how information can serve as a fundamental concept for the study of the hierarchic and functional forms of complexity presented elsewhere (Schroeder, 2014, 2015b). Both forms can be considered as consequences of the dualism of selective and structural manifestations. If we agree that selection of elements from some multiplicity must be related to their own structures (absence of structures corresponds to lack of information and therefore to purely random selection) and that every structure can be considered a selection of a particular configuration, we get a multiple layer hierarchic architecture of information systems.

On the way down of this hierarchy, the elements of a variety are themselves varieties with some structure. On the way up of the hierarchy, the structure on the variety in question is one of many possible structures, and therefore is an element of a higher level variety. This architecture is not necessarily infinite, as the layers may differ in the level of integration of information. Completely integrated and completely disintegrated information systems may serve as lower and upper bounds for the finite hierarchy.

Functional complexity can be considered as dual to structural, as every function consists in the selection of the course of dynamic evolution of information systems. Therefore the study of functional complexity requires a reference to the appropriate dynamics of information. Basic outline of the dynamics of information is outlined elsewhere (Schroeder, 2013b).

Bibliography

Archibald, R. C. (1914). Time as a Fourth Dimension. *Bull. Amer. Math. Soc.*, 20 (8), 409-412.

Aristotle (1955). *Aristotle: Selections*, ed. W. D. Ross, New York, NY: Charles Scribner's Sons.

Artz, F. B. (1980). *The Mind of the Middle Ages: An Historical Survey*, 3rd ed. Chicago, IL: Chicago Univ. Press.

Balcazar, J. L., Diaz, J., and Gabarro, J. (1988). *Structural Complexity*. Berlin/Heidelbeg/New York: Springer.

Barnes, J. (2001). *Early Greek Philosophy*. 2nd rev. ed. London: Penguin Books.

Berkeley, G. (1948-1957). Siris: A chain of philosophical reflections and inquiries concerning the virtues of tar-water, and divers other subjects connected together and arising one from another. In A. A. Luce, T. E. Jessop. *The Works of George Berkeley, Bishop of Cloyne*. 9 vol. London: Thomas Nelson & Sons, 5, pp. 31-164.

Birkhoff, G. (1967). *Lattice Theory*, 3rd ed. Vol XXV, Providence, R. I.: American Mathematical Society Colloquium Publications.

Brillouin, L. (1956). *Science and Information Theory*. New York: Academic Press.

Burgin, M. (2005). *Super-recursive Algorithms*. Berlin/Heidelberg/New York: Springer.

Burgin, M. (2012). *Structural Reality*. New York: Nova Science Publ.

Cantor, G. (1883). Uberunendliche, lineare Punktmannigfaltigkeiten, 5. *Math. Ann.*, 21, 545-586.

Chaitin, G. J. (1966). On the length of programs for computing finite binary sequences. *J. ACM*, 13(4), 547-569.

Clagett, M. (1968). *Nicole Oresme and the Medieval Geometry of Qualities and Motions; A Treatise on the Uniformity and Difformity of Intensities Known as Tractatus de Configurationibus qualitatum et Motuum.* Madison, Wi: University of Wisconsin Press.

Duhem, P. (1969). *To Save the Phenomena: An Essay on the Idea of Physical Theory from Plato to Galileo.* Transl. E. Doland and C. Maschler. Chicago: Chicago Univ. Press.

Evans, J., Berggren, J. L. (2006). *Geminos's Introduction to the Phenomena: A Translation and Study of a Hellenistic Survey of Astronomy.* Princeton, NJ: Princeton Univ. Press.

Gell-Mann, M. (1995). What is complexity? *Complexity,* 1 (1), 16-19.

Gell-Mann, M. (1996). Let's call it plectics. *Complexity,* 1 (5), 3.

Goldstein, B. R. (1997). Saving the phenomena: The background to Ptolemy's planetary theory. *J. History Astronomy,* 28, 1-12.

Husserl, E. (1891). *Philosophie der Arithmetik.* Halle: Pfeffer.

Izard, V., Sann, C., Spelke, E. S., Streri, A. (2009). Newborn infants perceive abstract numbers. *Proc. Natl. Acad. Sci. USA* 106 (25), 10382-10385.

Kolmogorov, A. N. (1965). Three approaches to the definition of the quantity of information. *Problems Inform. Transmission,* 1, 3-11.

Laplace, P. S. (1951). *A Philosophical Essay on Probabilities.* F.W. Truscott, F.L. Emory (transl.) New York, NY: Dover.

Lindley, R. H. (1966). Recording as a function of chunking and meaningfulness. *Psychonomic Sci.,* 6, 393-394.

Losee, J. (1972). *A Historical Introduction to the Philosophy of Science.* Oxford: Oxford Univ. Press.

Maturana, H. R. & Varela, F. J. (1980). *Autopoiesis and Cognition: The Realization of the Living.* Boston Studies in the Philosophy of Science, vol. 42, Dordrecht: D. Reidel.

McKeon, R. (ed.) (1941). *The Basic Works of Aristotle.* New York, NY: Random House.

Miller, G. (1956). The magical number seven, plus or minus two: some limits on our capacity for processing information. *Psychol. Rev.* 63, 81-97 (reprinted in 1994, 101 (2), 343-352).

Nolte, D. D. (2010). The tangled tale of phase space. *Physics Today,* 63 (4), 33-39.

Ortiz Hill, C., Rosado Haddock, G. (2000). *Husserl or Frege, Meaning, Objectivity and Mathematics.* Chicago: Open Court.

Rashevsky, N. (1965). The representation of organisms in terms of (logical) predicates. *Bull. Math. Biophys.*, 27, 477-491.

Rashevsky, N. (1972). *Organismic Sets: Some Reflections on the Nature of Life and Society.* Holland, Michigan: Mathematical Biology, Inc.

Rescher, N. (1998). *Complexity: A Philosophical Overview.* New Brunswick, N.J.: Transaction Publ.

Rosen, R. (1958). The representation of biological systems from the standpoint of the theory of categories. *Bull. Math. Biophys.*, 20, 317-341.

Rosen, R. (1987). Some epistemological issues in physics and biology. In B. J. Hiley and F. D. Peat (Eds.) *Quantum Implications: Essays in Honour of David Bohm.* London: Routledge & Kegan Paul.

Rosen, R. (1991) *Life Itself: A Comprehensive Inquiry into the Nature, Origin, and Fabrication of Life.* New York: Columbia University Press.

Schroeder, M. J. (2004). An Alternative to Entropy in the Measurement of Information. *Entropy,* 6, 388-412.

Schroeder, M. J. (2005). Philosophical Foundations for the Concept of Information: Selective and Structural Information. In Proceedings of the Third International Conference on the Foundations of Information Science, Paris, July 2005, http://www.mdpi.org/fis2005/proceedings. html/ Accessed 19 July 2014.

Schroeder, M. J. (2009). Quantum coherence without quantum mechanics in modeling the unity of consciousness. In P. Bruza *et al.* (eds.) *QI 2009,* LNAI, Vol. 5494, Heidelberg: Springer, pp. 97-112.

Schroeder, M. J. (2011a). From philosophy to theory of information. *International J. Inform. Theor. Appl.,* 18 (1), 56-68.

Schroeder, M. J. (2011b). Concept of information as a bridge between mind and brain. *Information,* 2(3), 478-509 (2011). Available at http://www.mdpi.com/2078-2489/2/3/478/

Schroeder, M. J. (2012a). Search for syllogistic structure of semantic information. *J. Appl. Non-Classical Logic,* 22, 101-127.

Schroeder, M. J. (2012b) The role of information integration in demystification of holistic methodology. In P. L. Simeonov, L. S. Smith, A. C. Ehresmann (eds.) *Integral Biomathics: Tracing the Road to Reality* (pp. 283-296). Berlin: Springer.

Schroeder, M. J. (2013a). The complexity of complexity: structural vs. quantitative approach. In *Proceedings of the International Conference on Complexity, Cybernetics, and Informing Science CCISE 2013,* Porto, Portugal, http://www.iiis-summer13.org/ccise/VirtualSession/viewpaper. asp?C2=CC195GT&vc=58/ Accessed 18 July 2014.

Schroeder, M. J. (2013b). Dualism of selective and structural manifestations of information in modelling of information dynamics, In G. Dodig-Crnkovic, R. Giovagnoli (eds.) *Computing Nature, SAPERE* 7. Berlin, Germany: Springer, pp. 125-137.

Schroeder, M. J. (2013c). From proactive to interactive theory of computation. In M. Bishop and Y. J. Erden (eds.) *The 6th AISB Symposium on Computing and Philosophy: The Scandal of Computation – What is Computation?* The Society for the Study of Artificial Intelligence and the Simulation of Behaviour, pp. 47-51.

Schroeder, M. J. (2014). Algebraic model for the dualism of selective and structural manifestations of information. In M. Kondo (ed.), *RIMS Kokyuroku*, No. 1915. Kyoto: Research Institute for Mathematical Sciences, Kyoto University, pp. 44-52.

Schroeder, M. J. (2015a). Structural and quantitative characteristics of information and complexity. In M. Kondo (ed.), *RIMS Kokyuroku*, No. 1964, Kyoto: Research Institute for Mathematical Sciences, Kyoto University, pp. 88-97.

Schroeder, M. J. (2015b). Hierarchic information systems in a search for methods to transcend limitations of complexity. *Philosophies,* 1, 1-14.

Schrödinger, E. (1945). *What is Life?* Cambridge: Cambridge University Press.

Shannon, E. C. (1948). A mathematical theory of communication. *Bell Sys. Tech. J.,* 27, 379-423, 623-656.

Singer, C. (1958). *From Magic to Science: Essays on the Scientific Twilight.* New York: Dover.

Solomonoff, R. (1964). A formal theory of inductive inference part I. *Inform. Control,* 7 (1), 1–22.

Smuts, J. C. (1926). *Holism and Evolution.* London: Macmillan.

Thom, R. (1975). *Structural Stability and Morphogenesis.* Reading, MA: Benjamin

Turing, A. M. (1936). On computable numbers, with an application to the Entscheidungsproblem. *Proc. London Math. Soc.,* (2), 42, 230-265, correction 43, 544-546.

Von Bertalanffy, L. (1950). An outline of general system theory. *British J. Philos. Sci.,* 1, 134-165.

Weaver, W. (1948). Science and complexity. *American Scientist,* 36 (4), 536-544.

Chapter 7

Multiscale Information Theory for Complex Systems: Theory and Applications

Blake C. Stacey

Physics Department, University of Massachusetts Boston
100 Morrissey Blvd., Boston, MA 02125, USA

Benjamin Allen

Department of Mathematics, Emmanuel College
400 The Fenway, Boston, MA 02115, USA

Program for Evolutionary Dynamics, Harvard University
1 Brattle Square, Cambridge, MA 02138, USA

Yaneer Bar-Yam

New England Complex Systems Institute
210 Broadway Suite 101, Cambridge, MA 02139, USA

Abstract

The science of complex systems requires a general way to represent and understand structure. We review a mathematical formalism that uses information theory to make precise the intuition that a complex system exhibits structure at multiple scales. We show that structure can be seen as the totality of relationships among a system's components, and information theory can quantify these relationships. Beginning with fundamental axioms that specify the properties that a function must satisfy in order to be an information measure, we develop quantitative indices that summarize system structure, namely the complexity profile (CP) and the marginal utility of information (MUI). We demonstrate the applicability of our formalism with examples from evolutionary biology, economics and finite geometry.

7.1. Introduction

A century and odd years ago, the philosopher William James asked,[1]

What shall we call a *thing* anyhow? It seems quite arbitrary, for we carve out everything, just as we carve out constellations, to suit our human purposes. For me, this whole 'audience' is one thing, which grows now restless, now attentive. I have no use at present for its individual units, so I don't consider them. So of an 'army,' of a 'nation.' But in your own eyes, ladies and gentlemen, to call you 'audience' is an accidental way of taking you. The permanently real things for you are your individual persons. To an anatomist, again, those persons are but organisms, and the real things are the organs. Not the organs, so much as their constituent cells, say the histologists; not the cells, but their molecules, say in turn the chemists.

The Jamesian view is that each of these scientific disciplines is as "fundamental" as the others. A discipline must prove its own worth by way of its pragmatic utility, at its level of organizational description. This attitude is counter to a common temperament in modern thinking about science, which holds that the noblest aspiration is to seek the most elementary constituents of matter. The right way to theorize, so the training goes, is to separate molecules into atoms, atoms into electrons and nuclei, nucleons into quarks.

But this approach has limitations. There is no difference between quarks that are part of a person and those within a rock. The inter-component relationships that have been abandoned become the very essence of what we are often interested in understanding. These relationships are characterized by information specific to the system, and this is the subject of this paper.

Quantifying these relationships presents challenges that are difficult to address with traditional statistical thinking. While it is easy to consider a solid object, it is much harder to consider dynamically dependent entities that are partially or sometimes dependent on each other, e.g., a human audience or a flock of birds that coalesces over some interval and maintains flexible relationships for a time. However, such dependencies are essential to understanding the structure and behaviors of the world we live in. Formalizing and quantifying them is essential to scientific inquiry.

In the study of complex systems, we face this directly. A complex system exhibits structure at many scales of organization. For example, one can study human beings at any magnification, from the molecular level to the societal, and an entire science flourishes at each level. We have

Information and Complexity

developed a formalism for making this intuition mathematically precise
and quantitatively useful, employing the tools of information theory.[2-7] To
explore how this formalism can be used, and to make clear the intricacies
of multiscale information theory, we shall in this essay apply that theory
to an illustrative set of problems.

One general lesson drawn from practical experience with complex-
systems science is that *partial descriptions* of a system can have increased
utility if they can exploit patterns and redundancies. Furthermore, the way
the utility of a description increases as we allow more information to be used
tells us about the structure of the system we are describing. This approach
is different from the way information theory has typically been used in the
past, because we are considering *scale* and information as *complementary
quantities*.[2] We measure the effort which goes into a description in units
of information, whereas the effectiveness of that description is the scale of
what it captures.

We now turn to mathematizing this idea, following our earlier work
on multiscale structure and information theory. The resulting formalism
will be applicable at levels from the intracellular to the societal. This will
allow us to discuss descriptions, utilities and related concepts beginning
from an axiomatic starting point. With these concepts developed and some
illustrative examples analyzed, we will then apply them to evolutionary dynamics. Subsequently, we will demonstrate the generality of our formalism
by studying abstract systems defined in terms of discrete geometry.

7.1.1. *Information-theoretic axioms for structured systems*

For convenience, we review the basic axioms of the multiscale information
formalism which we developed in earlier work.[2] The crucial idea of this
formalism is that in order to develop a viable, quantitative notion of "complexity," we need to augment the concept of *information* with that of *scale*.
Often, "scale" is thought of in terms of length or time (for example, the
James quote above organizes the learned disciplines essentially by the geometrical dimensions of what they study). For an axiomatic development,
a more general definition is appropriate, and so for our purposes, "scale"
will refer to the *number of components* within a system which are involved
in an interrelationship.

In this formalism, a *system* is defined by a set of components, A, and an
information function, H, which assigns a nonnegative real number to each
subset $U \subset A$. This number $H(U)$ is the amount of information needed to

describe the components in U. It is the information function that captures the structure of the system. For example, a system composed of parts that act independently of each other has a different structure from a system whose parts act in concert, even if the systems have the same number of components. These two systems would have different information functions. To qualify as an information function, H must satisfy two axioms:

- *Monotonicity:* The information in a subset U that is contained in a subset V cannot have more information than V. That is, $H(U) \leq H(V)$.
- *Strong subadditivity:* Given two subsets, the information contained in both cannot exceed the information in each of them separately minus the information in their intersection:

$$H(U \cup V) \leq H(U) + H(V) - H(U \cap V). \qquad (7.1)$$

The Shannon information of a joint probability distribution for a set of random variables satisfies these axioms. Other examples of information functions include set cardinality and vector space dimension.[2] Proving theorems from the above axioms allows us to establish results that apply to all information functions.

Given an information function H, we can construct functions which express different kinds of possible relationships among a system's components, such as the mutual information, which is the difference between the total information of two components considered separately and the joint information of those two components taken together:

$$I(a;b) = H(a) + H(b) - H(a,b). \qquad (7.2)$$

By extension,[8] we can also define the tertiary mutual information

$$I(a;b;c) = H(a) + H(b) + H(c) - H(a,b) - H(b,c) - H(a,c) + H(a,b,c). \qquad (7.3)$$

This can be extended to higher scales in the same fashion, defining *shared information* for sets of four or more components.

One way to understand the meaning of our axioms is the following. Take a set of questions, which are all mutually independent in the sense that answering one does not help to answer any other, or any combination of others. Each question pertains to one or more components of a system, in the sense that an answer will specify certain aspects of these components. Components have nonzero shared information if one or more questions pertain to both of them.

7.1.2. *Indices of structure*

To specify the structure of a system according to our definition, it is necessary to specify the information content of each subset $U \subset A$. Because the number of such subsets grows exponentially with the number of components, complete descriptions of structure are impractical for large systems. Therefore, we require statistics which can convey the general character of a system's structure without specifying it completely. Using an *index of structure*, we can summarize how a system is organized and compare that pattern of organization to the patterns manifested by other systems.

One such index of structure is the *complexity profile*, introduced in[4] to formalize the intuition that a genuinely complex system exhibits structure at multiple scales. The complexity profile is a real-valued function $C(k)$ that specifies the amount of information contained in interdependencies of scale k and higher. $C(k)$ can be computed using a combinatorial formula which takes as input the values of the information function H on all subsets $U \subset A$.[2-7] First, we define the quantity $Q(j)$ as the sum of the joint information of all collections of j components:

$$Q(j) = \sum_{i_1,\dots,i_j} H(a_{i_1},\dots,a_{i_j}). \tag{7.4}$$

The complexity profile can be computed using the formula

$$C(k) = \sum_{j=N-k}^{N-1} (-1)^{j+k-N} \binom{j}{j+k-N} Q(j+1), \tag{7.5}$$

where $N = |A|$ is the number of components in the system. We shall illustrate this in the next section with a few examples.

The complexity profile satisfies a *conservation law*: the sum of $C(k)$ over all scales k is

$$\sum_k C(k) = \sum_{a \in A} H(a). \tag{7.6}$$

That is, the sum of the complexity over all scales is given by the individual information assigned to each component, regardless of the components' interrelationships.

Another useful index of structure is the Marginal Utility of Information, or MUI.[2] While the complexity profile characterizes the amount of information that is present in the system behavior at different scales, the MUI is based on descriptive utility of limited information through its ability to describe behavior of multiple components. Informally speaking, we describe a system by "investing" a certain amount of information, and for any amount of information invested, an *optimal* description yields the best possible characterization of the system. The MUI expresses how the usefulness of an optimal description increases as we invest more information. We can define the MUI precisely, starting with the basic axioms of information functions, by using notions from linear programming.[2]

In general outline, one constructs the MUI as follows. Let $\mathcal{A}$ be a system, defined per our formalism as a set of components A and an information function H. Then, let d be a *descriptor,* an entity which conveys information about the system $\mathcal{A}$. To express this mathematically, we consider the new, larger system made by conjoining d with the set of components A and defining an information function on the subsets of this expanded set. The information function for the augmented system reduces to that of the original for all those interdependencies which do not involve the descriptor d, and it expresses the shared information between d and the original system. The *utility* of d is the sum of the shared information between d and each component within $\mathcal{A}$:

$$u(d) = \sum_{a \in A} I(d; a). \tag{7.7}$$

This counts, in essence, the total scale of the system's organization that is captured by d. We define the *optimal utility* $U(y)$ as the utility of the best possible descriptor having $H(d) = y$. The MUI is then the derivative of $U(y)$.

The complexity profile is an amount of information as a function of scale, while the MUI is a scale as a function of increasing information. How do these structure indices capture the organization of a system? We can illustrate the general idea by way of a conceptual example. Consider a crew of movers, who are carrying furniture from a house to a truck. They can be acting largely independently, as when each mover is carrying a single chair, or they can be working in concert, transporting a large item that requires collective effort to move, like a grand piano. In the former case, knowing what any one mover is doing does not say much about what specific act any other mover is engaged with at that time. Information about the crew applies at the scale of an individual mover. By contrast, in the latter case, the behavior of one mover can be inferred from that of another, and information about their actions is applicable at a larger scale. From these general considerations, it follows that for a system of largely independent movers, $C(k)$ is large at small k and drops off rapidly, whereas when the movers are working collectively, $C(k)$ is small for low k

and remains nonzero for larger k. To understand the MUI, consider that when the movers act mostly independently, we cannot do much better at *describing* their behavior than by specifying the behavior of each mover in turn. Therefore, as we invest more information into describing the system, the gain in utility of our description remains essentially constant. For the case of independent movers, then, the MUI curve is low and flat. On the other hand, when the movers are acting in concert, a brief description can have a high utility, so the MUI curve is peaked at the origin and falls off sharply. Heuristically speaking, we can in this example think of the complexity profile and the MUI as reflections, i.e., inverses, of each other. When we develop these indices quantitatively, we find in fact that in a broad class of systems, the complexity profile is exactly the inverse of the MUI.[2]

Both the complexity profile and the MUI obey a convenient sum rule. If a system separates into two independent subsystems, the complexity profile of the whole is the sum of the profiles of the pieces, and likewise for the MUI. This property of both structure indices follows from the basic information-function axioms.[2] In the next section, we will see examples of systems which illustrate the sum rule for both the MUI and the complexity profile.

7.1.3. *Three-component systems*

To explore the consequences of our definitions, it is helpful to begin with simple examples. Following the recent review article about the multiscale complexity formalism,[2] we study the following four systems, each of which contains three binary variables.

- *Example **A**: Three independent bits:* The system comprises three components, and knowing the state of any one bit provides no information about the state of any other. As a whole, the system can be in any one of eight possible configurations, with no preference given to any of the eight possibilities.
- *Example **B**: Three completely interdependent bits:* The system as a whole is either in state 000 or state 111, with no preference given to either option. Knowing the value of any one bit allows the inference of both other bits.
- *Example **C**: Independent blocks of dependent bits:* Each component is equally likely to take the value 0 or 1; however, the first two

components always take the same value, while the third can take either value independently of the coupled pair.

- *Example* **D**: *The* $2+1$ *parity bit system*: Three bits which can exist in the states 110, 101, 011, or 000 with equal probability. Each of the three bits is equal to the parity (0 if even; 1 if odd) of the sum of the other two. Any two of the bits are statistically independent of each other, but the three as a whole are constrained to have an even sum.

Figures 7.1 and 7.2 show the complexity profiles and the MUI curves for these example systems.

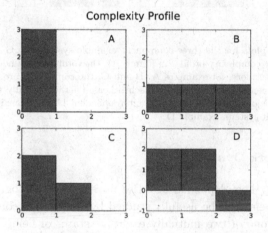

Fig. 7.1. Complexity profiles for the three-component example systems **A**, **B**, **C** and **D**, computed using Eq. (7.5). Examples **A** and **B** illustrate the general fact that highly interdependent systems have tall and narrow complexity profiles, whereas the profiles of systems with largely independent components are low and wide. Example **C**, which we can think of as the combination of two independent subsystems, illustrates the complexity profile's sum rule. Finally, example **D**, the parity-bit system, showcases the emergence of negative shared information. Note that the total signed area bounded by each curve is 3 units.

In the following sections, we will apply the multiscale complexity formalism to systems with more components. First, we will study a type of stochastic system that has practical applications, and in which an overall symmetry property simplifies the calculation of the complexity profile. Then, we will turn to more abstract mathematical examples that do not depend upon the idea of probability.

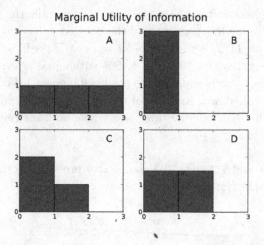

Fig. 7.2.   MUI plots for the three-component example systems **A**, **B**, **C** and **D**. Note that, as with the complexity profiles in Figure 7.1, the total area bounded by each curve is 3 units. Furthermore, for examples **A**, **B** and **C**, the complexity profile and the MUI are reflections (generalized inverses) of each other. This is generally true for systems which are the disjoint union of internally interdependent blocks,[2] but it is not the case for the parity-bit system, example **D**.

7.2.   Network Dynamics

Understanding how dependencies arise in real world biological and socio-economic systems can be usefully studied by considering components that are found in one of two mutually exclusive states of being. Shannon information theory captures the role of probabilities of those variables in uncertainty about the existing state. Our formalism is designed to capture the way dependencies between them influence the space of possible states of the system as a whole.

We idealize a phenomenon by treating it as composed of binary random variables, possibly correlated, or having dependencies of other kinds that affect which combined states are possible. We might postulate that each organism in a population can follow one of two survival strategies. For example, a male bower bird can maraud, attacking other birds' bowers, or it can remain at its own bower, guarding its own mating display from marauders.[9,10] Or, we might postulate that a gene comes in two variant forms. Each instance of the gene in the idealized population is then a binary random variable. We can make an analogous approximation when modeling social and economic systems. For example, an individual voter

· can choose between one of two political parties. Or, in a simplified but still instructive model for a stock market, the price of a company's stock can be going either up or down.[11]

A specific implementation of this idea is the *Moran model,* which was originally formulated in biology but can be applied more broadly.[11] Consider a haploid population of N individuals, and a gene which comes in two alleles. The genetic character of the population can change as individuals are born and die. One simple dynamical model for this process picks an individual at random with each tick of a discrete-time clock. The chosen, or *focal,* individual mates with one of the other $N-1$ organisms and produces an offspring, which then takes the place of the focal individual. The allele carried by the offspring is that carried by one of its two parents, the choice of which parent being made randomly with equal probability either way.

Reframing the Moran model in network-theory language turns out to be convenient for developing extensions, such as treatments including structured populations, wherein mating is not uniformly random. Furthermore, doing so broadens the range of systems to which the mathematics can be applied. Moving away from the specifically biological terminology makes it more explicit that the Moran model can be applied equally well to biological evolution or to other problems such as social dynamics, becoming a universal model of influence.[11]

The components of our system will be the N nodes of a network. Each node is a random variable which can take the values 0 and 1. In addition to these N nodes, we augment the system with a number N_0 of nodes whose states are all fixed at 0, and a quantity N_1 of nodes whose states are fixed to be 1.

At each time step, we pick one of the variable nodes at random. We then choose, stochastically, whether or not to change that node's value. With probability p, we keep the node value the same, and with probability $1-p$, we assign to it the value of another node, chosen at random from a pool of candidates. This pool contains the neighborhood of the node in the network topology, both the variable nodes and those of the $N_0 + N_1$ fixed nodes to which it is connected. In this way, the fixed nodes represent the possibility of mutation: even if all the dynamical population has allele 1, there remains the opportunity of picking up a 0, and vice versa. For a complete graph, the steady-state behavior of this dynamical system can actually be found analytically.[12] The probability that exactly m nodes out of the N whose value can vary will be in state 1 is

$$q(m) = A(N, N_0, N_1)\frac{\Gamma(N_1 + m)\Gamma(N + N_0 - m)}{\Gamma(N - m + 1)\Gamma(m + 1)}, \qquad (7.8)$$

where the normalization constant A is given by

$$A(N, N_0, N_1) = \frac{\Gamma(N + 1)\Gamma(N_0 + N_1)}{\Gamma(N + N_0 + N_1)\Gamma(N_0)\Gamma(N_1)}. \qquad (7.9)$$

We illustrate $q(m)$ for networks of $N = 10$ nodes and different values of N_0 and N_1 in Figure 7.3. The function $q(m)$ is an example of the *beta-binomial distribution*.

Because the gamma function can take noninteger values, we can compute the probability $q(m)$ even for nonintegral N_0 and N_1. This is useful if we wish to examine the low-mutation-rate limit.

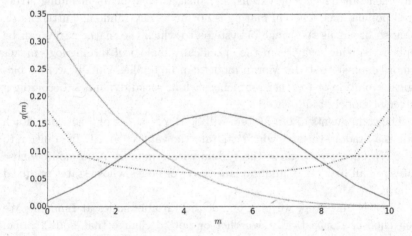

Fig. 7.3. Probability that exactly m nodes out of 10 will be in the 1-state, for different values of N_0 and N_1. Solid: $N_0 = N_1 = 5$; dashed: $N_0 = N_1 = 1$; dash-dotted: $N_0 = N_1 = 0.5$; dotted: $N_0 = 5$ and $N_1 = 1$.

If the network topology is that of a complete graph, then the system has *exchange symmetry,* an invariance under permutations which simplifies the calculation of structure indices.[2] This simplification follows from the fact that if exchange symmetry holds, all subsets having the same number of components can be taken to contain the same quantity of information. Formally, for each set $U \subset A$, the information of U is a function of the cardinality $|U|$, which we can write as a subscript, $H(U) = H_{|U|}$.

Recalling that the complexity profile $C(k)$ indicates the information in dependencies of scale k and higher, the information specific to scale k is

$$D(k) = C(k) - C(k+1). \tag{7.10}$$

The sum of $D(k)$ over all scales k is $C(1)$. For any fixed scale k, the complexity $D(k)$ is (up to a prefactor) the binomial transform of the sequence $a_l \equiv H_{l+N-k}$.

$$D(k) = \binom{N}{k} \sum_{l=0}^{k} (-1)^{l+1} \binom{k}{l} H_{l+N-k}. \tag{7.11}$$

We can calculate H_n from the probability distribution $q(m)$, as given by Eq. (7.8). Knowing H_n, we can compute $D(k)$, from which we can find the complexity profile $C(k)$. Figure 7.4 illustrates the results.

We see that $C(k)$ depends upon the numbers of fixed influence nodes, N_0 and N_1. When $C(k)$ is concentrated at $k = 1$, the nodes are changing their values almost independently of one another. This is the case, for example, when $N_0 = N_1 = 5$. For those parameter values, the external influences are stronger than those of the variable nodes upon each other, while being equally balanced in both directions. This creates a situation in which knowing the status of any one variable node provides very little information about the status of any other. On the other hand, when $C(k)$ is highly elevated at larger values of k, then nonnegligible amounts of information apply at higher scales. This occurs when the external influences are weaker than the internal dynamics, causing the variable nodes to act collectively.

The Moran model has been applied to real stock-market data, and the empirical chronicles of the numbers of upward- and downward-moving stock prices fit the model well.[11] The overall result of the analysis is that collective behavior, of the kind indicated by a longer-tailed $C(k)$, is a sign of an *unhealthy market economy*: it shows a vulnerability to panic that can lead to a crash.

7.3. Frequency-Dependent Moran Process

The principle of natural selection states that the genetic composition of a population can change over time due to the preferential survival of organisms carrying certain traits. Which traits are beneficial depends upon the organism's environment, and that environment will typically include *other organisms*. The effect of any action that a living being takes will naturally

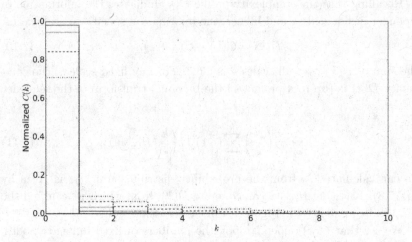

Fig. 7.4. Complexity profiles for the cases illustrated in Figure 7.3. Each curve is normalized so that the total area under it is 1. Elevated complexity $C(k)$ at larger k indicates collective behavior at larger scales. Solid: $N_0 = N_1 = 5$; dashed: $N_0 = N_1 = 1$; dash-dotted: $N_0 = N_1 = 0.5$; dotted: $N_0 = 5$ and $N_1 = 1$.

depend on what other organisms are doing at the same time.[13,14] A simple, albeit approximate, way to represent the state of an ecosystem, as well as its influence on the survival and reproduction of organisms, is by specifying the frequencies of abundance or population densities for the types which are present. In this context, we can speak of *frequency-dependent fitness*: the reproductive success of an organism type or an evolutionary strategy can be a function of the current population densities.

The simplest kind of frequency dependence is a linear relationship between population density and fitness. As before, we consider two varieties, and we keep the total population size constant, so the frequencies of both types can be given in terms of a single variable x. We take the reproductive rates of type-0 and type-1 organisms to be given by

$$f_0(x) = A_{01}x + A_{00}(1 - x), \qquad (7.12)$$

$$f_1(x) = A_{11}x + A_{10}(1 - x). \qquad (7.13)$$

In game-theoretic language, the coefficient A_{ij} can be considered to be the payoff which a type-i player gains by playing with a type-j player. Different values of the matrix A represent different interactions between evolutionary strategies.

Allowing for random mutations that change individuals between the two types, the evolution of a population is a stochastic process resulting in a probability distribution that reflects the *mutation-selection equilibrium* which is the steady state of a frequency-dependent Moran process. We can find this distribution numerically by iterating the appropriate update rule, which we can represent as multiplication by a transition matrix. The next step is to construct this matrix. Having done so, we will be able to compute $q(m)$ as we did above and thence obtain the complexity profile, as before. The result will typically depend both upon the payoff matrix A and on the mutation rate.

Let the total population size be N, and let m denote the number of type-1 individuals. We suppose that mutations occur at rate u. That is, an offspring inherits its parent's type with probability $1 - u$, while with probability u, we pick the offspring's type at random. A nonzero mutation rate implies that the population does not have to get stuck in a uniform configuration: even if all individuals have the same type, a mutation can create an organism of the opposite type in the next generation. This is a necessary requirement for having a steady-state probability distribution which is not concentrated entirely at $m = 0$ or $m = N$.

In the frequency-dependent Moran process,[15] the probability that m will decrease by 1 is

$$p_{m \to m-1} = \frac{m}{N} \left((1-u) \frac{(N-m)f_0 \left(\frac{m}{N} \right)}{mf_1 \left(\frac{m}{N} \right) + (N-m)f_0 \left(\frac{m}{N} \right)} + \frac{u}{2} \right). \tag{7.14}$$

And the probability of m increasing by 1 is

$$p_{m \to m-1} = \frac{N-m}{N} \left((1-u) \frac{mf_1 \left(\frac{m}{N} \right)}{mf_1 \left(\frac{m}{N} \right) + (N-m)f_0 \left(\frac{m}{N} \right)} + \frac{u}{2} \right). \tag{7.15}$$

With these equations, we can find the steady-state probability distribution $q(m)$, which will depend on the payoff matrix A and the mutation rate u. Knowing $q(m)$, we can as before find the complexity profile $C(k)$. The resulting curve tells us about the scales of organization which arise within the population as a consequence of the evolutionary game dynamics.

To connect with the literature,[15] we carry out this calculation for the payoff matrix

$$A = \begin{pmatrix} 6 & 4 \\ 7 & 5 \end{pmatrix}, \tag{7.16}$$

which defines an instance of the *Prisoner's Dilemma*. One application of this to biology is the case of the bower birds mentioned earlier.[9, 10] Simplifying somewhat, a male bower bird has two strategies available to it: to guard its own bower, or to maraud and attempt to damage others. Designate guarding as strategy 0 and marauding as strategy 1. The matrix element A_{ij} denotes the payoff to a bird following strategy i against an opponent who plays strategy j. In this example, a guardian (row 0) who plays against a marauder (column 1) obtains a score of 4. The highest payoff is A_{10}, the score obtained by a marauder who plays against a guardian. In fact, it is better to maraud than to guard, when facing either kind of foe:

$$A_{10} > A_{00}, \text{ and also } A_{11} > A_{01}. \qquad (7.17)$$

So far, it looks like the thing to do is to maraud. However, the payoff obtained when both birds follow this strategy is A_{11}, which is *less* than the payoff A_{00} they would have obtained if they had both stayed home.

The particular choice of numbers here is arbitrary, but the relationships between the numbers are representative of typical conditions in the wild. As Gonick[10] summarizes, "Seemingly forced by the game's logic into a hostile strategy, they end up worse off than if they had only cooperated!" A wide variety of biological scenarios can be considered as examples of this game.[16,17] A primary concern is to identify the conditions under which cooperation (for example, both bower birds guarding rather than marauding) is evolutionarily favorable.

This type of situation is designated a "Prisoner's Dilemma" because it is usually introduced with an example of two people apprehended for a crime and interrogated by the police. Each player can choose to say nothing, or to inform on the other player. The payoff matrix is such that it is better to inform than to stay silent, whatever option the other player takes; however, if both players keep quiet, they fare better than if they both inform on each other.

Figure 7.5 shows the probability distribution for the Moran process in mutation-selection equilibrium with this payoff matrix, given two different mutation rates. Note that the effect of varying the mutation rate is quite dramatic. As before, we can compute the complexity profile, which we plot in Figure 7.6. When $C(k)$ is elevated at larger values of k, the population exhibits collective behavior at larger scales. Here, "collective behavior" refers to birds employing the same strategy at the same time, not necessarily to birds cooperating with one another. For higher levels of mutation the strategies are more varied, i.e., independent, while for lower mutation rates, the strategies are more coherent across the population, and the complexity profile quantifies the degree to which this is the case.

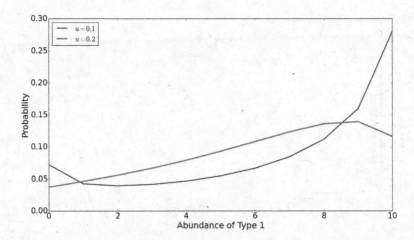

Fig. 7.5. Equilibrium probability that exactly m agents out of 10 will be in the 1-state (marauding), for the Prisoner's Dilemma game defined by Eq. (7.16). Thinner line: $u = 0.1$; thicker line: $u = 0.2$.

7.4. Multiscale Challenges and Evolution

In the previous section, we considered the scales of organization which can arise as an evolutionary process develops stochastically. We can also apply our mathematical formalism of multiscale structure to other aspects of evolutionary theory.

Consider an organism that lives within an environment which changes in significant ways over time intervals shorter than the cycling of generations. For example, a plant might flower annually, while the presence of different herbivore species might change seasonally, and weather conditions fluctuate on a day-to-day basis. Some of these short-term changes may be severe enough that the organism must mount active responses in order to survive them, e.g., adopting new foraging patterns, producing different sets of digestive enzymes, etc. If the flexibility of the organism is insufficient to meet the variability of the environment, the organism will die.

This suggests a way of thinking about natural selection in terms of *multiscale variety*:[2] A life form, or a collection of them, can use information pertaining to a particular scale of the environment to take a self-preserving action of corresponding scale. A mismatch between the variety of challenges that the environment can pose at a given scale and the variety of possible responses at that scale will be costly. Natural selection will tend to penalize such discrepancies.

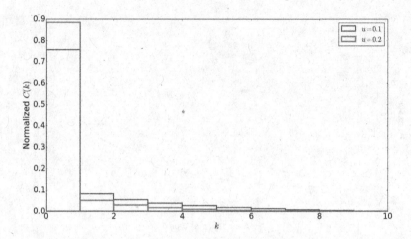

Fig. 7.6. Complexity profiles for the cases illustrated in Figure 7.5. Each curve is normalized so that the total area under it is 1. Elevated complexity C at larger k indicates collective behavior at larger scales. Thinner line: $u = 0.1$; thicker line: $u = 0.2$.

Within an individual organism, multiple scales of environmental challenges are met by different scales of system responses.[18] For example, organisms have a range of ways to protect themselves against infection: physical barriers like skin, generic physiological responses like clotting, and highly specialized adaptive immune responses. This incorporates multiple responses that include relatively large- and small-scale countermeasures.[19]

On scales larger than the individual, groups of organisms can take collective actions. Indeed, within species like social insects,[20] we can identify distinct scales of individual, colony and species. This hints that we can apply multiscale cybernetics to the evolution of social behavior. Following the same logic as above, we expect that scales of organization within a population—the scales, for example, of groups or colonies—will evolve to match the scales of the challenges which the environment presents.

7.5. Complexity of Incidence Geometries

To develop additional intuition about our information-theoretic formalism, and to build a bridge between different areas of mathematics, we shall apply the information theory of multicomponent systems to *incidence geometry*. The premise of incidence geometry is that one has a set of points and a set of lines which connect them, satisfying some conditions which abstract basic notions of geometry. To wit, for any incidence geometry, every line contains at least two distinct points, and for every line, there exist one or more points not lying on that line. We relate geometry to information theory in the following way: A line corresponds to a component of the system and the information associated with that component is the number of points that the line intersects. Since each point has a unit of information we can think of a point as a binary variable, or more generally as a degree of freedom. When two or more lines intersect in a point those components share that information. Since the standard definitions of incidence geometry require a line to have two or more points, it excludes the case of components with a single degree of freedom. This convention avoids examples that are, perhaps, trivial geometrically, but not trivial for systems. It focuses attention on the cases where components all have two or more units of information, which can therefore be shared with other components in non-trivial ways. Incidence geometry regards two lines that have all the same points as the same line, so there are no cases where two different components are informationally equivalent.

The examples we shall consider from incidence geometry will illustrate most of the key features of the multiscale information theory formalism. The noteworthy exception is that incidence geometry does not provide examples of negative multivariate mutual information. This is a subtlety which can arise when one considers dependencies among three or more components,[2] as we saw in example **D**.

The simplest possible incidence geometry contains 3 points and 3 lines. If we denote the three lines by l_1, l_2 and l_3, as in Figure 7.7, then because each line contains exactly two points, we have

$$H(l_1) = H(l_2) = H(l_3) = 2, \tag{7.18}$$

while because any two lines intersect in exactly one point,

$$I(l_1; l_2) = I(l_2; l_3) = I(l_1; l_3) = 1. \tag{7.19}$$

The joint information of all three components taken together is the total number of points in the geometry:

$$H(l_1, l_2, l_3) = 3. \tag{7.20}$$

From these three observations, we can deduce that the tertiary mutual information of the three components vanishes:

$$C(3) = I(l_1; l_2; l_3) = 0. \tag{7.21}$$

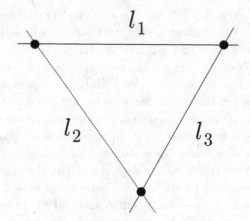

Fig. 7.7.   The simplest possible incidence geometry. Each of the three lines contains two distinct points, and for each line, there exists exactly one point which does not lie on that line. When we associate a unit of information to each point, the shared information of any pair of lines is the information ascribed to their point of intersection.

This is the information-theoretic restatement of the geometric fact that the three lines do not all come together at a single point. All together, the complexity profile of the minimal incidence geometry is given by

$$C(k) = \begin{cases} 3, & k \in \{1,2\}, \\ 0, & k = 3. \end{cases} \qquad (7.22)$$

The information-theoretic relationships among the three system components l_1, l_2 and l_3 can be expressed in a three-circle Venn diagram, shown in Figure 7.8.

It is also illuminating to consider the other structure index, the MUI. We can deduce the MUI of the minimal incidence geometry using the properties of the MUI established in Ref. 2. First, a descriptor d must have at least 3 units of information to capture all of the information associated to the geometry. Expanding on an *optimal* descriptor, i.e., one that wastes nothing, brings no benefit beyond a descriptor length of $H(d) = 3$. Therefore, the marginal utility $M(y)$ will equal zero for $y \geq 3$. In addition, because the integral of the MUI curve is the utility of a full description—that is, the total scale-weighted information of the system—we know the integral of the MUI for this geometry will be 6. Furthermore, we can constrain the height of the MUI curve, using the following property:

- If there are no nontrivial interdependencies of degree k or higher— formally, if $I(a_1; \ldots; a_k) = 0$ for all collections $a_1, \ldots, a_k$ of k distinct components—then $M(y) \leq k$ for all y (see §VII.B in Ref. 2).

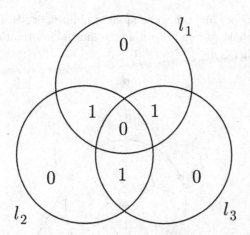

Fig. 7.8. Information diagram for the minimal incidence geometry depicted in Figure 7.7. The total information within each circle is 2 units: $H(l_1) = H(l_2) = H(l_3) = 1 + 1 = 2$. Within each of the three circles, all of the regions which contain nonzero information are regions of overlap with another circle. This is the information-theoretic consequence of the geometrical fact that each point belongs to more than one line. Note that the central region, where all three circles overlap, contains no information.

Here, this means that $M(y) \leq 3$. Furthermore, we know that $M(y)$ is the derivative of a piecewise linear function, so $M(y)$ is piecewise constant. For the minimal geometry, then, we expect the MUI should be

$$M(y) = \begin{cases} 2, & 0 \leq y < 3, \\ 0, & y \geq 3. \end{cases} \tag{7.23}$$

Note that the MUI curve is the reflection of the complexity profile $C(k)$ in Eq. (7.22).

Quite generally, for any incidence geometry, the MUI vanishes for y larger than the number of points used to build the geometry, the integral of the MUI is the total scale-weighted information, and the MUI is bounded above by one plus the maximal number of lines which mutually intersect at a common point. We can relate the MUI and the complexity profile by noting that the areas bounded by both curves are the same, and moreover, the width of the MUI curve $M(y)$ is the height of the complexity profile $C(1)$, because both are given by the number of points in the geometry.

7.5.1.   *Fano plane*

The Fano plane, Figure 7.9, has 7 points, 7 lines, 3 points on every line, and 3 lines through every point. The total scale-weighted information is the number of points per line times the number of lines, or 21. The information content of the whole system is 7, while the mutual information between any line and any other is 1.

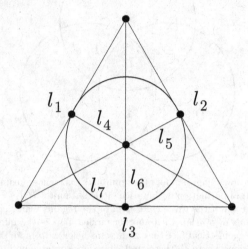

Fig. 7.9.   The Fano plane: a symmetrical arrangement of seven points and seven lines. The shared information between any two lines is 1, but the shared information at higher scales depends on which set of lines we choose.

For the Fano plane, there are two possible scenarios involving three distinct lines. If the three lines do not meet at a common point, as for example l_1, l_2 and l_3, then the tertiary mutual information of those three components is zero. If the three lines do meet at a common point, as with l_1, l_3 and l_5, then the tertiary mutual information is 1.

$$I(l_1; l_2; l_3) = 0, \text{ but } I(l_1; l_3; l_5) = 1. \tag{7.24}$$

The tertiary mutual information $I(l_i; l_j; l_k)$ can never be greater than 1, because any two lines come together in one and exactly one point. This uniqueness of intersections also implies that, in any three-circle Venn diagram, the lens-shaped regions where two circles overlap always contain a total of 1 unit of information. If the inner region of triple overlap, corresponding to $I(l_i; l_j; l_k)$, contains the value 1, then the outer region, $I(l_i; l_j | l_k)$, must contain the value 0, and vice versa. In addition, the total information content enclosed by each of the three circles is always 3 units, the number of points per line. Together, these facts constrain the possible three-circle Venn diagrams for subsets of the Fano-plane system, leaving only the two possibilities depicted in Figure 7.10.

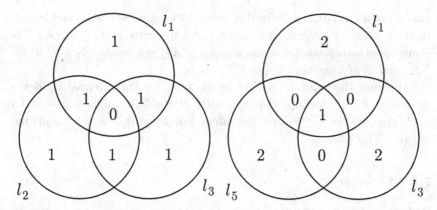

Fig. 7.10.   Illustrative examples of the two possible three-circle Venn diagrams for three-component subsets of the Fano-plane system. Note that the information in the central region is zero in one case but nonzero in the other.

The Fano plane illustrates a commonplace occurrence in complex systems: *higher-order structure that cannot be resolved into lower-order interrelationships.* In this case, we see there exists a variety of relationships among triples of components which cannot be inferred from considering pairs. The Fano-plane system does not fall within the particular special classes of systems studied as examples in Ref. 2, since not all subsets of the same size have the same information content.

We can deduce the complexity profile $C(k)$ of the Fano-plane system by counting points lying on k or more lines, or by computation using Eq. (7.5). If we take the latter approach, with 7 components there are $2^7 - 1 = 127$ nonempty subsets U for which we must find the information content $H(U)$. However, the high degree of symmetry simplifies the calculation for the different possible subsets of the component set. Because there exist 3 lines through any point, eliminating 1 line (component) can only reduce the number of lines through any point down to 2. So, the information content of any six-component set is still 7. To eliminate all lines through a point, we must remove at least three components. From such considerations, we can deduce $C(k)$ by explicit computation. Thus, the complexity profile is given by

$$C(k) = \begin{cases} 7, & 1 \leq k \leq 3, \\ 0, & 4 \leq k \leq 7. \end{cases} \qquad (7.25)$$

The result we have obtained by calculation from Eq. (7.5) can be obtained more directly and intuitively by recalling that, generally, $C(k)$ captures the amount of information contained in interrelationships of scale k and higher. In the context of incidence geometry, the complexity profile $C(k)$ has the geometrical interpretation as *the number of distinct points which lie at the intersection of k or more lines.*

Applying the same properties as we used for the minimal incidence geometry, we can deduce that the MUI of the Fano plane vanishes for descriptor lengths $y \geq 7$, that the integral of $M(y)$ is $7 \cdot 3 = 21$, and that $M(y) \leq 4$ for all y.

7.6. Summary

Reductionism and traditional statistical thinking are inadequate for the study of complex systems. Motivated by this shortcoming, we have developed an axiomatic framework for the ideas of information and scale, which we have shown ought to be regarded as complementary quantities. Characterizing structure and thereby quantifying complexity are important tasks for the progress of complex-systems science. Our formalism builds on the understanding that these concepts are ultimately related to the dependencies among components. The structure of a system can be expressed in terms of the amount of information associated to each possible set of components within that system. Two different yet related indices, the complexity profile and the Marginal Utility of Information, can summarize that structure. We have applied our multiscale formalism to examples from evolutionary biology, a fertile source of complex phenomena, and we have also seen that notions of scale and information are relevant to pure mathematics as well. Further extensions along both of these avenues are possible.[21]

Bibliography

1. W. James, *Pragmatism: A New Name for Some Old Ways of Thinking.* (Penguin (2000 reprint), 1907). URL `https://en.wikisource.org/wiki/Pragmatism:_A_New_Name_for_Some_Old_Ways_of_Thinking`.
2. B. Allen, B. C. Stacey, and Y. Bar-Yam, An information-theoretic formalism for multiscale structure in complex systems, *Preprint.* (2014). URL `http://necsi.edu/research/multiscale/`.
3. Y. Bar-Yam, A mathematical theory of strong emergence using multiscale variety, *Complexity.* **9**(6), 15–24, (2004).
4. Y. Bar-Yam, Multiscale complexity/entropy, *Advances in Complex Systems.* **7**, 47–63, (2004).

5. Y. Bar-Yam, Multiscale variety in complex systems, *Complexity.* **9**(4), 37–45, (2004).

6. S. Gheorghiu-Svirschevski and Y. Bar-Yam, Multiscale analysis of information correlations in an infinite-range, ferromagnetic Ising system, *Physical Review E.* **70**, 066115, (2004).

7. R. Metzler and Y. Bar-Yam, Multiscale complexity of correlated Gaussians, *Physical Review E.* **71**, 046114, (2005).

8. C. M. Caves. 'Is there a mutual information for three random variables?' [note to M. Nielsen]. http://info.phys.unm.edu/~caves/reports/reports.html, (1996).

9. S. Pruett-Jones and M. Pruett-Jones, Sexual competition and courtship disruptions: why do male bowerbirds destroy each other's bowers?, *Animal Behaviour.* **47**(3), 607–20, (1994). doi: 10.1006/anbe.1994.1084.

10. L. Gonick, The bowerbird's dilemma, *Discover.* **1994**(10), 138–9, (1994). URL http://www.msri.org/ext/larryg/pages/15.htm.

11. D. Harmon, M. De Aguiar, D. Chinellato, D. Braha, I. Epstein, and Y. Bar-Yam, Anticipating economic market crises using measures of collective panic, *PLOS One.* **10**(7), e0131871, (2015). doi: 10.1371/journal.pone.0131871. URL http://www.necsi.edu/research/economics/economicpanic.html.

12. M. A. M. de Aguiar and Y. Bar-Yam, The Moran model as a dynamical process on networks and its implications for neutral speciation, *Physical Review E.* **84**, 031901, (2011). doi: 10.1103/PhysRevE.84.031901.

13. B. Allen and M. A. Nowak, Games on graphs, *EMS Surveys in Mathematical Sciences.* **1**(1), 113–51, (2014). doi: 10.4171/EMSS/3.

14. B. Allen and M. A. Nowak, Games among relatives revisited, *Journal of Theoretical Biology.* **378**, 103–16, (2015). doi: 10.1016/j.jtbi.2015.04.031.

15. B. Allen and C. E. Tarnita, Measures of success in a class of evolutionary models with fixed population size and structure, *Journal of Mathematical Biology.* **68**(1–2), 109–43, (2014). doi: 10.1007/s00285-012-0622-x. URL http://scholar.princeton.edu/ctarnita/files/AxiomSuccessPublished.pdf.

16. P. E. Turner and L. Chao, Prisoner's dilemma in an RNA virus, *Nature.* **398**, 441–43, (1999). doi: 10.1038/18913.

17. D. Grieg and M. Travisano, The prisoner's dilemma and polymorphism in yeast *SUC* genes, *Proceedings of the Royal Society B.* **271**, S25–S26, (2004). doi: 10.1098/rsbl.2003.0083.

18. Y. Bar-Yam. Complexity of military conflict: Multiscale complex systems analysis of littoral warfare. Technical report, NECSI, (2003). URL http://www.necsi.edu/projects/yaneer/SSG_NECSI_3_Litt.pdf.

19. B. C. Stacey and Y. Bar-Yam. Principles of security: Human, cyber, and biological. Technical Report 2008-06-01, NECSI, (2008). URL http://www.necsi.edu/research/military/cyber/.

20. W. R. Tschinkel and E. O. Wilson, Scientific natural history: Telling the epics of nature, *BioScience.* **64**(5), 438–43, (2014). doi: 10.1093/biosci/biu033.

21. B. C. Stacey. *Multiscale Structure in Eco-Evolutionary Dynamics.* PhD thesis, Brandeis University, (2015). URL http://arxiv.org/abs/1509.02958.

Chapter 8

Bounds on the Kolmogorov Complexity Function for Infinite Words

Ludwig Staiger

Institut für Informatik, Martin-Luther-Universität
Halle-Wittenberg D06099 Halle (Saale), Germany

Abstract

The Kolmogorov complexity function of an infinite word ξ maps a natural number to the complexity $K(\xi \restriction n)$ of the n-length prefix of ξ. We investigate the maximally achievable complexity function if ξ is taken from a constructively describable set of infinite words. Here we are interested in linear upper bounds where the slope is the Hausdorff dimension of the set. As sets we consider Π_1-definable sets obtained by dilution and sets obtained from constructively describable infinite iterated function systems. In these cases, for a priori and monotone complexity, the upper bound coincides (up to an additive constant) with the lower bound, thus verifying the existence of oscillation-free maximally complex infinite words.

8.1. Introduction

The *Kolmogorov complexity* of a finite word w, $K(w)$, is, roughly speaking, the length of a shortest input (program) π for which a universal algorithm prints w.[1] For infinite words (ω-words) its asymptotic Kolmogorov complexity might be thought of as

$$\lim_{n \to \infty} \frac{K(\xi \restriction n)}{n}, \qquad (8.1)$$

where $\xi \restriction n$ denotes the prefix of length n of ξ.

Since this limit need not exist, the quantities

$$\underline{\kappa}(\xi) := \liminf_{n \to \infty} \frac{K(\xi \restriction n)}{n} \text{ and } \kappa(\xi) := \limsup_{n \to \infty} \frac{K(\xi \restriction n)}{n}.$$

were considered (see [1–4]).

---

[1] We require that w and π be words over the same finite (not necessarily binary) alphabet X of cardinality ≥ 2.

These limits are also known as constructive dimension or constructive strong dimension, respectively, introduced in [5] and [6], respectively. For more details about this see [7].

In these papers mainly the following approach was pursued: Given a set of infinite words (a so-called ω-language) F, bound the maximum possible Kolmogorov complexity $\underline{\kappa}(\xi)$ or $\kappa(\xi)$ for $\xi \in F$. In the present paper we are not only interested in this asymptotic case but also in bounds on the Kolmogorov complexity function $K(\xi \restriction n)$ of maximally complex infinite words (ω-words) $\xi \in F$.

In this asymptotic case, Ryabko [1] showed that for arbitrary ω-languages F the Hausdorff dimension, $\dim F$, is a lower bound to $\underline{\kappa}(F) := \sup\{\underline{\kappa}(\xi) : \xi \in F\}$, but Example 3.18 of [2] shows that already for simple computable ω-languages the Hausdorff dimension is not an upper bound to $\kappa(F) := \sup\{\kappa(\xi) : \xi \in F\}$ in general. In [2,4], we showed that for restricted classes of computably definable ω-languages F its Hausdorff dimension is also an upper bound to $\underline{\kappa}(F)$, thus giving a partial completion to Ryabko's lower bound.

The present paper focuses on a more detailed consideration of the Kolmogorov complexity function $K(\xi \restriction n)$ of infinite words in ω-languages F. Thus, in contrast to the asymptotic case where it is not relevant which kind of complexity is used, in the case of the Kolmogorov complexity function it matters which one of the complexities we consider.

Lower and upper bounds on the Kolmogorov complexity function are closely related to partial randomness. Partial randomness was investigated in the papers [8] and [9]. It is a linear generalization of the concept of random sequences (see the textbooks [10, 11]). The concept of partial randomness tries to specify sequences as random to some degree ε, $0 < \varepsilon \leq 1$, where the case $\varepsilon = 1$ coincides with usual randomness. In [8] and [9] several different generalizations of the concepts for partially random sequences were given.

A simple idea what could be an example of a binary $\frac{1}{2}$-random infinite word is the following. Take $\xi = x_1 x_2 \cdots x_i \cdots$ to be a (1-)random infinite word and dilute it by inserting zeros at every other position to obtain $\xi' = x_1 0 x_2 0 \cdots x_i 0 \cdots$ (cf. [2]).

As one observes easily the description complexity of the n-length prefix of a diluted word ξ' is about the complexity of the $\varepsilon \cdot n$-length prefix of the original word ξ where ε is the dilution coefficient (e.g. $\varepsilon = \frac{1}{2}$ in the above example). This was a motivation to consider the asymptotic complexity of an infinite word as the limit of the quotient of the complexity of the n-length prefix and the length n (see [1, 2]).

The aim of our paper is to survey several results concerning the Kolmogorov complexity function $K(\xi \restriction n)$ of infinite words contained in computably describable ω-languages. Here we investigate under which conditions certain simple construction principles yield ω-languages having maximally complex elements ξ with a linear complexity slope, that is, $K(\xi \restriction n) = \gamma \cdot n + O(1)$. As complexities we consider besides the usual plain complexity also variants like *a priori* complexity and monotone complexity. The construction principles presented here are dilution, e.g. as described above and infinite concatenation. Infinite concatenation is closely related to self-similarity. Instead of producing infinite words as products of finite ones (taken from a fixed language) one may regard this also as a process of shrinking the set of all infinite words successively by application of metric similitudes related to the words in the fixed language. This brings into play as a second dimension the similarity dimension known from Fractal Geometry. It turns out that under certain conditions – like in Fractal Geometry – similarity dimension and Hausdorff dimension coincide.

The paper is organized as follows. After introducing some notation, Cantor space and Hausdorff dimension in Section 8.3 introduces the plain, *a priori* and monotone complexity of finite words. The last part of this section presents the concept of lower bounding the slope of the Kolmogorov complexity functions by Hausdorff dimension. The fourth section deals with dilution. As a preparation we investigate expansive prefix-monotone functions (see [3]) and connect them to Hölder conditions known from Fractal geometry (see [12]). The last section is devoted to self-similar sets of infinite words and maximally achievable complexity functions of their elements. Here we present mainly results from [13] which show tight linear upper bounds on these complexity functions.

8.2. Notation and Preliminary Results

Next we introduce the notation used throughout the paper. By $\mathbb{N} = \{0, 1, 2, \ldots\}$ we denote the set of natural numbers, $\mathbb{Q}$ is the set of rational numbers and $\mathbb{R}_+$ is the set of non-negative reals. Let X, Y be alphabets of cardinality $|X|, |Y| \geq 2$. Usually we will denote the cardinality of X by $|X| = r$. X^* is the set (monoid) of words on X, including the *empty word* e, and X^ω is the set of infinite sequences (ω-words) over X. $|w|$ is the *length*[2] of the word $w \in X^*$ and $\mathbf{pref}(B)$ is the set of all finite prefixes of

---

[2]If there is no danger of confusion, for a set M we use the same notation $|M|$ to denote its *cardinality*.

strings in $B \subseteq X^* \cup X^\omega$. We shall abbreviate $w \in \mathbf{pref}(\eta)$ $(\eta \in X^* \cup X^\omega)$ by $w \sqsubseteq \eta$.

For $w \in X^*$ and $\eta \in X^* \cup X^\omega$ let $w \cdot \eta$ be their *concatenation*. This concatenation product extends in an obvious way to subsets $W \subseteq X^*$ and $B \subseteq X^* \cup X^\omega$. Thus X^n is the set of words of length n over X, and we use $X^{\leq c}$ as an abbreviation for $\{w : w \in X^* \wedge |w| \leq c\}$. For a language W let $W^* := \bigcup_{i \in \mathbb{N}} W^i$ be the *submonoid* of X^* generated by W, and $W^\omega := \{w_1 \cdots w_i \cdots : w_i \in W \setminus \{e\}\}$ is the set of infinite strings formed by concatenating words in W.

A language $V \subseteq X^*$ is called *prefix-free* provided for arbitrary $w, v \in V$ the relation $w \sqsubseteq v$ implies $w = v$.

We consider the set X^ω as a metric space (Cantor space) (X^ω, ρ) of all ω-words over the alphabet X, $|X| = r$, where the metric ρ is defined as follows.

$$\rho(\xi, \eta) := \inf\{r^{-|w|} : w \sqsubset \xi \wedge w \sqsubset \eta\}.$$

The open balls in this space are sets of the form $w \cdot X^\omega$, their diameter is $\mathrm{diam}(w \cdot X^\omega) = r^{-|w|}$, and $\mathcal{C}(F) := \{\xi : \mathbf{pref}(\xi) \subseteq \mathbf{pref}(F)\}$ is the *closure* of the set F (smallest closed subset containing F) in (X^ω, ρ).

Another way to describe ω-languages (sets of infinite words) by languages $W \subseteq X^*$ is the δ-limit $W^\delta := \{\xi : \xi \in X^\omega \wedge |\mathbf{pref}(\xi) \cap W| = \infty\}$ (see [14, 15]).

The mapping $\Phi_w(\xi) := w \cdot \xi$ is a contracting similitude if only $w \neq e$. Thus a language $W \subseteq X^* \setminus \{e\}$ defines a possibly infinite IFS (IIFS) in (X^ω, ρ). Its (maximal) *fixed point* is the ω-power W^ω of the language W. It was observed in [16] that, in general, the IIFS $(\Phi_w)_{w \in W}$ has a great variety of fixed points, that is, solutions of the equation $\bigcup_{w \in W} \Phi_w(F) = F$. All of these fixed points are contained in W^ω, and, except for the empty set $\emptyset$, their closure equals $\mathcal{C}(W^\omega)$, which is the *attractor* of $(\Phi_w)_{w \in W}$.

Next we recall the definition of the Hausdorff measure and Hausdorff dimension of a subset of (X^ω, ρ) (see [12, 17]). In the setting of languages and ω-languages this can be read as follows (see [2]). For $F \subseteq X^\omega$ and $0 \leq \alpha \leq 1$ the equation

$$\mathbb{L}_\alpha(F) := \lim_{l \to \infty} \inf\left\{\sum_{w \in W} r^{-\alpha \cdot |w|} : F \subseteq W \cdot X^\omega \wedge \forall w(w \in W \to |w| \geq l)\right\}$$
$$(8.2)$$

defines the α-dimensional metric outer measure on X^ω. The measure $\mathbb{L}_\alpha$ satisfies the following.

Corollary 8.1. *If $\mathbb{L}_\alpha(F) < \infty$ then $\mathbb{L}_{\alpha+\varepsilon}(F) = 0$ for all $\varepsilon > 0$.*

Then the *Hausdorff dimension* of F is defined as

$$\dim F := \sup\{\alpha : \alpha = 0 \vee \mathbb{L}_\alpha(F) = \infty\} = \inf\{\alpha : \mathbb{L}_\alpha(F) = 0\}.$$

It should be mentioned that dim is countably stable and shift invariant, that is,

$$\dim \bigcup_{i \in \mathbb{N}} F_i = \sup\{\dim F_i : i \in \mathbb{N}\} \quad \text{and} \quad \dim w \cdot F = \dim F. \qquad (8.3)$$

8.3.   Description Complexity of Finite Words

In this section we briefly recall the concept of description complexity of finite words. For a more comprehensive introduction see the textbooks [10, 11, 18] and the paper [19]. We start with plain complexity.

8.3.1.   *Plain complexity*

Recall that the plain complexity (Kolmogorov) of a string $w \in X^*$ w.r.t. a partial computable function $\varphi : X^* \to X^*$ is $K_\varphi(w) = \inf\{|\pi| : \varphi(\pi) = w\}$. It is well-known that there is a universal partial computable function $U : X^* \to X^*$ such that

$$K_U(w) \le K_\varphi(w) + c_\varphi$$

holds for all strings $w \in X^*$. Here the constant c_φ depends only on U and φ but not on the particular string $w \in X^*$. We will denote the complexity K_U simply by K.

Plain complexity satisfies the following property.

Proposition 8.2. *If $\varphi : X^* \to X^*$ is a partial computable function then there is a constant c such that*

$$K(\varphi(w)) \le K(w) + c \text{ for all } w \in X^*. \qquad (8.4)$$

We conclude this section by a generalization of Theorem 2.9 of [2].

Theorem 8.3. *Let $W \subseteq X^*$ or $X^* \setminus W$ be computably enumerable, ε, $0 < \varepsilon < 1$, be a computable real number and let $\sum_{i=0}^{m} |W \cap X^i| \le c \cdot r^{\varepsilon \cdot m}$ for some constant $c > 0$ and all $m \in \mathbb{N}$. Then*

$$\exists c' \Big(c' > 0 \wedge \forall w (w \in W \to K(w) \le \varepsilon \cdot |w| + c') \Big).$$

Proof. Let $c \le r^{\varepsilon \cdot m_0}$. Then $\sum_{i=0}^{m} |W \cap X^i| \le |X^l|$ for $l \ge \varepsilon \cdot (m + m_0)$.

If W is computably enumerable define a partial computable function $\varphi : X^* \to X^*$ as follows.

$$\varphi(\pi) := \text{the } \pi\text{th word of length} \leq \lceil \tfrac{|\pi|-m_0}{\varepsilon} \rceil \text{ in the enumeration of } W. \tag{8.5}$$

Here we interpret a word $\pi \in X^n$ as a number between 0 and $r^n - 1$.

If $w \in X^*$, $|w| = m$, choose the smallest $l \in \mathbb{N}$, $l_{\min}$ say, such that $|X^l| \geq |W \cap X^{\leq m}|$. This $l_{\min}$ satisfies $\lfloor \tfrac{l_{\min}}{\varepsilon} \rfloor - m_0 = m$ and thus $l_{\min} \leq \varepsilon \cdot (m + m_0) + 1$. By the above remark there is a $\pi \in X^{l_{\min}}$ such that $\varphi(\pi) = w$. Consequently, $K_\varphi(w) \leq l_{\min} \leq \varepsilon \cdot |w| + \varepsilon \cdot m_0 + 1$.

If $X^* \backslash W$ is computably enumerable define a partial computable function $\psi : X^* \to X^*$ as follows.

Set $m := \lfloor \tfrac{|\pi|}{\varepsilon} \rfloor - m_0$ and enumerate $X^* \backslash W$ until $\sum_{i=0}^m r^i - r^{|\pi|}$ elements of length $\leq m$ are enumerated. Then take from the rest the πth word of length $\leq m$ as $\psi(\pi)$.

If $w \in W$, $|w| = m$, again choose the smallest $l_{\min} \in \mathbb{N}$ such that $|X^{l_{\min}}| \geq \sum_{i=0}^m |W \cap X^i|$. Observe that in view of $|W \cap X^{\leq m}| \leq |X^{l_{\min}}|$ this rest contains $W \cap X^{\leq m}$. As in the above case when W was assumed to be computably enumerable we obtain that for $w \in W$ there is a π such that $\psi(\pi) = w$ and $|\pi| = l_{\min}$. Then the proof proceeds as above. $\qquad \Box$

8.3.2. *Monotone and a priori complexity*

In this section we consider *a priori* and monotone complexity. We derive some elementary properties needed in the sequel.

We start with the notion of a continuous (cylindrical) semi-measure on X^*. A *continuous (cylindrical) semi-measure* on X^* is a function $m : X^* \to \mathbb{R}_+$ which satisfies $m(e) \leq 1$ and $m(w) \geq \sum_{x \in X} m(wx)$, for $w \in X^*$. If there is no danger of confusion, in the sequel we will refer to continuous (semi-)measures simply as measures.

If $m(w) = \sum_{x \in X} m(wx)$ the function m is called a *measure*. A semi-measure m has the following property.

Proposition 8.4. *If* $C \subseteq w \cdot X^*$ *is prefix-free then* $m(w) \geq \sum_{v \in C} m(v)$.

Thus, if $C \subseteq X^*$ is infinite and prefix-free, for every $\varepsilon > 0$, there is a word $v \in C$ such that $m(v) < \varepsilon$.

A function $m : X^* \to \mathbb{R}_+$ is referred to as *left-computable* or *approximable from below*, provided the set $\{(w, q) : w \in X^* \land Q \in \mathbb{Q} \land 0 \leq q < m(w)\}$ is computably enumerable. *Right-computability* is defined analogously, and m is referred to as *computable* if it is right- and left-computable.

In [20] the existence of a universal left-computable semi-measure $\mathbf{M}$ is proved: There is a left-computable semi-measure $\mathbf{M}$ which satisfies

$$\exists c_m > 0 \, \forall w \in X^* : m(w) \leq c_m \cdot \mathbf{M}(w), \tag{8.6}$$

for all left-computable semi-measures m. $\mathbf{M}$ has the following property.

Proposition 8.5. *If $\xi \in X^\omega$ is a computable ω-word then there is a constant $c_\xi > 0$ such that $\mathbf{M}(w) \geq c_\xi$, for all $w \in \mathbf{pref}(\xi)$.*

Proof. If $\xi \in X^\omega$ is a computable ω-word then $\mathbf{pref}(\xi)$ is a computable subset of X^*. Construct a semi-measure m_ξ such that

$$m_\xi(w) = \begin{cases} 1 & \text{if } w \in \mathbf{pref}(\xi) \text{ and} \\ 0 & \text{otherwise.} \end{cases}$$

Then m_ξ is a computable cylindrical measure and the assertion follows from Eq. (8.6). □

8.3.2.1. *A priori complexity*

The *a priori complexity* of a word $w \in X^*$ is defined as

$$\mathrm{KA}(w) := \lceil - \log_{|X|} \mathbf{M}(w) \rceil. \tag{8.7}$$

The properties of the semi-measure $\mathbf{M}$ imply $\mathrm{KA}(w) \leq \mathrm{KA}(w \cdot v)$ and $\sum_{v \in C} |X|^{-\mathrm{KA}(v)} \leq \mathbf{M}(e)$ when $C \subseteq X^*$ is prefix-free.

From Proposition 8.5 we obtain that KA does not satisfy the property of usual plain or prefix complexity that for arbitrary partial computable functions $\varphi : X^* \to X^*$ it holds $\mathrm{KA}(\varphi(w)) \leq \mathrm{KA}(w) + O(1)$.

Example 8.6. Let $X = \{0, 1\}$ and define $\varphi(w) := w \cdot 1$. We consider the set $0^* = \mathbf{pref}(0^\omega) \subseteq X^*$. Then, in view of Proposition 8.5 $\mathrm{KA}(w) \leq c$ for all $w \in 0^*$ and some constant c. Now, the set $\varphi(0^*) = 0^* \cdot 1$ is prefix-free and according to Proposition 8.4 the complexity $\mathrm{KA}(\varphi(v))$, $v \in 0^* \cdot 1$, is unbounded. □

The aim of this section is to prove the fact that an property analogous to Proposition 8.2 holds for a subclass of partial computable functions.

Definition 8.7. A partial mapping $\varphi : \subseteq X^* \to Y^*$ is referred to as *prefix-monotone* (or *sequential*) provided $w, v \in \mathrm{dom}(\varphi)$ and $w \sqsubseteq v$ imply $\varphi(w) \sqsubseteq \varphi(v)$.

Let $\mathbf{U}_\varphi(w) := \mathrm{Min}_{\sqsubseteq}\{v : v \in \mathrm{dom}(\varphi) \wedge w \sqsubseteq \varphi(v)\}$ be the upper quasi-inverse for φ (see [14]). Here $\mathrm{Min}_{\sqsubseteq}W$ is the set of all minimal elements w.r.t. the prefix ordering $\sqsubseteq$ in the language $W \subseteq X^*$. Then $\mathbf{U}_\varphi$ has the following properties.

Lemma 8.8. *Let φ be a prefix-monotone partial function mapping $\mathrm{dom}(\varphi) \subseteq X^*$ to Y^*. Then for $w \in Y^*, y, y' \in Y$ and $y \neq y'$ the following hold.*

(1) $\mathbf{U}_\varphi(wy) \cap \mathbf{U}_\varphi(wy') = \emptyset$.

(2) $\bigcup_{y \in Y} \mathbf{U}_\varphi(wy)$ is prefix-free, and if $v' \in \mathbf{U}_\varphi(wy)$ then there is a $v \in \mathbf{U}_\varphi(w)$ such that $v \sqsubseteq v'$.

(3) If μ is a cylindrical semi-measure on X^* then $\mu(\mathbf{U}_\varphi(w)) \geq \sum_{y \in Y} \mu(\mathbf{U}_\varphi(wy))$.

Proof. (1) holds, since $wy, wy' \sqsubseteq \varphi(v)$ implies $y = y'$.

(2) According the definition of $\mathbf{U}_\varphi$ and to 1. $\bigcup_{y \in Y} \mathbf{U}_\varphi(wy)$ is a union of pairwise disjoint prefix-free sets. Assume $u \in \mathbf{U}_\varphi(wy)$ and $v \in \mathbf{U}_\varphi(wy')$ where $u \sqsubset v$. Then $y \neq y'$ and $wy, wy' \sqsubseteq \varphi(v)$ which is impossible.

(3) follows from 2. and Proposition 8.4. $\qquad\square$

Lemma 8.9. *If φ is a prefix-monotone mapping and μ is a semi-measure then $\mu_\varphi : X^* \to \mathbb{R}_+$ defined by the equation*

$$\mu_\varphi(w) := \sum_{v \in \mathbf{U}_\varphi(w)} \mu(v) \tag{8.8}$$

is also a semi-measure.

Proof. We use from Lemma 8.8 the fact that the sets $\mathbf{U}_\varphi(w)$ are prefix-free and that for $y, y' \in Y$, $y \neq y'$ no pair words $v \in \mathbf{U}_\varphi(wy)$ and $u \in \mathbf{U}_\varphi(wy')$ satisfies $v \sqsubseteq u$ or $u \sqsubseteq v$. According to Lemma 8.8(2) $\bigcup_{y \in Y} \mathbf{U}_\varphi(wy)$ is a disjoint union and prefix-free.

Moreover, for every $v' \in \mathbf{U}_\varphi(wy)$ there is a $v \in \mathbf{U}_\varphi(w)$ such that $v \sqsubseteq v'$, and since μ is a semi-measure, $\mu(v) \geq \sum_{v' \in C} \mu(v')$ whenever $C \subseteq v \cdot X^*$ is prefix-free.

Consequently,

$$\mu_\varphi(w) = \sum_{v \in \mathbf{U}_\varphi(w)} \mu(v) \geq \sum_{x \in X} \sum_{v \in \mathbf{U}_\varphi(wx)} = \sum_{x \in X} \mu_\varphi(wx). \qquad\square$$

This will allow us to prove the following.

Theorem 8.10. *If $\mu : X^* \to \mathbb{R}_+$ is a left computable semi-measure and $\varphi : X^* \to X^*$ is a partial computable prefix-monotone mapping then $\mu_\varphi : X^* \to \mathbb{R}_+$ defined by Eq. (8.8) is a left-computable semi-measure.*

Proof. By Lemma 8.9 μ_φ is a semi-measure. It remains to show that μ_φ is left computable.

To this end we start with a computable monotone approximation $m(w, s)$ of μ satisfying (cf. the proof of [11, Theorem 3.16.2])

(1) $\mu(w) \geq m(w, s + 1) \geq m(w, s)$ and
(2) for all $w \in X^*$, we have $m(w, t) \geq \sum_{x \in X} m(wx, t)$.

It is obvious that every mapping $m(\cdot, s)$ is a computable semi-measure.

Moreover, we consider the partially defined prefix-monotone mapping $\varphi_t(w) := \varphi(w)$ if $w \in \mathrm{dom}^{(t)}(\varphi)$ where $\mathrm{dom}^{(t)}(\varphi)$ is the set consisting of the first t elements in a computable enumeration of $\mathrm{dom}(\varphi)$.[3]

Define $\mu_\varphi^{(t)}(w) := \sum_{v \in \mathbf{U}_{\varphi_t}} m(v, t)$ as in Lemma 8.9. Then $\mu_\varphi^{(t)}$ is a computable semi-measure.

Since for every $v' \in \mathbf{U}_{\varphi_t}(w)$ there is a $v \sqsubseteq v'$ such that $v \in \mathbf{U}_{\varphi_{t+1}}(w)$ and t for $v \in \mathbf{U}_{\varphi_{t+1}}(w)$ the set $\{v' : v \sqsubseteq v' \wedge v' \in \mathbf{U}_{\varphi_t}(w)\}$ is prefix-free, we obtain $\mu_\varphi^{(t)}(w) \leq \mu_\varphi^{(t+1)}(w)$ for $t \in \mathbb{N}$ and $w \in X^*$ from Proposition 8.4.

Finally, we prove $\lim_{t \to \infty} \mu_\varphi^{(t)}(w) = \mu_\varphi(w) = \sum_{v \in \mathbf{U}_\varphi(w)} \mu(v)$. To this end choose, for $\varepsilon > 0$, a finite subset $\{v_1, \ldots, v_\ell\} \subseteq \mathbf{U}_\varphi(w)$ with $\sum_{i=1}^{\ell} \mu(v_i) \geq \mu_\varphi(w) - \varepsilon$ a $t \in \mathbb{N}$ such that $\{v_1, \ldots, v_\ell\} \subseteq \mathrm{dom}^{(t)}(\varphi)$ and $m(v_i, t) \geq \mu(v_i) - \varepsilon \cdot 2^{-i}$. Then, clearly, $\mu_\varphi^{(t)}(w) \geq \mu_\varphi(w) - 2\varepsilon$. $\square$

As a corollary we obtain the required inequality.

Corollary 8.11. *Let $\varphi : X^* \to X^*$ be a partial computable prefix-monotone function. Then there is a constant c_φ such that $\mathrm{KA}(\varphi(w)) \leq \mathrm{KA}(w) + c_\varphi$ for all $w \in X^*$.*

Proof. Let $\mu := \mathbf{M}_\varphi$. Then μ is a left-computable semi-measure. Thus $\mu(w) = \mathbf{M}(\varphi(w)) \leq c \cdot \mathbf{M}(w)$ for some constant c and all $w \in X^*$. $\square$

8.3.2.2.   *Monotone complexity*

In this section we introduce the monotone complexity along the lines of [21] (see [19]). To this end let $E \subseteq X^* \times X^*$ be a description mode (a computably

---

[3]If $|\mathrm{dom}(\varphi)| < t$ set $\mathrm{dom}^{(t)}(\varphi) := \mathrm{dom}(\varphi)$.

enumerable set) universal among all description modes which satisfy the condition.

$$(\pi, w), (\pi', v) \in E \wedge \pi \sqsubseteq \pi' \rightarrow w \sqsubseteq v \vee v \sqsubseteq w. \tag{8.9}$$

Then $K_E(w) := \inf\{|\pi| : \exists u(w \sqsubseteq u \wedge (\pi, u) \in E)\}$ is the *monotone complexity* of the word w. In the sequel we use the term $\mathrm{Km}(w)$.

Similar to KA the monotone complexity satisfies also an inequality involving partial computable sequential functions.

Corollary 8.12. *Let* $\varphi : X^* \rightarrow X^*$ *be a partial computable prefix-monotone function. Then there is a constant* c_φ *such that* $\mathrm{Km}(\varphi(w)) \leq \mathrm{Km}(w) + c_\varphi$ *for all* $w \in X^*$.

Proof. Define $E_\varphi := \{(\pi', \varphi(w)) : \exists \pi(\pi \sqsubseteq \pi' \wedge (\pi, w) \in E)\}$. Then E_φ is computably enumerable and satisfies Eq. (8.9).

Since E is a universal description mode satisfying Eq. (8.9), we have $K_{E_\varphi}(\varphi(w)) \leq K_E(w) + c_\varphi$. □

Like *a priori* complexity monotone complexity has also relations to semi-measures [19, 22].

Proposition 8.13. *Let* $\mu : X^* \rightarrow \mathbb{R}_+$ *be a computable continuous semi-measure. Then* $\mathrm{Km}(w) \leq -\log \mu(w) + O(1)$.

Finally we mention some relations between the complexities K, KA and Km (see [11, 19]).

$$KA(w) \leq \mathrm{Km}(w) + O(1), \tag{8.10}$$

$$|K_1(w) - K_2(w)| \leq O(\log |w|) \text{ for } K_i \in \{K, KA, \mathrm{Km}\} \tag{8.11}$$

8.3.3. *Bounds via Hausdorff dimension*

In this section two bounds on the Kolmogorov complexity function from [2] and [23] are presented. Both are lower bounds which illustrate the principle that large sets contain complex elements. The first bound is for plain complexity K. Moreover, we present an asymptotic upper bound for some computably describable ω-languages from [4].

Lemma 8.14 ([2, Lemma 3.13]). *Let* $F \subseteq X^\omega$ *and* $\mathbb{L}_\alpha(F) > 0$. *Then for every* $f : \mathbb{N} \rightarrow \mathbb{N}$ *satisfying* $\sum_{n \in \mathbb{N}} r^{-f(n)} < \infty$ *there is a* $\xi \in F$ *such that* $K(\xi \restriction n) \geq_{\mathrm{ae}} \alpha \cdot n - f(n)$.

As a consequence we obtain Ryabko's bound [1].

$$\underline{\kappa}(F) \geq \dim F. \tag{8.12}$$

For the next lemma we mention that $\sum_{v \in C} r^{-\mathrm{KA}(v)} \leq \mathbf{M}(e)$ for every prefix-free language $C \subseteq X^*$.

Lemma 8.15 ([23, Theorem 4.6]). *Let $F \subseteq X^\omega$ and $\mathbb{L}_\alpha(F) > r^{-c} \cdot \mathbf{M}(e)$. Then there is a $\xi \in F$ such that $\mathrm{KA}(\xi \upharpoonright n) \geq_{\mathrm{ae}} \alpha \cdot n - c$.*

Proof. It is readily seen that the set of infinite words not fulfilling the asserted inequality is the δ-limit of $W_c = \{w : \mathrm{KA}(w) \leq \alpha \cdot n - c\}$.

Let $V_m = \mathrm{Min}_{\sqsubseteq}(W_c \cap X^m \cdot X^*)$. Then V_m is prefix-free and $W_c^\delta \subseteq V_m X^\omega$ for all $m \in \mathbb{N}$. Consequently, $\mathbb{L}_\alpha(W_c^\delta) \leq \sum_{v \in V_m} r^{-\alpha \cdot |v|} \leq \sum_{v \in V_m} r^{-\mathrm{KA}(v)-c} \leq r^{-c} \cdot \mathbf{M}(e)$. Then the inequality $\mathbb{L}_\alpha(F) > \mathbb{L}_\alpha(W_c^\delta)$ shows the assertion $F \not\subseteq W_c^\delta$. $\square$

Proposition 8.16. *If $F_i \subseteq X^\omega$ and $X^* \setminus \mathbf{pref}(F_i)$ is computably enumerable then $\underline{\kappa}(\bigcup_{i \in \mathbb{N}} F_i) = \dim \bigcup_{i \in \mathbb{N}} F_i$.*

8.4.   Dilution

It is evident that inserting fixed letters, e.g. zeroes in a computable way into complex infinite words results in infinite words of lower complexity (see [24]). This effect – called dilution – was used to obtain partially random infinite words (see [2,9]). Here we are interested in the result of diluting sets of infinite words via computable mappings. Dilution can be seen locally as the application of a (computable) prefix-monotone mapping $\varphi : X^* \to X^*$ to (the prefixes of) an infinite word.

The extension of this mapping to a partial mapping $\overline{\varphi} : \mathrm{dom}(\overline{\varphi}) \to X^\omega$ is given by a limit process: $\overline{\varphi}(\xi)$ is the infinite word having infinitely many prefixes of the form $\varphi(w), w \sqsubseteq \xi$. If the set $\{\varphi(w) : w \sqsubseteq \xi\}$ is finite we say that $\overline{\varphi}(\xi)$ is not defined, otherwise the identity $\mathbf{pref}(\overline{\varphi}(\xi)) = \mathbf{pref}(\varphi(\mathbf{pref}(\xi)))$ holds.

Using the δ-limit this process can be formulated as $\{\overline{\varphi}(\xi)\} = \{\varphi(w) : w \sqsubseteq \xi\}^\delta$ (see [14]). The mapping $\overline{\varphi}(\xi)$, however, need not be continuous on $\mathrm{dom}(\overline{\varphi})$. For more detailed results on the extension $\overline{\varphi}$ of (partially defined) prefix-monotone mappings $\varphi : X^* \to Y^*$ see [14]. We mention here only the following:

$$\overline{\varphi}(W^\delta) \subseteq \varphi(W)^\delta. \tag{8.13}$$

Proof. It is readily seen that $\{\overline{\varphi}(\xi)\} = \varphi(V_\xi)^\delta$ where V_ξ is any infinite subset of $\mathbf{pref}(\xi)$. Thus choose $V_\xi := \mathbf{pref}(\xi) \cap W$ for $\xi \in W^\delta$. Then $\bigcup_{\xi \in W^\delta} V_\xi \subseteq W$ implies $\overline{\varphi}(W^\delta) = \bigcup_{\xi \in W^\delta} \{\overline{\varphi}(\xi)\} = \bigcup_{\xi \in W^\delta} \varphi(V_\xi)^\delta \subseteq \varphi(W)^\delta$.

$\square$

8.4.1. *Expansiveness and Hausdorff dimension*

In an addendum to Section 3 of [3] a relation between the growth of the quotient $\frac{|w|}{|\varphi(w)|}$ on the prefixes of $\xi \in F$ and the Hausdorff dimension of the image $\overline{\varphi}(F), F \subseteq X^\omega$, was established. To this end we introduce the following.

Definition 8.17 ([3, 25]). A prefix-monotone mapping $\varphi : X^* \to Y^*$ is called γ-*expansive* on $\xi \in X^\omega$ provided $\liminf_{w \to \xi} \frac{|\varphi(w)|}{|w|} \geq \gamma$.

We say that $\varphi : X^* \to Y^*$ is γ-*expansive* on $F \subseteq X^\omega$ if it is γ-expansive on every $\xi \in F$.

Remark 8.18. Cai and Hartmanis [3] used $\limsup_{w \to \xi} \frac{|w|}{|\varphi(w)|} = \gamma$ as defining equation. This results in replacing γ by γ^{-1}.

Then Conjecture C of [3] claims the following.

Claim 8.19. *Let* $\dim F = \alpha$ *and let* φ *satisfy* $\limsup_{w \to \xi} \frac{|w|}{|\varphi(w)|} = \gamma$ *for all* $\xi \in F$. *Then* $\dim \overline{\varphi}(F) \leq \alpha \cdot \gamma$.

Moreover, if φ *and* $\overline{\varphi}$ *are one-one functions then* $\dim \overline{\varphi}(F) = \alpha \cdot \gamma$.

We can prove here only the first part of this conjecture, for the second part we derive a counter-example.

Example 8.20. Let $X = \{0,1\}$, $m_i := \sum_{j=0}^{2i} j!$ a sequence of rapidly growing natural numbers and define the prefix-monotone mapping $\varphi : \{0,1\}^* \to \{0,1\}^*$ as follows ($w \in \{0,1\}^*, x \in \{0,1\}$).

$$\varphi(e) := e$$
$$\varphi(wx) := \begin{cases} \varphi(w)x & \text{if } |\varphi(w)x| \notin \{m_i : i \in \mathbb{N}\}, \text{ and} \\ \varphi(w)x0^{(2i+1)!} & \text{if } |\varphi(w)x| = m_i. \end{cases}$$

that is φ dilutes the input by inserting sparsely long blocks of zeros. Then $\overline{\varphi}(\{0,1\}^\omega) = \prod_{i=0}^\infty \{0,1\}^{(2i)!} \cdot 0^{(2i+1)!}$ whence $\dim \overline{\varphi}(\{0,1\}^\omega) = 0$ (cf. [2, Example 3.18]).

On the other hand, $\limsup_{w \to \xi} \frac{|w|}{|\varphi(w)|} \leq \gamma$ implies $\gamma \geq 1$.

$\square$

For a proof of the first part we derive several auxiliary lemmas.

Lemma 8.21. *Let $\varphi : X^* \to Y^*$ be a prefix-monotone mapping and let $V \subseteq X^*$. If $c > 0$ and for almost all $v \in V$ the relation $|v| \le c \cdot |\varphi(v)|$ holds then there is an $n_0 \in \mathbb{N}$ such that for all $n \ge n_0$ we have $\varphi(V \cap X^{\le c \cdot n}) \supseteq \varphi(V) \cap Y^{\le n}$.*

Proof. Let $v_0 \in V$ be a longest word such that $|v_0| > c \cdot |\varphi(v_0)|$, and let $n \ge \frac{|v_0|}{c}$.

Let $w \in \varphi(V)$ and $|w| \le n$. Then there is a $v \in V$ such that $\varphi(v) = w$. If $|v| \le |v_0|$ then $|v| \le c \cdot n$ and if $|v| > |v_0|$ then $|v| \le c \cdot |\varphi(v)| \le c \cdot n$. In both cases $w \in \varphi(V \cap X^{\le c \cdot n})$. $\qquad\square$

Moreover, we use the fact that the Hausdorff dimension of an ω-language $F \subseteq X^\omega$ can be described via the entropy of languages $W \subseteq X^*$. Here for a language $W \subseteq X^*$ we define its *entropy* as usual[4] (cf. [2, 26]).

$$\mathbf{H}_W = \limsup_{n \to \infty} \frac{\log_r(|W \cap X^n| + 1)}{n} = \limsup_{n \to \infty} \frac{\log_r(|W \cap X^{\le n}| + 1)}{n}. \qquad (8.14)$$

The following identity gives a relation between Hausdorff dimension and entropy of languages (see [2, Eq. (3.11)]).

$$\dim F = \inf\{\mathbf{H}_W : W \subseteq X^* \wedge W^\delta \supseteq F\}. \qquad (8.15)$$

Lemma 8.22. *Let $\varphi : X^* \to Y^*$ be a prefix-monotone mapping which satisfies $\varphi(V \cap X^{\le c \cdot n}) \supseteq \varphi(V) \cap Y^{\le n}$ for almost all $n \in \mathbb{N}$. Then $\mathbf{H}_{\varphi(V)} \le c \cdot \log_{|Y|}|X| \cdot \mathbf{H}_V$.*

Proof. If $\varphi(V)$ is finite the inequality is obvious. Let $\varphi(V)$ be infinite. Then using Lemma 8.21 we obtain

$$
\begin{aligned}
\mathbf{H}_{\varphi(V)} &= \limsup_{n \to \infty} \frac{\log_{|Y|}|\varphi(V) \cap Y^{\le n}|}{n} \le \limsup_{n \to \infty} \frac{\log_{|Y|}|\varphi(V \cap X^{\le c \cdot n})|}{n} \\
&\le \limsup_{n \to \infty} \frac{\log_{|Y|}|V \cap X^{\le c \cdot n}|}{n} = c \cdot \log_{|Y|}|X| \cdot \limsup_{n \to \infty} \frac{\log_{|X|}|V \cap X^{\le c \cdot n}|}{c \cdot n} \\
&\le c \cdot \log_{|Y|}|X| \cdot \limsup_{n \to \infty} \frac{\log_{|X|}|V \cap X^{\le n}|}{n}.
\end{aligned}
$$

$\qquad\square$

Then it holds (see also [3, Conjecture C] and [25, Proposition 1.19]).

Theorem 8.23. *Let $\varphi : X^* \to Y^*$ be a prefix-monotone mapping such that for all $\xi \in F$ the inequality $\liminf_{w \to \xi} \frac{|\varphi(w)|}{|w|} \ge \gamma$ is true. Then $\dim \overline{\varphi}(F) \le \frac{1}{\gamma} \cdot \log_{|Y|}|X| \cdot \dim F$.*

---

[4]The +1 in the numerator is added to avoid $\mathbf{H}_W = -\infty$ for finite W.

Proof. Using Eq. (8.15) it suffices to show that for every $c > \frac{1}{\gamma}$ the inequality $\dim \overline{\varphi}(F) \leq c \cdot \log_{|Y|} |X| \cdot \dim F$ holds true.

Let $W_c := \{w : \frac{|\varphi(w)|}{|w|} \geq \frac{1}{c}\}$. Since $c > \frac{1}{\gamma}$, for every $\xi \in F$ the set $\mathbf{pref}(\xi) \setminus W_c$ is finite. Now, consider a $W \subseteq X^*$ such that $W^\delta \supseteq F$. Then for $\zeta \in F$ the set $(\mathbf{pref}(\zeta) \cap W) \setminus W_c$ is finite, too, whereas $(\mathbf{pref}(\zeta) \cap W)$ is infinite. Hence $F \subseteq (W \cap W_c)^\delta$.

Now Eq. (8.13) implies $\overline{\varphi}(F) \subseteq \overline{\varphi}((W \cap W_c)^\delta) \subseteq \varphi(W \cap W_c)^\delta$.

Then Lemma 8.22 yields $\mathbf{H}_{\varphi(W \cap W_c)} \leq c \cdot \log_{|Y|} |X| \cdot \mathbf{H}_{W \cap W_c}$ and thus $\dim \overline{\varphi}(F) \leq \mathbf{H}_{\varphi(W \cap W_c)} \leq c \cdot \log_{|Y|} |X| \cdot \mathbf{H}_{W \cap W_c}$. Taking the infimum on the right hand side yields the assertion. $\qquad\square$

8.4.2. *Uniform dilution and Hölder condition*

Our Theorem 8.23 is closely related to the Hölder condition (see [12, Prop. 2.2 and 2.3]). Whereas Theorem 8.23 holds also for not necessarily continuous mappings $\overline{\varphi} : \mathrm{dom}(\overline{\varphi}) \to Y^\omega$ the Hölder condition implies continuity but yields also bounds on Hausdorff measure.

Theorem 8.24. *Let $F \subseteq X^\omega$ and $\Phi : F \to Y^\omega$ be a mapping such that for $c > 0$ and $\gamma > 0$ the condition $\forall \xi \forall \eta (\xi, \eta \in F \to \rho(\Phi(\xi), \Phi(\eta)) \leq c \cdot \rho(\xi, \eta)^\gamma)$ is fulfilled. Then $\mathbb{L}_{\alpha/\gamma}(\Phi(F)) \leq c^{\alpha/\gamma} \cdot \mathbb{L}_\alpha(F)$ for all $\alpha \in [0, 1]$.*

The condition $\exists c(c > 0 \wedge \forall \xi \forall \eta (\xi, \eta \in F \to \rho(\Phi(\xi), \Phi(\eta)) \leq c \cdot \rho(\xi, \eta)^\gamma))$ is also known as Hölder condition of exponent γ. The following lemma gives a connection between Hölder condition of exponent γ and γ-expansive prefix-monotone mappings.[5]

Lemma 8.25. *Let $F \subseteq X^\omega$ and $\Phi : F \to Y^\omega$ be a mapping such that for $c > 0$ and $\gamma > 0$ the condition $\forall \xi \, \forall \eta \, (\xi, \eta \in F \to \rho(\Phi(\xi), \Phi(\eta)) \leq c \cdot \rho(\xi, \eta)^\gamma)$ is fulfilled.*

Then there is a γ-expansive prefix-monotone mapping $\varphi : X^* \to Y^*$ such that $\overline{\varphi}(\xi) = \Phi(\xi)$ for all $\xi \in F$.

Proof. Let $m \in \mathbb{N}$ be chosen such that $c \leq r^m$. Then in view of $\rho(\Phi(w \cdot \xi), \Phi(w \cdot \eta)) \leq c \cdot r^{-\gamma \cdot |w|} \leq r^{-\gamma \cdot |w| + m}$ for $w \cdot \xi, w \cdot \eta \in F$, every $\zeta \in \Phi(w \cdot X^\omega \cap F)$ has the same word v_w of length $\lceil \gamma \cdot |w| - m \rceil$ as prefix. Thus define $\varphi(w) := v_w$ for $w \in \mathbf{pref}(F)$ and φ is γ-expansive. $\qquad\square$

From the proof of Lemma 8.25 we see that a Hölder condition of exponent γ puts a more restrictive requirement on a prefix-monotone mapping than

---

[5]This is also the reason why we altered the definition of [3].

the mere γ-expansiveness.

If, for some strictly increasing function $g : \mathbb{N} \to \mathbb{N}$, the prefix-monotone mapping $\varphi : X^* \to X^*$ satisfies the conditions $|\varphi(w)| = g(|w|)$ and for every $v \in \mathbf{pref}(\varphi(X^*))$ there are $w_v \in X^*$ and $x_v \in X$ such that

$$\varphi(w_v) \sqsubset v \sqsubseteq \varphi(w_v \cdot x_v) \wedge \forall y(y \in X \wedge y \neq x_v \to v \not\sqsubseteq \varphi(w_v \cdot y)) \quad (8.16)$$

then we call φ a *dilution function* with modulus g. If φ is a dilution function then $\overline{\varphi}$ is a one-to-one mapping. The condition of Eq. (8.16) is equivalent to the fact that for every $w \in X^*$ and every pair of letters $x, y \in X, x \neq y$, the words $\varphi(w \cdot x)$ and $\varphi(w \cdot y)$ differ in the letter immediately after $\varphi(w)$, in particular, the words $\varphi(w \cdot x)$ and $\varphi(w \cdot y)$ are incomparable w.r.t. $\sqsubseteq$.

As an illustration we consider the following dilution functions. Let $0 < \gamma < 1$ and define $g(n) := \lceil n/\gamma \rceil$ and $\varphi : X^* \to X^*$ via $(w \in X^*, x \in X)$

$$\varphi(e) := e, \text{ and}$$
$$\varphi(wx) := \varphi(w) \cdot x^{g(n+1)-g(n)}.$$

Since $g(n) - 1 < \frac{n}{\gamma} \leq g(n) < \frac{n}{\gamma} + 1$ and, consequently, $\gamma \cdot g(n) - \gamma < n \leq \gamma \cdot g(n) < n + \gamma$, the dilution function φ satisfies $\rho(\overline{\varphi}(\xi), \overline{\varphi}(\eta)) = r^{-g(n)} \iff \rho(\xi, \eta) = r^{-n}$, that is, $\overline{\varphi}$ and $\overline{\varphi}^{-1}$ satisfy the following Hölder conditions on X^ω or $\overline{\varphi}(X^\omega)$, respectively.

$$\rho(\overline{\varphi}(\xi), \overline{\varphi}(\eta)) \leq r^{-n/\gamma} = \rho(\xi, \eta)^{1/\gamma}, \text{ and}$$
$$\rho(\xi, \eta) \leq r^{-\gamma \cdot n + \gamma} = r^\gamma \cdot \rho(\overline{\varphi}(\xi), \overline{\varphi}(\eta))^\gamma.$$

As a consequence we obtain $\mathbb{L}_\gamma(\overline{\varphi}(X^\omega)) \leq \mathbb{L}_1(X^\omega) = 1 \leq r \cdot \mathbb{L}_\gamma(\overline{\varphi}(X^\omega))$ setting $\alpha = 1$ or $\alpha = \gamma$ in Theorem 8.24.

Thus we can state the following properties of computably diluted ω-languages.

Proposition 8.26. *Let $1 > \gamma > 0$ be a computable real number, $g(n) := \lceil \frac{n}{\gamma} \rceil$ and $\varphi : X^* \to X^*$ a computable dilution function with modulus g. Then $\dim \overline{\varphi}(X^\omega) = \gamma$, $\mathbb{L}_\gamma(\overline{\varphi}(X^\omega)) > 0$ and there is a $\xi \in \overline{\varphi}(X^\omega)$ such that $\mathrm{KA}(\xi \upharpoonright n) \geq \gamma \cdot n - c$ for some constant c.*

Moreover, the complexity functions $K(\xi \upharpoonright n)$, $K \in \{\mathrm{K}, \mathrm{KA}, \mathrm{Km}\}$, are bounded by $\gamma \cdot n + c'$ for some constant c'.

Proof. The first assertion is shown above, and the lower bound follows from Lemma 8.15.

Using Proposition 8.2 and Corollaries 8.11 and 8.12 we have the bounds $K(\varphi(w)) \leq \gamma \cdot |w| + c$. Since the differences $|\varphi(wx)| - |\varphi(w)|$ are bounded by $\frac{1+\gamma}{\gamma}$, the intermediate values $K(v), w \sqsubseteq v \sqsubseteq wx$, cannot exceed the value $\gamma \cdot |v|$ too much. $\square$

The most complex ω-words in $\overline{\varphi}(X^\omega)$ satisfy $|\text{KA}(\xi \upharpoonright n) - \gamma \cdot n| = O(1)$, a behavior which for $\gamma = 1$ characterizes random ω-words. Thus their behavior might be seen as a scaled down by factor γ randomness, a case of partial randomness. Partial randomness allows for oscillations above the slope $\gamma \cdot n$ (see [8, 9]). The partially random ω-words in $\overline{\varphi}(X^\omega)$, however, exhibit an oscillation-free randomness (see also [13, 27]).

8.5. Infinite Products and Self-Similarity

Another way to describe sets of infinite words is to concatenate them as infinite products with factors chosen from a given set of finite words V. This resembles one of defining a subset $F \subseteq X^\omega$ via the recurrence $F = V \cdot F$. Since the mappings $\Phi_w(\xi) := w \cdot \xi$ of the space (X^ω, ρ) into itself are metric similarities, the sets

$$F = V \cdot F = \bigcup_{w \in V} \Phi_w(F) \tag{8.17}$$

are self-similar sets in the space (X^ω, ρ). An equation like Eq. (8.17) may, however, have a great variety of solutions (see [16]). Fortunately, there is a unique maximal w.r.t. set inclusion solution which is the ω-power V^ω of the language V. Relations between self-similarity and ω-power languages were investigated e.g. in [8, 28, 29].

In this section we focus on iterated function systems $(\Phi_v)_{v \in V}$ where $V \subseteq X^*$ is prefix-free. Thus the mappings Φ_v map the space (X^ω, ρ) into pairwise disjoint parts. A special rôle here plays the similarity dimension of the system $(\Phi_v)_{v \in V}$. It turns out that it coincides with the Hausdorff dimension of the infinite product V^ω.

8.5.1. *Dimension and asymptotic complexity*

In this part we review some results on the Hausdorff dimension of ω-power languages and their asymptotic complexities.

We start with some results on the Hausdorff dimension of ω-power languages W^ω (see [2] or, in a more general setting [28]).

Eq. (6.2) of [2] yields the following connection between the entropy of W^* and the Hausdorff dimension of W^ω.

$$\dim W^\omega = \mathbf{H}_{W^*}. \tag{8.18}$$

Next we review some results on the upper and lower asymptotic complexity for ω-power languages W^ω.

Proposition 8.27 ([2, Lemma 6.7]). *If $W^* \subseteq X^*$ or its complement $X^* \setminus W^*$ are computably enumerable languages then $\underline{\kappa}(W^\omega) = \underline{\kappa}((W^*)^\delta) = \dim W^\omega$.*

Moreover W^ω contains always an ω-word of highest upper Kolmogorov complexity (see [2]) and, moreover, its closure $\mathcal{C}(W^\omega)$ in (X^ω, ρ) has the same upper bound (see Corollary 6.11 and Eq. (6.13) of [2]).

Lemma 8.28. $\kappa(W^\omega) = \kappa(\mathcal{C}(W^\omega)) = \max\{\kappa(\xi) : \xi \in W^\omega\} \geq \mathbf{H}_{\mathbf{pref}(W^*)}$.

For computably enumerable languages W we have the following exact bound.

Proposition 8.29 ([2, Proposition 6.15]). *If $W \subseteq X^*$ is computably enumerable then $\kappa(W^\omega) = \mathbf{H}_{\mathbf{pref}(W^*)}$.*

8.5.2. *Similarity dimension*

Let $V \subseteq X^*$ and $\mathbf{t}_1(V) := \sup\{t : t \geq 0 \wedge \sum_{i \in \mathbb{N}} |V \cap X^i| \cdot t^i \leq 1\}$. Then the parameter $-\log_r \mathbf{t}_1(V)$ is the *similarity dimension* of the system $(\Phi_v)_{v \in V}$. If V is finite $(\Phi_v)_{v \in V}$ is a usual IFS and $-\log_r \mathbf{t}_1(V)$ is the (unique) solution of the equation $\sum_{v \in V} r^{-\alpha \cdot |v|} = 1$, so one may replace $\leq$ by $=$ in the definition of $\mathbf{t}_1(V)$.

The value $\mathbf{t}_1(V)$ fulfils the following (see [2,26]).

Lemma 8.30. *If $V \subseteq X^*$ is prefix-free then $-\log_r \mathbf{t}_1(V) = \mathbf{H}_{V^*}$.*

Thus, for prefix-free languages $V \subseteq X^*$ Eq. (8.18) and Lemma 8.30 imply $\sum_{v \in V} r^{-\alpha \cdot |v|} \leq 1$ for $\alpha = \dim V^\omega$.

In [30] for certain ω-power languages a necessary and sufficient condition to be of non-null α-dimensional Hausdorff measure was derived. In this respect, for a language $V \subseteq X^*$, the *α-residue of V derived by w*, the value $\mathrm{res}_\alpha(V, w) := r^{-\alpha |w|} \sum_{v \in V} r^{-\alpha |v|} = \sum_{wv \in V} r^{-\alpha |v|}$ for $w \in \mathbf{pref}(V)$ plays a special rôle.

Theorem 8.31 ([30]). *Let $V \subseteq X^*$ be prefix-free and $\sum_{v \in V} r^{-\alpha |v|} = 1$. Then $\alpha = \dim V^\omega$, and, moreover $\mathbb{L}_\alpha(V^\omega) > 0$ if and only if the α-residues $\mathrm{res}_\alpha(V, w)$ of V are bounded from above.*

Thus in view of Lemma 8.15 such V^ω contain sequences ξ having a linear lower complexity bound $\alpha \cdot n - c$ for *a priori* complexity. It is interesting to observe that bounding the α-residues of V from below yields a linear upper bound on the slope α on the complexity of ω-words in the closure $\mathcal{C}(V^\omega)$.

8.5.3. Plain complexity

First we show that bounding the α-residues of V from below results in an upper bound on the number of prefixes of V^ω. Then we apply Theorem 8.3 to computably enumerable prefix-free languages V to show that a positive lower bound to the α-residues of V implies a linear upper bound on the complexity function $K(\xi \restriction n)$ for $\xi \in \mathcal{C}(V^\omega)$.

Lemma 8.32. *Let $V \subseteq X^*$ be prefix-free, $\sum_{v \in V} r^{-\alpha|v|} \leq 1$ and $\sum_{wv \in V} r^{-\alpha|v|} \geq c' > 0$ for all $w \in \mathbf{pref}(V)$. Then $|\mathbf{pref}(V^*) \cap X^l| \leq c \cdot r^{\alpha \cdot l}$ for some constant $c > 0$ and all $l \in \mathbb{N}$.*

Proof. We have $\mathbf{pref}(V^*) \cap X^l = \mathbf{pref}(V^l) \cap X^l$ for $l \in \mathbb{N}$.

Let $a := \sum_{v \in V} r^{-\alpha|v|}$. Since V is prefix-free, $a^l = \sum_{v \in V^l} r^{-\alpha|v|} = \sum_{|w|=l, w \in \mathbf{pref}(V^*)} \left(r^{-\alpha \cdot l} \cdot \sum_{wv \in V^l} r^{-\alpha|v|} \right)$.

If $w = v_1 \cdots v_{i_w - 1} \cdot w'$ with $v_j \in V$ and $w' \in \mathbf{pref}(V)$ then $\{v : wv \in V^l\} \supseteq \{v : w'v \in V^{l-i_w+1}\} \supseteq \{v : w'v \in V\} \cdot V^{l-i_w}$.

Thus, $\sum_{wv \in V^l} r^{-\alpha|v|} \geq \sum_{w'v \in V} r^{-\alpha|v|} \cdot a^{l-i_w} \geq c' \cdot a^{l-i_w} \geq c' \cdot a^l$ and we obtain $a^l \geq r^{-\alpha \cdot l} \cdot |\mathbf{pref}(V^*) \cap X^l| \cdot c' \cdot a^l$ which proves our assertion. $\square$

Now, the fact that $\mathbf{pref}(V^*)$ is computably enumerable if only V is computably enumerable yields our result.

Lemma 8.33 ([13, Lemma 7]). *Let $V \subseteq X^*$ be a computably enumerable and prefix-free, α be right-computable and $\sum_{v \in V} r^{-\alpha \cdot |v|} = a \leq 1$.*

If there is a $c > 0$ such that $\sum_{wv \in V} r^{-\alpha \cdot |v|} \geq c$ for all $w \in \mathbf{pref}(V)$ then there is a constant c such that

$$K(\xi \restriction n) \leq \alpha \cdot n + c \text{ for every } \xi \in \mathcal{C}(V^\omega).$$

8.5.4. A priori and monotone complexity

Lemma 8.32, however, is not applicable to *a priori* and monotone complexity. To this end we construct, for prefix-free languages $V \subseteq X^*$ and values $\alpha \in \mathbb{R}_+$ such that $\sum_{v \in V} r^{-\alpha \cdot |v|} \leq 1$ a continuous semi-measure μ satisfying $\mu(w) = r^{-\alpha \cdot |w|}$ for $w \in V^*$ (see the proof of [27, Lemma 3.9]).

Proposition 8.34. *Let $V \subseteq X^*$ be a prefix-free language, $\alpha > 0$ and*

$\sum_{v \in V} r^{-\alpha \cdot |v|} \leq 1$. Then $\mu : X^* \to \mathbb{R}_+$ where

$$\mu(w) = \begin{cases} 0 & \text{if } w \notin \mathbf{pref}(V^*), \\ r^{-\alpha \cdot |w|} & \text{if } w \in V^*, \\ \displaystyle\sum_{wv \in V} r^{-\alpha|wv|} & \text{if } w \in \mathbf{pref}(V) \setminus \{e\}, \\ \mu(u) \cdot \mu(v) & \text{if } w = u \cdot v, \\ & \text{with } u \in V \cdot V^* \wedge v \in \mathbf{pref}(V) \setminus V \end{cases} \qquad (8.19)$$

is a continuous semi-measure on X^*. If, moreover, $\sum_{v \in V} r^{-\alpha \cdot |v|} = 1$ then μ is a continuous measure.

Proof. We have to show that $\mu(w) \geq \sum_{x \in X} \mu(wx)$. We prove this by induction.

The equation $\mu(w) \geq \sum_{x \in X} \mu(wx)$ for $w \in \mathbf{pref}(V) \setminus V$ follows directly from the requirement $\sum_{v \in V} r^{-\alpha \cdot |v|} \leq 1$ and the third line of the construction. Observe that $\mu(e) > \sum_{x \in X} \mu(x) = \sum_{v \in V} r^{-\alpha \cdot |v|}$ if $\sum_{v \in V} r^{-\alpha \cdot |v|} < 1$.

Let $w \in V \cdot \mathbf{pref}(V^*)$. Since V is prefix-free, the decomposition in the last line of the construction is unique. Thus $w = u \cdot v$ where $u \in V \cdot V^*$ and $v \in \mathbf{pref}(V) \setminus V$. Consequently, $\mu(w) = \mu(u) \cdot \mu(v) \geq \mu(u) \cdot \sum_{x \in X} \mu(vx) = \sum_{x \in X} \mu(wx)$.

Finally, if $w \notin V \cdot \mathbf{pref}(V^*) \cup \mathbf{pref}(V) = \mathbf{pref}(V^*)$ then also $wx \notin \mathbf{pref}(V^*)$, and the inequality is trivially satisfied.

If $\sum_{v \in V} r^{-\alpha \cdot |v|} = 1$ then $\mu(w) = \sum_{x \in X} \mu(wx)$ for $w \in \mathbf{pref}(V) \setminus V$ and the identity $\mu(w) = \sum_{x \in X} \mu(wx)$ follows by induction. $\qquad \square$

Now we can prove the announced bounds.

Lemma 8.35 ([13, Lemma 3]). *Let $V \subseteq X^*$ be a computably enumerable prefix-free language. Let α be right-computable such that $\sum_{v \in V} r^{-\alpha \cdot |v|} = a \leq 1$ and the α-residues $\mathrm{res}_\alpha(V, w) := \sum_{wv \in V} r^{-\alpha|v|}$ of V derived by $w \in \mathbf{pref}(V)$ are bounded from below. Then there is a constant c such that for every $\xi \in \mathcal{C}(V^\omega)$*

$$\mathrm{KA}(\xi \restriction n) \leq \alpha \cdot n + c.$$

Proof. First we show that the semi-measure μ constructed in the previous proposition is left-computable.

To show that μ is left-computable we successively approximate the value $\mu(w)$ from below. Let V_i be the set of the first i elements in the enumeration of V and α_i the ith approximation of α from the right. We start with $\mu^{(j)}(e) = 1$ for $j > 0$ and $\mu^{(0)}(w) := 0$ for $w \neq e$. Suppose that the jth approximation $\mu^{(j)}$ for all words shorter than w is already computed. If there is a $v \in V_j$ with $w = v \cdot w'$, $w' \neq e$, then $\mu^{(j)}(w')$ is defined and we set $\mu^{(j)}(w) = \mu^{(j)}(v) \cdot \mu^{(j)}(w')$. Otherwise, if $w \in \mathbf{pref}(V_j)$ we set $\mu^{(j)}(w) = \sum_{v \in V_j \wedge w \sqsubseteq v} r^{-\alpha_j \cdot |v|}$. If $w \notin \mathbf{pref}(V_j) \cup V_j \cdot X^*$ then $\mu^{(j)}(w) = 0$.

From the construction in Proposition 8.34 we obtain that $\mu(w) = r^{-\alpha|u|} \cdot \sum_{vv' \in V} r^{-\alpha|vv'|} = r^{-\alpha|w|} \cdot \mathrm{res}_\alpha(V, v)$ when $w = u \cdot v$ is the unique decomposition of $w \in \mathbf{pref}(V^*)$ into factors $u \in V^*$ and $v \in \mathbf{pref}(V) \setminus V$.

Let $c_{\inf} := \inf \{\mathrm{res}_\alpha(V, v) : v \in \mathbf{pref}(V)\}$. Since μ is a left-computable semi-measure, the following inequality holds true.

$$\mathbf{M}(w) \cdot c_\mu \geq \mu(w) \geq r^{-\alpha|w|} \cdot c_{\inf}.$$

Taking the negative logarithm on both sides of the inequality we obtain $\mathrm{KA}(w) \leq \alpha \cdot |w| + \log \frac{c_\mu}{c_{\inf}}$ for every $w \in \mathbf{pref}(V^*)$. $\qquad\square$

The following example shows, that in Lemma 8.35 we cannot omit the condition that the α-residues are bounded from below. To this end we use a computable prefix-free language constructed in Example (6.4) of [2].

Example 8.36. Let X$=\{0,1\}$ and consider $W := \bigcup_{i \in \mathbb{N}} 0^{i+1} \cdot 1 \cdot X^{i+1} \cdot 0^{4 \cdot i + 3}$. The language W is a prefix-free. Its ω-power, W^ω, satisfies $\alpha = \dim W^\omega = \dim \mathcal{C}(W^\omega) = \frac{1}{3}$ and $\mathbb{L}_\alpha(W^\omega) = \mathbb{L}_\alpha(\mathcal{C}(W^\omega))$. For every $w \in \bigcup_{i \in \mathbb{N}} 0^{i+1} \cdot 1 \cdot X^{i+1}$ we have $W \cap w \cdot X^* = w \cdot \{0^{4 \cdot i + 3}\}$. Thus $\sum_{wv \in W} r^{-\alpha \cdot |v|} = r^{-\alpha \cdot (4 \cdot i + 3)}$ and, consequently, $\inf\{\sum_{wv \in W} r^{-\alpha \cdot |v|} : w \in \mathbf{pref}(W)\} = 0$.

Since $\mathbf{pref}(W) \supseteq \bigcup_{i \in \mathbb{N}} 0^{i+1} \cdot 1 \cdot X^{i+1}$, we have $\mathbf{H}_{\mathbf{pref}(W)^*} \geq \frac{1}{2}$. Now Proposition 8.29 shows $\sup_{\xi \in W^\omega} \limsup_{n \to \infty} \frac{\mathrm{KA}(\xi \upharpoonright n)}{n} = \kappa(W^\omega) \geq \frac{1}{2} > \frac{1}{3} = \dim W^\omega$. $\qquad\square$

In connection with Theorem 8.31 our Lemma 8.35 yields a sufficient condition for ω-powers V^ω to contain ω-words ξ satisfying $|\mathrm{KA}(\xi \upharpoonright n) - \alpha \cdot n| = O(1)$.

Corollary 8.37. *Let $V \subseteq X^*$ be a computably enumerable prefix-free language and α right-computable such that $\sum_{v \in V} r^{-\alpha \cdot |v|} = 1$ and the α-residues $\mathrm{res}_\alpha(V, w)$ of V derived by $w \in \mathbf{pref}(V)$ are bounded from above and below. Then there is a $\xi \in V^\omega$ such that $|\mathrm{KA}(\xi \upharpoonright n) - \alpha \cdot n| = O(1)$.*

The results of Section 3.2 of [27] show that Corollary 8.37 is valid for prefix-free languages definable by finite automata. The subsequent example verifies that there are also non-regular prefix-free languages which satisfy the hypotheses of Corollary 8.37.

Example 8.38. Let $X = \{0,1\}$ and consider the Łukasiewicz language L defined by the identity $L = 0 \cup 1 \cdot L^2$. This language is prefix-free and Kuich [26] showed that $\sum_{w \in L} 2^{-|w|} = 1$. Thus the language V defined by $V = 00 \cup 11 \cdot V^2$ is also prefix-free and satisfies $\sum_{v \in V} 2^{-\frac{1}{2} \cdot |w|} = 1$. By induction one shows that for $v \in \mathbf{pref}(V)$ we have $V/v = w' \cdot V^k$ for suitable $k \in \mathbb{N}$ and $|w'| \leq 1$. Therefore the α-residues of V derived by $v \in \mathbf{pref}(V)$ are bounded from above and below. $\qquad\square$

For the monotone complexity Km a result similar to Lemma 8.35 can be obtained for a smaller class of ω-languages. We start with an auxiliary result.

Proposition 8.39. *Let* $V \subseteq X^*$ *be computably enumerable.*

(1) If $\sum_{v \in V} r^{-\alpha|v|} = 1$ *then* α *is left-computable.*
(2) If $\sum_{v \in V} r^{-\alpha|v|} = 1$ *and* α *is right-computable then* V *is computable.*

Proof. The proof of part 1 is obvious. To prove part 2 we present an algorithm to decide whether a word w is in V or not.

Let V_j be the set of the first j elements in the enumeration of V and α_j the jth approximation of α from the right.

```
Input w
j := 0
  repeat
     j := j + 1
     if w ∈ Vⱼ then accept and exit
  until r^(-αⱼ|w|) + ∑_(v∈Vⱼ) r^(-αⱼ|v|) > 1
reject
```

If $w \notin V$ then the repeat until loop terminates as soon as $\sum_{v \in V_j} r^{-\alpha_j|v|} > 1 - r^{-\alpha_j|w|} \geq 1 - r^{-\alpha|w|}$ because $\sum_{v \in V_j} r^{-\alpha_j|v|} \to 1$ for $j \to \infty$. $\qquad\square$

Now we can prove our result on monotone complexity.

Lemma 8.40 ([13, Lemma 4]). *Let* $V \subseteq X^*$ *be a computably enumerable prefix-free language. If* α *is right-computable such that* $\sum_{v \in V} r^{-\alpha \cdot |v|} = 1$ *and the* α-*residues* $\mathrm{res}_\alpha(V, w)$ *derived by* $w \in \mathbf{pref}(V)$ *are bounded from below then there is a constant* c *such that* $\mathrm{Km}(\xi \upharpoonright n) \leq \alpha \cdot n + c$ *for every* $\xi \in \mathcal{C}(V^\omega)$.

Proof. We construct μ as in Proposition 8.34. Then $\sum_{v \in V} r^{-\alpha \cdot |v|} = 1$ implies that μ is a measure and Lemma 8.35 shows that μ is left-computable.

Because of Proposition 8.39 we can assume that α is a computable real number and V is computable. Then for every $v \in V^*$ the number $\mu(v) =$ is computable. Since V is a computable prefix-free language, for every $w \in X^*$ we can compute the unique decomposition $w = v \cdot w'$ with $v \in V^*$ and $w' \notin V \cdot X^*$. Now

$$\mu(w) = \mu(v) \cdot \left(1 - \sum_{v' \in V \wedge w \not\sqsubseteq vv'} r^{-\alpha |v'|} \right)$$

shows that μ is also right-computable. If $w' \notin \mathbf{pref}(V)$ then the last factor is zero.

Again let $c_{\inf} := \inf \left\{ \sum_{wv \in V} r^{-\alpha \cdot |v|} : w \in \mathbf{pref}(V) \right\}$. In view of Proposition 8.13 we get the bound

$$\mathrm{Km}(w) \leq - \log \mu(w) + c_\mu \leq \alpha \cdot |w| + c_\mu - \log c_{\inf}$$

for every $w \in \mathbf{pref}(V^*)$. $\qquad\square$

As for Lemma 8.35 we obtain a sufficient condition for ω-powers V^ω to contain ω-words ξ satisfying $|\mathrm{Km}(\xi \upharpoonright n) - \alpha \cdot n| = O(1)$.

Corollary 8.41. *Let $V \subseteq X^*$ be a computably enumerable prefix-free language and α right-computable such that $\sum_{v \in V} r^{-\alpha \cdot |v|} = 1$ and the α-residues $\mathrm{res}_\alpha(V, w)$ of V derived by $w \in \mathbf{pref}(V)$ are bounded from above and below. Then there is a $\xi \in V^\omega$ such that $|\mathrm{Km}(\xi \upharpoonright n) - \alpha \cdot n| = O(1)$.*

8.6. Concluding Remark

Proposition 8.26 and the Lemmas 8.35 and 8.40 show that in certain computably describable ω-languages the strings of maximal complexity have (up to an additive constant) linear oscillation-free complexity functions w.r.t. a priori and monotone complexity. Though in the case of plain complexity we have also linear upper bounds Theorems 4.8 and 4.12 of [2] show that maximally complex infinite strings in ω-languages definable by finite automata (in particular, those of the form V^ω with V definable by a finite automaton) exhibit complexity oscillations similar to random infinite strings (cf. Theorem 6.10 of [10] or Lemma 3.11.1 in [11]).

For prefix complexity (see [10, Section 4.2] or [11, Section 3.5]), however, it seems to be not as simple to obtain linear upper bounds on the complexity function (see [31, 32]) let alone to detect an oscillation-free behavior as mentioned above. In fact, Theorem 5 of [33] shows that the oscillation-free behavior w.r.t. to prefix complexity differs substantially from the one of a priori complexity.

Bibliography

[1] B. Y. Ryabko, Noise-free coding of combinatorial sources, Hausdorff dimension and Kolmogorov complexity, *Problemy Peredachi Informatsii* **22**, 3, pp. 16–26 (1986).

[2] L. Staiger, Kolmogorov complexity and Hausdorff dimension, *Inform. and Comput.* **103**, 2, pp. 159–194 (1993), doi:10.1006/inco.1993.1017, http://dx.doi.org/10.1006/inco.1993.1017.

[3] J.-Y. Cai and J. Hartmanis, On Hausdorff and topological dimensions of the Kolmogorov complexity of the real line, *J. Comput. System Sci.* **49**, 3, pp. 605–619 (1994), doi:10.1016/S0022-0000(05)80073-X.

[4] L. Staiger, A tight upper bound on Kolmogorov complexity and uniformly optimal prediction, *Theory Comput. Syst.* **31**, 3, pp. 215–229 (1998), doi:10.1007/s002240000086, http://dx.doi.org/10.1007/s002240000086.

[5] J. H. Lutz, The dimensions of individual strings and sequences, *Inform. Comput.* **187**, 1, pp. 49–79 (2003).

[6] K. B. Athreya, J. M. Hitchcock, J. H. Lutz and E. Mayordomo, Effective strong dimension in algorithmic information and computational complexity, *SIAM J. Comput.* **37**, 3, pp. 671–705 (2007), doi:10.1137/S0097539703446912, http://dx.doi.org/10.1137/S0097539703446912.

[7] L. Staiger, Constructive dimension equals Kolmogorov complexity, *Inform. Process. Lett.* **93**, 3, pp. 149–153 (2005), doi:10.1016/j.ipl.2004.09.023, http://dx.doi.org/10.1016/j.ipl.2004.09.023.

[8] K. Tadaki, A generalization of Chaitin's halting probability Ω and halting self-similar sets, *Hokkaido Math. J.* **31**, 1, pp. 219–253 (2002).

[9] C. S. Calude, L. Staiger and S. A. Terwijn, On partial randomness, *Ann. Pure Appl. Logic* **138**, 1-3, pp. 20–30 (2006), doi:10.1016/j.apal.2005.06.004, http://dx.doi.org/10.1016/j.apal.2005.06.004.

[10] C. S. Calude, *Information and Randomness*, 2nd edn., Texts in Theoretical Computer Science. An EATCS Series. Springer-Verlag, Berlin (2002), ISBN 3-540-43466-6, doi:10.1007/978-3-662-04978-5, http://dx.doi.org/10.1007/978-3-662-04978-5, an algorithmic perspective, With forewords by Gregory J. Chaitin and Arto Salomaa.

[11] R. G. Downey and D. R. Hirschfeldt, *Algorithmic Randomness and Complexity*, Theory and Applications of Computability. Springer, New York (2010), ISBN 978-0-387-95567-4, doi:10.1007/978-0-387-68441-3, http://dx.doi.org/10.1007/978-0-387-68441-3.

[12] K. Falconer, *Fractal Geometry*. John Wiley & Sons Ltd., Chichester (1990), ISBN 0-471-92287-0.

[13] J. Mielke and L. Staiger, On oscillation-free ε-random sequences II, in A. Bauer, P. Hertling and K.-I. Ko (eds.), *Computability and Complexity in Analysis, Dagstuhl Seminar Proceedings*, Vol. 09003. Schloss Dagstuhl - Leibniz-Zentrum für Informatik, Germany (2009), http://drops.dagstuhl.de/opus/volltexte/2009/2269.

[14] L. Staiger, Sequential mappings of ω-languages, *RAIRO Inform. Théor. Appl.* **21**, 2, pp. 147–173 (1987).

[15] L. Staiger, The Kolmogorov complexity of infinite words, *Theoret. Comput. Sci.* **383**, 2-3, pp. 187–199 (2007), doi:10.1016/j.tcs.2007.04.013, http://dx.doi.org/10.1016/j.tcs.2007.04.013.

[16] L. Staiger, On ω-power languages, in G. Păun and A. Salomaa (eds.), *New Trends in Formal Languages*, Lecture Notes in Computer Science, Vol. 1218. Springer-Verlag, Berlin, ISBN 3-540-62844-4, pp. 377–394 (1997), ISBN 3-540-62844-4, control, cooperation, and combinatorics.

[17] G. Edgar, *Measure, topology, and fractal geometry*, 2nd edn., Undergraduate Texts in Mathematics. Springer, New York (2008), ISBN 978-0-387-74748-4, doi:10.1007/978-0-387-74749-1, http://dx.doi.org/10.1007/978-0-387-74749-1.

[18] A. Nies, *Computability and Randomness*, Oxford Logic Guides, Vol. 51. Oxford University Press, Oxford (2009), ISBN 978-0-19-923076-1, doi:10.1093/acprof:oso/9780199230761.001.0001, http://dx.doi.org/10.1093/acprof:oso/9780199230761.001.0001.

[19] V. A. Uspensky and A. Shen, Relations between varieties of Kolmogorov complexities, *Math. Systems Theory* **29**, 3, pp. 271–292 (1996), doi:10.1007/BF01201280, http://dx.doi.org/10.1007/BF01201280.

[20] A. K. Zvonkin and L. A. Levin, The complexity of finite objects and the basing of the concepts of information and randomness on the theory of algorithms, *Uspekhi Mat. Nauk* **25**, 6(156), pp. 85–127 (1970).

[21] A. K. Shen', Algorithmic variants of the notion of entropy, *Dokl. Akad. Nauk SSSR* **276**, 3, pp. 563–566 (1984).

[22] V. A. Uspenskiĭ, A. L. Semenov and A. K. Shen', Can an (individual) sequence of zeros and ones be random? *Uspekhi Mat. Nauk* **45**, 1(271), pp. 105–162 (1990), doi:10.1070/RM1990v045n01ABEH002321, http://dx.doi.org/10.1070/RM1990v045n01ABEH002321.

[23] J. Mielke, Refined bounds on Kolmogorov complexity for ω-languages, in [34], pp. 181–189 (2008), doi:10.1016/j.entcs.2008.12.016, http://dx.doi.org/10.1016/j.entcs.2008.12.016, Hagen, August 21–24, 2008.

[24] R. P. Daley, The extent and density of sequences within the minimal-program complexity hierarchies, *J. Comput. System Sci.* **9**, pp. 151–163 (1974).

[25] J. Reimann, *Computability and Fractal Dimension*, Ph.D. thesis, Ruprecht-Karls-Universität Heidelberg (2004).

[26] W. Kuich, On the entropy of context-free languages, *Inform. Control* **16**, pp. 173–200 (1970).

[27] L. Staiger, On oscillation-free ε-random sequences, in Ref. 34, pp. 287–297 (2008), doi:10.1016/j.entcs.2008.12.024, http://dx.doi.org/10.1016/j.entcs.2008.12.024, Hagen, August 21–24, 2008.

[28] H. Fernau and L. Staiger, Iterated function systems and control languages, *Inform. Comput.* **168**, 2, pp. 125–143 (2001), doi:10.1006/inco.2000.2912, http://dx.doi.org/10.1006/inco.2000.2912.

[29] L. Staiger, Codes, simplifying words, and open set condition, *Inform. Process. Lett.* **58**, 6, pp. 297–301 (1996), doi:10.1016/0020-0190(96)00074-9, http://dx.doi.org/10.1016/0020-0190(96)00074-9.

[30] L. Staiger, Infinite iterated function systems in Cantor space and the Hausdorff measure of ω-power languages, *Internat. J. Found. Comput. Sci.* **16**, 4, pp. 787–802 (2005), doi:10.1142/S0129054105003297, http://dx.doi.org/10.1142/S0129054105003297.

[31] C. S. Calude, N. J. Hay and F. Stephan, Representation of left-computable ε-random reals, *J. Comput. System Sci.* **77**, 4, pp. 812–819 (2011), doi:10.1016/j.jcss.2010.08.001, http://dx.doi.org/10.1016/j.jcss.2010.08.001.

[32] K. Tadaki, A new representation of Chaitin Ω number based on compressible strings, in C. S. Calude, M. Hagiya, K. Morita, G. Rozenberg and J. Timmis (eds.), *Unconventional Computation*, Lecture Notes in Computer Science, Vol. 6079. Springer, ISBN 978-3-642-13522-4, pp. 127–139 (2010), ISBN 978-3-642-13522-4.

[33] L. Staiger, On oscillation-free Chaitin h-random sequences, in M. J. Dinneen, B. Khoussainov and A. Nies (eds.), *Computation, Physics and Beyond*, Lecture Notes in Computer Science, Vol. 7160. Springer, Heidelberg, ISBN 978-3-642-27653-8, pp. 194–202 (2012), ISBN 978-3-642-27653-8.

[34] V. Brattka, R. Dillhage, T. Grubba and A. Klutsch (eds.), *Proceedings of the Fifth International Conference on Computability and Complexity in Analysis (CCA 2008)*, Electronic Notes in Theoretical Computer Science, Vol. 221. Elsevier, Amsterdam (2008), Hagen, August 21–24, 2008.

PART 2

Quantum Information and Complexity

Chapter 9

Quantum Computational Complexity in Curved Spacetime

Marco Lanzagorta

US Naval Research Laboratory, Washington DC, USA

Jeffrey Uhlmann

Department of Computer Science, University of Columbia-Missouri, USA

Abstract

In this article we examine how computational complexity analysis of quantum algorithms may be compromised when implicit assumptions of flat spacetime are violated. In particular, we show that in curved spacetime, i.e., all practical contexts, the complexity of standard formulations of Grover's algorithm (and other iterative quantum algorithms) may reduce to that of classical alternatives. In addition, we discuss the implications of these results for quantum error correction and fault tolerant quantum computation.

9.1. Introduction

The principal goal of quantum information science is to harness quantum phenomena to improve the performance of information processing systems [Nielsen and Chuang (2000); Lanzagorta and Uhlmann (2009)]. There has been substantial progress in the development of quantum communication, computation, and sensing devices, and some have even reached a level of technological maturity sufficient to find commercial applications. However, optimism about their potential advantage over classical alternatives is invariably founded on theoretical analysis that implicitly assumes a flat spacetime operating environment, i.e., that their operations will not be influenced by local gravitation.

Gravity affects quantum information [Lanzagorta (2013)], especially in the case of spin-based quantum hardware. Indeed, spin is an intrinsically relativistic concept that can only be formally described within the context of relativistic quantum field theory [Weinberg (1995)]. In this context, spin is

227

simply defined as the degrees of freedom of a quantum state that transform in a non-trivial manner by a Poincare transformation. This group-theoretic definition embodies the invariance of physical laws under special relativity[1]. Because spin emerges from a relativistic concept, any spin-based representation of quantum information is subject to a direct coupling to classical gravitational fields as described by Einstein's general theory of gravity; therefore, any complete analysis of the time evolution of quantum information must consider the effects of gravitation.

The fact that quantum information invariably gravitates has deep philosophical implications about the nature of information. Indeed, classical information is a completely abstract mathematical construction, and therefore it is meaningless to inquire about the gravitation of a classical bit. In this regard, as one could have expected, quantum information has a strong connection to the physical world.

This paper begins with an examination of Wigner rotations on the amplitudes of states in the computational basis. We then consider orbiting qubits in Schwarzschild spacetime (i.e. in the static and isotropic curved spacetime produced by a spherically symmetric black hole). From here we examine the effects of gravitational perturbation on Grover's quantum search algorithm and Shor's quantum factoring algorithm.

The principal contribution of this article lies in the last section, which discusses the implications of gravity to quantum error correction and fault tolerant quantum computation. To this end, we show that gravitation induces perturbations that cannot generally be treated using models which assume locally independent errors/noise. Finally, we discuss conclusions that can be drawn and directions for future work.

9.2. The Wigner Rotation

The interaction between spin and gravity is best expressed through a rotation in physical space [Lanzagorta (2013)]. Thus, the effect of gravity can be described by the rotation operator:

$$\hat{D} = \mathcal{T} \exp\left(\frac{i}{2} \int_{\tau_1}^{\tau_2} \boldsymbol{\sigma} \cdot (\vartheta_{23}, \vartheta_{31}, \vartheta_{12}) \, d\tau \right), \tag{9.1}$$

---

[1]Note that this definition avoids the problematic conception of spin as an "intrinsic angular momentum". Indeed, for the case of photons moving at the speed of light it is impossible to find an inertial frame where the photon is at rest so the photon's intrinsic angular momentum is undefined.

where $\boldsymbol{\sigma} = (\sigma_x, \sigma_y, \sigma_z)$ is the vector of Pauli spin matrices and ϑ_{ij} are the *infinitesimal Wigner angles*. The integration is done over the proper time of the particle that follows a path in spacetime from τ_1 to τ_2.

The time ordering operator $\mathcal{T}$ is necessary in the expression because, in general, the infinitesimal rotations will not commute with each other. In the very particular case where the infinitesimal rotations are restricted to take place along a single direction (e.g. the y direction), there is no need for $\mathcal{T}$ and the expression for the rotation operator reduces to:

$$
\begin{aligned}
\hat{D}_y &= \exp\left(\frac{i}{2}\int_{\tau_1}^{\tau_2}\sigma_y\vartheta_{31}d\tau\right) \\
&= \exp\left(\frac{i\,\sigma_y}{2}\int_{\tau_1}^{\tau_2}\vartheta_{31}d\tau\right) \\
&= \exp\left(i\sigma_y\frac{\Omega}{2}\right),
\end{aligned}
\tag{9.2}
$$

where Ω is called the *Wigner angle.* Then, as a spin-based qubit moves in curved spacetime, its spin will rotate by $\Omega/2$ along the y direction:

$$
|\psi\rangle = \alpha|0\rangle + \beta|1\rangle = \begin{pmatrix}\alpha\\\beta\end{pmatrix} \longrightarrow \begin{pmatrix}\cos\dfrac{\Omega}{2} & \sin\dfrac{\Omega}{2}\\[2mm]-\sin\dfrac{\Omega}{2} & \cos\dfrac{\Omega}{2}\end{pmatrix}\begin{pmatrix}\alpha\\\beta\end{pmatrix},
\tag{9.3}
$$

where $|0\rangle$ and $|1\rangle$ are spin eigenstates in the σ_z basis, and Ω will depend in a non-trivial manner on the gravitational field and the path followed by the qubit.

It is important to remark that this is a general relativistic effect that emerges as a consequence of the qubit moving through a curved manifold. That is, the Wigner angle is strictly zero in Newtonian gravitation. As a consequence, *gravitation rotates spin-based qubits in a non-trivial manner.*

To clarify what we mean by a non-trivial rotation, let us consider a spinning particle moving in a circular orbit around a static and spherically symmetric massive object. As conceptually shown in Figure 9.1, in the context of Newtonian gravitation, the spin of the particle is constant along the orbit, so it always points upwards. As the orbit is completed, the spin returns to its original position ($\mathbf{S}_1 = \mathbf{S}_9$).

On the other hand, in the context of Einstein's general theory of relativity, spacetime curvature affects the rotation of the spin. That is, when the particle completes an orbit, the spin state does not return to its original value ($\mathbf{S}_1 \neq \mathbf{S}_9$). Notice that once the particle starts its orbital motion, the spin no longer points upwards. Thus, after completion of a single orbit, the spin is transformed by a trivial rotation of 2π (as it moves around the

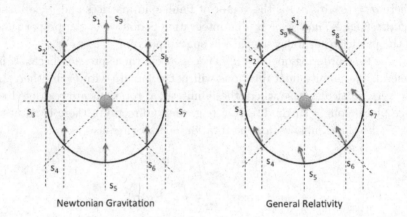

Fig. 9.1. Conceptual description of spin rotation in Newtonian gravity and in General Relativity. Notice that due to spacetime curvature, the spin does not reach its original value ($S_1 \neq S_9$) after completion of a single circular orbit. Once the orbit has been completed, the angle between S_1 and S_9 is proportional to the Wigner angle Ω.

central object) and a non-trivial rotation given by the Wigner angle Ω due to the spacetime curvature caused by the central object. As illustrated in the figure, after a single orbit, Ω is proportional to the angle between S_1 and S_9. In the context of general relativity for classical macroscopic bodies, this effect is known as *geodetic precession* or *de Sitter precession* [Hobson (2006)]. An explicit expression for Ω in the simple case of a spherically symmetric gravitational field will be described in the following section.

The effect of gravity on quantum information is clear. For instance, suppose we define the computational basis using as a quantization axis the direction established by the imaginary vertical line that connects an orbiting satellite with a distant star (e.g. the parallel vertical dotted lines in Figure 9.1). In the case of Newtonian gravity, the orientation of states prepared in the computational basis aboard the satellite will remain invariant as the satellite orbits the massive object. That is, if we prepare the state $|0\rangle$, then the particle will remain in the $|0\rangle$ state as the satellite performs its orbital motion.

On the other hand, in the context of General Relativity, the orientation of states prepared in the computational basis aboard the satellite will slowly rotate as the satellite orbits around the massive object. That is, if we prepare the state $|0\rangle$, as the satellite moves, the onboard observer will have a non-zero probability to measure states orthogonal to $|0\rangle$.

The gravitation interaction is important to consider because spin-based qubits in a quantum computer will clearly interact with Earth's gravitational field and their states will therefore change with time even if the computer is in the idle state. In other words, qubit-encoded quantum information will invariably suffer gravitation-induced drift determined by its environment of operation.

Furthermore, it can be shown that *uncorrected* errors can undermine the asymptotic computational complexity advantage of most (if not all) quantum algorithms with respect to classical alternatives [Lanzagorta and Uhlmann (2012)]. In this chapter we examine the perturbative effects of gravitation on the evolution of quantum systems and their implications for quantum computation. Although the effects are small, they cannot generally be mitigated by the use of conventional quantum error correcting codes and can therefore impose limits on the scalability of quantum algorithms.

9.3. Gravitational Drifting of Qubit States

In this section we will briefly discuss how gravity affects 1-qubit vector states, 1-qubit mixed states, and 2-qubit vector states. Generalization to higher dimensional systems is straightforward.

9.3.1. *1-Qubit vector states*

We begin by considering a single qubit in the uniform superposition, i.e., it will be measured as "0" or "1" with equal probability:

$$|\psi_1\rangle = \frac{|0\rangle + |1\rangle}{\sqrt{2}}. \tag{9.4}$$

In the presence of gravity this state will "drift" into:

$$|\psi_1\rangle \longrightarrow \frac{\cos\frac{\Omega}{2} + \sin\frac{\Omega}{2}}{\sqrt{2}}|0\rangle + \frac{\cos\frac{\Omega}{2} - \sin\frac{\Omega}{2}}{\sqrt{2}}|1\rangle. \tag{9.5}$$

The behavior of the probability of measuring "1" and "0" with respect to Ω is shown in Figure 9.2. Notice that the expressions for the probabilities have a 2π period with the value of Ω determining the relative probability of measuring "1" or "0" (i.e., Ω has the effect of amplifying the probability of measuring one state relative to the other), and of course the sum of the probabilities is unity.

Note also that, in general, the Wigner rotation angle is a function of time, $\Omega = \Omega(t)$, which depends on the existing gravitational fields and

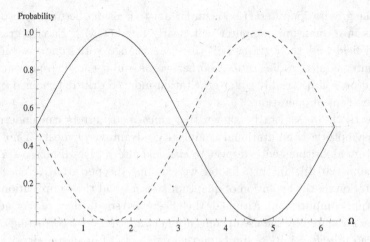

Fig. 9.2. Drifting of the probability of measuring "1" (solid line) and "0" (dashed line) for a 1 qubit state in the uniform superposition in the presence of a gravitational field described by the Wigner rotation angle $\Omega(t)$.

the trajectory of the qubit. For example, consider the static and isotropic gravitational field produced by a spherically symmetric body of mass M described by the Schwarzschild metric [Lanzagorta (2013); Alsing, Stephenson and Kilian (2009); Terashima and Ueda (2004)]. If the qubit is following a circular orbit of radius r then the Wigner angle per orbital period is given by:

$$\Omega = 2\pi\sqrt{f}\left(1 - \frac{Kr_s}{2rf}\frac{1}{K+\sqrt{f}}\right) - 2\pi,\qquad(9.6)$$

where:

$$K \equiv \frac{1-\frac{r_s}{r}}{\sqrt{1-\frac{3r_s}{2r}}},\qquad f \equiv 1-\frac{r_s}{r},\qquad r_s \equiv 2M\qquad(9.7)$$

all given in natural units $(G = 1, c = 1)$. That is, once a qubit has completed an entire circular orbit in Schwarzschild spacetime, Ω is the total rotation of the spin solely due to the presence of a gravitational field. This is a purely relativistic effect due to the interaction of a spin-$\frac{1}{2}$ quantum field with a classical gravitational field.

Figure 9.3 shows the behavior of Ω with respect to r_s/r for a qubit that has completed a circular orbit in Schwarzschild spacetime. On the other hand, Figure 9.4 shows the behavior of the probability of measuring "1" and "0" with respect to r_s/r for a qubit after completion of a single orbit in Schwarzschild spacetime.

In particular, note that if the Wigner rotation angle is very small, $\Omega \ll 1$, then:

$$P_0 = |\langle 0|\psi_1\rangle|^2 \approx \frac{1}{2} + \frac{\Omega}{2},$$
$$P_1 = |\langle 1|\psi_1\rangle|^2 \approx \frac{1}{2} - \frac{\Omega}{2}, \tag{9.8}$$

where P_0 and P_1 are the probabilities of measuring "0" and "1", respectively. Thus, the measurement error in weak gravitational fields is approximately given by $\Omega/2$.

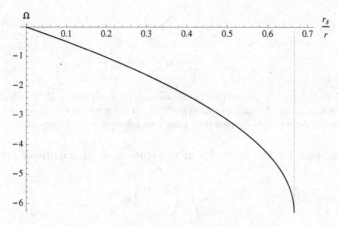

Fig. 9.3.   Wigner angle Ω for a qubit that has completed a circular orbit of radius r in the Schwarzschild spacetime produced by an object of mass $r_s/2$.

9.3.2.   1-Qubit mixed states

Let us now consider the case of a single qubit mixed state given by the density matrix:

$$\rho = \begin{pmatrix} a_{11} & a_{12} \\ a_{21} & a_{22} \end{pmatrix}. \tag{9.9}$$

Then, under the effect of gravity, the state will transform into:

$$\tilde{\rho} = \hat{U}_g^\dagger \, \rho \, \hat{U}_g \tag{9.10}$$

with components:

$$\tilde{\rho}_{11} = a_{11}\cos^2(\Omega/2) - (a_{12} + a_{21})\sin(\Omega/2)\cos(\Omega/2) + a_{22}\sin^2(\Omega/2),$$
$$\tilde{\rho}_{12} = (a_{11} - a_{22})\sin(\Omega/2)\cos(\Omega/2) + a_{12}\cos^2(\Omega/2) - a_{21}\sin^2(\Omega/2),$$
$$\tilde{\rho}_{21} = (a_{11} - a_{22})\sin(\Omega/2)\cos(\Omega/2) - a_{12}\sin^2(\Omega/2) + a_{21}\cos^2(\Omega/2),$$
$$\tilde{\rho}_{22} = a_{11}\sin^2(\Omega/2) + (a_{12} + a_{21})\sin(\Omega/2)\cos(\Omega/2) + a_{22}\cos^2(\Omega/2).$$

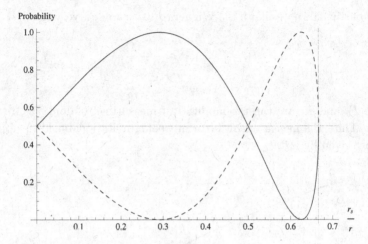

Fig. 9.4. Drifting of the probability of measuring "1" (solid line) and "0" (dashed line) for a 1 qubit state in the uniform superposition after completion of a circular orbit of radius r in the Schwarzschild spacetime produced by an object of mass $r_s/2$.

We notice that for the case of a mixed state with no coherence terms, we have:

$$\rho_0 = \begin{pmatrix} a & 0 \\ 0 & b \end{pmatrix} \tag{9.11}$$

and under gravity:

$$\tilde{\rho}_0 = \begin{pmatrix} a\cos^2(\Omega/2) + b\sin^2(\Omega/2) & (a-b)\sin(\Omega/2)\cos(\Omega/2) \\ (a-b)\sin(\Omega/2)\cos(\Omega/2) & a\sin^2(\Omega/2) + b\cos^2(\Omega/2) \end{pmatrix}. \tag{9.12}$$

That is, if $a \neq b$, gravity induces coherence terms. However, as expected, the degree of purity of the state remains the same:

$$\mathrm{Tr}(\rho^2) = \mathrm{Tr}(\tilde{\rho}^2) = a^2 + b^2. \tag{9.13}$$

9.3.3. *2-Qubit states*

Consider now a 2-qubit state uniform superposition:

$$|\psi_2\rangle = \frac{|00\rangle + |01\rangle + |10\rangle + |11\rangle}{2} \tag{9.14}$$

which under the presence of gravity is transformed into:

$$|\psi_2\rangle \rightarrow \frac{\left(\cos\frac{\Omega}{2} - \sin\frac{\Omega}{2}\right)^2}{2}|00\rangle + \frac{\cos^2\frac{\Omega}{2} - \sin^2\frac{\Omega}{2}}{2}|01\rangle \tag{9.15}$$

$$+ \frac{\cos^2\frac{\Omega}{2} - \sin^2\frac{\Omega}{2}}{2}|10\rangle + \frac{\left(\cos\frac{\Omega}{2} + \sin\frac{\Omega}{2}\right)^2}{2}|11\rangle,$$

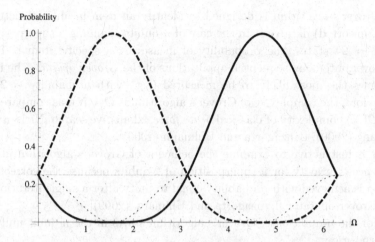

Fig. 9.5. Drifting of the probability of measuring "00" (solid line), "01" and "10" (dotted line), and "11" (dashed line) for a 2 qubit state in the uniform superposition in the presence of a gravitational field described by the Wigner rotation angle $\Omega(t)$.

where we have assumed that the two qubits have negligible spatial separation so that their Wigner angles are identical.

The drifting of the 2-qubit state in the uniform superposition with respect to the Wigner angle is shown in Figure 9.5. Note that the probability of measuring "00" and "11" is amplified and/or reduced in a periodic fashion. On the other hand, the probability of measuring "01" or "10" is always smaller than the original $1/4$ probability of the uniform superposition. This suggests the intriguing possibility that drifting qubits could be used to measure gravitational fields. This is certainly the case if the qubits are near a black hole and the Wigner angle is large. Indeed, if $\Omega \approx \pi/2$ then the measurement of the "11" qubit state will be very close to 1.

9.4. 2-Qubit Grover's Algorithm

Grover's algorithm is the quintessential example of an *amplitude amplification algorithm* [Nielsen and Chuang (2000); Lanzagorta and Uhlmann (2009)]. Such algorithms consist of a series of qubit operations that transforms a quantum state in such a way that, after a certain number of iterations, measurements of some states are much more likely than other states. In other words, these quantum algorithms amplify the amplitudes of solution states so that they are more likely to be measured.

Grover's algorithm is designed to identify an item in an unstructured (e.g., unsorted) database. In the case of n-qubits spanning a superposition of $N = 2^n$ states, the probability of measuring a specific item is $1/N$. However, after $\sqrt{N}$ sequential applications of the *Grover operator* the item becomes the most likely to be measured (e.g., with probability $\approx 2/3$). Therefore, the complexity of Grover's algorithm is $\mathcal{O}(\sqrt{N})$, as compared to the $\mathcal{O}(N)$ complexity of classical *brute force* exhaustive search [Nielsen and Chuang (2000); Lanzagorta and Uhlmann (2009)].

It is instructive to examine the behavior of Grover's algorithm in the presence of gravity for a superposition of 2-qubits because the correct solution is achieved with probability equal to unity after a single iteration of the Grover operator [Lanzagorta and Uhlmann (2009)].

For the n-qubit case, Grover's algorithm starts in the n-qubit uniform superposition:

$$|\psi_n\rangle = \frac{1}{\sqrt{N}} \sum_{i=1}^{N} |i\rangle \qquad (9.16)$$

and the n-qubit Grover operator is given by:

$$\hat{G}_n = \hat{M}_n \times \hat{O}_n, \qquad (9.17)$$

where $\hat{M}_n$ is the n-qubit *inversion around the mean* and $\hat{O}_n$ is the n-qubit *oracle* [Lanzagorta and Uhlmann (2009)]. In particular, for the 2-qubit case, the inversion operator is given by:

$$\hat{M}_2 = -\frac{1}{2} \begin{pmatrix} 1 & -1 & -1 & -1 \\ -1 & 1 & -1 & -1 \\ -1 & -1 & 1 & -1 \\ -1 & -1 & -1 & 1 \end{pmatrix}. \qquad (9.18)$$

If the "00" element represents the solution state then the effect of the 2-qubit oracle can be represented in matrix form as:

$$\hat{O}_2 = \begin{pmatrix} -1 & 0 & 0 & 0 \\ 0 & 1 & 0 & 0 \\ 0 & 0 & 1 & 0 \\ 0 & 0 & 0 & 1 \end{pmatrix} \qquad (9.19)$$

so that the oracle "marks" the solution by changing the phase of the corresponding state. In the absence of gravity the state after a single Grover iteration is given by:

$$\hat{G}_2|\psi_2\rangle = |00\rangle \qquad (9.20)$$

and, therefore, the probability of measuring "00" is exactly 1. By contrast, a classical brute force search may require up to 4 comparison operations, one for each element in the dataset.

In the presence of gravity, however, the operator that must be applied to the uniform state is approximated by:

$$\hat{D}_2(\Omega_2) \times \hat{G}_2 \times \hat{D}_2(\Omega_1)|\psi_2\rangle, \tag{9.21}$$

where $\hat{D}_2(\Omega_i)$ is the 2-qubit Wigner rotation for the qubit moving in the time interval Δt_i. That is, the quantum register is initialized to the uniform superposition, then incurs the gravitational drift $\hat{D}_2(\Omega_1)$ during the time interval Δt_1 before the application of the Grover operator $\hat{G}_2$, and then incurs an additional gravitational drift $\hat{D}_2(\Omega_2)$ during the time interval Δt_2 prior to the measurement.

Notice that, in general, $\Omega_1 \neq \Omega_2$. Indeed, the effect of gravity will be different in Δt_1 and Δt_2 if the particle moves in an arbitrary path across a non-uniform gravitational field. However, we can assume a perfectly regular quantum computer that performs operations at regular intervals so that $\Delta t_1 \approx \Delta t_2$. In addition, we can assume that the qubits are moving in an uniform gravitational field (this would be the case of qubits separated by a negligible distance aboard a satellite moving in a circular orbit in Schwarzschild spacetime). If these assumptions remain valid, then we can approximate $\Omega_1 \approx \Omega_2$.

Under such approximation, the probability P_{ab} of measuring the state "ab" is given by:

$$P_{00} = \cos^4\left(\frac{\Omega}{2}\right), \qquad P_{11} = \sin^4\left(\frac{\Omega}{2}\right), \qquad P_{01} = P_{10} = \frac{1}{4}\sin^2\Omega,$$

where the nonzero Wigner rotation $\Omega \equiv \Omega_{1,2}$ reduces the probability of correctly measuring the desired state "00". The effect of Ω on the respective probabilities of measuring "00", "01" and "10", and "11" is shown in Figure 9.6, where Ω represents the Wigner angle accrued during the time between two consecutive operations. That is, if the quantum computer operates at 1 Hz then the Wigner angle is the rotation due to the drifting of the qubit in the gravitational field during the time span of 1 second.

The probability of success of Grover's algorithm diminishes in the presence of a gravitational field. In the case of a quantum computer near a black hole with $\frac{\pi}{2} < \Omega < \frac{3\pi}{2}$ the probability of success is less than $1/n$, i.e., worse than classical, and is near zero for $\Omega \approx \pi$. While Ω may be small near the surface of the earth, its impact on the probability of success

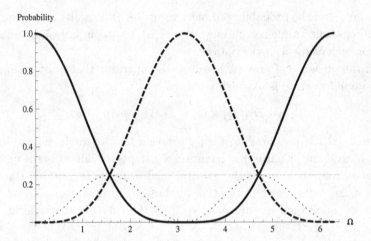

Fig. 9.6. Probability of measuring "00" (solid line), "01" and "10" (dotted line), and "11" (dashed line) for a 2 qubit state after a single iteration of the Grover operator in the presence of a gravitational field described by the Wigner rotation angle $\Omega(t)$.

for Grover's algorithm can become significant as the number of qubits and quantum operations is increased.

Furthermore, it is worth to remark that the Wigner rotation is an unitary operation, and as a consequence, in principle one could always find the inverse transformation. However, in practice it may be an unfeasible task to find and implement the exact inverse Wigner rotation at each computational step. Indeed, for such a task we would require perfect knowledge of the gravitational field at any given point.

9.5. 3-Qubit Grover Algorithm

Consider now Grover's algorithm initialized with a 3-qubit state in the uniform superposition. In the absence of gravity the probability of measuring the correct solution (say "000") after two iterations is 0.945313.

In analogy to the 2-qubit case, the net effect of two iterations of the Grover operator in the presence of gravity is given by:

$$\hat{D}_3 \times \hat{G}_3 \times \hat{D}_3 \times \hat{G}_3 \times \hat{D}_3 |\psi_3\rangle, \qquad (9.22)$$

where $\hat{D}_3$ is the Wigner rotation operator for 3-qubits. Then, the probability of measuring the right solution ("000") after two Grover iterations is:

$$P_{000} = \left(\begin{array}{c} (66\sin(x) - 24\sin(3x) - 21\sin(7x) \\ +\sin(9x) + 66\cos(x) + 24\cos(3x) \\ +96\cos(5x) - 3\cos(7x) - 7\cos(9x)) \end{array} \right)^2 \frac{1}{32768}, \qquad (9.23)$$

where for notational simplicity we have defined:

$$x \equiv \frac{\Omega}{2}. \qquad (9.24)$$

The probability of measuring a non-solution state, e.g., "111", is given by:

$$P_{111} = \left(\begin{array}{c} (-18\sin(x) - 48\sin(3x) + 72\sin(5x) \\ -3\sin(7x) + 7\sin(9x) - 78\cos(x) \\ +48\cos(3x) + 24\cos(5x) + 21\cos(7x) \\ +\cos(9x)) \end{array} \right)^2 \frac{1}{32768}. \qquad (9.25)$$

Note that for small Wigner angles $x \ll 1$ we have:

$$P_{000} \approx 0.945313 - 1.54688\,x, \qquad (9.26)$$
$$P_{111} \approx 0.0078125 + 0.234375\,x.$$

Figure 9.7 shows the probability of measuring "000" (solid line) and "111" (dashed line) for a 3-qubit state after two iterations of the Grover operator in the presence of a gravitational field described by the Wigner rotation angle Ω. Once again, depending on the value of Ω, Grover's algorithm may not be able to provide the solution to the search problem with high probability.

It is also important to note that, in the case of two qubits, the probabilities P_{00} and P_{11} were the same, but shifted by π in the value of Ω (see Figure 9.6). On the other hand, for three qubits, the probabilities P_{000} and P_{111} are completely different functions of Ω. This suggests that, in general, we cannot expect that the influence of gravity on the Grover measurement probabilities will possess some easy to identify symmetry.

9.6. General Iterative Algorithm

Consider now a quantum computer running an algorithm that iteratively applies a quantum operation to an initial n-qubit quantum state represented by the density matrix $\rho^{(0)}$. We can examine the result of this computation in the noiseless (i.e., flat spacetime) and weak-field regimes.

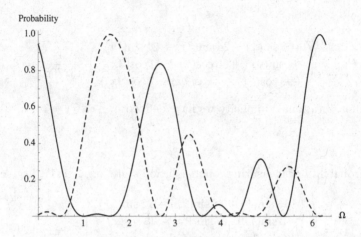

Fig. 9.7. Probability of measuring "000" (solid line) and "111" (dashed line) for a 3 qubit state after two iterations of the Grover operator in the presence of a gravitational field described by the Wigner rotation angle $\Omega(t)$.

9.6.1. *Noiseless operation*

Suppose the quantum algorithm performs m sequential applications of a single multi-qubit gate $\hat{U}$. The system has n qubits that represent $N = 2^n$ possible states. In the absence of gravity, and ignoring all possible sources of noise and error, the state's density matrix after the first computational step is:

$$\rho^{(1)} = \hat{U}\rho^{(0)}\hat{U}^\dagger \tag{9.27}$$

and the state after m iterations is given by:

$$\rho^{(m)} = \hat{U}^m\rho^{(0)}\hat{U}^{\dagger m}. \tag{9.28}$$

9.6.2. *Weak Field Approximation*

By contrast, the state after one iteration in the presence of a weak gravitational field is:

$$\rho^{(1)} = \hat{D}\hat{U}\rho^{(0)}\hat{U}^\dagger\hat{D}^\dagger, \tag{9.29}$$

where $\hat{D}$ is the unitary operation that represents the n-qubit Wigner rotation between computational steps. After two iterations the state will be:

$$\rho^{(2)} = \hat{D}\hat{U}\hat{D}\hat{U}\rho^{(0)}\hat{U}^\dagger\hat{D}^\dagger\hat{U}^\dagger\hat{D}^\dagger \tag{9.30}$$

and so on. In this case the Wigner rotation can be written as:

$$\hat{D} = \bigotimes_{j=1}^{n} e^{i\hat{\Sigma}_j \cdot \Omega_j / 2}, \tag{9.31}$$

where Ω_j is the vector of Wigner rotation angles for the jth qubit and $\hat{\Sigma}_j$ is the vector of spin rotation generators that acts on the jth qubit. This expression reflects the fact that, in general, qubits will occupy different positions in spacetime, their spins may be aligned in different directions, and the quantization axes may be different for each of them. To simplify the analysis we assume not only that the gravitational field is weak but also that all qubits undergo the exact same Wigner rotation Ω such that:

$$|\Omega_j - \Omega| \ll 1 \quad \forall j, \tag{9.32}$$

where in the weak field limit $\Omega \ll 1$.

In the weak field limit, the qubit rotation operator $\hat{D}$ can be expressed as:

$$\hat{D} \approx \mathbb{I} + \frac{i\Omega}{2} \sum_{j=1}^{n} \hat{\Sigma}_j + \mathcal{O}(\Omega^2), \tag{9.33}$$

where $\hat{\Sigma}_j$ is a unitary operator that acts in a non-trivial manner only on the jth-qubit:

$$\hat{\Sigma}_j = \underbrace{\mathbb{I} \otimes \mathbb{I} \otimes \cdots \otimes \mathbb{I}}_{j-1} \otimes \sigma \otimes \underbrace{\mathbb{I} \otimes \mathbb{I} \otimes \cdots \otimes \mathbb{I}}_{n-j}, \tag{9.34}$$

where the under-brace denotes the number of single-qubit identity operators in the tensor product and σ is the spin rotation generator over a given axis.

As a consequence, at order $\mathcal{O}(\Omega)$ the state after one iteration can approximately be written as:

$$\rho^{(1)} \approx \left(1 + \frac{i\Omega}{2} \sum_{j=1}^{n} \hat{\Sigma}_j \right) \hat{U} \rho^{(0)} \hat{U}^\dagger \left(1 - \frac{i\Omega}{2} \sum_{k=1}^{n} \hat{\Sigma}_k^\dagger \right) + \mathcal{O}(\Omega^2) \tag{9.35}$$

$$\approx \hat{U} \rho^{(0)} \hat{U}^\dagger + \frac{i\Omega}{2} \sum_{j=1}^{n} (\hat{\Sigma}_j \hat{U} \rho^{(0)} \hat{U}^\dagger - \hat{U} \rho^{(0)} \hat{U}^\dagger \hat{\Sigma}_j^\dagger) + \mathcal{O}(\Omega^2).$$

Defining Ξ as:

$$\Xi(\rho) \equiv \frac{i}{2} \sum_{j=1}^{n} (\hat{\Sigma}_j \hat{U} \rho \hat{U}^\dagger - \hat{U} \rho \hat{U}^\dagger \hat{\Sigma}_j^\dagger) \tag{9.36}$$

$$= \frac{i}{2} \sum_{j=1}^{n} [\hat{\Sigma}_j, U \rho \hat{U}^\dagger]$$

allows $\rho^{(1)}$ at first order in Ω to be expressed as:

$$\rho^{(1)} \approx \hat{U}\rho^{(0)}\hat{U}^\dagger + \Omega\ \Xi(\rho^{(0)}). \tag{9.37}$$

Thus, the second iteration is:

$$\begin{aligned}
\rho^{(2)} &\approx \hat{U}\rho^{(1)}\hat{U}^\dagger + \Omega\ \Xi(\rho^{(1)}) \\
&\approx \hat{U}\hat{U}\rho^{(0)}\hat{U}^\dagger\hat{U}^\dagger + \Omega\hat{U}\ \Xi(\rho^{(0)})\hat{U}^\dagger + \Omega\ \Xi(\hat{U}\rho^{(0)}\hat{U}^\dagger) + \mathcal{O}\left(\Omega^2\right) \\
&\approx \hat{U}\hat{U}\rho^{(0)}\hat{U}^\dagger\hat{U}^\dagger + \Omega(\hat{U}\ \Xi(\rho^{(0)})\hat{U}^\dagger + \Xi(\hat{U}\rho^{(0)}\hat{U}^\dagger)) + \mathcal{O}\left(\Omega^2\right)
\end{aligned} \tag{9.38}$$

and the state after m iterations will be of the form:

$$\rho^{(m)} \approx (\hat{U})^m\rho^{(0)}(\hat{U}^\dagger)^m + \Omega\underbrace{(...)}_{m} + \mathcal{O}(\Omega^2), \tag{9.39}$$

where the underbrace denotes how many n-sum terms Ξ are contained inside the parentheses.

At this point it is clear that the presence of a gravitational field affects the probability of measuring the correct final state of the system. The exact deviation from the expected performance of the quantum algorithm will depend in a non-trivial manner on the type and number of quantum gates, data qubits, ancillary qubits, and error correction encoding used to implement the computation. While it is notationally straightforward to represent all gravitational effects in the form of a single unitary transformation, the actual identification of that transformation at each computational step may not be feasible.

If it is assumed/conjectured that the gravitational field of the operating environment can only be estimated with bounded accuracy then the probability of measuring the correct result after m iterations can be expressed as:

$$p \gtrsim (1 - n\epsilon)^m \approx 1 - nm\epsilon + \mathcal{O}(\epsilon^2), \tag{9.40}$$

where $\epsilon = \mathcal{O}(\Omega)$ and we have used a small limit approximation $n\epsilon \lesssim 1$. Under these conditions the error probability for the quantum algorithm is approximately bounded by:

$$e \lesssim 1 - (1 - n\epsilon)^m. \tag{9.41}$$

In principle it would seem that the algorithm could be iterated to increase the probability of success to satisfy any desired threshold. For example, after k runs of the entire algorithm, the bound for the probability of error could be reduced to:

$$e^k \lesssim \left(1 - (1 - n\epsilon)^m\right)^k \tag{9.42}$$

and k is chosen such that:

$$e^k \approx \delta \tag{9.43}$$

where δ is the maximum error probability desired for the computational process. That is, k is given by:

$$k \lesssim \frac{\log \delta}{\log\left(1 - (1 - n\epsilon)^m\right)}. \tag{9.44}$$

In the asymptotic limit for large m we have:

$$k \lesssim -\log \delta \times \left(\frac{1}{1 - n\epsilon}\right)^m = \mathcal{O}\left(\left(\frac{1}{1 - n\epsilon}\right)^m\right) \tag{9.45}$$

and the *true complexity* of the algorithm (i.e. the total number of iterations necessary to complete the computational task with error probability δ) is:

$$\mathcal{O}\left(m \times k\right) \approx \mathcal{O}\left(m \times \left(\frac{1}{1 - n\epsilon}\right)^m\right). \tag{9.46}$$

Thus, as the number of qubits n grows – approaching the value $1/\epsilon$ – the algorithmic complexity becomes exponential in the number of iterations m. In other words, the presence of gravity increases the computational dependence on m from linear to exponential. This motivates an examination of the specific consequences of this for practical n-qubit applications of Grover's algorithm and Shor's algorithm.

9.7. n-Qubit Grover's Algorithm

In light of the analysis of the previous section, uncorrected gravitation-induced errors increase the complexity of Grover's algorithm to search an N-element database from $\mathcal{O}(\sqrt{N})$ to:

$$\mathcal{O}\left(\sqrt{N} \times \left(\frac{1}{1 - n\epsilon}\right)^{\sqrt{N}}\right) \tag{9.47}$$

which is exponential in N for $n = \log N$ qubits.

There is of course a distinction to be made between behavior in the asymptotic limit of large N and the practically-observed scaling behavior of the algorithm for reasonable values of n and m and gravitation typical at the earth's surface. It is not possible to precisely quantify all possible runtime constants, but we can treat them as *all* being equal to 1 as a rough approximation. If we further assume that $n\epsilon \ll 1$ so that we can use a Taylor series to estimate the value of k, then for finite N we obtain:

$$k \approx \left(\frac{1}{1 - n\epsilon}\right)^{\sqrt{N}} \approx 1 + n\epsilon\sqrt{N} \tag{9.48}$$

Under these assumptions we may estimate that the number of iterations necessary for Grover's algorithm is given by:

$$\mathcal{O}(\sqrt{N} + n\epsilon N) = \mathcal{O}(nN) = \mathcal{O}(N \log N) \qquad (9.49)$$

which is worse than classical. However, $n\epsilon N$ only becomes significant when:

$$n\epsilon N \approx \sqrt{N} \qquad (9.50)$$

which implies:

$$\sqrt{N} \log N \approx \frac{1}{\epsilon}. \qquad (9.51)$$

Therefore, if the quantum processor operates at 1 Hz on the surface of Earth, then $\epsilon \approx \Omega \approx 10^{-14}$, which implies that Grover's algorithm could outperform classical brute force for datasets of size up to $N \approx 2^{80}$. This breakeven analysis is of course very crude, but it does suggest the possibility of a practical performance advantage of Grover's algorithm over classical despite what is implied by our asymptotic analysis. On the other hand, a slightly more complete and/or detailed analysis may yield an opposite conclusion.

9.8. Shor's Algorithm

For completeness we now consider the other major quantum algorithm, Shor's algorithm, which can factorize an n-bit co-prime number using $\mathcal{O}(\log N)$ quantum computational steps with probability close to one [Nielsen and Chuang (2000)]. In the presence of gravity, however, the complexity becomes:

$$\mathcal{O}\left(\log N \times \left(\frac{1}{1 - \epsilon \log N} \right)^{\log N} \right) \qquad (9.52)$$

or, equivalently, in terms of number of qubits:

$$\mathcal{O}\left(n \times \left(\frac{1}{1 - n\epsilon} \right)^{n} \right) \qquad (9.53)$$

which is exponential in n.

Clearly, Shor's algorithm is more resilient to the effects of gravitation than Grover's algorithm. The reason is that Shor's algorithm has linear dependency on the number of qubits while the dependency of Grover's algorithm is exponential.

9.9. Implications for Quantum Error Correction

The magnitude of gravitation-induced errors clearly can be reduced but will never be zero, só the greater challenge for reliable, scalable quantum computation is to limit their *cumulative* effect.

The cumulative effect of qubit errors induced by gravity is somewhat similar to the case of GPS. Indeed, GPS satellites can maintain bounded-error state estimates in a defined global coordinate frame by measuring and correcting with respect to fixed anchor points which define that coordinate frame. Said another way, the GPS problem admits a Newtonian formulation wherein non-Newtonian sources of error can be corrected to arbitrary precision by a measurement-and-correction process with respect to an absolute coordinate frame. The quantum computation problem, by contrast, can only be formulated to admit an analogous type of "absolute" measurement-and-correction of qubits in the limit of classical information, i.e., bits.

Fundamentally, quantum error correction (QEC) uses redundancy to reduce the magnitude and/or probability of error associated with the result of a computational step [Nielsen and Chuang (2000); Gaitan (2008); Lidar and Brun (2013)]. For example, if a computational process is known to produce a correct solution with probability p then the probability of not obtaining a solution from k *independent* executions of the process is reduced to $(1-p)^k$, i.e., the probability of failure diminishes exponentially with the degree of redundancy k. This is why error correction (redundancy) can be applied effectively with minimal effect on the computational complexity of the overall computational process [Aharonov and Ben-Or (1997, 1999); Kitaev (1997a,b); Preskill (1998); Knill, Laflamme and Zurek (1998a,b)].

While some computational processes may produce results that can be unambiguously recognized as either "correct" or "incorrect", the more general problem for error correction requires a determination of what constitutes the "correct" result based on k executions of the process. This determination may be made based on a plurality consensus, weighted average, or any of a multitude of other functions of the k results. Regardless of the specifics, the efficacy of error correction is premised on an assumption that redundant executions provide independent samples from a stationary error process. The errors introduced by gravitation clearly do not satisfy this assumption because each of the k executions will be transformed similarly, i.e., their errors will not be statistically independent, during the time interval of the overall computation.

Gravitational interactions imply non-stationary error processes at all levels of analysis for a given quantum computing system because all components of the system are transformed by the same field, i.e., the net error associated with the system cannot be recursively defined as a linear combination of independent errors from a set of spatially separated subsystems. This would seem to violate an assumption critical for the filtration exploited by all lightweight (polylog overhead) recursive quantum error correction protocols, thus limiting the applicability of QEC. In particular, the celebrated *quantum threshold theorem* for scalable quantum computation relies on assumptions that appear to be violated by gravitation[Aharonov and Ben-Or (1997, 1999); Aharonov, Kitaev and Preskill (2006)]. More specifically, the following is a necessary assumption for fault-tolerance according to the quantum threshold theorem [Aliferis (2011)]:

> *Faults that act collectively on many qubits are highly suppressed in probability or in amplitude depending on the noise model. Furthermore, the noise strength, ϵ, must be a sufficiently small constant that is independent of the size of the computation.*

The critical element of this assumption is that the noise strength must be sufficiently small that it can be treated analytically as *independent of the size of the computation*. This cannot be assumed in the case of gravitation because it acts coherently on all components of the system throughout the duration of its computation. In other words, the effective noise strength from gravitation increases (integrates) with the size of the computation both in terms of the number of system components involved in the computation and in terms of the temporal length of the computation.

In summary, while the effects of gravitation may be much smaller than those of more mundane sources of error for short-duration computations, errors due to gravitation will asymptotically dominate with time. This implies that many computational complexity results for quantum algorithms technically require a flat-spacetime assumption.

9.10.   Conclusions

In this chapter, we have examined the impact of gravitation on the maintenance and processing of quantum information. The principal conclusion is that uncorrected gravitation-induced errors undermine the theoretical computational complexity advantages of most quantum algorithms, e.g., Grover's and Shor's, with respect to classical alternatives. However, we have also argued that the effective scaling of quantum algorithms in the regime of practical computing problems may be considerably better than what is suggested by asymptotic analysis.

We have discussed the limitations of conventional quantum error correction to mitigate errors introduced when an entire quantum computing system is continuously transformed by a gravitational field. This motivates the need for improved methods to measure this field for purposes of mitigation. To this end we have suggested that instead of viewing the gravitational drift of qubits as an "error" process that it can equally be viewed as a means for measuring the influence of gravitation [Lanzagorta (2013); Lanzagorta, Uhlmann and Venegas-Andraca (2015); Lanzagorta (2012); Lanzagorta and Salgado (2015)]. Thus, a quantum computer could be augmented with sets of "reference qubits" to determine the inverse transformations necessary to reduce errors during computation. This represents a direction for future research.

Bibliography

P. Aliferis, *Level Reduction and the Quantum Threshold Theorem*, CalTech PhD thesis (2007), http://arxiv.org/pdf/quant-ph/0703230v2.pdf, 2011.

M.A. Nielsen and I.L. Chuang, *Quantum Computation and Quantum Information*, Cambridge University Press, 2000.

M. Lanzagorta and J. Uhlmann, *Quantum Computer Science*, Morgan & Claypool, 2009.

M. Lanzagorta, *Quantum Information in Gravitational Fields*, Institute of Physics, 2013.

S. Weinberg, *The Quantum Theory of Fields*, Vol. 1, Cambridge University Press, 1995.

P.M. Alsing, G.J. Stephenson, and P. Kilian, "Spin-induced non-geodesic motion, gyroscopic precession, Wigner rotation and EPR correlations of massive spin-$\frac{1}{2}$ particles in a gravitational field", arXiv:0902.1396v1 [quant-ph], 2009.

H. Terashima and M. Ueda, "Einstein-Rosen correlation in gravitational field", *Phys. Rev. A* **69** 032113, 2004.

M.P. Hobson, G. Efstathiou, and A.N. Lasenby, *General Relativity: An Introduction for Physicists*, Cambridge University Press, 2006.

M. Lanzagorta and J. Uhlmann, "Error scaling in fault tolerant quantum computation", *Appl. Math. Comp.*, Vol. 219, No. 1, 24-30, 2012.

F. Gaitan, *Quantum Error Correction and Fault Tolerant Quantum Computing*, CRC Press, 2008.

D.A. Lidar and T.A. Brun, *Quantum Error Correction*, Cambridge University Press, 2013.

D. Aharonov and M. Ben-Or, "Fault tolerant computation with constant error", *Proceedings of the 29th Annual ACM Symposium on the Theory of Computing*, 1997.

D. Aharonov and M. Ben-Or, "Fault tolerant quantum computation with constant error rate", quant-ph/9906129, 1999.

A.Y. Kitaev, "Quantum Computations: Algorithms and Error Correction", *Russ. Math. Surv.*, 52(6):1191-1249, 1997.

A.Y. Kitaev, "Quantum error correction with imperfect gates", *Quantum Communication, Computing, and Measurement*, A.S. Holevo, O. hirota, and C.M. Caves (eds.), Plenum Press, 1997.

J. Preskill, "Reliable quantum computers", *Proc. R. Soc. London A*, 454, 1998.

E. Knill, R. Laflamme, and W.H. Zurek, "Resilient quantum computation", *Science*, 279(5349), 1998.

E. Knill, R. Laflamme, and W.H. Zurek, "Resilient quantum computation: error models and thresholds", *Proc. R. Soc. London A*, 459(1969), 1998.

D. Aharonov, A. Kitaev, and J. Preskill, "Fault-tolerant quantum computation with long-range correlated noise", *Phys. Rev. Lett.* 96(5), 050504, 2006.

M. Lanzagorta, J. Uhlmann, and S. Venegas-Andraca, "Quantum sensing in the maritime environment", *Proceedings of the MTS/IEEE Oceans Conference*, Washington DC, 2015.

M. Lanzagorta, "Effect of Gravitational frame dragging on orbiting qubits", arXiv:1212.2200v1 [quant-ph], 2012.

M. Lanzagorta and M. Salgado, "Detection of gravitational frame dragging using orbiting qubits", to appear in *Quant. Class. Grav.*, 2016.

Chapter 10

A Silk Road from Leibniz to Quantum Information

Rossella Lupacchini

Department of Philosophy, University of Bologna, Italy

Abstract

At the roots of quantum physics we find two "specular" principles: a principle of *distinguishability*, which arranges the "uncertainty" of quantum measurement, and a principle of *continuity*, which drives the evolution of quantum systems. The vital link between the two principles was sharply captured by Leibniz. In his *Theodicy*, the issue of continuity (and *indivisibles*) is presented as one of "the two famous labyrinths" in which our reason can lose its way; the other concerns "the great question of *freedom* and *necessity*." According to Leibniz, *only geometry can provide a thread for the labyrinth of continuity*. However, escaping from the labyrinth of Fate, Fortune, and Freedom requires a different perspective on nature. Leibniz's perspective on the mechanism of nature is significantly different from Descartes' or Newton's. It reveals notable affinities with the Chinese *correlative thinking*. Surprisingly, the rationale behind these affinities may find a coherent setting in quantum information.

10.1.   Introduction

While meditating on the relationship between "continuity axiom" and need
for complex numbers in quantum physics, as brought into focus by Lucien
Hardy (2001), I came across the following passage of Leibniz's letter to the
theologian Antoine Arnould (September 1687):

> For all substances should be in mutual harmony and in-
> terrelation, and all should express within themselves the
> same universe and its universal cause, which is the will of
> their Creator, and the decrees or laws which he has set up
> so that they may adjust themselves to each other in the
> best way possible. This mutual correspondence of differ-
> ent substances (which cannot act upon each other, speak-
> ing with metaphysical rigor, and which nevertheless agree
> as though they were acting upon each other) is also *one of
> the strongest proofs of the existence of God* or of a common
> cause which each effect must always express according to
> its point of view and its capacity. (Leibniz, 1969, p. 341)

What caught my attention was not simply that Leibniz's substances and
quantum particles seem to show similar aspects in broad sense, but that
both involve a *principle of continuity* and *specular symmetries* in their conceptual structure. May we plausibly regard Leibniz's "monads" as remote
ancestors of qubits? Monads express the perfect harmony of causal determinism, while qubits are born from a "genuinely random" theory. How
could they be related? This paper seeks a thread in Leibniz's fascina-
tion with China. In particular, certain affinities between Leibniz's pre-
established harmony and the Chinese "correlative thinking", emphasized
by Joseph Needham (1956), encourage placing Leibniz at the confluence of
rays going back to the roots of the celebrated "Chinese wisdom" and forth
to quantum *randomness*. Thus, Leibniz's philosophical reflection may offer
insight into the nature of probability and information.

10.2. Continuity and Distinguishability in Leibniz's Universe

Leibniz's philosophical reflection[1] aims to establish a general system of knowledge. It is grounded in the "law of continuity." Its path leads from logic to geometry and, through the infinitesimal calculus and metaphysics, from geometry to the theory of nature. Introduced as a general principle of order, the idea of continuity guides the construction of the geometric concepts. Its rationale stems from Leibniz's "perspectival view." If the Renaissance painters – think in particular of Piero della Francesca or Albrecht Dürer – regard perspective as an art of measure drawn from the Euclidean geometry, Leibniz's conceptual analysis aims rather to extract a "theory of measure" from an Albertian perspectival view. Thus, one should call Leibniz's view a *perspective renverse*, or a "doctrine of shadows".[2]

10.2.1. *Reversing perspective*

In the Euclidean geometry as in perspective painting, continuity seems not at issue, but simply given. In his search for a general *geometric characteristic*, however, Leibniz ponders over the fundamental ingredients of geometry.

> Imagine taking two points in space, hence conceiving the indeterminate straight line through them; one thing is that each point is regarded individually as single, another thing is that both are regarded as simultaneously existing; besides the two points, something else is needed for seeing them as co-existent in their respective positions. When we consider one of the two points as if we took its position and looked at the other (point), what the mind determines is called *direction*. (Leibniz, 1995, p. 278)

What is missing, or has to be brought to light, is the idea of continuity. As Leibniz puts it: "Continuum is also where parts are indefinite, or solely mentally designated" (*Continuum autem est in quo partes sunt indefinitae, sive in quo partes mente tantum designantur*). Continuity does not concern things, but order: "it inheres in the order according to which everything can be allotted [*assignari*] its location [*locus*] at a given time." Time enters

---

[1] My reading of Leibniz's thought is primarily inspired by [Cassirer (1902)].

[2] As Leibniz writes in the *Préceptes pour avancer les sciences*: "The doctrine of shadows is nothing but a reverse perspective; it is drawn from perspective once the light replaces the eye, the opaque replaces the object, and the shadow replaces the projection" (Erdmann, 1840, p. 170).

geometry and transforms the concept of space: "Space is the continuity
in the 'order of co-existence' according to which, given the co-existence
relation in the present and the law of changes [*lege mutationis*], the co-
existence relation in any given time can be defined." Hence, a line is the
extension described by a point's *motion* (*linea est extensum quod describitur
motu puncti*). In the light of continuity, what does not change through the
ideal motion (of a point) between two sites, or what is shared by two points
ideally separated becomes "clear and distinct". Focusing on the *situs* that
a point can take, Leibniz regards the Euclidean points as "viewpoints" and
therefore replaces the Cartesian *res extensa* (the extended *thing*) with a
"*subject* extending oneself" (*sujet qui s'étende*):

> As the extension is just something abstract, it requires a
> thing to be extended. It needs a subject, as it is something
> concerning this subject, like the duration. It also presup-
> poses something in this subject. It supposes a quality, an
> attribute, a nature that extends itself, stretches itself, that
> continues in this subject. The extension is the diffusion of
> such a quality or nature.[3]

When continuity allows a point to stretch out the quality of extension
over a line, it also allows the embryonic concept of "quantity" to be brought
about in its intuitive form. This guides Leibniz to solve the logical contrast
between measure and conceptual determination, which arises from the distinction between a *quantitative* property of things (to be determined *via*
sensory experience) and a *qualitative* property (as a character to be defined
by means of concepts). The relation between an element and what results
from its extension finds a parallel in the relation between the concepts of
differential and integral. The differential defines the changeable quality of
the variable x, while the integral is the quantity determined as a "sum"
of infinitesimal elements, namely the area under a curve. In this way, the
area is "given" as a function conceptually well defined. On the other hand,
finding areas reverses finding tangents. The nature of tangents lies in the
law of direction. Whereas the intuitive interpretation regards a point as
an ultimate unity, not further divisible into parts, Leibniz regards a point
as a "principle of change". He extracts the direction of the tangent, hence
the construction of a curve, from a point. In his view, the rationale behind
the law of continuity demands both unfolding the infinite multiplicity of

---

[3] *Examen des principes du R. P. Malebranche*, 1711 (Erdmann, 1840, p. 692).

possible cases and holding the logical value of quantity while its intuitive
meaning vanishes in the concept of limit.

> Although it is not rigorously true that rest is a kind of mo-
> tion, or equality a kind of inequality, and it is also not true
> that the circle is a kind of regular polygon, nevertheless,
> one can say that rest, equality, and the circle terminate
> the motions, the [in]equalities, and the regular polygons
> which vanish through a continuous change. Even if these
> terminations are exclusive, namely not rigorously included
> in the set they delimit, nevertheless they share the proper-
> ties of the set, as if they were included, according to that
> language of the infinite or infinitesimals which takes a cir-
> cle as a regular polygon with an infinite number of sides.
> Otherwise, the law of continuity would be violated.[4]

Through the conceptual analysis of the problem of quantities, the ancient vision of the infinite is taken to its limits. The infinite is not defined
as a negation of the finite, but it is rather required to determine the finite.
Those quantities, which were claimed "incommensurable" with respect to
the intuitive unity of measure, become conceptually commensurable. Thus,
understanding the incommensurable allows fixing the distinction between
the limits of ideal vision and the limits of sensory measure. Plato's separation of the world of ideas from the world of things and Aristotle's distinction
between potentiality and actuality give way to the correlation of ideal and
real. Insofar as the infinite is needed to ground the correlation, the infinitesimal gives expression to the fabric of reality through the continuous
process of its ideal calculus:

> ... if someone refuses to admit infinite and infinitesimal
> lines in a rigorous metaphysical sense and as real things,
> he can still use them with confidence as ideal concepts
> which shorten his reasoning, similar to what we call imagi-
> nary roots in the ordinary algebra [...] Furthermore, imag-
> inary roots likewise have a real foundation (*fundamentum
> in re*) [...] So it can also be said that infinites and in-
> finitesimals are grounded in such a way that everything in
> geometry, and even in nature, takes place as if they were

---

[4] *Justification du Calcul des infinitésimales par celui de l'Algèbre ordinaire* (Gerhardt,
1849-55, IV, p. 106).

perfect realities. (Letter to Varignon, 1702; Leibniz, 1969,
pp. 543-544).

Leibniz's "ideal concepts" stand as a bridge between the mathematical rules of perspective drawing and Hilbert's "intuitive" view of geometry.[5] On the one hand, they can be traced back to the vanishing points of linear perspective; on the other hand, they pave the way for Hilbert's ideal elements.[6] In this respect, the idea of continuity, as a leading principle of the geometric constructions, stems from Alberti's *lineamentum*. It does not lead the painter to represent in two dimensions what is actually seen in perspective, it rather leads the architect to imagine in three dimensions what appears in a plan, hence to choose the best solution and make it real.

10.2.2. *God's vision & the order of the universe*

In creating the universe, the divine architect has chosen the best solution and made it real. How did he observe all of the possible solutions? How did he make his decision?

Leibniz is not content with the answer that our universe is the best simply because God has made it. If this were so, he argues in the *Discourse on Metaphysics* (1686), God, as its author, would not have had to evaluate it afterwards and find it good, as the Sacred Scriptures testify. It is rather by considering his works that one can recognize him as the author. "God's works must therefore carry his mark in themselves." That God is an "absolutely perfect being" must be inferred from his works according to *rules* of goodness and perfection. Leibniz is not content either with the answer that the best solution has been solely determined by God's *will*. The eternal truths of metaphysics and geometry and consequently also the rules of goodness, justice, and perfection are not "merely the effects of the will of God; instead, [...] they are only the consequences of his *understanding*, which, assuredly, does not depend on his will, any more than his essence" (Leibniz, 1989).[7]

In Leibniz's thought, the divine understanding is so comprehensive as

---

[5] For an insightful treatise on the role of visual intuition in geometry, see Hilbert and Cohn-Vossen (1952).

[6] For more on ideal elements in Hilbert's geometry, see Stillwell (2014).

[7] The existence of eternal truths is also taken as a proof for the existence of God. As existing things cannot derive from anything but existing things, the eternal truths must have "their existence in a certain absolute or metaphysically necessary *subject*, that is, in God, through whom those things which would otherwise be imaginary are realized" (*On the Ultimate Origination of Things*, 1697; see Leibniz, 1989, p. 152).

to include and distinguish all possible universes in all possible combinations, that is to say, the totality of God's ideas is *complete*, or has *no gaps*. Everything not internally contradictory is possible and, therefore, exists in the mind of God. As Leibniz writes in his *Monadology* (1714): "God is not only the source of existences, but also that of essences insofar as they are real" (Leibniz, 1987, p. 43).[8] The essences contain all the "reality" existing in possibility, which we may interpret as what makes possibility feasible. Hence, without God "not only would nothing exist, but also nothing would be possible." God's understanding is defined as "the realm of eternal truths or that of the ideas on which they depend."

Besides understanding or knowledge, God also possesses will, which springs from his goodness and is driven by his wisdom, and power which makes his decisions effective: *power* is the source of everything, *knowledge* contains the diversity of ideas, *will* brings about changes and products in accordance with the principle of the best (M 48). Although power precedes understanding and will, as the *Theodicy* explains: "it operates as the one displays and as the other requires" (Leibniz, 1951, §149). In Leibniz's portrait of God as divine author, the divine architect teams up with the divine legislator. Consequently, the perfection of the architect's creation "expresses" the most perfect order. The skills of the architect and of the legislator coalesce into God's decision. Since there is an infinity of possible universes in God's ideas, and since only one of them can exist (M 53), the decision is made in two steps. First, all possible universes must be *distinguishable* from each other in the vision of the architect; second, there must be a *sufficient reason* for determining the choice of the legislator. Then, "God the architect pleases in every respect God the legislator" (M 89).

In Leibniz's metaphysics, God's vision is captured in the "network of monads". A monad is a *simple substance* and a *unity of perceptions*. As a simple substance, it enters into compounds and has no parts (like a point). As a unity of perceptions, it is not properly a thing that is perceived, but rather a "subject" that perceives (similar to consciousness). Now as elements of things, the monads are "the true atoms of nature"; and yet, because they have no parts, they have neither extension, nor shape, hence they are *not* observable. Moreover, "the monads have no windows through which something can enter or leave [...] Thus, neither substance nor accident can enter a monad from without" (M 7). But then, how can monads be distinguishable from one another? How can they change? Leibniz takes for

---

[8] All quotations of *Monadology* are taken from Leibniz (1989).

granted that, like every created thing, also a monad is subject to continual changes.

Since monads cannot differ in magnitude, they must have some "qualities", or *modes*. Since they have no windows, their "natural changes" must come from an *internal principle*; "no external cause would be able to influence their inner being." Leibniz makes it clear that, "besides the principle of change, there must be *diversity* [*un détail*] in that which changes, which produces, so to speak, the specification and variety of simple substances" (M 8-12). More precisely, "this diversity must involve a multitude in the unity," and such a multitude is spanned by a changeable set of states or relations. Finally, "the passing state which involves and represents a multitude in the unity or in the simple substance is nothing other than what one calls *perception*" (M 13-14). As an example of a simple substance with an internal diversity, Leibniz mentions first the soul (M 16). Then, claiming that monads have in themselves a certain perfection, a sufficiency that makes them the sources of their internal actions, he speaks of "incorporeal automata" (M 18).

Leibniz's idea of perception inherits its genes from geometry. Like the extension, it needs a subject. Like the direction, it is a mutual relation between (view) points, which does not influence their inner being. "Thus we attribute *action* to a monad insofar as it has distinct perceptions, and *passion*, insofar as it has confused perceptions" (M 49). As a ray determined by two monads, each perception defines a branch of their "network". As monads have no windows, however, each branch must perform as a mirror. As Leibniz explains:

> This *interconnection* or accommodation of all created things to each other, and each to all the others, brings it about that each simple substance has relations that express all the others, and consequently, that each simple substance is a perpetual *living mirror* of the universe. (M 56)

> Just as the same city viewed from different directions appears entirely different and, as it were, multiplied *perspectively*, in just the same way it happens that, because of the infinite multitude simple substances, there are, as if were, just as many different universes, which are, nevertheless, only perspectives on a single one, corresponding to the different points of view of each monad. (M 57)

Here is how the thorough vision of God is depicted. The infinite perspectives provide "the way of obtaining as much variety as possible, but with the greatest order possible, that is, it is the way of obtaining as much perfection as possible" (M 58). Here is how Leibniz states his "criterion of perfection", i.e., the maximum of variety with the maximum of order.[9]

What remains to be spelled out is how a particular configuration can be selected from the whole. What makes a particular universe the one entitled to exist? The idea of *perfection* provides the key to answer this question. To explain the passage from the "metaphysical" truths of every possible universe to the "physical" truths of ours, Leibniz[10] appeals to the "very fact" that essence in itself tends to exist. This entails that "all possible things, or things expressing an essence or possible reality, tend towards existence with equal right in proportion to the quantity of essence or reality, or to the degree of perfection which they involve; for *perfection is nothing but quantity of essence*" (Leibniz, 1969, p. 487). The conclusion is that the rules of perfection require *maximizing existence*. Hence, out of all possible universes, God chooses the one through which the greatest amount of essence, i.e., feasible possibility, is brought into existence. "And this is the cause of the existence of *the best*, which wisdom makes known to God, which his goodness makes him choose, and which his power makes him produce" (M 55).

Reversing perspective, Leibniz's metaphysics also reverses Leonardo's viewpoint on nature and artifice. In his *Trattato della Pittura* (I.24), Leonardo asserts that painting, as a science, triumphs over nature. The claim finds its reason in the primacy of geometry over the discontinuous terms of arithmetic, for the continuity of forms in space inspires the painter to create infinite works while the constituent parts of nature are finite (Leonardo, 1890). For Leibniz instead, nature as divine art infinitely surpasses all human art (M 64). Again a mathematical reason supports the claim, as the infinitesimal calculus assists the divine architect in the construction of nature.

> And the author of nature has been able to practice this divine and infinitely marvellous artifice, because each portion of matter is not only divisible to infinity, as the ancients have recognized, but is also actually subdivided without end, each part divided into parts having some *motion* of

---

[9] For a more comprehensive discussion on this point, see Perkins (2004).
[10] In his essay *On the Radical Origination of Things*, 1697 (Leibniz, 1969).

their own: otherwise, it would be impossible for each por-
tion of matter to express the whole universe. (M 65)

Once geometry has guided Leibniz to see the Euclidean points as *view-points*, and metaphysics to see perceptions as rays, the artifice of monads would now require rays to be also endowed with a *phase*. But metaphysics bans complex numbers from its land:

It is true that in my system there is no infinity and the infinitesimals are not magnitudes. My metaphysics bans them from its lands. It gives them retreat solely in the imaginary spaces of the geometrical calculus, where these notions are admitted as well as the roots that are called imaginary. (Letter to Fontenelle; Leibniz, 1854)

The point still at issue, however, is the rationale of nature itself. If monads are living mirrors, the passage from geometry to the theory of nature may require mirrors to become glasses.

10.2.3. *The nature of the artifice*

The difference between the divine artifice and human art, Leibniz comments, is that each part of the divine machine is still a machine, as it encodes the characters of the whole.

For a machine constructed by man's art is not a machine in each of its parts. For example, the tooth of a brass wheel has parts or fragments which, for us, are no longer artificial things, and no longer have any marks to indicate the machine for whose the wheel was intended. But natural machines, that is, living bodies, are still machines in their least parts, to infinity. (M 64)

Here is why each organic body of a living thing is a kind of divine machine, or natural automaton, which infinitely surpasses all artificial automata.[11] But does nature also accommodate inorganic matter? Are there things, which dwell in nature, without an organized physical structure?

---

[11] For a subtle account of a path from exact sciences to life phenomena, which could help elaborate Leibniz's approach, unconventional for his time and still open to discussion, see [Longo (2009)].

Where is the boundary between the organic and the inorganic? How can a "thinking thing" be separated from an extended thing?

In contrast to the Cartesian separation between *res cogitans* and *res extensa*, which implies the separation between mathematical thought and physical world, "logical subject" and "physical object" overlap in Leibniz's concept of *being*. It grows out of the mathematical concept of differential, as a principle of change as well as a unity of *measure*. It incorporates the topological determination of the monad, as a viewpoint, and the multitude of its relational properties (within a unity). As a result, Leibniz's system of nature embodies the intelligence of monads. At this stage, Cassirer (1902) notices, the key role of continuity in Leibniz's thought becomes apparent as a leading principle from the mere geometry of point to the being of nature. Continuity and distinguishability hold as basic principles.

What makes monads able to trigger interactions is their essentially relational character, namely, their *perceptive function*. What makes each monad different from any other is its own set of perceptions, or attributes. The crucial point is that this set is changeable. Indeed, all the *internal actions* of simple substances consist only in perceptions and their changes (M 17). As a ray between two monads, each perception lights a mode, or attribute, of the (simple) substance shared by the two monads. Perkins (2004) comments that Leibniz agrees with Spinoza in claiming that any interaction must involve modes of one substance rather than distinct substances. For Spinoza, however, this means that there is only one substance, while for Leibniz it means that each substance expresses the entire universe, from a different perspective. Thus, each substance is determined insofar as its modes are determined. In his *Primary Truths* (1686?), Leibniz writes:

> Indeed, *all individual substances are different expressions of the same universe* and different expressions of the same universal cause, namely God. But the expressions vary in perfection, just as different representations or drawings of the same town from different points of view do. (Leibniz, 1989, p. 33)

The main concern is how to figure out the relation between monads and created things, as the monads do not interact. It is here that Leibniz asks for the intervention of God. God alone knows from the beginning of things what every monad rightly demands (M 51). This is why he is the "primitive unity", or the first [*originaire*] simple substance, from which all monads are generated (M 47). Being grounded in the primitive unity, interactions must meet criteria of equity and symmetry:

> Actions and passions among creatures are mutual. For God, comparing two simple substances, finds in each reasons that require him to adjust the other to it; and consequently, what is active in some respects is passive from another point of view: *active* insofar as what is known distinctly in one serves to explain what happens in another; and *passive* insofar as the reason for what happens in one is found in what is known distinctly in another. (M 52)

Can we explain perception in physical terms, putting aside the metaphysical notion of substance? How can we measure a perception? Indisputably, perception is a qualitatively different sort of entity from all the attributes of a physical system. Leibniz feels obliged to admit: "*perception*, and what depends on it, *is inexplicable in terms of mechanical reasons*, that is, through shapes and motions." His argument goes as follows:

> If we imagine that there is a machine whose structure makes it think, sense, and have perceptions, we could conceive it enlarged, keeping the same proportions, so that we could enter into it, as one enters into a mill. Assuming that, when inspecting its interior, we will only find parts that push one another, and we will never find anything to explain a perception. And so, we should seek perception in the simple substance and not in the composite or in the machine. (M 17)

Despite inspecting every part of the machine, as it pertains a simple substance, perception is not observable. The distinct character of the natural automaton then is that "the parts that push one another" must also *express* one another. Leibniz defines his understanding of "expression" in the letter to Arnould mentioned above:

> One thing expresses another, in my usage, when there is a constant and regular relation between what can be said about one and about the other. It is in this way that a projection in perspective expresses a geometric figure. (Leibniz, 1969, p. 339)

Natural processes unfold through series of transformations mutually related. To make these series knowable to one another, there must be a "constant and regular" relation mapping every given element of one series exactly to one element of the other. Thus, the possibility to establish univocal relations between two series of changes rests on continuity. It is continuity that attributes a sequence of a motion's states to the same mobile system. However, a sharp definition of the infinite multiplicity of states in the trajectory of a system, *per se* one and the same, involves an "act of reason".

What distinguishes us from animals and gives us *reason* is the knowledge of necessary and eternal truths. "It is also through the knowledge of necessary truths and through their abstractions that we rise to *reflective acts*, which enable us to think of that which is called 'I' and enable us to consider that this or that is in *us*." That is what we call the rational soul, or *mind* (M 29-30). The necessary and eternal truths are "truth of reasoning". Yet there are also "truths of fact", concerning the series of things distributed throughout the universe of creatures. They must have a sufficient reason as well. Now the search for this reason involves other prior or more detailed contingencies, and it might go on *ad infinitum* on account of the immense differentiation of nature (M 37). Therefore, it must lie outside the sequence or *series* of this multiplicity of contingencies, however infinite it may be:

> And this is why the ultimate reason of things must be in
> a necessary substance in which the diversity of changes is
> only eminent, as in its source. This is what we call God.
> (M 38)

10.3. Chinese Interlude

In the correspondence with Arnould, Leibniz intends to answer two central questions: how the soul perceives the motions of its body, and how an individual entity could contain once for all everything that will ever happen to it. He proceeds in a "natural way" from the notion of substance towards his design of the *pre-established* harmony:

> By the concept of substance or of a completed being in
> general, which implies that its present state is always a
> natural result of its precedent state, it follows that it is

the nature of each individual substance, and consequently
of each soul, to express the universe. It has been created
from the beginning in such a way that by virtue of the laws
of its own nature it must come to agree with all that takes
place in bodies and particularly in its own [...] After all
this I cannot guess where one can still find the slightest
shadow of difficulty, unless we are to deny that God can
create substances so constituted from the beginning that
by virtue of their own nature they thereafter agree with
the phenomena of all the others. (Leibniz, 1969, p. 340)

Through the doctrine of creation, the harmony of God's plan can flow
into the real world. The invisible cosmos of monads gives shape to the
created matter, and animates the organic bodies of nature.

Philosophers have been greatly perplexed about the origin
of forms, entelechies, or souls. But today, when exact inquiries on plants, insects, and animals have shown us that
organic bodies in nature are never produced from chaos or
putrefaction, but always through seeds in which there is,
no doubt, some *preformation*, it has been judged that, not
only the organic body was already there before conception,
but there was also a soul in this body; in brief, the animal itself was there, and through conception this animal
was merely prepared for a great transformation, in order
to become an animal of another kind. (M 74)

Joseph Needham praises the originality of Leibniz's metaphysics of monads and pre-established harmony in the frame of European culture, and emphasized the affinities with the (ancient) Chinese thought. In his *Science
and Civilization in China*, he claims:

It would be hardly wrong to say that Leibniz's monads
were the first appearance of organisms upon the stage
of occidental theorising [...] His pre-established harmony
(though couched in theist terms, as for a European milieu
it had to be) seems strangely familiar to those who have
become accustomed to the Chinese world-picture. That
things should not react upon one another but all work
together by a harmony of wills was no new idea for the

Chinese; it was the foundation of their correlative thinking. (Needham, 1956, p. 292)

Accordingly, Needham seeks to shows that Chu Hsi, the "greatest Chinese thinker", developed in the 12th century a "philosophy of organism",
which finds no analogue in Europe. If Chu Hsi can be regarded as a lucid
heir of the long tradition of the Chinese correlative coordinative thinking,
Leibniz is the first European philosopher who would benefit from his legacy.
In contrast with European philosophy, which tended to find reality in *substance*, Chinese philosophy tended to find it in *relation* (Chang Tung-Sun,
1939).[12] It is very sensible to conjecture that Leibniz compared his conception of expression with the Chinese attention to the alternation of aspects in
natural phenomena. In Chinese thought, as Needham remarks, two aspects
are not connected by a cause and effect relationship, but "rather 'paired'
like the obverse and the reverse of something, or to use a metaphor from
the Book of Changes, like echo and sound, or shadow and light."

Leibniz's interest in China is well known and documented, but there is
no clear evidence that his philosophy is indebted to Chinese thought in general, or to Neo-Confucianism in particular. Leibniz's philosophical system,
as we have seen, has a strong mathematical structure, while mathematics
plays no significant role in the philosophical speculations of the ancient
Chinese. Moreover, the fundamental ideas of the *Monadology* are already
in the *Discourse on Metaphysics* (1686), while Leibniz's first contacts with
the Jesuits' reports from China date back to the 1690s and his first writings on China to 1698-1699 (preface to *Novissima Sinica*). Nevertheless,
certain similarities are striking. Those similarities, Perkins (2004) argues,
could serve to advance Leibniz's avowedly ecumenical ends. His main concern is in cross-cultural interaction and understanding. Even two worlds
separated by an enormous distance, like Europe and China, may mutually
instruct and enlighten one another (Bernard, 1937). It is through synthesis,
more than through analysis, that different cultures can discover unifying
elements beyond the ideas and coordinate them into a "whole".

---

[12] As is written in a passage of the Han apocrypha, the *Li Wei Chi Ming Chêng*: "The
movements of the rites accord with the *chhi* of the Heaven and the *chhi* of the Earth.
When the four seasons are in mutual accord, when the Yin and Yang complement each
other, when the sun and the moon give forth their light (unimpeded by fogs or eclipses),
and when superiors and inferiors are in intimate harmony with one another, then (all)
things, (all) persons and (all) animals, are in accord with their own natures and functions
(*ju chhi hsing ming*)" (quoted in Needham, 1959, p. 290).

Leibniz exposes his view on Chinese thought and religion in a long letter to M. de Remond written in March 1716, published as *Discours sur la Théologie naturelle des Chinois* (1987). Stressing the superiority of the ancient Chinese doctrines over the moderns, Leibniz aims to set down a proper method for a profitable dialogue with China. More than a treatise on philosophy, the *Discours* provides a refined argument for encouraging the Chinese to join the family of Christian Church. Jesuits must show them the truth, "but not simply by quoting from the Bible and giving them telescopes; show them also how both theological and *scientific* truth could be read in their own most ancient writings" (Cook and Rosemont, 1981). The four and last section of the *Discours* explains Leibniz's understanding of the development of Chinese thought, and his strategy to convince both the Chinese and the Europeans that Confucian views were compatible with Christian doctrine. The section concerns the Book of Changes (*Yi Jing*), a "metaphysics of numbers" in which Father Bouvet recognizes the system of Pythagoras and Plato.[13] As Leibniz says:

> Father Bouvet and I discovered the very literal significance,
> of the characters of Fuxi, the founder of the emperor. They
> only consist of combinations of broken or solid lines, and
> are regarded as the most ancient and the simplest of China.
> There are 64 figures in the Book of Changes [...] The con-
> necting structure is a binary arithmetic which that great
> ruler seems to have possessed and that I have found anew
> some thousands of years later [...] This also shows how the
> ancient Chinese overtook the moderns, not only in devo-
> tion (which is the most perfect moral), but also in science.

Notwithstanding the theological weaknesses of the modern Chinese, a *natural theology* consistent with Christianity seems incorporated in the ancient texts. Leibniz intends to light the mathematical reason behind that consistency. Besides theological ideas consonant to Christian ideas, those texts also reveal – in the hexagrams composed of broken and solid lines – mathematical concepts analogues to his new binary system. This system clearly shows how all things are created out of unity and nothingness; indeed, the origin of numbers provides the best demonstration of God's almighty power.

---

[13]For an illuminating analysis of the figures of the *Yi Jing*, see Jullien (1993).

Although the *Yi Jing*'s code does not parallel the "universal characteristic" that Leibniz is pursuing, i.e., a universal language formed from concepts instead of arbitrary symbols, it might show the "common structure" of natural theology. The figures of the ancient Book of Changes appear to suggest, through binary arithmetic, "a mystical model that related God to creation" (Swetz, 2003). Thus, "it was their very high level of rationality that made the Chinese people the most likely non-Christian candidates for true Christian conversion without any missionary compromises nor even a reliance on Revelation" (Cook and Rosemont, 1981).

The doctrine of creation, however, proves to be one of the main obstacles for Chinese conversion to Christianity.[14] Creation provides evidence of the pre-determined harmony in God's design. Similarly, the ancient Chinese recognized a fundamental harmony in the world, i.e., a harmony of resonant possibilities. But they never saw this harmony as having a reason, conceived of as an "intentional action". For the ancient Chinese, as Granet (1934) puts it: "The idea of correspondence has a great significance and replaces the idea of causality, for things are connected rather than caused." In fact, the *Yi Jing* does not contain laws of inference, but rules connecting the natural situations represented by the hexagrams. And the relevant hexagram is to be determined at random by tossing coins. If both the *Yi Jing* and the Bible intend to describe the rationale of the world, the former does not secure any internal "truth" to be proved or unraveled. The *Yi Jing* shows the "reason of things" in their interconnection, in the *logic of immanence* (Jullien, 1993).

When looking at Chinese painting, as Jullien (2003) suggests, it is illuminating to consider the essential lesson of Shitao. He focuses on the passage from the informal to the form: the simplest one, just a stroke, is already complete as it contains all the possible forms (*yi hua*). This first stroke, which develops on the paper, reproduces the continuous process of the "creation-formation" of things, of the emergence of the visible from the invisible background. It shows the passage from the original "it is not there", the without-form of the non-differentiated background (the great simplicity – *tai pu*, or the "non-separated" – *hun-dun*), to the "it is there", which constructs the diversity of forms in continuous motion. In a universe dwelled neither by God nor by a demiurge, it is this first and unique stroke of brush that is in charge of performing all those fictions. Here is the vanishing point of the artifice. Does Leibniz see it?

---

[14]For more about this, see Perkins (2004, Chap. 3).

10.4.   From Natural Theology to Quantum Information

Once the doctrine of creation has come into question, we may take up the challenge and play the game: How to build from scratch the most perfect universe? How to accommodate it in a suitable representation space?

10.4.1.   *In the reverse perspective*

Descartes conceived the extension as an "inert substance", and used real numbers as coordinates to distinguish the points in a given space. In contrast with Descartes' "*metric* geometry", Leibniz's "*geometric* analysis" breathes continuity into points which become "moving subjects". In the sight of a point, the extension of space emerges from its visual field. A "line" springs from a visual ray, a "plane" grows out of an angle of view. The divergence between classical and quantum physics may be seen as a switch from a Cartesian to a Leibnizian perspective. Classical physics describes the world by adding the laws of motion to "punctual" initial conditions; quantum physics draws the description of the world from unitary transformations. Which is the one that could fit the world of monads?

Passing from essence (*beable*) to existence (*being*) monads must perform in the guise of *glasses* rather than mirrors. Hence, let perceptions become *observable* as physical states. Indeed, *esse est percipi*. But first and foremost, perception (as a direction) needs *two* points to be determined. Thus, the simple constituents of created things (physical systems) must come into existence as pairs. This imposes one constraint on any virtual creation, overlooked in Leibniz's *Monadology*. Given the infinity of perceptions, the number of created things must be the logarithm to the base two of that infinity. Therefore, the matter is not *actually* divisible without end (M 65). Incidentally, Kronecker was right for God just needs to create the natural numbers. On the other hand, Leibniz's principle of continuity holds for the evolution of each monad, i.e., for its *passing state* of perception (M 14). Replacing monads with physical systems, this means that there must be a continuous reversible transformation on a physical system between any two distinct states of that system (Hardy, 2001). What else is needed for the harmony of monads?

10.4.2.   *God's will and quantum randomness*

For Leibniz, there must be a reason to cause things to happen. The harmony of creation has an ultimate reason in God, the original unity. The need for a principle of sufficient reason is claimed in a letter to M. de Remond, written in 1714:[15]

> So far we have just spoken as simple *physicists*; now we
> must raise to *metaphysics*, by making use of the *great prin-
> ciple*, little used, commonly, that *nothing takes place with-
> out sufficient reason*, that is, that nothing happens without
> it being possible for someone who knows enough things to
> give a reason sufficient to determine why is so and not
> otherwise. (Leibniz, 1989, p. 210)

Thus, "reasonable" means "possible for someone who knows why is so and not otherwise." Since no reason for the world can be found in any one of its states, as Leibniz explains in his essay *On the Ultimate Origination of Things* (1697), the reason must be found outside the chain of natural processes. "For in eternal things, even if there is no cause, we must still understand there to be a reason" (*Ibid.*, p. 149). In the *Theodicy*, Leibniz's argues against a conception of will as freedom emerging from indifference. The will cannot find a way without a reason to determine it:

> It is as if one were to suppose that God had decreed to
> make a material sphere, with no reason for making it of
> any particular size. This decree would be useless, it would
> carry with it that which would prevent its effect. It would
> be quite another matter if God decreed to draw from a
> given point one straight line to another given straight line,
> without any determination of the angle, either in the decree
> or in its circumstances. For in this case the determination
> would spring from the nature of the thing, the line would
> be perpendicular, and the angle would be right, since that
> is all that is *determined and distinguishable*. It is thus
> one must think of the creation of the best of all possible
> universes, all the more since God not only decrees to cre-
> ate a universe, but decrees also to create the best of all.
> (Leibniz, 1951, §196)

What springs from the nature of things is all that is "determined and distinguishable". Even though for the principle of sufficient reason the

---

[15]Published as *Principles of Nature and Grace*, 1714 (Leibniz, 1989).

harmony is pre-established in the divine intellect, the structure of that
harmony is the "nature" of things. In Leibniz's words:

> What, therefore, is the ultimate reason for the divine will?
> The divine intellect [...] What then is the reason for the
> divine intellect? The harmony of things. What is the
> reason for the harmony of things? *Nothing*. For example,
> no reason can be given for the ratio of 2 to 4 being the
> same as that of 4 to 8, not even in the divine will. This
> depends on the essence itself, or the idea of things. For
> the essences of things are numbers, as it were, and contain
> the possibility of being which God does not make as he
> does existence, since these possibilities or ideas of things
> coincide rather in God himself.[16]

What numbers then contain the *possibility* of being? Those numbers
must be the bricks of the construction.

In classical physics, a complete description of the (initial) state of a system is encapsulated in a point of the phase space, and a continuous function
(the Hamiltonian) describes how the system evolves from one state to another. The *deterministic* character of the theory relies on some metaphysical assumptions (Hughes, 1989) such as: (a) measuring a physical quantity
for a system, we can think of this quantity as a *property* of the system; (b)
a measurement of one particular quantity of a system does not affect the
other properties of the system.

In quantum physics also, the evolution of systems is described by a continuous function, the Schrödinger wave function. This function is not only
continuous, but also *complex*. Indeed, complex numbers capture the essence
of quantum systems. If Leibniz understands complex numbers as "amphib-
ians between being and not being,"[17] Dirac (1930) regards a quantum state
as "intermediate", for it results from the *superposition* of pure states, given

---

[16]Letter to Magnus Wedderkopf, May 1671 (Loemker, 1969, p. 146; *my italics*).

[17]Despite complex numbers originate in the late Renaissance, their formal properties remain unclear until Hamilton's definition (1835), and their usefulness for physics remains
unexploited until quantum theory. Girolamo Cardano, who first introduces "imaginary
roots" in his *Ars Magna* (1545), refers to them as quantities "as subtle as useless". Leibniz pairs them with infinitesimals, as "useful fictions" with a *fundamentum in re*. For
more on Cardano's attitude to complex numbers and probability, and their synergy in
quantum physics, see Ekert (2008).

by the wave function. The *indeterministic* character of quantum theory flows by projecting pure states on to real physical quantities.

As we have seen, monads change *continuously* from one set of perceptions to another. Leibniz asks for more than simple continuous changes: "There must be *diversity in that which changes*," for no external cause can affect the inner being of monads. Hence, diversity involves an original *multitude in the unity*. In physical terms, this diversity can be spanned by a finite set of pure states. Therefore, a monad can be observed in some finite number of distinguishable states. As simple substances, monads demand just a two-state system. In line with the image of perception as a ray, distinguishable states can be thought of as antipodes through the "unite sphere" of the monad. All this strongly suggests that monads may dwell in a quantum universe. But how can "the perfect *harmony* between the perceptions of the monad and the motions of bodies" (Leibniz, 1989, p. 208) be consistent with *quantum randomness*?

Threading his way on the edge of Cartesian dualism, as shown in the first section, Leibniz is led to conceive of continuity as what makes the *ideal* a mathematical object. To help clarify what it means for the ideal to become an *object*, we may think of the concepts of limit, of irrational number, or of imaginary root. All these concepts are born by taking the *reason* for mathematical construction to its vanishing point; hence, they bring about the visual field of the whole construction. In Leibniz's perspective, monads may help think what it means to view a physical system from the inside as opposed to the outside.

From the outside, we view physical systems as points on a vector space, and the connecting mechanism is given by the equations of motion. Monads ask for a reverse perspective. Mechanism, for Leibniz, requires a foundation in individual substances whose principle of activity is "mind" (Arthur, 2001). On the inside, every monad contains the entire universe in the unity of perceptions. The internal action consists of a constant change of perceptions that leave invariant the total unity. So it may be expressed by a unitary transformation. To find a way out, the monad needs to choose one direction first, and set its visual field accordingly. Since the opposite way involves a rotation of $\pm\pi$, each direction opens an ideal visual angle of 2π. Notice that the orthogonal direction ($\pm\pi/2$) defines a visual angle of π. Then rotating its visual plane about one axis, the monad can set a mapping of perceptions over a unit sphere in a two dimensional complex space. Thus to chart their universe, monads may well use complex numbers. To fulfil their temptation to exist, however, they must count on bodies. This requires them to make a decision about *which* way out, and let perception become *real*.

From the outside, there is no access to the internal view of monads. Therefore, which perception will occur is unknown, or uncertain. Quantum theory uses projection operators to tabulate probabilities of the system being in a particular state. Leaving the space of the ideal view, the imaginary and the real overlap in the space of actual measurements. Thus, probability amplitudes must be squared to provide real probabilities. The metaphysical assumption that physical systems are created with unchangeable features gives shape to the notion of probability as *ignorance*. On the inside, however, the "passing state" evolves continuously and the symmetrical distribution of internal states does not privilege any particular direction. Choosing one way out, perception enters the real world. But from a monad's point of view, there is no reason for choosing one way instead of another. A perfect harmony of possibilities decrees that the choice must be *random*.[18]

10.4.3.   *The nature of information*

At first sight, a pair of monads looks very much like an EPR pair. Indeed, perception, as a possibility of relation, needs two monads to be measured. And, since any relation between monads can be thought of as a channel through "glass beads", the shared perception (observable) can be detected either in one way (state) or in the opposite. But how does the measurement take place? Where is the observer? In this setting, the possibility of "correlations at the source" is not a question to be solved by measurement, but rather an "axiom". Both monads and each of them are a *primitive* unity of perceptions. All information about the universe is encapsulated in every monad from the absolute beginning. No further information comes from, or goes through, measurement.

It is the action of an internal principle, as Leibniz says, that governs the change from one perception to another[19] (M 15). The *substance* of the monad, then we may say, is grasped by a unitary transformation. In

---

[18]As Leibniz admits in his *Theodicy*: "This so-called *fatum*, which binds even the Divinity, is nothing but God's own nature, his own understanding, which furnishes the rules for his wisdom and his goodness; it is a happy necessity, without which he would be neither good nor wise" (Leibniz, 1951, §191). For a clarifying conceptual analysis of the notion of randomness as relative unpredictability, see Calude and Longo (2015).

[19]Leibniz warns that "perception must be carefully distinguished from *apperception* or conscious awareness" (M 14).

the *Monadology*, the simple substance coincides with the continuity principle of the disclosure of itself. There is no external relation between single substances: if monads had windows, they would lose their own "identity". What is related, within the substance, is the primitive capability of perception with its effects. The "essence" of the substance is not rest, but motion; its life is in continuously changing from one state to another. Solely the original unity must be preserved. Therefore, every monad must be also endowed with an original capability of *representing*, which makes it able to generate the whole ensemble of phenomena. Knowledge is a kind of awakening, or revelation: "The ideas of things that we are not actually thinking about are in our mind as the shape of Hercules is in rough marble."[20] Leibniz's causal determinism rests on his claim that "substance is change"; it is a *metaphysical* determinism. Here, however, we may also see the matrix of quantum randomness. Here is the ontological character of quantum probability.

Leibniz's determinism is a "metaphysical mathematicism" (Cassirer, 1936). Both Leibniz and Descartes avouch the identity of mathematics and nature, but they conceive of a theory of nature in different ways. Koyré (1950) emphasizes that while Descartes fails in his attempt to "reconstruct the world" on the identity of matter and space, Newton manages to establish a mathematical physics by distinguishing the *corpuscular* matter from the *empty* space and adapting the mathematical entities to the requirements of physics. Leibniz's calculus, by contrast, grows out of his vision of geometry, where the law of continuity has replaced the Cartesian *res extensa*. A physical theory drawn from the metaphysics of monads may well be like a Pythagorean representation of nature by means of complex numbers. Indeed, quantum theory provides such a picture. Not surprisingly, monads and qubits pose a similar problem as to how to gain access to their infinite internal information. But what is information?

In the *Monadology*, perception plays a rather subtle role, encouraging comparison of its meaning with that of information. Perception is defined as the internal *passing state*. Its range varies from one, i.e., just a single (perception) state, to infinity, i.e., the entire unity. It is something *ideal*, or an "abstraction", as "is inexplicable in terms of mechanical reasons." It is a function of correlation, as it enables monads to express each other. Can it be understood as information for the monad? In contrast with the sense of information as a "measure of one's freedom of choice when

---

[20]Cf. *Meditations on Knowledge, Truth, and Ideas*, 1687 (Leibniz, 1989).

one selects a message" (Weaver and Shannon, 1949), perception cannot measure monad's freedom of choice, because, as a passing state, it is the choice itself. Here is the reason for seeing the substance of a monad as a unitary transformation in a complex space. But a unitary transformation does not describe a "qubit", it rather describes a *computation step*.

Investigating the meaning of information, Deutsch and Marletto (2014) discern two heterogeneous components – logical and physical – in the notion. "Despite being physical," they say, "information also has a counterfactual character: an object in a particular physical state cannot be said to carry information unless it *could have been* in a different state." Therefore, they suggest a more coherent "physical" definition of the concept of information in terms of computation. Their "constructor theory of information" may be considered, in broad sense, in Leibniz's path as it derives *difference* (information) from *change* (computation). Indeed, it rests on "first understanding a spontaneous change" (in a physical system) as a *computation*. Hence, an *information variable* is defined as a "cloneable computation variable." But what needs to be "cloned" in the real world is just *given* in the complex space.

A monad can also define information in terms of change. Indeed it cannot do otherwise, as its substance is change. In the complex space where monads should dwell, change is expressed by unitary transformation. But any unitary transformation has its *dual*, and both overlap with the same orthogonal transformation in the real space. For a monad, the *passing state* of perception, involves *two* states and, therefore, conveys a "unity of information". Information is *what* a simple change can bring about, its ideal domain. Continuity is the ideal extension of the *motion* involved in change, from one *situs* to its dual (clone or reflection). Distinguishability is the ideal *duality* of states involved in change. Thus, continuity and distinguishability are the basic ingredients of any ideal construction which dispenses with a creator. Change is the brick of the construction.

10.5. Conclusion

"I take it to be an unassailable truth," Hughes (1989) remarks in *The Structure and Interpretation of Quantum Mechanics*, "that what Taoism, Confucianism, Zen Buddhism [...] have in common, they have in common with quantum mechanics. As truths go, however, this one isn't illuminating. Quantum mechanics [...] is essentially a mathematical theory; one will gain little genuine insight into it without some awareness of the mathematical models it employs." Leibniz not only concurs with Hughes in conceiving of mathematics as essential to gain genuine insight into a physical theory, but also relies on mathematics for securing the "archetypes", eternal and unchangeable, of being. Thus, he supposes that the figures of the ancient Book of Changes (*Yi Jing*) might contain a "metaphysics of numbers" which relates God to creation and, therefore, provides a common language for Chinese conversion to Christianity.

In fact, the connecting structure of those figures, which emerges from combinations of broken and solid lines, is analogue to Leibniz's binary arithmetic. But Leibniz wants more than an "arithmetic" language; he wants a *universal* language. For the alphabet of such a language to express the "alphabet of thought", its symbols must secure the substance of ideas. Rather than from binary compounds, Leibniz would expect to gain some insight into those symbols from Chinese ideograms. Then, the mechanism of the *Yi Jing*, if it were there, might offer a key. As a mirror of the mechanism of universe, Leibniz's universal language is supposed to result from an alphabet of concepts processed in the simplest and most perfect way, namely, by symbolic calculation.

It may appear ironic that, after inventing an almost "automatic" notation for the differential and integral calculus (Davis, 2000), Leibniz seems to have overlooked the universal character of binary digits, i.e., the symbols of his own binary arithmetic. We may well blame metaphysics for blinding his eyes. Once the Kantian revolution has been accomplished, Hilbert (1922) clearly sees the significance of Shitao's lesson for his *New Groundings of Mathematics*: "In the beginning was the sign." So, we may say that Turing's computational model expresses Leibniz's *calculus ratiocinator* in Hilbert's terms and, therefore, fulfils Leibniz's visionary dream of a *universal characteristic* only in part.

But what is obscured by metaphysics is enlightened by geometry. The ideal, meaningful character that Leibniz asks for the symbols of his alphabet has "imaginary roots". Once complex numbers reveal the harmony of quantum bits, Leibniz's dream appears fulfilled entirely by quantum computation. As to the reason for the harmony, we may just gain some insight from the *Glass Bead Game*:

> Nothing is harder, yet nothing is more necessary, than
> to speak of certain things whose existence is neither

demonstrable nor probable. The very fact that serious and conscientious men treat them as existing things brings them a step closer to existence and to the possibility of being born. (Hesse, 1943)

Bibliography

Arthur, T. W. (2001) Introduction to Leibniz (2001).

Bernard, H. (1937) Chü Hsi's Philosophy and Its Interpretation by Leibniz, *Thien Hsia*, Vol. 5, N. 9 (Shangai), pp. 9-18.

Calude, C. S. and Longo, G. (2015) Classical, Quantum and Biological Randomness as Relative Unpredictability, *Natural Computing*, Vol. 14, N. 4.

Cassirer, E. (1902) *Leibniz' System in seinen wissenschaftlichen Grundlagen*. (Elwert, Marburg).

Cassirer, E. (1936) *Determinism and Indeterminism in Modern Physics*. (Yale University Press, New Haven).

Chang Tung-Sun (1939) A Chinese Philosopher's Theory of Knowledge, *Yenching Journal of Social Studies, I*.

Cook, D. J. and Rosemont, H. Jr. (1981) The Pre-Established Harmony between Leibniz and Chinese Thought, *Journal of the History of Ideas*, Vol. 42, N. 2, pp. 253-267.

Davis, M. (2000) *The Universal Computer. The Road from Leibniz to Turing* (W. W. Norton & Company, New York).

Dirac, P.A.M. (1930) *The Principles of Quantum Mechanics*. (Clarendon Press, Oxford).

Deutsch, D. and Marletto, C. (2014) Constructor Theory of Information, *Proceedings of the Royal Society A* Vol. 471, 20140540.

Ekert, A. (2008). Complex and Unpredictable Cardano, *International Journal of Theoretical Physics*, 47, 2101-2119.

Erdmann, J. E. (1840) *Leibnitii opera omnia*. (Berlin)

Gerhardt, C. I. (1849-55) *G. W. Leibniz: Mathematische Schriften*, 7 Vols. (Berlin)

Granet, M. (1934) *La pensée chinoise* (La Renaissance du Livre, Paris).

Hesse, H. (1943) *Das Glasperlenspiel*. (Henry Holt & Co., New York).

Hardy, L. (2001) Quantum theory from five reasonable axioms, (quant-ph 0101012).

Hilbert, D. (1922) New Groundings of Mathematics. *From Kant to Hilbert: A Source Book in the Foundations of Mathematics*, Vol. 2, ed. Ewald, W. B. (Oxford Univ. Press, Oxford 1996).

Hilbert, D. and Cohn-Vossen, S. (1952) *Geometry and the Imagination*. (Chelsea Publishing Co., New York).

Hughes, R. I. G. (1989) *The Structure and Interpretations of Quantum Mechanics*. (Harvard Univ. Press, Cambridge, MA).

Jullien, F. (1993) *Figures de l'immanence. Pour une lecture philosophique du Yi king, le Classique du changement*. (Éditions Grasset & Fasquelle, Paris).

Jullien, F. (2003) *La grande image n'a pas de forme.* (Édition du Seuil, Paris).

Koyré, A. (1950) La synthése newtonienne. *Études newtoniennes.* (Gallimard, Paris).

Leibniz, G.W. (1854) *Lettres et opuscules inédits de Leibniz 1702-1704,* ed. Foucher de Coreil, A. (Ladrange, Paris).

Leibniz, G.W. (1951) *Theodicy.* (Routledge and Kegan Paul, London).

Leibniz, G.W. (1969) *Philosophical Papers and Letters,* ed. Loemker, L. E. (Reidel, Dordrecht).

Leibniz, G.W. (1987) *Discourse on the Natural Theology of the Chinese* (Monographs of the Society for Asian and Comparative Philosophy, N. 4) (University of Hawaii Press, Honolulu).

Leibniz, G.W. (1989) *Philosophical Essays,* eds. Ariew, R. and Garber, D. (Hackett Publishing Company, Indianapolis & Cambridge)

Leibniz, G.W. (1995) *La caractétistique géométrique,* eds. Echeverría, J. and Parmentier, M. (Librairie philosophique J. Vrin, Paris).

Leibniz, G.W. (2001) *The Labyrinth of the Continuum. Writings on the Continuum Problem, 1672-1686,* ed. Arthur, R.T.W. (Yale Univ. Press, New Haven and London).

Leonardo da Vinci (1890) *Trattato della Pittura.* Codice Vaticano Urbinate 1270. (Unione Cooperativa Editrice, Rome).

Longo, G. (2009). From Exact Science to Life Phenomena: Following Schödinger and Turing on Programs, Life and Causality, *Information and Computation,* 207, pp. 545-558.

Needham, J. (1956) *Science and Civilization in China,* Vol. 2. (Cambridge Univ. Press, Cambridge).

Perkins, F. (2004) *Leibniz and China. A Commerce of Light.* (Cambridge Univ. Press, Cambridge).

Stillwell, J. (2014). Ideal Elements in Hilbert's Geometry, *Perspectives on Science,* Vol. 22, N. 1, pp. 35-55.

Swetz, F.J. (2003) Leibniz, the Yijing, and the Religious Conversion of the Chinese, *Mathematical Magazine,* Vol. 76, N. 4, pp. 276-291.

Weaver, J.A. and Shannon, C.E. (1949) *The Mathematical Theory of Communication.* (University of Illinois Press, Urbana).

Chapter 11

Generalized Event Structures and Probabilities

Karl Svozil

Institute for Theoretical Physics, Vienna University of Technology
Wiedner Hauptstraße 8-10/136, A-1040 Vienna, Austria
svozil@tuwien.ac.at
http://tph.tuwien.ac.at/~svozil

Abstract

For the classical mind, quantum mechanics is boggling enough; nevertheless more bizarre behaviour could be imagined, thereby concentrating on propositional structures (empirical logics) that transcend the quantum domain. One can also consistently suppose predictions and probabilities which are neither classical nor quantum, but which are subject to subclassicality; that is, the additivity of probabilities for mutually exclusive, co-measurable observables, as formalized by admissibility rules and frame functions.

11.1. Specker's Oracle

In his first, programmatic, article on quantum logic Ernst Specker – one of his sermons is preserved in his *Selecta* [Specker (1990), pp. 321-323] – considered a parable [Specker (1960)] which can be easily translated into the following oracle: imagine that there are three boxes on a table, each of which either contains a gem or does not. Your task is to correctly choose two of the boxes that will either both be empty or both contain a gem when opened.

Note that, according to combinatorics (or, more generally, Ramsey theory), for all classical states there always exist two such boxes among the three boxes satisfying the above property of being "both empty or both filled."

After you place your guess the two boxes whose content you have attempted to predict are opened; the third box remains closed. In Specker's malign oracle scenario it turns out that you always fail: no matter how often you try and what you choose to forecast, the boxes you have predicted as both being empty or both being full always have mixed content – one box is always filled and the other one always empty. That is, phenomenologically, or, if you like, epistemically, Specker's oracle is defined by the following behavior: if e and f denote the empty and the filled state, respectively, and $*$ stands for the third (unopened) box, then one of the following six configurations are rendered: $ef*$, $fe*$, $e*f$, $f*e$, $*ef$, or $*fe$.

Is such a Specker oracle realizable in Nature? Intuition tends to negate this. Because, more formally, per box there are two classical states e and f, and thus 2^3 such classical "ontological" configurations or classical three-box states, namely eee, eef, efe, fee, eff, fef, ffe, and fff, which can be grouped into four classes: those extreme cases with all the boxes filled and empty, those with two empty and one filled boxes, and those with two filled and one empty boxes. These can be represented by the four-partitioning (into equivalence classes with respect to the number of filled and empty boxes) of the set of all states $\{\{eee\}, \{fff\}, \{eef, efe.fee\}, \{eff, fef, eff\}\}$.

Now, on closer inspection, in any unbiased prediction (or unbiased preparation) scenario there is an ever decreasing chance that you will not hit the right prediction eventually, because for all eight possible configurations there always is at least one right prediction (either two empty or two full boxes).

Of course, if I am in command of the preparation process, and if you and me chose to conspire in such a way that I always choose to prepare, say, either eee or eef or efe or fee, and you always choose to predict ff, than you will never win. But such a scenario is hilariously biased. Also with adaptive, that is, *a posteriori,* preparation *after* the prediction, the Specker parable is realizable – in hindsight I can always ruin your prediction. But if you allow no restrictions on predictions (or preparations), and no *a posteriori* manipulation, there are no classical means to realize Specker's oracle.

Can this system be realized quantum mechanically? That is, can one find a quantum state and projection measurements rendering that kind of performance? I guess (but have no proof of it) not, because in any finite dimensional Hilbert space the associated empirical logic [von Neumann (1932); Birkhoff and von Neumann (1936)] is a merging through identifying common elements, called a *pasting* [Navara and Rogalewicz (1991)], of (possibly a continuum of) Boolean subalgebras with a finite number of atoms or, used synonymously, contexts [Svozil (2009a); Abbott *et al.* (2015a)]. And any subalgebra, according to the premises of Gleason's theorem [Gleason

(1957); Dvurečenskij (1993); Pitowsky (1998); Peres (1992)], in terms of probability theory, is classically Boolean.

As has already been pointed out by Specker, the phenomenology of the oracle suggests, that $e_i \rightarrow f_j$, and, conversely $f_i \rightarrow e_j$ for different Boxes $i, j \in \{1, 2, 3\}$, that is, "the first opened box always contains the complement of the second opened box"; and otherwise – that is, by disregarding the third (unopened) box – they are classical. Thus one could say that the contents of the two opened boxes represent the two atoms of a Boolean subalgebra 2^2. There are three such subalgebras associated with opening two of three boxes, namely $(1, 2)$, $(1, 3)$, and $(2, 3)$ which need to be pasted into the propositional structure at hand; in the quantum case this is quantum logic.

This can be imagined in two ways, by interpreting the situation as follows: (i) The first option would be to attempt to paste or "isomorphically bundle" the three subalgebras 2^2 into a three-atomic subalgebra 2^3. Clearly this attempt is futile, since this would imply transitivity, and thus yield a complete contradiction, by, say $e_1 \rightarrow f_2 \rightarrow e_3 \rightarrow f_1$. (ii) The second option would circumvent transitivity by means of complementarity (as argued originally by Specker), through a *horizontal pasting* of the three Boolean algebras, amounting to a logic of the Chinese lantern form MO_3. This is a common quantum logic rendered, for instance, by spin-$\frac{1}{2}$ measurements along different spatial directions; as well as by the quasi-classical partition logics [Svozil (2005)] of automata and generalized urn models [Wright (1990)]. But clearly, such a logic does not deal with the three boxes of Specker's oracle equally; rather the third, unopened box could be considered as a "space holder" or "indicator" labeling the associated context.

Within such a context one could, for example, attempt to consider a general wave function in eight dimensional Hilbert space $|\Psi\rangle = \sum_{i,j,k \in \{e,f\}} \alpha_{ijk} |ijk\rangle$, geometrically representable by $|e\rangle \equiv (1, 0)$ and $|f\rangle \equiv (0, 1)$, and thus $|\Psi\rangle \equiv (\alpha_{eee}, \alpha_{eef}, \ldots, \alpha_{fff})$. All three measurements (i.e. projections onto $|ijk\rangle$) commute; so one can open the boxes "independently." By listing all the associated "unbiased" measurement scenarios (including partial traces over the third box), there is no quantum way one could end up with the type of behavior one expects from Specker's oracle. Ultimately, because a general quantum state is a coherent superposition of classical states, one cannot "break outside" this extended classical domain.

So, I guess, if one insists on treating all the three boxes involved in Specker's oracle equally, this device requires supernatural means. And yet it is imaginable; and that is the beauty of it.

11.2. Observables Unrealizable by Quantum Means

In what follows we shall enumerate, as a kind of continuation of Specker's oracle, hypothetical "weird" propositional structures, in particular, certain anecdotal "zoo of collections of observables" constructed by pastings of contexts (or, used synonymously, blocks, subalgebras) containing "very few" atoms. We shall compare them to logical structures associated with very low-dimensional quantum Hilbert spaces. (Actually, the dimensions dealt with will never exceed the number of fingers on one hand.)

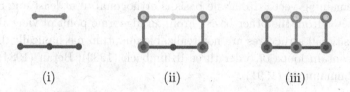

(i) (ii) (iii)

Fig. 11.1. Orthogonality diagrams with mixed two- and three-atomic contexts, drawn in different colors.

It is not too difficult to sketch propositional structures which are not realizable by any known physical device. Take, for instance, the collection of observables whose Greechie or, by another wording, orthogonality diagram [Greechie (1971)] is sketched in Fig. 11.1. In Hilbert space realizations, the straight lines or smooth curves depicting contexts represent orthogonal bases, and points on these straight lines or smooth curves represent elements of these bases; that is, two points being orthogonal if and only if they are on the same these straight line or smooth curve. From dimension three onwards, bases can intertwine [Gleason (1957)] by possessing common elements.

The propositional structure depicted in Fig. 11.1 consists of four contexts of mixed type; that is, the contexts involved have two and three atoms. No such mixed type phenomenology occurs in Nature; on the contrary, regardless of the quantized system the number of (mutually exclusive) physical outcomes, reflected by the dimension of the associated Hilbert space, always remains the same.

You may now say that this was an easy and almost trivial cheat; but what about the triangular shaped propositional structures depicted in Fig. 11.2? They surely look inconspicuous, yet none of them has a

representation as a quantum logic; simply because they have no realization
in two- and three-dimensional Hilbert space: The propositional structure
depicted in Fig. 11.2(i) has too tightly intertwining contexts, which would
mean that two different orthogonal bases in two-dimensional Hilbert space
can have an element in common (which they cannot have, except when
the bases are identical). By a similar argument, the propositional structure depicted in Fig. 11.2(ii) has "too tightly intertwined" contexts to be
representable in three-dimensional Hilbert space: in dimension three, for
two non-identical but intertwined orthogonal bases with one common vector (if they have two common elements they would have to be identical) it
is impossible to "shuffle" the remaining vectors around such that at least
one remaining vector from one basis is orthogonal to at least one remaining vector from the other basis. From an algebraic point of view all these
propositional structures are not realizable quantum mechanically, because
they contain loops of order three [Kalmbach (1983); Beran (1984); Pták
and Pulmannová (1991)].

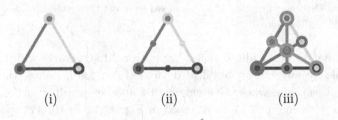

Fig. 11.2. Orthogonality diagrams representing tight triangular pastings of two- and
three-atomic contexts.

Indeed, for reasons that will be explicated later, the propositional structure depicted in Fig. 11.2(i) has no two-valued (admissible [Abbott *et al.*
(2012, 2014, 2015b)]) state equivalent to a frame function [Gleason (1957)];
a fact that can be seen by ascribing one element a "1," forcing the remaining
two to be "0." (There cannot be only zeroes in a context.) This means that
it is no quasi classical partition logic. The logic depicted in Fig. 11.2(ii) has
sufficiently many (indeed four) two-valued measures to be representable by
a partition logic [Svozil (2014a)]. The propositional structure depicted in
Fig. 11.2(iii) is too tightly interlinked to be representable by a partition
logic – it allows only one two-valued state.

In a similar manner one could go on and consider orthogonality diagrams of the "square" type, such as the ones depicted in Fig. 11.3. All

these propositional structures are not realizable quantum mechanically, because they contain loops of order four [Kalmbach (1983); Beran (1984); Pták and Pulmannová (1991)]. The propositional structure in Fig. 11.3(i) has two two-valued measures, but the union of them is not "full" because it cannot separate opposite atoms. Figs. 11.3(ii) as well as (iii) represent propositional structures with "sufficiently many" two-valued measures (e.g. separating two arbitrary atoms by different values), which are representable as partition (and, in particular, as generalized urn and automaton) logics. Actually, the number of two-valued measures for the propositional structures in Figs. 11.3(i) as well as (iii) can be found by counting the number of permutations, or permutation matrices: these are 2! and 3!, respectively. Because of the too tightly intertwined contexts the propositional structure in Fig. 11.3(iv) has no two-valued state.

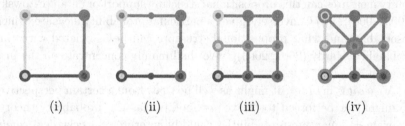

(i)   (ii)   (iii)   (iv)

Fig. 11.3. Orthogonality diagrams representing tight square type pastings of two- and three-atomic contexts.

Let us now come back to the collection of observables represented in Fig. 11.1. Are they in some form realizable, maybe even in ways "beyond" quantum realizability? Again, as long as there are "sufficiently many" two-valued measures [Wright (1978)], partition logics as well as their generalized urn and automaton models [Svozil (2005)] are capable of reproducing these phenomenological schemes. One construction yielding the pasting described in Fig. 11.1(ii) would involve a four color (associated with the four contexts) scheme; with three symbols "+," "−," and "0" in two colors representing the Boolean algebra 2^3 of two contexts, and with two symbols "+," and "−" in two colors representing the Boolean algebra 2^2 of two contexts. (I leave it to the Reader to find a concrete realization; one systematic way would be the enumeration of all two-valued measures.) Fig. 11.1(iii) does not possess a quasi-classical *simulacrum* in terms of a partition logic. For the sake of a proof by contradiction [Greechie (1971)], suppose there exist a two-valued state. Any such two-valued state needs to have exactly two

1s on the horizontal contexts, whereas it needs to have exactly three 1s on the vertical contexts; but both contexts yield (two- and three-atomic) partitions of the entire set of atoms; thus implying $2 = 3$, which is clearly wrong.

So, in a sense, one could say that the collection of observables represented in Fig. 11.1(iii) is "weirder" than the ones represented in Figs. 11.1(i)-(iii).

11.3. Generalized Probabilities Beyond the Quantum Predictions

When it comes to observables and probabilities there are two fundamental questions: (i) Given a particular collection of observables; what sort of probability measures can this propositional structure support or entail [Pitowsky (2003, 2006)]? (ii) Conversely, given a particular probability measure; which observables and what propositional structure can be associated with this probability [Hardy (2001, 2003)]? We shall mainly concentrate on the first question.

A *caveat* is in order: it might as well be that, from a certain perspective, we might not be forced to "leave" or modify classical probability theory: for example, quantum probabilities could be interpreted as classical *conditional* probabilities [Khrennikov (2015)], where conditioning is with respect to fixed experimental settings, in particular, with respect to the context measured.

11.3.1. *Subclassicality and frame functions*

In order to construct probability measures on non-Boolean propositional structures which can be obtained by pasting together contexts we shall adhere to the following assumption which we would like to call *subclassicality: every context (i.e., Boolean subalgebra, block) is endowed with classical probabilities*. In particular, any probability measure on its atoms is additive. This is quite reasonable, because it is prudent to maintain the validity of classical probability theory on those classical substructures of the propositional calculus that containing observables which are mutually co-measurable.

Subclassicality can be formalized by frame functions in the context of Hilbert spaces [Gleason (1957); Dvurečenskij (1993); Pitowsky (1998); Peres (1992)] as follows: A frame function of unit weight for a separable Hilbert space H is a real-valued function f defined on the (surface of the) unit sphere of H such that if $\{e_i\}$ is an orthonormal basis of H then $\sum_i f(e_i) = 1$. This can be translated for pastings of contexts by identifying the set of atoms $\{a_i\}$ in a particular context C with the set of vectors in one basis, and by requiring that $\sum_i f(a_i) = 1$ for all contexts C involved.

For pastings of contexts on value definite systems of observables, admissibility, which originally has been conceived as a formalization of "partial value definiteness" and value indefiniteness [Abbott *et al.* (2012, 2014, 2015b)] is essentially equivalent to the requirements imposed upon frame functions; that is, subclassicality. Nevertheless, one could also request generalized admissibility rules as follows. Let O be a set of atoms in a propositional structure, and let $f : O \to [0,1]$ be a probability measure. Then f is *admissible* if the following condition holds for every context C of O: for any $a \in C$ with $0 \leq f(a) \leq 1$, $\sum_i f(b_i) = 1 - f(a)$ for all $b_i \in C \setminus \{a\}$. Likewise, for two-valued measures v on value definite systems of observables, admissibility [Abbott *et al.* (2012, 2014, 2015b)] can be defined in analogy to frame functions: for any context $C = \{a_1, \ldots, a_n\}$ of O, the two-valued measure on the atoms $a_1, \ldots, a_n$ has to add up to one; that is, $\sum_i v(a_i) = 1$.

For the sake of a (quasi-) classical formalization, define a *two-valued measure* (or, used synonymously, *valuation,* or *truth assignment*) v on a single context $C = \{a_1, \ldots, a_n\}$ to acquire the value $v(a_i) = 1$ on exactly one a_i, $1 \leq i \leq n$ of the atoms of the context, and the value zero on the remaining atoms $v(a_{j \neq i}) = 0$, $1 \leq j \leq n$. Any (quasi-) classical probability measure, or, used synonymously, *state,* or *non-negative frame function* f (of weight one), on this context can then be obtained by a convex combination of all m two-valued measures; that is,

$$f = \sum_{1 \leq k \leq m} \lambda_k v_k, \text{ with}$$
$$1 = \sum_{1 \leq k \leq m} \lambda_k, \text{ and } \lambda_k \geq 0. \tag{11.1}$$

As far as classical physics is concerned, that is all there is – the classical probabilities are just the convex combinations of the m two-valued measures on the Boolean algebras 2^m.

This convex combination can be given a geometrical interpretation: First encode every two-valued measure on C as some m-tuple, whereby the i'th component of the m-tuple is identified with the value $v(a_i)$ of that valuation on the i'th atom of the context C; and then interpret the resulting set of m-tuples as the set of the vertices of a convex polytope.

By the Minkoswki-Weyl representation theorem [Ziegler (1994), p.29], every convex polytope has a dual (equivalent) description: either as the convex hull of its extreme points (vertices); or as the intersection of a finite number of half-spaces. More generally, one can do this not only on the atoms of one context, but also on a selection of atoms and joint probabilities of two or more contexts [Pitowsky (1989, 1991, 1994); Pitowsky and Svozil (2001)]. This results in what Boole [Boole (1958, 1862)] called *"conditions of possible experience"* for the *"concurrence of events."* In an Einstein-Podolsky-Rosen setup one ends up in Bell-type inequalities, which are prominently violated by quantum probabilities and correlations. Alas, the quantum correlations do not violate the inequalities maximally, which has led to the introduction of so-called "nonlocal boxes" [Popescu (2014)], which may be obtained by "sharpening" the two-partite quantum correlations to a Heaviside function [Krenn and Svozil (1998)].

As long as there are "sufficiently many" two-valued measures (e.g. capable of separating two arbitrary atoms) one might generalize this strategy to non-Boolean propositional structures. In particular, one could obtain quasi-classical probability measures by enumerating all two-valued measures, and by then taking the convex combination (11.1) thereof [Svozil (2009a)]. One can do this because a two-valued measure has to "cover" all involved contexts simultaneously: if subclassicality is assumed, then the same two-valued measure defined on one context contributes to all the other contexts in such a way that the sums of that measure, taken along any such context has to be additive and yield one.

11.3.2. *Cat's cradle configurations*

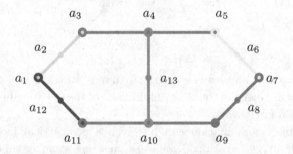

Fig. 11.4. Orthogonality diagram of a cat's cradle logic which requires that, for two-valued measures, if $v(a_1) = 1$, then $v(a_7) = 0$. For a partition logic as well as for a Hilbert space realization see Refs. [Svozil and Tkadlec (1996); Svozil (2009a)].

Consider a propositional structure depicted in Fig. 11.4. As Pitowsky [Pitowsky (2003, 2006)] has pointed out, the reduction of some probabilities of atoms at intertwined contexts yields

$$p_1 + p_7 = \frac{3}{2} - \frac{1}{2}(p_{12} + p_{13} + p_2 + p_6 + p_8) \leq \frac{3}{2}, \qquad (11.2)$$

because all probabilities p_i are non-negative. Indeed, if one applies the standard quantum mechanical Born (trace) rule to a particular realization enumerated in Fig. 4 of Ref. [Svozil and Tkadlec (1996)], then, as $a_1 \equiv \frac{1}{\sqrt{3}}(\sqrt{2}, -1, 0)$ and $a_7 \equiv \frac{1}{\sqrt{3}}(\sqrt{2}, 1, 0)$, the quantum probability of finding the quantum in a state spanned by a_7 if it has been prepared in a state spanned by a_1 is $p_7(a_1) = \langle a_7|a_1\rangle^2 = \frac{1}{9}$. Together with $p_1(a_1) = \langle a_1|a_1\rangle^2 = 1$ we obtain $p_1(a_1) + p_7(a_1) = \frac{10}{9}$, which satisfies the classical bound $\frac{3}{2}$.

Indeed, a closer look at the quantum probabilities reveals that, with $a_{13} \equiv (0, 1, 0)$, $a_{6,8} \equiv \frac{1}{2\sqrt{3}}(-1, \sqrt{2}, \pm 3)$, $p_{12}(a_1) = p_2(a_1) = 0$, $p_{13}(a_1) = \frac{1}{3}$, and $p_6(a_1) = p_8(a_1) = \frac{4}{9}$, the classical bounds of probability (11.2) – Boole's conditions of possible experience – are perfectly satisfied by the quantum predictions, since $1 + \frac{1}{9} = \frac{3}{2} - \frac{1}{2}(0 + \frac{1}{3} + 0 + \frac{2}{9} + \frac{2}{9})$. This was to be expected, as Eq. (11.2) has been derived by supposing subclassicality which is satisfied both by quasi-classical (e.g. generalized urn as well as automata) models as well as quantum mechanics.

But does that mean that the classical and quantum predictions coincide? The quantum predictions, computed under the assumption that the system is prepared in state a_1 and thus $p_1(a_1) = 1$, are enumerated in Fig. 11.5(i). Note that the sum of the probabilities of each context has to sum up to unity.

In contrast to the quantum predictions, with the same preparation, the classical predictions cannot yield any $p_7(a_1)$ other than zero, because by the way the logic is constructed there does not exist any two-valued measure satisfying $p_1(a_1) = p_7(a_1) = 1$. (This is easily derivable by proving the impossibility of any such measure [Svozil (2009b)].) They are enumerated in Fig. 11.5(ii). The full parametrization of all conceivable classical probabilities is depicted in Fig. 11.5(iii).

So, if one interprets this argument in terms of a (state dependent) Boole-Bell type inequality, all it needs is to prepare a three-state quantum system in a state along $a_1 \equiv \frac{1}{\sqrt{3}}(\sqrt{2}, -1, 0)$ and measure the projection observable along $a_7 \equiv \frac{1}{\sqrt{3}}(\sqrt{2}, 1, 0)$. In a generalized beam splitter setup [Reck *et al.* (1994)], once the detector associated with a_7 clicks on the input associated with port a_1 one knows that the underlying physical realization is "quantum-like" and not classical. This represents another type of violation of Boole's conditions of possible experience by quantized systems.

There exist more quantum predictions contradicting (quasi-) classical predictions based on additivity: suppose a tandem cat's cradle logic, which are just two cat's cradle logics intertwined at three contexts per copy, with a non-separating set of two-valued states already discussed by Kochen and Specker [Kochen and Specker (1967), Γ_3, p. 70], and explicitly parameterized in three-dimensional real Hilbert space by Tkadlec [Tkadlec (1998), Fig. 1], thereby continuing the observables and preparations already used earlier. Classical predictions based on this set of observables would require that that if one prepares a quantized system in $a_1 \equiv \frac{1}{\sqrt{3}}\left(\sqrt{2},-1,0\right)$ and measure it along $b \equiv \frac{1}{\sqrt{3}}\left(-1,\sqrt{2},0\right)$, the measurement would always yield a positive result, because every two-valued measure v on that logic must satisfy $v(a_1) = v(b) = 1$. However, the quantum predictions, also satisfying subclassicality, are $\langle b|a_1\rangle^2 = \frac{8}{9}$.

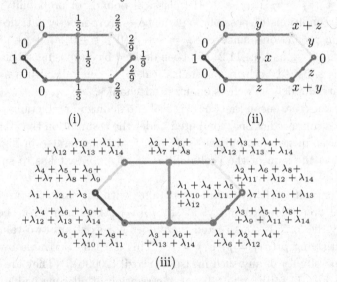

Fig. 11.5. Orthogonality diagram of the logic depicted in Fig. 11.4 with overlaid (i) quantum and (ii) classical prediction probabilities for a state prepared along a_1. The classical predictions require that x, y and z are non-negative and $x + y + z = 1$. (iii) The full parametrization of classical probabilities; with non-negative $\lambda_1, \ldots \lambda_{14} \geq 0$, and $\lambda_1 + \cdots + \lambda_{14} = 1$. Note that the special case (ii) is obtained by identifying with $\lambda_1 = x$, $\lambda_2 = y$, $\lambda_3 = z$, and $\lambda_4, \ldots \lambda_{14} = 0$.

The full hull computation [Fukuda (2000, 2015)] reveals the Boole-Bell type conditions of possible experience

$$p_1 + p_2 + p_6 \geq p_4 + p_8,$$
$$p_1 + p_2 \geq p_4,$$
$$p_1 + 2p_2 + p_6 \geq 2p_4 + p_8,$$
$$p_2 + p_6 \geq p_4, \ldots$$
$$p_{10} + p_2 + p_6 \geq p_4 + p_8,$$
$$p_4 + p_8 + 1 \geq p_1 + p_{10} + p_2 + p_6,$$
$$p_8 + 1 \geq p_1 + p_{10} + p_2,$$
$$p_4 + 1 \geq p_1 + p_2 + p_6, \tag{11.3}$$
$$p_4 + p_5 \geq p_1 + p_2,$$
$$p_1 + p_2 + p_6 + p_7 \geq p_4 + 1,$$
$$p_4 + p_8 + p_9 \geq p_1 + p_2 + p_6,$$
$$p_1 + p_{10} + p_{11} + p_2 + p_6 \geq p_4 + p_8 + 1,$$
$$p_{12} + p_4 + p_8 \geq p_{10} + p_2 + p_6,$$
$$p_{10} + p_{13} + p_4 \geq 1$$

as bounds of the polytope spanned by the two-valued measures interpreted as vertices. Some of these classical bounds are enumerated in Eq. (11.3). A fraction of these, in particular, $p_2 + p_6 \geq p_4$ is violated by the quantum probabilities mentioned earlier, as $p_2 = 0$, $p_6 = \frac{2}{9}$, and $p_4 = \frac{1}{3}$.

11.3.3. *Pentagon configuration*

There exist, however, probabilities that are neither quasi-classical nor quantum-like although they satisfy subclassicality, and although the underlying logic can be realized both quasi-classically by partition logics as well as quantum mechanically. For the sake of an example, we shall discuss Wright's dispersionless state [Wright (1978)] on the logic whose orthogonality diagram is a pentagon, as depicted in Fig. 11.6(ii).

What are the probabilities of prediction associated with such structures? The propositional structure depicted in Fig. 11.6(i) has no two-valued state, and just allows a single probability measure which is constant on all atoms; that is, $p_1 = p_3 = p_5 = p_7 = p_9 = \frac{1}{2}$.

This prediction or oracle is still allowed by the subclassicality rule even if one adds one atom per block. But, as has been pointed out by Wright [Wright (1978)], it can neither be operationally realized by any quasi-classical nor by any quantum oracle. For quasi-classical systems, this

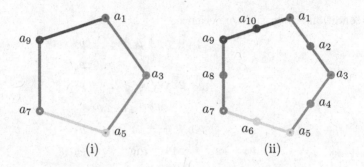

Fig. 11.6. Orthogonality diagram of the reduced pentagon (i), and of the pentagon logic (ii). A realization of (ii) in terms of partition logic is enumerated in Eq. (11.4); an explicit quantum realization can be found in Ref. [Svozil and Tkadlec (1996)].

can explicitly be demonstrated by enumerating all two-valued measures on this "pentagon logic" of Fig. 11.6(ii), as depicted in Fig. 11.7. Note that no measure exists which is non-zero only on the atoms located at intertwining contexts; that is, which does not vanish at one (or more) atoms at intertwining contexts, and at the same time vanishes at all the "middle" atoms belonging to only one context. Because the quasi-classical probabilities are just the convex sum Eq. (11.1) over all the two-valued measures it is clear that no classical probability vanishes at all non-intertwining atoms; in particular one which is $\frac{1}{2}$ on all intertwining atoms.

A straightforward extraction [Svozil (2005, 2009a)] based on two-valued measures in Fig. 11.7 yields the partition logic – which is the pasting of subalgebras specified by partitions of the set $\{1, 2, \ldots, 11\}$ in such a way that any atom is represented by the set of indices of two-valued measures acquiring the value one on that atom – of indices of the two-valued measures enumerated in Eq. (11.4); that is, in terms of the subscripts of the two-valued measures (i.e., $v_i \to i$),

$$\begin{aligned}
\{\{\{1, 2, 3\}, \{7, 8, 9, 10, 11\}, \{4, 5, 6\}\}, \\
\{\{4, 5, 6\}, \{1, 3, 9, 10, 11\}, \{2, 7, 8\}\}, \\
\{\{2, 7, 8\}, \{1, 4, 6, 10, 11\}, \{3, 5, 9, 3\}\}, \\
\{\{3, 5, 9, 3\}, \{1, 2, 4, 7, 11\}, \{6, 8, 10\}\}, \\
\{\{6, 8, 10\}, \{4, 5, 7, 9, 11\}, \{1, 2, 3\}\}\}.
\end{aligned} \qquad (11.4)$$

These partitions directly translate into the classical probabilities which are, for instance, realizable by generalized urn or automaton models.

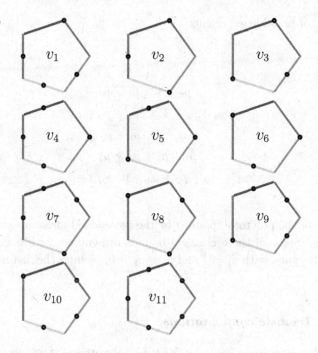

Fig. 11.7. Two-valued measures on the pentagon logic of Fig. 11.6.

Fig. 11.8 parameterizes all classical probabilities through non-negative $\lambda_1, \ldots, \lambda_{11} \geq 0$ with $\lambda_1 + \cdots + \lambda_{11} = 1$, subject to subclassicality.

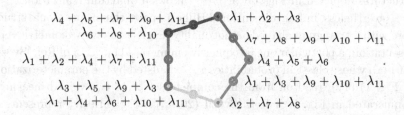

Fig. 11.8. Classical probabilities on the pentagon logic.

The hull computation [Fukuda (2000, 2015)] reveals the Boole-Bell type conditions of possible experience

$$p_4 + p_8 \geq p_1, \ldots$$
$$p_4 + 1 \geq p_1 + p_2 + p_6,$$
$$p_4 + p_8 + 1 \geq 2p_1 + p_2 + p_6,$$
$$p_1 + p_2 \geq p_4,$$
$$p_1 + p_2 + p_6 \geq p_4 + p_8,$$
$$2p_1 + p_{10} + p_2 + p_6 \geq p_4 + p_8 + 1$$

$$(11.5)$$

as bounds of the polytope spanned by the two-valued measures interpreted as vertices. Some of these classical bounds are enumerated in Eq. (11.5). Wright's measure, with $p_1 = \frac{1}{2}$ and $p_4 = p_8 = 0$, violates the first inequality.

11.3.4. *Triangle configurations*

Very similar arguments hold also for the propositional structures depicted in Figs. 11.2(i) and 11.2(ii): Fig. 11.9(i) represents a trivial classical prediction with equal probabilities. Fig. 11.9(ii) represents all classical predictions; the probability measures being read off from the partition logic $\{\{\{1\}, \{3\}, \{2\}\}, \{\{2\}, \{1\}, \{3\}\}, \{\{3\}, \{2\}, \{1\}\}\}$ obtained from the three two-valued states on the logic in Fig. 11.2(ii). Figs. 11.9(i) and 11.2(iii) represent predictions $\frac{1}{2}$ for all atoms at which the three contexts intertwine. Fig. 11.9(iii) represents a Wright prediction. None of the propositional structures depicted in Figs. 11.9(i)–(iii) allows a quantum realization.

Nevertheless, in four-dimensional Hilbert space, the propositional structure with a triangular shaped orthogonality diagram allows a geometric representation; a particular one is explicitly enumerated in Fig. 4 of Ref. [Svozil (2014a)] whose classical probabilities are exhausted by the parameterization in Fig. 11.9(v), read off from the complete set of 14 two-valued measures enumerated in Fig. 5 of Ref. [Svozil (2014a)]. Fig. 11.9(iv) represents a Wright prediction, which cannot be realized classically as well as quantum mechanically for the same reasons as mentioned earlier. In the quantum case, the proof of Theorem 2.2 of Ref. [Wright (1978)] can be directly transferred to the four-dimensional configuration.

The hull computation [Fukuda (2000, 2015)] reveals the Boole-Bell type

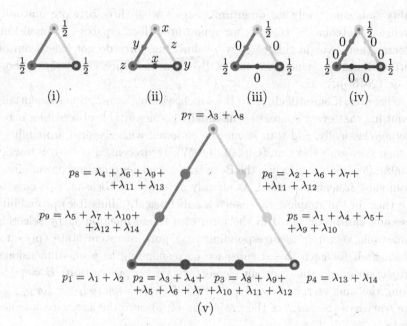

Fig. 11.9.   Classical probabilities (i) and (ii) of the tight triangular pastings of two- and three-atomic contexts introduced in Figs. 11.9(i) and 11.9(ii); with $x, y, z \geq 0$, and $x + y + z = 1$. The prediction probabilities represented by (iii) as well as (iv) are neither classical nor quantum mechanical. The classical probabilities on the triangle logic with four atoms per context are enumerated in (v); again $\lambda_1, \ldots, \lambda_{14} \geq 0$ and again $\lambda_1 + \cdots + \lambda_{14} = 1$.

conditions of possible experience

$$p_5 + p_6 \geq p_1, \ldots$$
$$p_5 + p_6 + 1 \geq 2p_1 + p_2 + p_3 + p_8,$$
$$p_1 + p_2 + p_3 \geq p_5 + p_6, \tag{11.6}$$
$$p_5 + p_6 + p_7 \geq p_1 + p_2 + p_3$$
$$2p_1 + p_2 + p_3 + p_8 + p_9 \geq p_5 + p_6 + 1$$

as bounds of the polytope spanned by the two-valued measures interpreted as vertices. Some of these classical bounds are enumerated in Eq. (11.6). Wright's measure, with $p_1 = \frac{1}{2}$ and $p_5 = p_6 = 0$, violates the first inequality.

11.3.5.   *Gleason theorem and Kochen-Specker configurations*

The strategy to obtain predictions and probabilities by taking the convex sum of (sufficiently many) two-valued measures satisfying subclassicality fails completely for quantum systems with three or more mutually exclusive outcomes – that is, for quantum Hilbert spaces of dimensions greater than two: in this case, two-valued measures do not exist even on certain finite substructures thereof [Kochen and Specker (1967); Abbott *et al.* (2015b)].

However, if one still clings to the subclassicality assumption – essentially requiring that every context of maximally co-measurable observables is behaving classically, and thus should be endowed with classical probabilities – then Gleason's theorem [Gleason (1957); Dvurečenskij (1993); Pitowsky (1998); Peres (1992)] derives the Born (trace) rule for quantum probabilities from subclassicality. Indeed, as already observed by Gleason, it is easy to see that, in the simplest case, such a subclassical (admissible) probability measure can be obtained in the form of a frame function f_ρ by selecting some unit vector $|\rho\rangle$, corresponding to a pure quantum state (preparation), and, for each closed subspace corresponding to a one-dimensional projection observable (i.e. an elementary yes-no proposition) $E = |e\rangle\langle e|$ along the unit vector $|e\rangle$, and by taking $f_\rho(|e\rangle) = \langle\rho|e\rangle\langle e|\rho\rangle = |\langle e|\rho\rangle|^2$ as the square of the norm of the projection of $|\rho\rangle$ onto the subspace spanned by $|e\rangle$.

The reason for this is that, because an arbitrary context can be represented as an orthonormal basis $\{|e_i\rangle\}$, an *ad hoc* frame function f_ρ on any such context (and thus basis) can be obtained by taking the length of the orthogonal (with respect to the basis vectors) projections of $|\rho\rangle$ onto all the basis vectors $|e_i\rangle$, that is, the norm of the resulting vector projections of $|\rho\rangle$ onto the basis vectors, respectively. This amounts to computing the absolute value of the Euclidean scalar products $\langle e_i|\rho\rangle$ of the state vector with all the basis vectors. In order that all such absolute values of the scalar products (or the associated norms) sum up to one and yield a frame function of weight one, recall that $|\rho\rangle$ is a unit vector and note that, by the Pythagorean theorem, these absolute values of the individual scalar products – or the associated norms of the vector projections of $|\rho\rangle$ onto the basis vectors – must be squared. Thus the value $f_\rho(|e_i\rangle)$ of the frame function on the argument $|e_i\rangle$ must be the square of the scalar product of $|\rho\rangle$ with $|e_i\rangle$, corresponding to the square of the length (or norm) of the respective projection vector of $|\rho\rangle$ onto $|e_i\rangle$. For complex vector spaces one has to take the absolute square of the scalar product; that is, $f_\rho(|e_i\rangle) = |\langle e_i|\rho\rangle|^2$.

Pointedly stated, from this point of view the probabilities $f_\rho(|e_i\rangle)$ are just the (absolute) squares of the coordinates of a unit vector $|\rho\rangle$ with respect to some orthonormal basis $\{|e_i\rangle\}$, representable by the square $|\langle e_i|\rho\rangle|^2$ of the length of the vector projections of $|\rho\rangle$ onto the basis vectors $|e_i\rangle$. The squares come in because the absolute values of the individual components do not add up to one; but their squares do. These considerations apply to Hilbert spaces of any, including two, finite dimensions. In this non-general, *ad hoc* sense the Born rule for a system in a pure state and an elementary proposition observable (quantum encodable by a one-dimensional projection operator) can be motivated by the requirement of subclassicality for arbitrary finite dimensional Hilbert space.

Note that it is possible to generate "Boole-Bell type inequalities (sort of)" if one is willing to *abandon subclassicality*. That is, suppose one is willing to accept that, within any particular context mutually excluding observables are not mutually exclusive any longer. In particular, one could consider two-valued measures in which all or some or none of the atoms acquire the value zero or one (with subclassicality, the two-valued measure is one at only a single atom; all other atoms have measure zero). With these assumptions one can, for every context, define a "correlation observable" as the product of the (non-subclassical) measures of all the atoms in this context. For instance, for any particular i'th context C_i with atoms $a_{i,1}, \ldots, a_{i,n}$; then the "joint probabilities" P_i or "joint expectations" E_i of a single context C_i take on the values

$$P_i = \prod_{j=1}^{n} v(a_{i,j}) = v(a_{i,1}) \cdots v(a_{i,n}),$$

$$E_i = \prod_{j=1}^{n} [1 - 2v(a_{i,j})] = [1 - 2v(a_{i,1})] \cdots [1 - 2v(a_{i,n})].$$

(11.7)

A geometric interpretation in terms of convex correlation polytopes is then straightforward – the tuples representing the edges of the polytopes are obtained by the enumeration of the "joint probabilities" P_i or the "joint expectations" E_i for all the involved contexts C_i.

For example, solving the hull problem for the "correlation polytope" of a system of observables introduced in Ref. [Cabello *et al.* (1996)] and depicted in Fig. 11.10 yields, among 274 facet inequalities,

$$0 \leq P_1 \leq 1$$
$$P_1 + 3 \geq P_2 + P_6 + P_7 + P_8$$
$$P_1 + P_3 + P_5 + 4 \geq P_2 + P_4 + P_6 + P_7 + P_8 + P_9$$
$$\ldots$$
$$-1 \leq E_1 \leq 1,$$
$$E_1 + 7 \geq E_2 + E_3 + E_4 + E_5 + E_6 + E_7 + E_8 + E_9,$$
$$E_1 + E_8 + E_9 + 7 \geq E_2 + E_3 + E_4 + E_5 + E_6 + E_7,$$
$$E_1 + E_6 + E_7 + E_8 + E_9 + 7 \geq E_2 + E_3 + E_4 + E_5,$$
$$E_1 + E_4 + E_5 + E_6 + E_7 + E_8 + E_9 + 7 \geq E_2 + E_3,$$
$$E_1 + E_2 + E_3 + E_4 + E_5 + E_6 + E_7 + E_8 + E_9 + 7 \geq 0.$$

$$(11.8)$$

The last bound has been introduced in Ref. [Cabello (2008)]. It is violated both by classical models (satisfying subclassicality) as well as by quantum mechanics, because both cases obey subclassicality, thereby rendering the value "-1" for any "correlation observable" $E_1, \ldots, E_9$ of all nine tightly intertwined contexts $C_1, \ldots, C_9$: in each context, there is an odd number of "-1"-factors. For the sake of demonstration, Fig. 11.10 also explicitly enumerates one (of 1152 non-admissible, non-subclassical) value assignments yielding the bound seven.

However, note that the associated observables, and also the two-valued measures and frame functions, have been allowed to disrespect subclassicality; because otherwise no two-valued measure exists.

Note also that similar calculations [Pitowsky (1989, 1991, 1994); Pitowsky and Svozil (2001)] for two- and three-partite correlations do not suffer from a lack of subclassicality, since in an Einstein-Podolsky-Rosen setup, the observables entering as factors in the product – coming from different particles – are independent (therefore justifying multiplication of single-particle probabilities and expectations), and not part of a one and the same single-particle context.

11.4. Discussion

We have discussed "bizarre" structures of observables and have considered classical, quantum and other, more "bizarre" probability measures on them. Thereby we have mostly assumed subclassicality, which stands for additivity within contexts, formalized by frame functions as well as

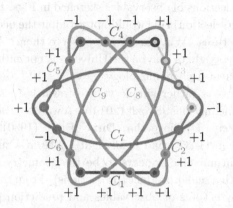

Fig. 11.10. Orthogonality diagram of a finite subset $C_1, \ldots, C_9$ of the continuum of blocks or contexts embeddable in four-dimensional real Hilbert space without a two-valued probability measure [Cabello *et al.* (1996)]; with one of the 1152 non-admissible value assignments yielding the bound seven, as derived in Ref [Cabello (2008)]. In contrast, subclassicality would require that, within each one of the nine contexts, exactly one observable would have value "-1," and the other three observables would have the value "$+1$."

admissibility [Gleason (1957); Dvurečenskij (1993); Pitowsky (1998); Peres (1992)].

From all of this one might conclude a simple lesson: in non-Boolean empirical structures which allow both a quantum as well as a quasi-classical representation (rendering a homeomorphic embedding into some larger Boolean algebra) the predictions from quantum and classical probabilities (rendered by the convex combination of two-valued measures) may be different. Which ones are realized depends on the nature of the system (e.g. quasi-classical generalized urn models or finite automata, or quantum states of orthohelium [Kochen and Specker (1967)]) involved.

Such structures may also allow (non-dispersive) probabilities and predictions which can neither be realized by (quasi-) classical nor be quantized systems. Stated pointedly: even if one assumes subclassicality – that is, the validity of classical predictions within contexts in the form of maximal subsets of observables which are mutually co-measurable – in general (i.e. in non-Boolean cases) the structure of observables does not determinate the probabilities completely.

Finally, let us speculate that if we were living in a computable universe capable of universal computation, then universality would imply we could see the types of collections of observables sketched in Figs. 11.1 and 11.2; at least if some (superselection) rule would not prohibit the occurrence of such propositional structures. Why do we not observe them? Maybe we have not looked closely enough, or maybe the Universe is not entirely "universal" in terms of fundamental phenomenology.

I personally have a rather simple stance towards these issues, which comes out of my inclinations [Svozil (2014b)] towards *"The Church of the larger Hilbert space."* I believe that Dirac [Dirac (1930)] and von Neumann [von Neumann (1932)] had it all right – alas in a surprising, literal way. The quantum universe appears to be the geometry of linear vector space equipped with a scalar product (projections). From this point of view, all those bizarre structures of observables and prediction probabilities do not show up just because, after all, our operationally accessible universe, at least on the most fundamental level, has to be understood in purely geometric terms, thereby disallowing some algebraic possibilities. This may be similar to the non-maximal violation of certain Boole-Bell type conditions of possible experience.

Acknowledgments

This research has been partly supported by FP7-PEOPLE-2010-IRSES-269151-RANPHYS. I gratefully acknowledge advice from Komei Fukuda with the `cddlib` package, as well as Alexander Svozil for his help installing it. I am also indebted to Alastair A. Abbot for a critical reading of the manuscript, as well as for suggesting improvements.

Bibliography

Abbott, A. A., Calude, C. S., Conder, J. and Svozil, K. (2012). Strong Kochen-Specker theorem and incomputability of quantum randomness, *Physical Review A* **86**, p. 062109, doi:10.1103/PhysRevA.86.062109, URL http://dx.doi.org/10.1103/PhysRevA.86.062109.

Abbott, A. A., Calude, C. S. and Svozil, K. (2014). Value-indefinite observables are almost everywhere, *Physical Review A* **89**, p. 032109, doi:10.1103/PhysRevA.89.032109, URL http://dx.doi.org/10.1103/PhysRevA.89.032109.

Abbott, A. A., Calude, C. S. and Svozil, K. (2015a). On the unpredictability of individual quantum measurement outcomes, in L. D. Beklemishev, A. Blass, N. Dershowitz, B. Finkbeiner and W. Schulte (eds.), *Fields of Logic and Computation II*, *Lecture Notes in Computer Science*, Vol. 9300 (Springer International Publishing, Cham, Heidelberg, New York, Dordrecht, London),

ISBN 978-3-319-23533-2, pp. 69–86, doi:10.1007/978-3-319-23534-9_4, URL
http://dx.doi.org/10.1007/978-3-319-23534-9_4.

Abbott, A. A., Calude, C. S. and Svozil, K. (2015b). A variant of the Kochen-Specker theorem localising value indefiniteness, doi:10.1063/1.4931658, URL http://dx.doi.org/10.1063/1.4931658.

Beran, L. (1984). *Orthomodular Lattices. Algebraic Approach* (D. Reidel, Dordrecht).

Birkhoff, G. and von Neumann, J. (1936). The logic of quantum mechanics, *Annals of Mathematics* **37**, 4, pp. 823–843, doi:10.2307/1968621, URL http://dx.doi.org/10.2307/1968621.

Boole, G. (1862). On the theory of probabilities, *Philosophical Transactions of the Royal Society of London* **152**, pp. 225–252, URL http://www.jstor.org/stable/108830.

Boole, G. (1958). *An Investigation of the Laws of Thought* (Dover, New York).

Cabello, A. (2008). Experimentally testable state-independent quantum contextuality, *Physical Review Letters* **101**, 21, 210401, doi:10.1103/PhysRevLett.101.210401, URL http://dx.doi.org/10.1103/PhysRevLett.101.210401.

Cabello, A., Estebaranz, J. M. and García-Alcaine, G. (1996). Bell-Kochen-Specker theorem: A proof with 18 vectors, *Physics Letters A* **212**, 4, pp. 183–187, doi:10.1016/0375-9601(96)00134-X, URL http://dx.doi.org/10.1016/0375-9601(96)00134-X.

Dirac, P. A. M. (1930). *The Principles of Quantum Mechanics* (Oxford University Press, Oxford).

Dvurečenskij, A. (1993). *Gleason's Theorem and Its Applications* (Kluwer Academic Publishers, Dordrecht).

Fukuda, K. (2000,2015). cdd program, URL http://www.inf.ethz.ch/personal/fukudak/cdd_home/, available at http://www.inf.ethz.ch/personal/fukudak/cdd_home/.

Gleason, A. M. (1957). Measures on the closed subspaces of a Hilbert space, *Journal of Mathematics and Mechanics (now Indiana University Mathematics Journal)* **6**, 4, pp. 885–893, doi:10.1512/iumj.1957.6.56050", URL http://dx.doi.org/10.1512/iumj.1957.6.56050.

Greechie, R. J. (1971). Orthomodular lattices admitting no states, *Journal of Combinatorial Theory* **10**, pp. 119–132, doi:10.1016/0097-3165(71)90015-X, URL http://dx.doi.org/10.1016/0097-3165(71)90015-X.

Hardy, L. (2001). Quantum theory from five reasonable axioms, eprint arXiv:quant-ph/0101012, URL https://arxiv.org/abs/quant-ph/0101012.

Hardy, L. (2003). Probability theories in general and quantum theory in particular, *Studies in History and Philosophy of Science Part B: Studies in History and Philosophy of Modern Physics* **34**, 3, pp. 381–393, doi:10.1016/S1355-2198(03)00034-0, URL http://dx.doi.org/10.1016/S1355-2198(03)00034-0.

Kalmbach, G. (1983). *Orthomodular Lattices* (Academic Press, New York).

Khrennikov, A. (2015). CHSH inequality: Quantum probabilities as classical conditional probabilities, *Foundations of Physics* **45**, 7, pp. 711–725, doi:10.1007/s10701-014-9851-8, URL http://dx.doi.org/10.1007/s10701-014-9851-8.

Kochen, S. and Specker, E. P. (1967). The problem of hidden variables in quantum mechanics, *Journal of Mathematics and Mechanics (now Indiana University Mathematics Journal)* **17**, 1, pp. 59–87, doi:10.1512/iumj.1968.17.17004, URL http://dx.doi.org/10.1512/iumj.1968.17.17004.

Krenn, G. and Svozil, K. (1998). Stronger-than-quantum correlations, *Foundations of Physics* **28**, 6, pp. 971–984, doi:10.1023/A:1018821314465, URL http://dx.doi.org/10.1023/A:1018821314465.

Navara, M. and Rogalewicz, V. (1991). The pasting constructions for orthomodular posets, *Mathematische Nachrichten* **154**, pp. 157–168, doi:10.1002/mana.19911540113, URL http://dx.doi.org/10.1002/mana.19911540113.

Peres, A. (1992). An experimental test for Gleason's theorem, *Physics Letters A* **163**, pp. 243–245, doi:10.1016/0375-9601(92)91005-C, URL http://dx.doi.org/10.1016/0375-9601(92)91005-C.

Pitowsky, I. (1989). From George Boole to John Bell: The origin of Bell's inequality, in M. Kafatos (ed.), *Bell's Theorem, Quantum Theory and the Conceptions of the Universe*, Fundamental Theories of Physics, Vol. 37 (Springer (Kluwer), Dordrecht), ISBN 978-90-481-4058-9, pp. 37–49, doi:10.1007/978-94-017-0849-4_6, URL http://dx.doi.org/10.1007/978-94-017-0849-4_6.

Pitowsky, I. (1991). Correlation polytopes their geometry and complexity, *Mathematical Programming* **50**, pp. 395–414, doi:10.1007/BF01594946, URL http://dx.doi.org/10.1007/BF01594946.

Pitowsky, I. (1994). George Boole's 'conditions of possible experience' and the quantum puzzle, *The British Journal for the Philosophy of Science* **45**, pp. 95–125, doi:10.1093/bjps/45.1.95, URL http://dx.doi.org/10.1093/bjps/45.1.95.

Pitowsky, I. (1998). Infinite and finite Gleason's theorems and the logic of indeterminacy, *Journal of Mathematical Physics* **39**, 1, pp. 218–228, doi:10.1063/1.532334, URL http://dx.doi.org/10.1063/1.532334.

Pitowsky, I. (2003). Betting on the outcomes of measurements: a bayesian theory of quantum probability, *Studies in History and Philosophy of Science Part B: Studies in History and Philosophy of Modern Physics* **34**, 3, pp. 395–414, doi:10.1016/S1355-2198(03)00035-2, URL http://dx.doi.org/10.1016/S1355-2198(03)00035-2, quantum Information and Computation.

Pitowsky, I. (2006). Quantum mechanics as a theory of probability, in W. Demopoulos and I. Pitowsky (eds.), *Physical Theory and its Interpretation*, The Western Ontario Series in Philosophy of Science, Vol. 72 (Springer Netherlands), ISBN 978-1-4020-4875-3, pp. 213–240, doi:10.1007/1-4020-4876-9_10, URL http://dx.doi.org/10.1007/1-4020-4876-9_10.

Pitowsky, I. and Svozil, K. (2001). New optimal tests of quantum nonlocality, *Physical Review A* **64**, p. 014102, doi:10.1103/PhysRevA.64.014102, URL http://dx.doi.org/10.1103/PhysRevA.64.014102.

Popescu, S. (2014). Nonlocality beyond quantum mechanics, *Nature Physics* **10**, pp. 264–270, doi:10.1038/nphys2916, URL http://dx.doi.org/10.1038/nphys2916.

Pták, P. and Pulmannová, S. (1991). *Orthomodular Structures as Quantum Logics* (Kluwer Academic Publishers, Dordrecht).

Reck, M., Zeilinger, A., Bernstein, H. J. and Bertani, P. (1994). Experimental realization of any discrete unitary operator, *Physical Review Letters* **73**, pp. 58–61, doi:10.1103/PhysRevLett.73.58, URL http://dx.doi.org/10.1103/PhysRevLett.73.58.

Specker, E. (1960). Die Logik nicht gleichzeitig entscheidbarer Aussagen, *Dialectica* **14**, 2-3, pp. 239–246, doi:10.1111/j.1746-8361.1960.tb00422.x, URL http://dx.doi.org/10.1111/j.1746-8361.1960.tb00422.x.

Specker, E. (1990). *Selecta* (Birkhäuser Verlag, Basel).

Svozil, K. (2005). Logical equivalence between generalized urn models and finite automata, *International Journal of Theoretical Physics* **44**, pp. 745–754, doi:10.1007/s10773-005-7052-0, URL http://dx.doi.org/10.1007/s10773-005-7052-0.

Svozil, K. (2009a). Contexts in quantum, classical and partition logic, in K. Engesser, D. M. Gabbay and D. Lehmann (eds.), *Handbook of Quantum Logic and Quantum Structures* (Elsevier, Amsterdam), ISBN 978-0-444-52869-8, pp. 551–586, doi:10.1016/B978-0-444-52869-8.50015-3, URL http://dx.doi.org/10.1016/B978-0-444-52869-8.50015-3.

Svozil, K. (2009b). Quantum scholasticism: On quantum contexts, counterfactuals, and the absurdities of quantum omniscience, *Information Sciences* **179**, pp. 535–541, doi:10.1016/j.ins.2008.06.012, URL http://dx.doi.org/10.1016/j.ins.2008.06.012.

Svozil, K. (2014a). Non-contextual chocolate ball versus value indefinite quantum cryptography, *Theoretical Computer Science* **560**, Part 1, pp. 82–90, doi:10.1016/j.tcs.2014.09.019, URL http://dx.doi.org/10.1016/j.tcs.2014.09.019.

Svozil, K. (2014b). Unscrambling the quantum omelette, *International Journal of Theoretical Physics* **53**, 10, pp. 3648–3657, doi:10.1007/s10773-013-1995-3, URL http://dx.doi.org/10.1007/s10773-013-1995-3.

Svozil, K. and Tkadlec, J. (1996). Greechie diagrams, nonexistence of measures in quantum logics and Kochen–Specker type constructions, *Journal of Mathematical Physics* **37**, 11, pp. 5380–5401, doi:10.1063/1.531710, URL http://dx.doi.org/10.1063/1.531710.

Tkadlec, J. (1998). Greechie diagrams of small quantum logics with small state spaces, *International Journal of Theoretical Physics* **37**, 1, pp. 203–209, doi:10.1023/A:1026646229896, URL http://dx.doi.org/10.1023/A:1026646229896.

von Neumann, J. (1932). *Mathematische Grundlagen der Quantenmechanik* (Springer, Berlin), English translation in Ref. [von Neumann (1955)].

von Neumann, J. (1955). *Mathematical Foundations of Quantum Mechanics* (Princeton University Press, Princeton, NJ).

Wright, R. (1978). The state of the pentagon. A nonclassical example, in A. R. Marlow (ed.), *Mathematical Foundations of Quantum Theory* (Academic Press, New York), pp. 255–274.

Wright, R. (1990). Generalized urn models, *Foundations of Physics* **20**, 7, pp. 881–903, doi:10.1007/BF01889696, URL http://dx.doi.org/10.1007/BF01889696.

Ziegler, G. M. (1994). *Lectures on Polytopes* (Springer, New York).

PART III
Applications

Chapter 12

An Upper Bound on the Asymptotic Complexity of Global Optimization of Smooth Univariate Functions

James M. Calvin

Department of Computer Science, New Jersey Institute of Technology, Newark, NJ 07102-1982, USA

Abstract

We study the problem of approximating the global minimum for a class of twice-continuously differentiable functions defined on the unit interval. For an algorithm that uses only function values, we show that the logarithm of the reciprocal of the error is asymptotically of order $n/\log(n)$ after n function evaluations.

12.1.   Introduction

Let f be a twice continuously differentiable function defined on the unit interval. We are interested in approximating the global minimum of f using a number of adaptively chosen function evaluations. The function can have many local minima, and so this is an example of what is called a global optimization problem.

In our study of the complexity of this problem we adopt a real-number model of computation. Furthermore, we focus on the cost of the computation in terms of the number of function evaluations.

Complexity results for global optimization are known for the worst-case, average-case, and asymptotic settings. It is well-known that in the worst case, global optimization is intractable. The following is a specialization of a result from [5]. Let $n(\epsilon, f)$ denote the minimal number of function and derivative evaluations that are required in order to obtain an approximation to the minimum of f with error at most ϵ. Let F denote the class of twice

continuously differentiable functions on the unit interval with the property
that

$$\max_{0 \le x \le 1} |f''(x)| \le 1.$$

Let A be any optimization algorithm that uses information obtained by
sequentially evaluating f and its partial derivatives, and assume that for
any $f \in F$, A is guaranteed to identify an x such that $f(x) - f^* \le \epsilon$. Then
there exists a function $f \in F$ such that algorithm A requires at least

$$n(\epsilon, f) \ge C \cdot \left(\frac{1}{\epsilon} \right)^{1/2}$$

evaluations for input f. This shows that even with uniform bounds on the
derivatives, the worst-case number of required function evaluations grows
exponentially in $\log(1/\epsilon)$.

If we know that f is convex, then there exist algorithms that obtain an ϵ
approximation with a number of evaluations that is polynomial in $\log(1/\epsilon)$
([9]). Therefore, one way to avoid intractability is to assume convexity (or
similar strong property) of the objective function. We emphasize that our
interest is in *not* restricting attention to such subclasses. We therefore seek
alternatives to the worst-case approach.

One approach is to fix the objective function and randomize the optimization algorithm. Then when applied to a suitable objective function,
the random time until an ϵ approximation is obtained can be analyzed.
This is the approach taken in [4] and [8].

Another approach is to view the objective function as a sample path
of a stochastic process or random field; that is, we randomize the objective function. Then we study the average number of function evaluations
required to obtain an ϵ-approximation. With the average case approach
there is a sharp difference between the power of adaptive and nonadaptive
algorithms.

Adaptive algorithms choose the next function evaluation point as a function of all previous information, while nonadaptive algorithms choose points
independently of past information. Examples of the latter class of algorithms are algorithms that choose points independently according to some
fixed probability distribution, or according to a fixed grid. Nonadaptive
global optimization algorithms are seldom used in practice, and there are
good theoretical reasons for why that is the case if we adopt a worst-case
perspective. Suppose that our objective function f is in some class of functions F, and assume that F is convex and symmetric. That is, for $0 \le \lambda \le 1$

and $f, g \in F$, $-f \in F$ and $\lambda f + (1 - \lambda)g \in F$. This type of class of objective functions provides a natural setting for global optimization problems (for example, r-times continuously differentiable functions). For such a class, adaptive algorithms are essentially no more powerful than nonadaptive algorithms. For any adaptive algorithm that obtains an error of at most ϵ with n function evaluations, there exists a nonadaptive algorithm using no more than $n + 1$ function evaluations that also obtains an error of at most ϵ (see [7]).

The average-case approach has resulted in upper (see [6]) and lower (see [1]) bounds for models based on Brownian motion. These studies have shown that adaptive methods are much more powerful than nonadaptive methods in this case. For example, any nonadaptive algorithm for optimizing a Brownian motion path has average error after n evaluations of order $n^{-1/2}$, while there are adaptive algorithms with error at most n^{-p}, for any positive p.

In this paper we adopt an asymptotic perspective and study the rate at which the error approaches zero for a particular algorithm. This gives an upper bound on the problem complexity. We are unaware of lower bounds for this setting.

12.2. Preliminary Definitions and Results

For continuous g, let

$$\|g\| \equiv \max_{0 \le t \le 1} |g(t)|.$$

Let $\hat{F} \subset C^2([0,1])$ denote the subset of $C^2([0,1])$ functions that have a finite number of global minimizers $x_j^* \in (0,1)$, with $f''(x_j^*) > 0$ for each global minimizer, and for which neither a global minimum or maximum occurs at 0 or 1. Our convergence rate bound will hold for functions in $\hat{F}$.

Note that $\hat{F}$ is convex and symmetric and so if we adopt a worst-case perspective adaptive algorithms can be essentially no more efficient than nonadaptive algorithms, for example a uniform grid of points, which has error after n evaluations of order $\|f''\| n^{-2}$.

Let $f^* \equiv \min_{0 \le t \le 1} f(t)$ denote the global minimum value of f. The difficulty of approximating f^* for $f \in \hat{F}$ depends on a function $\mathcal{I}_f$ defined for $x > 0$ by

$$\mathcal{I}_f(x) \equiv \int_0^1 \frac{dt}{\sqrt{f(t) - f^* + x}}.$$

The following lemma is proved in a similar manner to Lemma 3.2 of [3].

Lemma 12.1. *Suppose that $f \in \hat{F}$ with global minimizers $\{x_1^*, \ldots, x_\mu^*\}$. Define*

$$\alpha(f) \equiv \sum_{k=1}^{\mu} \left(\frac{1}{2} f''(x_k^*) \right)^{-1/2}.$$

Then

$$\lim_{\epsilon \downarrow 0} \frac{\mathcal{I}_f(\epsilon)}{\log(1/\epsilon)} = \alpha(f).$$

12.3. The Algorithm

We first introduce the notation for a general adaptive algorithm. Such an algorithm specifies a sequence of maps $t_k : \mathbb{R}^{k-1} \to [0,1]$, $k \geq 2$, that give the points at which to evaluate the function in terms of previously observed function values. Also specified are maps $M_k : \mathbb{R}^{k-1} \to \mathbb{R}$ that give the approximation to f^* as a function of the first k evaluations. The algorithm specifies a first point $t_1 \in [0,1]$ at which to evaluate $f(t_1)$. The algorithm then computes the second point $t_2 = t_2(f(t_1))$, and evaluates $f(t_2)$. Continuing on in this fashion, we evaluate

$$f(t_1), f(t_1), \ldots, f(t_n),$$

where $t_k = t_k(f(t_1), \ldots, f(t_{k-1}))$ for $k \leq n$.

Formally, we consider a sequence $\{A_n : n \geq 1\}$ of algorithms, where A_n stops after n function evaluations. However, we assume that each A_{n+1} makes the first n evaluations and approximations the same as algorithm A_n.

Denote the smallest function value after n evaluations by $M_n = \min_{1 \leq i \leq n} f(t_i)$ and the error by $\Delta_n \equiv M_n - f^*$.

Let t_i^n denote the ith smallest of the $\{t_j\}$, $1 \leq j \leq n$, so that $0 \leq t_1^n < t_2^n < \cdots < t_n^n \leq 1$ and $\{t_i^n : 1 \leq i \leq n\} = \{t_i : 1 \leq i \leq n\}$. For notational convenience set $t_0^n = 0$. Let $\tau_n = \min_{1 \leq i \leq n} t_i^n - t_{i-1}^n$ denote the smallest distance between function evaluation points.

We now define the specific algorithm that we will study. The first two observation points of the algorithm are fixed: $t_1 = 0$ and $t_2 = 1$. Define

$$g_n(x) = (2x \log(n))^2$$

for $0 < x \le 1/2$. For $n \ge 3$ and $1 \le i \le n$ set

$$\rho_i^n \equiv \frac{2(t_i^n - t_{i-1}^n)}{\left(f(t_{i-1}^n) - M_n + g_n(\tau_n)\right)^{1/2} + (f(t_i^n) - M_n + g_n(\tau_n))^{1/2}}.$$

The alternate equivalent integral form

$$\rho_i^n = \int_{s=t_{i-1}}^{t_i} \frac{ds}{\sqrt{L_n(s) - M_n + g_n(\tau_n)}} \tag{12.1}$$

will be useful, where $L_n(\cdot)$ is the linear interpolation of the function values:

$$L_n(s) = \frac{s - t_{i-1}^n}{t_i^n - t_{i-1}^n} f(t_i^n) + \frac{t_i^n - s}{t_i^n - t_{i-1}^n} f(t_{i-1}^n), \quad t_{i-1}^n \le s \le t_i^n.$$

The algorithm operates as follows. At step $n + 1$, choose the interval with the largest value of $\rho_i^n \equiv \rho^n$ and evaluate f at the point

$$s_i^n = t_{i-1}^n + r_n \left(t_i^n - t_{i-1}^n\right), \tag{12.2}$$

where $r_n = 1/2$ if a new smallest interval is about to be obtained or else $r_n = y_{i-1}^n / (y_{i-1}^n + y_i^n)$ where

$$y_i \equiv \sqrt{f(t_i^n) - M_n + g_n(\tau_n)}.$$

This means that only a bisection will result in a smallest interval.

For $n \ge 1$ and $1 \le i \le n$, let $T_i = T_i^n$ denote the ith interval. Suppose that at time n we are about to form a new smallest subinterval by bisecting interval T_i. This implies that $|T_i|/2 \le \tau_n$, and so

$$\rho^n \equiv \max_{1 \le i \le n} \rho_i^n = \frac{2(t_i^n - t_{i-1}^n)}{\left(f(t_{i-1}^n) - M_n + g_n(\tau_n)\right)^{1/2} + (f(t_i^n) - M_n + g_n(\tau_n))^{1/2}}$$

$$\le \frac{|T_i^n|}{2\tau_n \log(n)} \le \frac{2\tau_n}{2\tau_n \log(n)} = \frac{1}{\log(n)}. \tag{12.3}$$

The algorithm has the property that $\Delta_n \to 0$ for any continuous function f. Our main result is:

Theorem 12.2. *If $f \in \hat{F}$ with global minimizers $\{x_1^*, \ldots, x_\mu^*\}$. Then*

$$\Delta_n \le \exp\left(-\frac{1}{16}\alpha(f)\frac{n}{\log(n)}\right) \tag{12.4}$$

for all sufficiently large n.

This theorem improves on a result in [2] that gives an error bound of order $\exp(-c\sqrt{n})$ for a positive number $c = c(f)$.

The next section is devoted to a proof of this result.

12.4. Proof of Theorem 12.2

Note that

$$
\rho_i^n = \int_{s=t_{i-1}}^{t_i} \frac{ds}{\sqrt{f(s) - M + g_n}}
$$

$$
= \int_{s=t_{i-1}}^{t_i} \frac{ds}{\sqrt{L_n(s) - M_n + g_n}\sqrt{1 + \frac{(s-t_{i-1})(t_i-s)}{L_n(s)-M_n+g_n}\frac{f(s)-L_n(s)}{(s-t_{i-1})(t_i-s)} + \frac{M_n-M}{L_n(s)-M_n+g_n}}}.
$$

A routine computation shows that

$$
\max_{t_{i-1}\leq s\leq t_i} \frac{(s - t_{i-1})(t_i - s)}{L_n(s) - M_n + g_n} = \left(\frac{1}{2}\rho_i^n\right)^2.
$$

For the rest of this section we consider a fixed function $f \in \hat{F}$ and suppose that $n \geq n_1(f)$, where

$$
n_1(f) = \inf\left\{n \in \mathbb{N} : n \geq \exp\left(\|f''\|^{1/2}\right)\right\}. \tag{12.5}
$$

(Later we will further restrict n.)

Lemma 12.3. *For all $n \geq n_1(f)$,*

$$
\rho^n \leq \frac{2}{\log(n)}.
$$

Proof. Let $m \leq n$ be the last time before n that a smallest interval was about to be formed. Since smallest intervals are always formed through a bisection, $\tau_m = 2\tau_n$ and by (12.3),

$$
\rho^m \leq \frac{1}{\log(m)}. \tag{12.6}
$$

We will show by induction that

$$
\rho^{m+k} \leq \frac{2}{\log(m+k)}, \quad k = 1, 2, \ldots, n - m. \tag{12.7}
$$

Let us first consider $\{\rho_i^{m+1} : i \leq m + 1\}$. Suppose that i is the split interval at time m, and let j denote a non-split interval, so $\rho_j^m \leq \rho_i^m$. Then

$$\rho_j^{m+1} = \frac{2\left|T_j^{m+1}\right|}{\left(f(t_{j-1}^m) - M_{m+1} + g_{m+1}(\tau_n)\right)^{1/2} + \left(f(t_j^m) - M_{m+1} + g_{m+1}(\tau_n)\right)^{1/2}}$$

$$\leq \frac{2\left|T_j^{m+1}\right|}{\left(f(t_{j-1}^m) - M_m + g_{m+1}(\tau_n)\right)^{1/2} + \left(f(t_j^m) - M_m + g_{m+1}(\tau_n)\right)^{1/2}}$$

$$\leq \frac{2\left|T_j^{m+1}\right|}{\left(f(t_{j-1}^m) - M_m + g_m(\tau_m)\right)^{1/2} + \left(f(t_j^m) - M_m + g_m(\tau_m)\right)^{1/2}}$$

$$\times \left(\frac{g_m(\tau_m)}{g_{m+1}(\tau_n)}\right)^{1/2}$$

$$= \rho_j^m \frac{2\log(m)}{\log(m+1)}$$

$$< 2\rho_j^m$$

$$\leq \frac{2}{\log(m)}$$

by (12.6).

Next consider a child of the split subinterval T_i^m. Since we are forming a new smallest subinterval, $\tau_m = 2\tau_n$. Applying the mean value theorem to the integral form (12.1), there exists a point $c_i \in T_i^m$ such that (supposing that one child has index i at time $m+1$)

$$\rho_i^{m+1} = \frac{\left|T_i^m\right|/2}{\left(L_m(c_i) - M_{m+1} + g_{m+1}(\tau_{m+1})\right)^{1/2}}$$

$$\leq \frac{\tau_{m+1}}{g_{m+1}(\tau_{m+1})^{1/2}} = \frac{1}{2\log(m+1)}.$$

We have established the base case for the induction. Now let's consider iteration $m+k+1$, $1 \leq k < n - m$. For the induction hypothesis, assume that

$$\rho^{m+k} \leq \frac{2}{\log(m+k)}.$$

If j is a non-split interval then $\rho_j^{m+k+1} \leq \rho_j^{m+k}$ since the only possible change is a decrease in the record minimum M_{m+k+1}. If i is the split interval, then since we are not forming a smallest interval we subdivide the interval using the ratio r_i^{m+k}. Considering only the left child (having index

i),

$$\rho_i^{m+k+1} = \frac{2\left|T_i^{m+k+1}\right|}{y_{i-1}^{m+k+1} + y_i^{m+k+1}}$$

$$= \frac{2\left|T_i^{m+k}\right| r_i^{m+k}}{y_{i-1}^{m+k+1} + y_i^{m+k+1}}$$

$$\leq \frac{2\left|T_i^{m+k}\right| r_i^{m+k}}{y_{i-1}^{m+k} + y_i^{m+k+1}}$$

$$\leq \frac{2\left|T_i^{m+k}\right| r_i^{m+k}}{y_{i-1}^{m+k}}$$

$$= \frac{2\left|T_i^{m+k}\right| y_{i-1}^{m+k}/(y_{i-1}^{m+k} + y_i^{m+k})}{y_{i-1}^{m+k}}$$

$$= \frac{2\left|T_i^{m+k}\right|}{y_{i-1}^{m+k} + y_i^{m+k}}$$

$$= \rho_i^{m+k}.$$

A similar computation establishes the same bound for the right child.
The proof by induction of (12.7) is complete. □

We will use the following bound for the error in linear interpolation over
the interval $[t_{i-1}^n, t_i^n]$ (see, for example, [10]):

$$|f(t) - L(t)| \leq \frac{1}{2}(t - t_{i-1}^n)(t_i^n - t)\, \|f''\|, \quad t_{i-1}^n \leq t \leq t_i^n. \qquad (12.8)$$

Lemma 12.4. *Let τ_n^* denote the length of an interval containing a minimizer x^*. For $n \geq n_1$,*

$$\tau_n^* \leq 4\tau_n \qquad (12.9)$$

and

$$\Delta_n \leq \frac{1}{2}g_n(\tau_n). \qquad (12.10)$$

Proof. Suppose (to get a contradiction) that $|T_i^n| = \tau_n^*$, $|T_j^n| = \tau_n$, and
$\tau_n^* = 4\tau_n$, but yet we are about to split interval T_j^n, resulting in $\tau_n^* > 4\tau_n$;
that is, $\rho_j^n \geq \rho_i^n$:

$$\rho_j^n = \frac{\overbrace{|T_j^n| = \tau_n}}{(L_n(c_j) - M_n + g_n(\tau_n))^{1/2}} \geq \frac{\overbrace{|T_i^n| = \tau_n^* = 4\tau_n}}{(L_n(c_i) - M_n + g_n(\tau_n))^{1/2}} = \rho_i^n$$

for some $c_i \in T_i^n, c_j \in T_j^n$. This implies that

$$\frac{L_n(c_i) - M_n + g_n(\tau_n)}{L_n(c_j) - M_n + g_n(\tau_n)} \geq 4^2. \tag{12.11}$$

But $L_n(c_j) \geq M_n$ and

$$L_n(c_i) \leq M_n + \frac{1}{8} \|f''\| \, |T_i^n|^2 .$$

Thus

$$L_n(c_i) - L_n(c_j) \leq \frac{1}{8} \|f''\| \, \tau_n^2 4^2 .$$

This means that

$$
\begin{aligned}
\frac{L_n(c_i) - M_n + g_n(\tau_n)}{L_n(c_j) - M_n + g_n(\tau_n)} &= 1 + \frac{L_n(c_i) - L_n(c_j)}{L_n(c_j) - M_n + g_n(\tau_n)} \\
&= 1 + \frac{L_n(c_i) - L_n(c_j)}{\tau_n^2} \frac{\tau_n^2}{L_n(c_j) - M_n + g_n(\tau_n)} \\
&= 1 + \frac{L_n(c_i) - L_n(c_j)}{\tau_n^2} (\rho_j^n)^2 \\
&\leq 1 + \frac{1}{8} \|f''\| \, (4^2) \left(\frac{1}{\log(n)} \right)^2 \\
&= 1 + \frac{1}{8} \|f''\| \, (4^2) \frac{1}{\log(n)^2} \\
&\leq 1 + \frac{1}{8} \|f''\| \, (4^2) \frac{1}{\|f''\|} \\
&= 3.
\end{aligned}
$$

But this contradicts (12.11), and establishes (12.9).

The proof of (12.10) follows from

$$\frac{\Delta_n}{g_n(\tau_n)} \leq \frac{\frac{1}{8} \|f''\| \, (4\tau_n)^2}{(2\tau_n \log(n))^2} \leq \frac{\|f''\|}{2 (\log(n))^2} \leq \frac{1}{2} .$$

$\square$

The following lemma gives a lower bound for ρ^n that complements the upper bound provided by Lemma 12.3.

Lemma 12.5. *For $n \geq n_1(f)$,*

$$\rho^n \geq \frac{1}{\sqrt{6} \log(n)} .$$

Proof. Let T_n^* denote an interval containing a global minimizer at time n. Then $|T_n^*| = \tau_n^* \leq 4\tau_n$ by Lemma 12.4. For $s \in T_n^*$,

$$L_n(s) - M_n \leq \frac{1}{8} (4\tau_n)^2 \|f''\| = 2\tau_n^2 \|f''\| \leq 2\tau_n^2 \log(n)^2 = \frac{1}{2} g_n(\tau_n).$$

Therefore,

$$\rho^n \geq \int_{R_n^*} \frac{ds}{(L_n(s) - M_n + g_n(\tau_n))^{1/2}}$$

$$\geq \frac{\tau_n^*}{\left(\frac{1}{2} g_n(\tau_n) + g_n(\tau_n)\right)^{1/2}} \geq \frac{\tau_n}{2\tau_n \log(n) \left(1 + \frac{1}{2}\right)^{1/2}} = \frac{1}{\sqrt{6} \log(n)}.$$

$\square$

Lemma 12.6. *For $n \geq n_2(f) = 2n_1(f)$, we have the bounds*

$$\frac{1}{n} \sum_{i=1}^{n} \rho_i^n \leq \frac{2}{\log(n)} \tag{12.12}$$

and

$$\frac{1}{n} \sum_{i=1}^{n} \rho_i^n \geq \frac{1}{\sqrt{96} \log(n)}. \tag{12.13}$$

Proof. Equation (12.12) follows from Lemma 12.3.

For $n \geq n_1(f)$, the ρ values for the children of a split interval will not be much smaller than the parent. The largest possible decrease occurs if the values at the endpoints of T_i are constant, say with value $M_{m+k} + A$, and the new function values are the largest possible, namely $M_n + A + a$, where

$$a \leq \frac{1}{8} \|f''\| \, |T_i|^2.$$

Considering a child of the split interval (say with index i),

$$\rho_i^{n+1} \geq \frac{|T_i|/2}{(A + a + g_n(\tau_n))^{1/2}}$$

$$\geq \frac{|T_i|/2}{(A + g_n(\tau_n))^{1/2} \left(1 + \frac{a}{A + g_n(\tau_n)}\right)^{1/2}}$$

$$\geq \frac{|T_i|/2}{(A + g_n(\tau_n))^{1/2} \left(1 + \frac{\frac{1}{8}\|f''\||T_i|^2}{|T_i|^2} \frac{|T_i|^2}{A + g_n(\tau_n)}\right)^{1/2}}$$

$$\geq \frac{1}{2}\rho_i^n \frac{1}{\left(1 + \frac{\frac{1}{8}\|f''\|\|T_i\|^2}{|T_i|^2} \frac{|T_i|^2}{A+g_n(\tau_n)}\right)^{1/2}}$$

$$= \frac{1}{2}\rho_i^n \frac{1}{\left(1 + \frac{\frac{1}{8}\|f''\|\|T_i\|^2}{|T_i|^2} \left(\rho_i^n\right)^2\right)^{1/2}}$$

$$\geq \frac{1}{2}\rho_i^n \frac{1}{\left(1 + \frac{\frac{1}{8}\|f''\|\|T_i\|^2}{|T_i|^2} \left(\frac{2}{\log(n)}\right)^2\right)^{1/2}} \quad \text{(by Lemma 12.3)}$$

$$\geq \frac{1}{2}\rho_i^n \frac{1}{\left(1 + \frac{\frac{1}{8}\|f''\|\|T_i\|^2}{|T_i|^2} \left(\frac{2}{\|f''\|^{1/2}}\right)^2\right)^{1/2}} \quad \text{(since } n \geq n_1)$$

$$= \frac{1}{2}\left(3/2\right)^{-1/2}\rho_i^n.$$

Consider the average of the ρ values at time n that were the product of splits after time $n/2$. Over this time interval we have

$$\rho^k \geq \frac{(3/2)^{-1/2}}{2\log(k)}$$

by Lemma 12.5, since $n \geq 2n_1(f)$. Since the children ρ values are bounded below as described above,

$$\frac{1}{n}\sum_{i=1}^{n}\rho_i^n \geq \frac{1}{n}\frac{n/2}{n/2}\sum_{i=n/2}^{n}\rho^i \geq \frac{1}{2}\frac{1}{n/2}\sum_{i=n/2}^{n}\frac{(3/2)^{-1/2}}{2\log(i)} \geq \frac{1}{4}\frac{(3/2)^{-1/2}}{2\log(n)} = \frac{1}{\sqrt{96}\log(n)}.$$

$\square$

The following lemma gives an approximation needed to prove our error bound.

Lemma 12.7. *For $n \geq n_1(f)$,*

$$\sqrt{1/2}\,\mathcal{I}_f(g_n(\tau_n)) \leq \sum_{i=1}^{n}\rho_i^n \leq \sqrt{2}\,\mathcal{I}_f(g_n(\tau_n)). \qquad (12.14)$$

Proof. For some $c_i \in T_i$,

$$(f(c_i) - f^* + g_n(\tau_n))^{1/2} = (L_n(c_i) - M_n + g_n(\tau_n))^{1/2} \cdot$$

$$\left(1 + \frac{f(c_i) - L_n(c_i)}{|T_i|^2}\cdot\frac{|T_i|^2}{L_n(c_i) - M_n + g_n(\tau_n)} + \frac{M_n - f^*}{L_n(c_i) - M_n + g_n(\tau_n)}\right)^{1/2}\cdot$$

$$(12.15)$$

Using (12.8) we can bound the term

$$\frac{|f(c_i) - L_n(c_i)|}{|T_i|^2} \cdot \frac{|T_i|^2}{L_n(c_i) - M_n + g_n(\tau_n)} \leq \frac{1}{8} \|f''\| \left(\frac{2}{\log(n)}\right)^2 \leq \frac{1}{2}.$$

Recall that τ_n^* denotes the length of an interval containing a minimizer. Since $n \geq n_1$, $\tau_n^* \leq 4\tau_n$ by Lemma 12.4, and

$$M_n - f^* \leq L_n(x^*) - f(x^*) \leq \frac{1}{8} \|f''\| (\tau_n^*)^2 \leq \frac{4^2}{8} \|f''\| \tau_n^2$$

$$= 2 \|f''\| \tau_n^2 \leq 2 \log(n)^2 \tau_n^2 = \frac{1}{2} g_n(\tau_n).$$

Substituting these bounds in (12.15) gives

$$(f(c_i) - f^* + g_n(\tau_n))^{1/2} \leq (L_n(c_i) - M_n + g_n(\tau_n))^{1/2} \left(1 + \frac{1}{2} + \frac{1}{2}\right)^{1/2}$$

and

$$(f(c_i) - f^* + g_n(\tau_n))^{1/2} \geq (L_n(c_i) - M_n + g_n(\tau_n))^{1/2} \left(1 - \frac{1}{2}\right)^{1/2}.$$

Therefore, for $n \geq n_1(f)$,

$$\int_{[0,1]} (f(x) - f^* + g_n(\tau_n))^{-1/2} \, dx \leq (1/2)^{-1/2} \sum_{i=1}^{n} \rho_i^n$$

and

$$\int_{[0,1]} (f(x) - f^* + g_n(\tau_n))^{-1/2} \, dx \geq (2)^{-1/2} \sum_{i=1}^{n} \rho_i^n.$$

These inequalities imply (12.14).   □

There exists a number $n_3(f)$ such that for $n \geq n_3(f)$ and $\delta > 0$,

$$\log(1/\Delta_n) \geq (1 - \delta)\alpha(f)\mathcal{I}_f(\Delta_n)$$

by Lemma 12.1 and the fact that $\Delta_n \downarrow 0$. For $n \geq n_1(f)$, Lemma 12.7 implies that

$$\mathcal{I}_f(\Delta_n) \geq \sqrt{1/2} \sum_{i=1}^{n} \rho_i^n.$$

For $n \geq n_2(f)$, (12.13) of Lemma 12.6 implies that

$$\sum_{i=1}^{n} \rho_i^n \geq \frac{n}{\sqrt{96} \log(n)}.$$

Combining these gives the bound

$$\log(1/\Delta_n) \geq (1 - \delta)\alpha(f)\sqrt{1/2}\frac{n}{\sqrt{96}\log(n)},$$

valid for $n \geq \max\{n_1(f), n_2(f), n_3(f)\}$. Setting $1 - \delta = \sqrt{3/4}$ gives

$$\log(1/\Delta_n) \geq \frac{1}{16}\alpha(f)\frac{n}{\log(n)},$$

or

$$\Delta_n \leq \exp\left(-\frac{1}{16}\alpha(f)\frac{n}{\log(n)}\right)$$

for all sufficiently large n.

This completes the proof of Theorem 12.2.

Bibliography

[1] J. M. Calvin. A lower bound on complexity of optimization under the r-fold integrated Wiener measure. *Journal of Complexity*, 27:404–416, 2011.

[2] J. M. Calvin, Y. Chen, and A. Žilinskas. An adaptive univariate global optimization algorithm and its convergence rate for twice continuously differentiable functions. *Journal of Optimization Theory and Applications*, 155(2):628–636, 2012.

[3] J. M. Calvin and A. Žilinskas. On a global optimization of bivariate smooth functions. *Journal of Optimization Theory and Applications*, 163:528–547, 2014.

[4] V. V. Nekrutkin and A. S. Tikhomirov. Speed of convergence as a function of given accuracy for random search methods. *Acta Applicandae*, 33:89–108, 1993.

[5] A. S. Nemirovsky and D. B. Yudin. *Problem Complexity and Method Efficiency in Optimization*. John Wiley & Sons, Chichester, 1983.

[6] K. Ritter. Approximation and optimization on the Wiener space. *Journal of Complexity*, 6:337–364, 1990.

[7] K. Ritter. *Average-Case Analysis of Numerical Problems*. Springer, Berlin, 2000.

[8] A. S. Tikhomirov. On the Markov homogeneous optimization method. *Computational Mathematics and Mathematical Physics*, 3:361–375, 2006.

[9] S. Vavasis. Complexity issues in global optimization: a survey. In R. Horst and P. Pardalos, editors, *Handbook of Global Optimization*, volume 1, pages 27–41. Kluwer Academic Publishers, Dordrecht, 1995.

[10] S. Waldron. Sharp error estimates for multivariate positive linear operators which reproduce the linear polynomials. In C. K. Chui and L. L. Schumaker, editors, *Approximation Theory IX*, volume 1, pages 339–346. Vanderbilt University Press, 1998.

Chapter 13

Cellular Automata and Grossone Computations

Louis D'Alotto

Department of Mathematics and Computer Science York College
City University of New York, Jamaica, NY 11451, USA
The Doctoral Program in Computer Science
CUNY Graduate Center, USA

Yaroslav D. Sergeyev

University of Calabria, Italy
Lobachevsky State University of Nizhni Novgorod, Russia

Abstract

This work describes a new methodology that allows us to look at and understand infinities and infinitesimals in a new and innovative way that permits numerical computations with these quantities. The new methodology is then applied to the domain space of one-dimensional cellular automata to develop a metric that can allow infinitesimal computations and ultimately a dynamical classification. The classification is based on the number of cellular automaton sequences that equal a given sequence on a central window upon forward evolution (iteration) of the automaton function.

13.1. Introduction

A computational methodology introduced recently in [Sergeyev (2008a, 2010c, 2015c)] allows one to look at infinities and infinitesimals in a new way and to execute *numerical* computations with infinities and infinitesimals on the Infinity Computer patented in USA (see [Sergeyev (2010a)]) and other countries. This approach proposes a numeral system that uses *the same numerals* for several different purposes for dealing with infinities and infinitesimals: for measuring infinite sets; for indicating positions of elements in ordered infinite sequences; for working with functions and their derivatives that can assume different infinite, finite, and infinitesimal values

316

and can be defined over infinite and infinitesimal domains; for describing Turing machines, etc.

The new methodology is under an attentive study from both theoretical and applied viewpoints. On the one hand, papers connecting the new approach to the historical panorama of ideas dealing with infinities and infinitesimals (see [Lolli (2012, 2015); Margenstern (2011); Sergeyev and Garro (2010)]). In particular, relations of the new approach to bijections are studied in [Margenstern (2011)] and metamathematical investigations on the new theory and its non-contradictory can be found in [Lolli (2015)]. On the other hand, the new methodology has been successfully applied for studying cellular automata (see [D'Alotto (2012, 2013, 2015)]), Euclidean and hyperbolic geometry (see [Margenstern (2012, 2015)]), percolatión (see [Iudin *et al.* (2012, 2015); Vita *et al.* (2012)]), fractals (see [Sergeyev (2007, 2009a, 2011c, 2016); Vita *et al.* (2012)]), numerical differentiation and optimization (see [De Cosmis and De Leone (2012); Sergeyev (2009b, 2011a); Žilinskas (2012)]), infinite series and the Riemann zeta function (see [Sergeyev (2009c, 2011b); Zhigljavsky (2012)]), the first Hilbert problem, Turing machines, and lexicographic ordering (see [Sergeyev (2010b); Sergeyev and Garro (2010, 2013, 2015); Sergeyev (2015b)]), ordinary differential equations (see [Sergeyev (2013, 2015a)]), etc. The interested reader is invited to have a look also at surveys [Sergeyev (2008a, 2010c)] and the book [Sergeyev (2003, 2d electronic ed. 2013)] written in a popular way. Of particular interest, as presented in the article within, is the application to cellular automata. Cellular automata are well known computational models whereby even starting with complete disorder, self-organizing patterns can emerge. The application of the new methodology can actually measure, by counting, the quantity of information that can pass through a central viewing window under a cellular automaton rule. This is particularly interesting since it has been shown, see [Wolfram (2002)] and [Berlekamp *et al.* (2004)], that some cellular automata rules are capable of universal computation.

13.2. Expressing Infinite and Infinitesimal Quantities Using ①-Based Numerals

The numeral system is based on a new infinite unit of measure expressed by the numeral ① called *grossone* that is introduced as the number of elements of the set of natural numbers (notice that nowadays not only positive integers but also zero is frequently included in $\mathbb{N}$; however, since zero has been invented significantly later than positive integers used for counting objects, zero is not include in $\mathbb{N}$ in this text), i.e.,

$$\mathbb{N} = \{1, 2, 3, \dots \}. \tag{13.1}$$

Concurrently with the introduction of ① in the mathematical language all other symbols (like ∞, Cantor's ω, $\aleph_0, \aleph_1, \dots$, etc.) traditionally used to deal with infinities and infinitesimals are excluded from the language because ① and other numbers constructed with its help not only can be used instead of all of them but can be used with a higher accuracy. Analogously, when zero and the positional numeral system had been introduced in Europe, Roman numerals I, , IV, V, X, etc. had not been involved and in addition to the symbol 0 new symbols 1, 4, 5, etc. have been used to express numbers. The new element – zero expressed by the numeral 0 – had been introduced by describing its properties in the form of axioms. Analogously, ① is introduced by describing its properties postulated by the Infinite Unit Axiom added to axioms for real numbers (see [Sergeyev (2008a, 2010c)] for a detailed discussion). Let us comment upon some of properties of ①.

The introduction of ① allows us to write down the set of natural numbers as follows

$$\mathbb{N} = \left\{ 1, 2, \ \dots \ \frac{①}{2} - 2, \frac{①}{2} - 1, \frac{①}{2}, \frac{①}{2} + 1, \frac{①}{2} + 2, \ \dots \ ① - 2, \ ① - 1, \ ① \right\}. \tag{13.2}$$

Infinite natural numbers

$$\dots \ \frac{①}{2} - 2, \frac{①}{2} - 1, \frac{①}{2}, \frac{①}{2} + 1, \frac{①}{2} + 2, \ \dots \ ① - 2, ① - 1, ① \tag{13.3}$$

that are invisible if traditional numeral systems are used to observe the set of natural numbers can be viewed now thanks to the introduction of ①. The two records, (13.1) and (13.2), refer to the same set – the set of natural numbers – and infinite numbers (13.3) also take part[1] of $\mathbb{N}$. Both records, (13.1) and (13.2), are correct and do not contradict each other. They just use two different numeral systems to express $\mathbb{N}$. Traditional numeral systems do not allow us to see infinite natural numbers that we can observe now thanks to ①. Thus, we have the same object of observation – the set $\mathbb{N}$ – that can be observed by different instruments – numeral systems – with different accuracies.

Let us see now how one can write down different numerals expressing different infinities and infinitesimals and to execute computations with all of them. Instead of the usual symbol ∞ different infinite and/or infinitesimal

---

[1]This is a difference with respect to non-standard analysis where infinities it works with do not belong to $\mathbb{N}$.

numerals can be used thanks to ①. Indeterminate forms are not present and, for example, the following relations hold for infinite numbers ①, ①² and ①⁻¹, ①⁻² (that are infinitesimals), as for any other (finite, infinite, or infinitesimal) number expressible in the new numeral system

$$0 \cdot ① = ① \cdot 0 = 0, \quad ① - ① = 0, \quad \frac{①}{①} = 1, \quad ①^0 = 1, \quad 1^① = 1, \quad 0^① = 0,$$

$$0 \cdot ①^{-1} = ①^{-1} \cdot 0 = 0, \quad ①^{-1} > 0, \quad ①^{-2} > 0, \quad ①^{-1} - ①^{-1} = 0,$$

$$\frac{①^{-1}}{①^{-1}} = 1, \quad (①^{-1})^0 = 1, \quad ① \cdot ①^{-1} = 1, \quad ① \cdot ①^{-2} = ①^{-1},$$

$$\frac{①^{-2}}{①^{-2}} = 1, \quad \frac{①^2}{①} = ①, \quad \frac{①^{-1}}{①^{-2}} = ①, \quad ①^2 \cdot ①^{-1} = ①, \quad ①^2 \cdot ①^{-2} = 1.$$

The introduction of the numeral ① allows us to represent infinite and infinitesimal numbers in a unique framework. For this purpose a numeral system similar to traditional positional numeral systems was introduced in [Sergeyev (2003, 2d electronic ed. 2013, 2008a)]. To construct a number C in the numeral positional system with base ①, we subdivide C into groups corresponding to powers of ①:

$$C = c_{p_m} ①^{p_m} + \ldots + c_{p_1} ①^{p_1} + c_{p_0} ①^{p_0} + c_{p_{-1}} ①^{p_{-1}} + \ldots + c_{p_{-k}} ①^{p_{-k}}. \quad (13.4)$$

Then, the record

$$C = c_{p_m} ①^{p_m} \ldots c_{p_1} ①^{p_1} c_{p_0} ①^{p_0} c_{p_{-1}} ①^{p_{-1}} \ldots c_{p_{-k}} ①^{p_{-k}} \quad (13.5)$$

represents the number C, where all numerals $c_i \neq 0$, they belong to a traditional numeral system and are called *grossdigits*. They express finite positive or negative numbers and show how many corresponding units $①^{p_i}$ should be added or subtracted in order to form the number C. Note that in order to have a possibility to store C in the computer memory, values k and m should be finite.

Numbers p_i in (13.5) are sorted in the decreasing order with $p_0 = 0$

$$p_m > p_{m-1} > \ldots > p_1 > p_0 > p_{-1} > \ldots p_{-(k-1)} > p_{-k}.$$

They are called *grosspowers* and they themselves can be written in the form (13.5). In the record (13.5), we write $①^{p_i}$ explicitly because in the new numeral positional system the number i in general is not equal to the grosspower p_i. This gives the possibility to write down numerals without indicating grossdigits equal to zero.

The term having $p_0 = 0$ represents the finite part of C since $c_0①^0 = c_0$. Terms having finite positive grosspowers represent the simplest infinite parts of C. Analogously, terms having negative finite grosspowers represent the simplest infinitesimal parts of C. For instance, the number $①^{-1} = \frac{1}{①}$ mentioned above is infinitesimal. Note that all infinitesimals are not equal to zero. In particular, $\frac{1}{①} > 0$ since it is a result of division of two positive numbers.

A number represented by a numeral in the form (13.5) is called *purely finite* if it has neither infinite nor infinitesimals parts. For instance, 35.1 is purely finite and $35.1 + 78.2①^{-17.5}$ is not. All grossdigits c_i are supposed to be purely finite. Purely finite numbers are used on traditional computers and for obvious reasons have a special importance for applications. All of the numbers introduced above can be grosspowers, as well, giving thus a possibility to have various combinations of quantities and to construct terms having a more complex structure.

Notice that different numeral systems, if they have different accuracies, cannot be used together. For instance, records of the type $① + \omega$, $① - \aleph_0$, $①/\infty$, etc. have no sense because they include numerals developed under different methodological assumptions, in different mathematical contests, for different purposes, and, finally, numeral systems these numerals belong to have different accuracies.

By using the $①$-based numeral system it becomes possible to measure certain infinite sets. As we have seen above, relations of the type 'many' $+ 1 = $ 'many' and $\aleph_0 - 1 = \aleph_0$ are consequences of the weakness of numeral systems applied to express numbers (finite or infinite). Thus, one of the principles of the new computational methodology consists of adopting the principle 'The part is less than the whole' to all numbers (finite, infinite, and infinitesimal) and to all sets and processes (finite and infinite). Notice that this principle is a reformulation of Euclid's Common Notion 5 saying 'The whole is greater than the part'.

Let us show how, in comparison to the traditional mathematical tools used to work with infinity, the new numeral system allows one to obtain more precise answers in certain cases. For instance, Table 13.1 compares results obtained by the traditional Cantor's cardinals and the new numeral system with respect to the measure of a dozen of infinite sets (for a detailed discussion regarding the results presented in Table 13.1 and for more examples dealing with infinite sets see [Lolli (2015); Margenstern (2011); Sergeyev (2010b,c); Sergeyev and Garro (2010)]). Notice, that in $\mathbb{Q}$ and $\mathbb{Q}'$

Table 13.1 Measuring infinite sets using ①-based numerals allows one in certain cases to obtain more precise answers in comparison with the traditional cardinalities, $\aleph_0$ and $\mathcal{C}$, of Cantor.

Description of sets	Cardinality	Number of elements
the set of natural numbers $\mathbb{N}$	countable, $\aleph_0$	①
$\mathbb{N} \bigcup \{0\}$	countable, $\aleph_0$	①+1
$\mathbb{N} \setminus \{73, 124\}$	countable, $\aleph_0$	①-2
the set of even numbers $\mathbb{E}$	countable, $\aleph_0$	$\frac{①}{2}$
the set of odd numbers $\mathbb{O} \bigcup \{1,2,3,4\}$	countable, $\aleph_0$	$\frac{①}{2} + 2$
the set of integers $\mathbb{Z}$	countable, $\aleph_0$	2①+1
$\mathbb{Z} \setminus \{0,1,2,3\}$	countable, $\aleph_0$	2①-3
the set of square natural numbers $\mathbb{G} = \{x : x = n^2, x \in \mathbb{N}, n \in \mathbb{N}\}$	countable, $\aleph_0$	$\lfloor \sqrt{①} \rfloor$
the set of pairs of natural numbers $\mathbb{P} = \{(p,q) : p \in \mathbb{N}, q \in \mathbb{N}\}$	countable, $\aleph_0$	$①^2$
the set of numerals $\mathbb{Q}' = \{-\frac{p}{q}, \frac{p}{q} : p \in \mathbb{N}, q \in \mathbb{N}\}$	countable, $\aleph_0$	$2①^2$
the set of numerals $\mathbb{Q} = \{0, -\frac{p}{q}, \frac{p}{q} : p \in \mathbb{N}, q \in \mathbb{N}\}$	countable, $\aleph_0$	$2①^2 + 1$
the set of numerals A_2	continuum, $\mathcal{C}$	$2^①$
the set of numerals A_2'	continuum, $\mathcal{C}$	$2^① + 1$
the set of numerals A_{10}	continuum, $\mathcal{C}$	$10^①$
the set of numerals C_{10}	continuum, $\mathcal{C}$	$2 \cdot 10^①$

we calculate different numerals and not numbers. For instance, numerals $\frac{4}{1}$ and $\frac{8}{2}$ have been counted two times even though they represent the same number 4. Then, four sets of numerals having the cardinality of continuum are shown in Table 13.1 (these results are discussed more in detail in the next section). Among them we denote by A_2 the set of numbers $x \in [0,1)$ expressed in the binary positional numeral system, by A_2' the set being the same as A_2 but with x belonging to the closed interval $[0,1]$, by A_{10} the set of numbers $x \in [0,1)$ expressed in the decimal positional numeral system, and finally we have the set $C_{10} = A_{10} \cup B_{10}$, where B_{10} is the set of numbers $x \in [1,2)$ expressed in the decimal positional numeral system. It is worthwhile to notice also that grossone-based numbers from Table 13.1

can be ordered as follows

$$\lfloor\sqrt{①}\rfloor < \frac{①}{2} < \frac{①}{2} + 2 < ① - 2 < ① < 2① - 3 < 2① + 1 <$$

$$①^2 < 2①^2 + 1 < 2^① < 2^① + 1 < 10^① < 2 \cdot 10^①.$$

It can be seen from Table 13.1 that Cantor's cardinalities say only whether a set is countable or uncountable while the ①-based numerals allow us to express the exact number of elements of the infinite sets. However, both numeral systems – the new one and the numeral system of infinite cardinals – do not contradict one another. Both Cantor's numeral system and the new one give correct answers, but their answers have *different accuracies*. By using an analogy from physics we can say that the lens of our new 'telescope' used to observe infinities and infinitesimals is stronger and where Cantor's 'telescope' allows one to distinguish just two dots (countable sets and the continuum) we are able to see many different dots (infinite sets having different number of elements).

The ①-base numeral system, as all numeral systems, cannot express all numbers and give answers to all questions. Let us consider, for instance, the set of *extended natural numbers* indicated as $\widehat{\mathbb{N}}$ and including $\mathbb{N}$ as a proper subset

$$\widehat{\mathbb{N}} = \{\underbrace{1, 2, \ldots, ① - 1, ①,}_{\text{Natural numbers}} ① + 1, ① + 2, \ldots, 2① - 1, 2①, 2① + 1, \ldots$$

$$①^2 - 1, ①^2, ①^2 + 1, \ldots 10①^① - 1, 10①^①, 10①^① + 1, \ldots\}. \tag{13.6}$$

What can we say with respect to the number of elements of the set $\widehat{\mathbb{N}}$? The introduced numeral system based on ① is too weak to give an answer to this question. It is necessary to introduce in a way a more powerful numeral system by defining new numerals (for instance, ②, ③, etc.).

13.3.　Cellular Automata

Cellular automata, originally developed by von Neuman and Ulam in the 1940's to model biological systems, are discrete dynamical systems that are known for their strong modeling and self-organizational properties (for examples of some modeling properties see [Chopard and Droz (1998)], [D'Ambrosio *et al.* (2013)], [Trunfio *et al.* (2011)], and [Wolfram (2002)]). Cellular automata are defined on an infinite lattice and can be defined for all dimensions. In the one-dimensional case the integer lattice $\mathbb{Z}$ is used.

In the two-dimensional case, the lattice $\mathbb{Z} \times \mathbb{Z}$ is used[2]. An example of a two-dimensional cellular automata is John Conway's ever popular "Game of Life"[3]. Probably the most interesting aspect about cellular automata is that which seems to conflict our physical systems. While physical systems tend to maximal entropy, even starting with complete disorder, forward evolution of cellular automata can generate highly organized structure.

As with all dynamical systems, it is important and interesting to understand the long term or evolutionary behavior of cellular automata. Hence it makes sense to develop a classification based dynamical behavior. The concept of classifying cellular automata was initiated by Stephen Wolfram in the early 1980's, see [Wolfram (1983)] and [Wolfram (2002)]. Through numerous computer simulations, Wolfram noticed that if an initial configuration (sequence) was chosen at random the probability is high that a cellular automaton rule will fall within one of four classes.

The examples to follow are referred to by a rule numbering system developed by Wolfram, see [Wolfram (1983)] and [Wolfram (1984)]. In [Wolfram (1984)], one-dimensional cellular automata are partitioned into four classes depending on their dynamical behavior, see Figure 13.1 (Totalistic Rule 36) for an example of a Wolfram class 1 cellular automaton. Class 1 are the least chaotic, indeed Wolfram labeled these as automata that evolve to a uniform state. Figure 13.2 (Totalistic Rule 24) is an example of a Wolfram class 2 cellular automaton. Wolfram described the evolution of automata of this class as leading to simple stable or periodic structures. Figure 13.3 (Totalistic Rule 12) is an example of a Wolfram class 3 cellular automaton. In these automata the dynamical behavior is more complicated, however triangles and other small structures are seen to emerge in the form of a chaotic pattern. Figure 13.4 (Totalistic Rule 20) is an example of a class 4 cellular automaton. Wolfram labeled class 4 the most chaotic whereby localized complex structures emerge. In these figures it can be seen that a cellular automaton map starts with a given (random) initial configuration and evolves in a downward direction upon forward iterations (evolution) of the cellular automaton rule. It is interesting to note the two persisting structures that emerge in Figure 13.4 automaton. The structure on the left evolves straight down, while the structure on the right evolves on a diagonal. Eventually the one on the right will 'crash' into the structure on the

---

[2]For a study and classification of two-dimensional cellular automata using grossone, see [D'Alotto (2013)]

[3]For a complete description (including some of the more interesting structures that emerge) of "The Game of Life" see [Berlekamp *et al.* (2004)] Chapter 25.

left and they will either annihilate each other or produce another persisting structure.

A later and more rigorous classification scheme for one-dimensional cellular automata, see [Gilman (1987)], was developed by Robert Gilman. Here a probabilistic/measure theoretic classification scheme was developed based on the probability of choosing a configuration that will stay arbitrarily close to a given initial configuration under forward iteration (evolution)[4]. Gilman's classification partitions the cellular automata rules into three classes. Class A is the class of equicontinuous automata, whereby there is an open disk of configurations that stay arbitrarily close to the given initial configuration. Automata in class B conform to a stochastic analog of equicontinuity. Automata in this class have the property that the probability is positive that one can find (at random) another configuration that can stay arbitrary close to an initial configuration under forward evolution. Automata in class C have the property that the probability of finding another configuration that stays arbitrarily close to the initial under forward iterations is 0. Gilman called automata belonging to class C almost expansive automata. Owing to the fact that the lens of measure theory does not distinguish between countably infinite and uncountably infinite (in the Cantor sense) sets, it is noted that automata in all the classes have some indistinguishable dynamic similarities. For instance, in both Gilman classes A and B there are an infinite amount of configurations that can stay arbitrarily close to a given initial configuration under forward evolution. By applying the infinite unit axiom and grossone, the similarities are overcome by actually having a numeric representation for the number of configurations in each class that equal (or match) an initial configuration under forward evolution. Thus making the classes more distinguishable.

13.4.   Cellular Automata and the New Grossone Methodology

The new Grossone methodology fits very nicely to the theory of cellular automata. Indeed, since we will now have a numeric expression for the number of elements in the space $\mathbf{S}^{\mathbb{Z}}$ and an upper bound on this number of elements, cellular automata can now be partitioned, with respect to their dynamical behavior, into different classes.

Let S is an alphabet of size $s = |S|$ such that $s \geq 2$ and let $X = S^{\mathbb{Z}}$, i.e. the set of all maps from the lattice $\mathbb{Z}$ to the set S. That is, for $x \in X$,

---

[4]Gilman's classification is based on choosing an infinite product probability measure on the space of cellular automata.

Fig. 13.1.   Wolfram Rule 36.   Fig. 13.2.   Wolfram Rule 24.

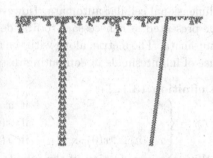

Fig. 13.3.   Wolfram Rule 12.   Fig. 13.4.   Wolfram Rule 20.

$x : \mathbb{Z} \to S$. One-Dimensional cellular automata (hence just called cellular automata from now on) are induced by arbitrary local maps:

$$F : S^{(2r+1)} \longrightarrow S.$$

These are usually called local rules or block maps in the literature, see [Gilman (1987)] and [Hedlund (1969)]. The value $r \in \mathbb{N}_0$ is called the range of the map. The automaton map f induced by F is defined by $f(x) = y$ with

$$y(i) = F[x(i - r), \ldots, x(i + r)].$$

The study of dynamical systems, in this case discrete dynamical systems, endeavors to understand the forward evolution (or forward iterations) of the system map and in this case the automaton rule. In this article, $\mathbb{N}_0$ is used to represent the set of $\mathbb{N} \cup \{0\}$. $f^t(x)$ is used to represent the tth iterate of the automaton map f. That is,

$$f^t(x) = f \circ f \circ f \cdots \circ f(x),$$

where $0 \le t \le \textcircled{1}$.

The restriction of $x \in X$ to a non-empty interval $[i,j]$ of $\mathbb{Z}$, where $-\text{①} \leq i \leq j \leq \text{①}$ is called a *word*. Words are written $x[i,j]$. The length of a word $w = x[i,j]$ is $|w| = j - i + 1$. It is important to note that, using ①, words (or the length of a word) can be infinite, however cannot have an endpoint greater than ① (nor less than $-\text{①}$). Also, for any $a \in S$, define $x_a \in X$ by $x(i) = a$, for $i \in \mathbb{Z}$. Words of infinite length are mentioned in [Gilman (1987)] but not much is done with them as the metric used cannot handle infinite computations. The introduction of the infinite unit axiom and grossone make infinite and infinitesimal computations possible. This article is concerned with the development of a classification of one-dimensional cellular automata. However, before a classification scheme can be presented, it is necessary to first define a metric on the space of cellular automata. The metric, along with the new grossone methodology, will make use of infinitesimals in computing distances.

Definition 13.1. Let
$$x \wedge y = \begin{cases} x & \text{if } x = y, \\ * & \text{if } x(0) \neq y(0) \text{ or } x(0) = *, \\ x(-n)\ldots x(0)\ldots x(n) & \text{if } x(i) = y(i) \; \forall i \in [-n,n] \text{ and } * \text{ outside.} \end{cases}$$
With the introduction of the infinite unit axiom, $-n$ can be infinite and equal $-\text{①} + k$ for some finite integer $k < 0$, similarly n can equal $\text{①} - k$ for some finite integer $k > 0$ (note that if $k = 0$, then $x = y$). Hence computations on infinite configurations are allowed. Thus, $x \wedge y$ is the place where two sequences agree on the largest symmetric window around 0 and is $*$ valued outside. Let λ be an arbitrary real-valued function defined on the alphabet S and taking values in the open interval $(0,1)$, i.e. $\lambda : S \to (0,1)$ where $\lambda_i = \lambda(x(i))$, hence $0 < \lambda_i < 1$. Keeping in line with the metric development in [D'Alotto (2012)], we need the following definition[5].

Definition 13.2.
$$F(x \wedge y) = \begin{cases} 1 & \text{if } x \wedge y = *, \\ \prod_{-n}^{n} \lambda_i & \text{if } x \wedge y = \ldots * * * x(-n)\ldots x(0)\ldots x(n) * * * \ldots. \end{cases}$$

We now form the following metric on the space of bi-infinite sequences:

Definition 13.3.
$$d(x,y) = \begin{cases} 0 & \text{if } x = y, \\ F(x \wedge y) & \text{otherwise.} \end{cases}$$

---

[5]The function $F : X \to (0,1]$ is called an evaluation function, see [D'Alotto (2012)] for a more formal development of a general nonarchimedean metric and [Narici *et al.* (1971)] for a complete reference on nonarchimedean analysis.

Example 13.4. Given $S = \{0, 1\}$, let

$$x = \overset{-①}{\overbrace{1}} \ldots 111\langle 1\rangle 111 \ldots \overset{①}{\overbrace{1}}$$

and

$$y = \overset{-①}{\overbrace{0}} \ \overset{-①+1}{\overbrace{0}} \ \overset{-①+2}{\overbrace{0}} \ 11 \ldots 111\langle 1\rangle 111 \ldots 1 \overset{①}{\overbrace{1}}$$

That is, x is the sequence of all 1's and y is the sequence of all 1's except for 3 zeros at the negative infinite indicated positions. In our examples, when not explicitly denoted, we will use the symbol $\langle \ \rangle$ to denote the zeroth place on the integer lattice. The sequences x and y agree completely on the right hand side, and don't agree at integral values $-①, -① + 1$, and $-① + 2$. Hence,

$$x \wedge y = x(-①+3), x(-①+4), \ldots, x(-1), x(0), x(1), \ldots, x(①-4), x(①-3).$$

and the evaluation function becomes

$$F(x \wedge y) = \lambda_1^{(2①-6)}.$$

If $\lambda_1 = \frac{1}{2}$, for example, then the distance becomes

$$d(x, y) = \frac{1}{2^{2①-6}}.$$

Note that the value of λ_0 was not needed since these configurations have only 1's where they agree, however the value should still be given and used when needed. Hence, the distance between the two points x and y is infinitesimal. Using grossone, there are obviously different representations of infinitesimal distances, depending on the choice of the λ_i's and the places where the sequences agree. Of course, as the following example shows, the above construction easily covers the finite distance case.

Example 13.5. Again, using the binary alphabet $S = \{0, 1\}$, let

$$x = \ldots 1110\langle 1\rangle 0011 \ldots \quad and \quad y = \ldots 1110\langle 1\rangle 0101 \ldots$$

Then

$$x \wedge y = \ldots * * * x(-1)x(0)x(1) * * * \ldots .$$

That is, the sequences differ in the 2nd integral position and hence is $*$ valued outside the central places where they agree. Therefore, depending on the values of λ_0 and λ_1,

$$d(x, y) = \lambda_0 \cdot \lambda_1 \cdot \lambda_0.$$

Note that, to compute their distance, we do not need to know the rest of these sequences past the 2nd and the -2nd integral positions, hence '...' is used to mean the sequences continue to the $-\textcircled{1}$ position on the left and the $\textcircled{1}$ position on the right.

Under the usual product topology, a *cylinder* is a set $C(i, j, w) = \{x \in X | x[i, j] = w\}$, where $|w| = j - i + 1$. We define the open disk of radius ε around x to be $C_{[-n,n]}(x) = C(-n, n, x[-n, n])$. Here, it is important to note, $\varepsilon > 0$ and that ε can be infinitesimal. It should be clarified that ε must be computed with respect to the metric defined above but first with the respective values of λ chosen. As the following example illustrates.

Example 13.6. Given the alphabet $S = \{0, 1\}$ and $\lambda_0 = \lambda_1 = 1/2$, then the disk centered at x and of radius $\varepsilon = 1/8$ is denoted by $C_{[-1,1]}(x)$[6].

It should also be noted that being a nonarchimedean metric space, given any two open disks, either one contains the other or they intersect trivially, see [Narici *et al.* (1971)] for a complete introduction to nonarchimedean spaces.

The following is a simple, but important, example of a cellular automaton of range $r = 1$. The evolutionary behavior of this automaton is clearly exhibited.

Example 13.7. Let $S = \{0, 1\}$ and let f be the automaton induced by the local rule $F : S^3 \to S$ by $F(1, 1, 1) = 1$ and $F(a, b, c) = 0$ otherwise. If we apply forward iterations of the induced automaton map f, all sequences eventually go to the quiescent state of x_0, except for the initial sequence x_1 which remains constant[7].

In the previous example, given any finite word $x[i, j]$ with at least one element in the word not equal to 1, every configuration will eventually evolve, under forward iterations, to the quiescent state of x_0. Moreover, if we choose an open disk $C_{[-n,n]}(x)$ around that point, every configuration in the open disk will eventually evolve to x_0. Hence it is important to determine how many elements are in these open disks. Using Theorem 5.2 of [Sergeyev (2008b)], this was answered in [D'Alotto (2012)]. Theorem

---

[6] We can also take the convention, once the λ values are fixed, to denote $C_{1/8}(x)$ as the disk of radius $1/8$.

[7] This is an example of a Gilman class A automaton. For this and other examples, including Gilman class B automata, see [Gilman (1987)]

13.8 and its corollaries below show the answer.

Theorem 13.8. *Given the space $S^{\mathbb{Z}}$ of bi-infinite sequences, the number of elements $x \in S^{\mathbb{Z}}$ is equal to $|S|^{2①+1}$.*

Proof. See [D'Alotto (2012)] for the proof. $\square$

Corollary 13.9. *The open disk $C_{[-n,n]}(x)$ around x contains $|S|^{2(①-n)}$ elements.*

Proof. Follows directly from Theorem 13.8, see [D'Alotto (2012)]. $\square$

Corollary 13.10. *If there are $|S|^{2①-2n}$ elements in an open disk $C_{[-n,n]}(x)$ of X, then there are $|S|^{2①-2n} \cdot (|S|^{2n+1} - 1)$ elements in the complement of $C_{[-n,n]}(x)^{8}$.*

Proof. See [D'Alotto (2015)].

$\square$

Given the definitions and the previous corollaries, it is allowable to define an open disk of infinitesimal radius. A disk of infinitesimal radius is an open disk around a word of infinite length. For example, the disk $C_{[-①+2,①-2]}(x)$ has exactly $|S|^{2①-(①-2+①-2)} = |S|^4$ elements. As is seen, open disks of infinitesimal radius can have very few elements. It should be noted that Corollaries 13.9 and 13.10 also apply to disks of infinitesimal radius.

13.5. Classes of One-Dimensional Automata

To understand the dynamics of cellular automata it is necessary to study the forward iterates of configurations that equal or match those of a given configuration, call it "x", on a given interval of $\mathbb{Z}$. Here the relation $x \sim y$ iff $\forall i \in \mathbb{N}_0$, $(f^i(y))[m,n] = (f^i(x))[m,n]$ forms an equivalence relation with equivalence classes denoted by $B_{m,n}(x)$. That is,

$$B_{m,n}(x) = \{y \mid (f^i(y))[m,n] = (f^i(x))[m,n] \ \forall i \in \mathbb{N}_0\}.$$

$B_{m,n}(x)$ is the set of y for which $(f^i(y))[m,n] = (f^i(x))[m,n]$, for $m \leq 0 \leq n$, under forward iterations of the cellular automaton function. That is, $\forall i \in \mathbb{N}_0$. Recall, $(f^i(y))[m,n]$ represents words and that the cellular automaton function, f is first applied to the entire configuration x (or y),

---

[8]M. Margenstern proves a general result, see [Margenstern (2011)] Proposition 1.

and then restricted to the interval $[m, n]$. Note that m can equal $-①+k$ and n can equal $①-k$, for some finite integer $k \geq 0$. In those cases the words are left-sided, right-sided or both sided infinite. Hence elements in the $B_{m,n}(x)$ classes will agree with, and so will their forward iterations, $x[m, n]$ and all forward iterations of $x[m, n]$ under the automaton map f. This will form the effect of an infinite vertical strip (column), not necessarily symmetric, around the central window.

Since we have an upper bound and a representation for the number of elements in the space $S^{\mathbb{Z}}$, we can develop a dynamical analysis of cellular automata. In this analysis we will use ① to count the number of elements in the class $B_{m,n}(x)$ whose forward iterates match those of x in the central window and develop a simple classification of one-dimensional cellular automata based on this count. Cellular automata rules are thus partitioned into three classes.

Definition 13.11. Define the classes of one dimensional cellular automata, f, as follows:

(1) $f \in \mathcal{A}$ if there is a $B_{m,n}(x)$ that contains at least $|S|^{2^{①}-k}$ elements, for some finite integer $k \geq 0$.
(2) $f \in \mathcal{B}$ if there is a $B_{m,n}(x)$ that contains at least $|S|^{\alpha^{①}-k}$ elements, for some finite integer $k \geq 0$, $0 < \alpha < 2$ and α not infinitesimal, but f does not belong to class $\mathcal{A}$.
(3) $f \in \mathcal{C}$ otherwise.

Class $\mathcal{C}$ is the most chaotic class of automata. Indeed, in this class there may only be finitely many elements or simple infinitely many elements in any $B_{m,n}(x)$ class. Hence, beginning with an initial configuration, most other configurations will diverge away from the initial configuration. Automata in class $\mathcal{A}$ are the least chaotic and most elements will equal an initial configuration upon repeated applications (iterations) of the automaton rule on the infinite strip. The following theorems show the relationship between an open disk and the number of configurations in a $B_{m,n}(x)$ class.

Theorem 13.12. *If there exists a $B_{m,n}(x)$, for cellular automaton f, that contains an open disk of non-infinitesimal radius, then $f \in \mathcal{A}$.*

Proof. See [D'Alotto (2015)]. □

Theorem 13.13. *If $f \in \mathcal{A}$ then there exists a $B_{m,n}(x)$ class that contains an open disk of non-infinitesimal radius.*

Proof. See [D'Alotto (2015)]. $\qquad\qquad\qquad\qquad\qquad\qquad\qquad\square$

Hence, the dynamical behavior of automata in class $\mathcal{A}$ is determined by a finite amount of information on the initial configuration x. This is not true for the other classes. For example, the forward (or backwards) dynamics of the right or left shift map cannot be determined by a finite amount of information.

The remainder of this section is dedicated to a few examples.

Example 13.14. By Theorem 13.12, the automaton defined in Example 13.7 above is an example of a class $\mathcal{A}$ automaton.

Example 13.15. The left shift map, σ, is a cellular automaton of range 1, defined by $\sigma(x_i) = x_{i+1}$. i.e. the map that shifts all symbols of a configuration to the left, as illustrated below:

$$
\begin{aligned}
x &= ...0\,1\,1\,1\,0\,0\,1\,1\,0\,1\,1\,\langle 1\rangle\,0\,1\,0\,0\,1\,0\,1\,0\,0\,0\,1\,1... \\
\sigma(x) &= ...1\,1\,1\,0\,0\,1\,1\,0\,1\,1\,1\,\langle 0\rangle\,1\,0\,0\,1\,0\,1\,0\,0\,0\,1\,1\,... \\
\sigma^2(x) &= ...1\,1\,0\,0\,1\,1\,0\,1\,1\,1\,0\,\langle 1\rangle\,0\,0\,1\,0\,1\,0\,0\,0\,1\,1\,...
\end{aligned}
$$

Obviously all configurations $y \in B_{m,n}(x)$ would have to agree with x to the right, out to ① and at the zeroth place. Therefore there are at least $|S|^{①-k}$ elements, for some finite $k > 0$ and at most $|S|^{①}$ elements in $B_{m,n}(x)$, hence $\sigma \in \mathcal{B}$.

Hence, under the shift as shown above, no finite amount of information can determine the behavior of a configuration on a central window. However, the quantity of information required is no more than $|S|^{①}$ symbols. This is opposed to the cellular automaton given in Example 13.7 and referenced again in Example 13.14. For that automaton, only a finite amount of information is needed to determine the configuration in a central viewing window.

13.6. Probabilities

In [Wolfram (1983)] the classification is based on the observation that if a configuration is chosen at random then the probability is high that the cellular automaton rule will lie in one of four classes. In [Gilman (1987)], the classification is based on the probability of finding another configuration that will stay arbitrarily close to the initial configuration. In this section we show and compute some of the probabilities, for the classification presented herein, of finding another configuration that stays arbitrarily close to an initial configuration. Here again the advantage of using the Infinite Unit Axiom is demonstrated. Grossone gives us the ability to actually compute real probabilities, with a higher degree of accuracy than shown in [Gilman (1987)]. Here we assume the equiprobable probability distribution. That is, given a finite alphabet S, the probability of each element occurring is

$$\frac{1}{|S|}.$$

For $f \in \mathcal{A}$ there is a $B_{m,n}(x)$ that contains at least $|S|^{2①-k}$ elements, for some finite $k \geq 0$. Hence the probability, $P(y)$, of randomly finding another configuration y that equals x on the central vertical strip (stays close to x), under forward iteration of the cellular automaton, is

$$\frac{1}{|S|^{k+1}} \leq P(y) \leq \frac{1}{|S|}.$$

Under the definitions, it is possible for the probability $P(y)$ to equal $\frac{1}{|S|}$, for example the automaton map that takes everything to the quiescent state of 0's. Hence everything gets mapped to 0 and the probability is $\frac{1}{|S|}$ that another randomly chosen configuration will equal the initial in the 0th place and then equal the initial under forward iterations.

For $f \in \mathcal{B}$ there is a $B_{m,n}(x)$ that contains at least $|S|^{\alpha①-k}$ elements, for some finite $k \geq 0$, $0 < \alpha < 2$ and α not infinitesimal, but $f \notin \mathcal{A}$. Hence the probability of finding another configuration y that stays arbitrarily close to x under forward iteration, is at most

$$\frac{1}{|S|^{(2-\alpha)①+k+1}}.$$

A simple computation will show this. For $f \in \mathcal{B}$, the probability of randomly finding another configuration, that will equal an initial configuration x in a central window upon forward iteration, is infinitesimal and hence highly improbable. However it is not impossible. Indeed, there are still a lot of configurations available. For a specific example see Example 13.15, the left (or right) shift map would have to have all other configurations agreeing with the initial on an infinite word out to the right (or left, respectively) and these values would have to be fixed without choice. In particular, choosing $B_{-1,1}(x)$ for the left shift map σ, the probability of finding another configuration that would equal the given x in the finite window $x[-1, 1]^9$ upon forward iterations of σ would equal

$$\frac{1}{|S|^{①+2}}.$$

It is obvious that this probability is infinitesimal however, as the following illustration shows, there are still an infinite number of configurations in the $B_{-1,1}(x)$ class.

$$
\begin{aligned}
&\qquad\qquad\qquad\qquad\overbrace{}^{①+2\ places\ fixed\ without\ choice} \\
x &= \ldots * * * * * * * * 1 \langle 1 \rangle 0\,1\,0\,0\,1\,0\,1\,0\,0\,0\,1\,1 \ldots \\
\sigma(x) &= \ldots * * * * * * * 1\,1 \langle 0 \rangle 1\,0\,0\,1\,0\,1\,0\,0\,0\,1\,1 \ldots \\
\sigma^2(x) &= \ldots * * * * * * 1\,1\,0 \langle 1 \rangle 0\,0\,1\,0\,1\,0\,0\,0\,1\,1 \ldots \\
&\vdots
\end{aligned}
$$

Here the $*$ means a wildcard choice for an element of alphabet S. Hence each element choice, on the fixed side, has a probability of occurrence of $\frac{1}{|S|}$.

For $f \in \mathcal{C}$ the probability of finding another configuration that equals a given initial configuration in a central window, under forward iterations, is much smaller and can possibly be 0.

13.7. Discussion and Conclusions

In this article, a discussion on the new methodology of the Infinite Unit Axiom and an application to the development of a classification scheme for one-dimensional (linear) cellular automata has been presented. The entire domain space of one-dimensional automata, $X = S^{\mathbb{Z}}$, contains $|S|^{2①+1}$ configurations and therefore puts an upper bound representation on the number of elements. Hence the space can be sub-divided into components (in this case three components) and used to build a classification on the number of configurations whose forward evolution, under a cellular automaton, equal those (on a central viewing window) of a given initial configuration.

This classification is in line with that of Wolfram and that of Gilman, however, due to the application of grossone, it is based on a numeric representation of counting elements in a set. Automata in class $\mathcal{A}$ are the least chaotic, having a very large number of configurations equaling those of a

---

[9]The reader is reminded that, according to the definitions, this does not have to be a symmetric central window but has to include the zeroth place.

given configuration, on some central window[10], upon forward iterations of the automaton map. Automata in class $\mathcal{B}$, such as the left shift automaton, are more chaotic than those in class $\mathcal{A}$. However, it seems that they can still be described without too much complexity. Automata in class $\mathcal{C}$ are more difficult to find and are the most chaotic in the respect that there are relatively very few other configurations that will follow and stay close to a given. Indeed, the number of configurations that stay close to a given initial configuration, upon forward iterations, is much less than the other classes and may be simple infinite (either ①, or ①^2, ..., or ①^n, or some part thereof), finite or a single configuration.

Wolfram class 1 and 2 (see Figures 13.1 and 13.2) seem to correspond to class $\mathcal{A}$ automata. By Theorem 13.12, Gilman's class A automata corresponds to the class $\mathcal{A}$ automata presented in this article, however there may be some overlap with Gilman's class B automata. The left (or right) shift map belongs in Gilman's class C automata, while they both belong to class $\mathcal{B}$ presented herein. This shows the classifications have some differences. Automata in Wolfram class 4, for example rule 20 as seen in Figure 13.4, seem to be similar to the shift map and hence are conjectured to fall into class $\mathcal{B}$. Wolfram class 3, as seen in rule 12 (see Figure 13.3), exhibit aperiodic behavior and seem to correspond to the most chaotic, class $\mathcal{C}$. However some of the Wolfram totalistic rules are conjectured to, and some were proven to, be capable of universal computation, see [Wolfram (2002)]. Due to the nature of universal computation, some of these automata can fall into class $\mathcal{C}$. It is left as an open problem to show these. On the whole, the presented classification would be stronger if there was an algorithm to determine membership in the different classes and we pose this as an open problem.

Acknowledgments

The work of Ya.D. Sergeyev was supported by the Russian Science Foundation, project No.15-11-30022 "Global optimization, supercomputing computations, and applications".

---

[10]Given the definition of the metric, it is allowable to say "staying close together" upon forward iterations.

Bibliography

Berlekamp, E., Conway, J., and Guy, R. (2004). *Winning Ways for Your Mathematical Plays, 2nd edition*, Vol. 4 (A. K. Peters).

Chopard, B. and Droz, M. (1998). *Cellular Automata Modeling of Physical Systems* (Cambridge University Press).

D'Alotto, L. (2012). Cellular automata using infinite computations, *Applied Mathematics and Computation* **218(16)**, pp. 8077–8082.

D'Alotto, L. (2013). A classification of two-dimensional cellular automata using infinite computations, *Indian Journal of Mathematics* **55**, pp. 143–158.

D'Alotto, L. (2015). A classification of one-dimensional cellular automata using infinite computations, *Applied Mathematics and Computation* **255**, pp. 15–24.

D'Ambrosio, D., Filippone, G., Marocco, D., Rongo, R., and Spataro, W. (2013). Efficient application of GPGPU for lava flow hazard mapping, *The Journal of Supercomputing* **65(2)**, pp. 630–644.

De Cosmis, S. and De Leone, R. (2012). The use of grossone in mathematical programming and operations research, *Applied Mathematics and Computation* **218(16)**, pp. 8029–8038.

Gilman, R. (1987). Classes of linear automata, *Ergodic Theory and Dynamical Systems* **7**, pp. 105–118.

Hedlund, G. A. (1969). Endomorphisms and automorphisms of the shift dynamical system, *Mathematical Systems Theory* **3**, pp. 51–59.

Iudin, D., Sergeyev, Y., and Hayakawa, M. (2012). Interpretation of percolation in terms of infinity computations, *Applied Mathematics and Computation* **218(16)**, pp. 8099–8111.

Iudin, D., Sergeyev, Y., and Hayakawa, M. (2015). Infinity computations in cellular automaton forest-fire model, *Communications in Nonlinear Science and Numerical Simulation* **20(3)**, pp. 861–870.

Lolli, G. (2012). Infinitesimals and infinites in the history of mathematics: A brief survey, *Applied Mathematics and Computation* **218(16)**, pp. 7979–7988.

Lolli, G. (2015). Metamathematical investigations on the theory of grossone, *Applied Mathematics and Computation* **255**, pp. 3–14.

Margenstern, M. (2011). Using grossone to count the number of elements of infinite sets and the connection with bijections, *p-Adic Numbers, Ultrametric Analysis and Applications* **3(3)**, pp. 196–204.

Margenstern, M. (2012). An application of grossone to the study of a family of tilings of the hyperbolic plane, *Applied Mathematics and Computation* **218(16)**, pp. 8005–8018.

Margenstern, M. (2015). Fibonacci words, hyperbolic tilings and grossone, *Communications in Nonlinear Science and Numerical Simulation* **21(1–1)**, pp. 3–11.

Narici, L., Beckenstein, E., and Bachman, G. (1971). *Functional Analysis and Valuation Theory* (Marcel Dekker, Inc.).

Sergeyev, Y. (2003, 2d electronic ed. 2013). *Arithmetic of Infinity* (Edizioni Orizzonti Meridionali, CS).

Sergeyev, Y. (2007). Blinking fractals and their quantitative analysis using infinite and infinitesimal numbers, *Chaos, Solitons & Fractals* **33**, 1, pp. 50–75.

Sergeyev, Y. (2008a). A new applied approach for executing computations with infinite and infinitesimal quantities, *Informatica* **19(4)**, pp. 567–596.

Sergeyev, Y. (2008b). A new applied approach for executing computations with infinite and infinitesimal quantities, *Informatica* **19 (4)**, pp. 567–596.

Sergeyev, Y. (2009a). Evaluating the exact infinitesimal values of area of Sierpinski's carpet and volume of Menger's sponge, *Chaos, Solitons & Fractals* **42(5)**, pp. 3042–3046.

Sergeyev, Y. (2009b). Numerical computations and mathematical modelling with infinite and infinitesimal numbers, *Journal of Applied Mathematics and Computing* **29**, pp. 177–195.

Sergeyev, Y. (2009c). Numerical point of view on Calculus for functions assuming finite, infinite, and infinitesimal values over finite, infinite, and infinitesimal domains, *Nonlinear Analysis Series A: Theory, Methods & Applications* **71(12)**, pp. e1688–e1707.

Sergeyev, Y. (2010a). *Computer system for storing infinite, infinitesimal, and finite quantities and executing arithmetical operations with them* (USA patent 7,860,914).

Sergeyev, Y. (2010b). Counting systems and the First Hilbert problem, *Nonlinear Analysis Series A: Theory, Methods & Applications* **72(3–4)**, pp. 1701–1708.

Sergeyev, Y. (2010c). Lagrange Lecture: Methodology of numerical computations with infinities and infinitesimals, *Rendiconti del Seminario Matematico dell'Università e del Politecnico di Torino* **68(2)**, pp. 95–113.

Sergeyev, Y. (2011a). Higher order numerical differentiation on the infinity computer, *Optimization Letters* **5(4)**, pp. 575–585.

Sergeyev, Y. (2011b). On accuracy of mathematical languages used to deal with the Riemann zeta function and the Dirichlet eta function, *p-Adic Numbers, Ultrametric Analysis and Applications* **3(2)**, pp. 129–148.

Sergeyev, Y. (2011c). Using blinking fractals for mathematical modelling of processes of growth in biological systems, *Informatica* **22(4)**, pp. 559–576.

Sergeyev, Y. (2013). Solving ordinary differential equations by working with infinitesimals numerically on the infinity computer, *Applied Mathematics and Computation* **219(22)**, pp. 10668–10681.

Sergeyev, Y. (2015a). Numerical infinitesimals for solving ODEs given as a blackbox, in S. T.E. and T. Ch. (eds.), *AIP Proc. of the International Conference on Numerical Analysis and Applied Mathematics 2014 (ICNAAM-2014)*, Vol. 1648 (Melville, New York), p. 150018.

Sergeyev, Y. (2015b). The olympic medals ranks, lexicographic ordering, and numerical infinities, *The Mathematical Intelligencer* **37(2)**, pp. 4–8.

Sergeyev, Y. (2015c). Un semplice modo per trattare le grandezze infinite ed infinitesime, *Matematica nella Società e nella Cultura: Rivista della Unione Matematica Italiana* **8(1)**, pp. 111–147.

Sergeyev, Y. (2016). The exact (up to infinitesimals) infinite perimeter of the Koch snowflake and its finite area, *Communications in Nonlinear Science and Numerical Simulation* **31(1–3)**, pp. 21–29.

Sergeyev, Y. and Garro, A. (2010). Observability of Turing machines: A refinement of the theory of computation, *Informatica* **21(3)**, pp. 425–454.

Sergeyev, Y. and Garro, A. (2013). Single-tape and multi-tape Turing machines through the lens of the Grossone methodology, *Journal of Supercomputing* **65(2)**, pp. 645–663.

Sergeyev, Y. and Garro, A. (2015). The grossone methodology perspective on Turing machines, in A. Adamatzky (ed.), *Automata, Universality, Computation, Emergence, Complexity and Computation*, Vol. 12 (Springer, New York), pp. 139–169.

Trunfio, G., D'Ambrosio, D., Rongo, R., Spataro, W., and Di Gregorio, S. (2011). A new algorithm for simulating wildfire spread through cellular automata, *ACM Transactions on Modeling and Computer Simulation* **22**, pp. 1–26.

Vita, M., Bartolo, S. D., Fallico, C., and Veltri, M. (2012). Usage of infinitesimals in the Menger's Sponge model of porosity, *Applied Mathematics and Computation* **218(16)**, pp. 8187–8196.

Wolfram, S. (1983). Statistical mechanics of cellular automata, *Reviews of Modern Physics* **55(3)**, pp. 601–644.

Wolfram, S. (1984). Universality and complexity in cellular automata, *Physica D* **10**, pp. 1–35.

Wolfram, S. (2002). *A New Kind of Science* (Wolfram Media, Inc.).

Zhigljavsky, A. (2012). Computing sums of conditionally convergent and divergent series using the concept of grossone, *Applied Mathematics and Computation* **218(16)**, pp. 8064–8076.

Žilinskas, A. (2012). On strong homogeneity of two global optimization algorithms based on statistical models of multimodal objective functions, *Applied Mathematics and Computation* **218(16)**, pp. 8131–8136.

Chapter 14

Cognition and Complexity

Yuri I. Manin

Max-Planck-Institut für Mathematik, Bonn, Germany

Abstract

The word "complexity" is most often used as a meta–linguistic expression referring to certain intuitive characteristics of a natural system and/or its scientific description. These characteristics may include: sheer amount of data that must be taken into account; visible "chaotic" character of these data and/or space distribution/time evolution of a system etc. This talk is centered around the precise mathematical notion of "Kolmogorov complexity", originated in the early theoretical computer science and measuring the degree to which an available information can be compressed.

In the first part, I will argue that a characteristic feature of basic scientific theories, from Ptolemy's epicycles to the Standard Model of elementary particles, is their splitting into two very distinct parts: the part of relatively small Kolmogorov complexity ("laws", "basic equations", "periodic table", "natural selection, genotypes, mutations") and another part, of indefinitely large Kolmogorov complexity ("initial and boundary conditions", "phenotypes", "populations"). The data constituting this latter part are obtained by planned observations, focussed experiments, and afterwards collected in growing databases (formerly known as "books", "tables", "encyclopaedias" etc). In this discussion Kolomogorov complexity plays a role of the central metaphor.

14.1. Summary

The word "complexity" is most often used as a metalinguistic expression referring to certain intuitive characteristics of a natural system and/or its scientific description. These characteristics may include: sheer amount of data that must be taken into account; visible "chaotic" character of these data and/or space distribution/time evolution of a system etc.

This paper is centered around the precise mathematical notion of "Kolmogorov complexity", originated in the early theoretical computer science and measuring *the degree to which an available information can be compressed.*

338

In the first section, I will argue that a characteristic feature of basic scientific theories, from Ptolemy's epicycles to the Standard Model of elementary particles, is their splitting into two very distinct parts: the part of relatively small Kolmogorov complexity ("laws", "basic equations", "periodic table", "natural selection, genotypes, mutations") and another part, of indefinitely large Kolmogorov complexity ("initial and boundary conditions", "phenotypes", "populations"). The data constituting this latter part are obtained by planned observations, focused experiments, and afterwards collected in growing databases (formerly known as "books", "tables", "encyclopedias" etc.). In this discussion Kolmogorov complexity plays a role of the central metaphor.

The second section is dedicated to more precise definitions and examples of complexity.

Finally, the last section briefly touches upon attempts to deal directly with Kolmogorov complex datasets and the "End of Science" prophecies.

14.2. Bipartite Structure of Scientific Theories

In this section, I will understand the notion of "compression of information" intuitively and illustrate its pervasive character with several examples from the history of science.

Planetary movements. Firstly, I will briefly remind the structure of several models of planetary motions in the chronological order of their development.

After the discovery that among the stars observable by naked eye on a night sky there exist several exceptional "moving stars" (planets), there were proposed several successful models of their movement that allowed predict the future positions of the moving stars.

The simplest of them placed all fixed stars on one celestial sphere that rotated around the earth in a way reflecting nightly and annual visible motions. The planets, according to Apollonius of Perga (3rd century B. C.), Hipparchus of Rhodes, and Ptolemy of Alexandria (2nd century A. D.), were moving in a more complicated way: along circular "epicycles" whose centers moved along another system of circles, "eccentrics" around Earth. Data about radii of eccentrics and epicycles and the speed of movements were extracted from observations of the visible movements, and the whole model was then used in order to predict the future positions at any given moment of observation.

As D. Park remarks ([Pa], p. 72), "[...] in the midst of all this empiricism sat the ghost of Plato, legislating that the curves drawn must be circles and nothing else, and that the planets and the various connecting points must move along them uniformly and in no other way."

Since in reality observable movements of planets involved accelerations, backward movements, etc., two circles in place of one for each planet at least temporarily saved face of philosophy. Paradoxically, however, much later and much more developed mathematics of modernity returned to the image of "epicycles", that could since then form an arbitrarily high hierarchy: the idea of Fourier series and, later, Fourier integral transformation does exactly that!

It is well known, at least in general outline, how Copernicus replaced these geocentric models by a heliocentric one, and how with the advent of Newton's

$$\text{gravity law } F = G\frac{m_1 m_2}{r^2}, \quad \text{dynamic law } F = ma,$$

and the resulting solution of the "two-body problem", planets "started moving" along ellipsoidal orbits (with Sun as one focus rather than center). It is less well known to the general public that this approximation as well is valid only insofar as we can consider negligible the gravitational forces with which the planets interact among themselves.

If we intend to obtain a more precise picture, we have to consider the system of differential equations defining the set of curves parametrised by time t in the $6n$-*dimensional phase space* where n is the number of planets (including Sun) taken in consideration:

$$\frac{d^2 q_i}{dt^2} = \sum_{i=1}^{n} \frac{m_i m_j ((q_i - q_j))}{|q_i - q_j|^3}.$$

Both Newton laws are encoded in this system.

The choice of one curve, corresponding to the evolution of our Solar system, is made when we input *initial conditions* $q_i(0)$, $\frac{dq_i}{dt}(0)$ at certain moment of time $t = 0$; they are supplied, with a certain precision, by observations.

At this level, a new complication emerges. Generic solutions of this system of equations, in the case of three and more bodies, cannot be expressed by any simple formulas (unlike the equations themselves). Moreover, even qualitative behavior of solutions depends in extremely sensitive way on the initial conditions: very close initial positions/velocities may produce widely divergent trajectories. Thus, the question whether our Solar system will persist for the next, say, 10^8 years (even without disastrous external interventions) cannot be solved unless we know its current parameters (masses of planets, positions of their centers of mass, and speeds) with unachievable precision. This holds even without appealing to much more precise Einstein's description of gravity, or without taking in account comets, asteroid belts and Moons of the Solar system (the secondary planets turning around planets themselves).

It goes without saying that a similarly detailed description of, say, our Galaxy, taking in account movements of all individual celestial bodies, constituting it, is unachievable from the start, because of sheer amount of these bodies. Hence, to understand its general space-time structure, we must first construct models involving averaging on a very large scale. And of course, the model of space-time itself, now involving Einstein's equations, will describe an "averaged" space-time.

Information compression: first summary. In this brief summary of consecutive scientific models, one can already see the following persisting pattern: the subdivision into a highly compressed part ("laws") and potentially indefinitely complex part. The first part in our brief survey was represented by formulas that literally became cultural symbols of Western civilization: Newton's laws, that were followed by Einstein's $E = mc^2$ and Heisenberg's $pq - qp = \frac{h}{2\pi i}$. The second part is kinematically represented by "initial" or "boundary" conditions, and dynamically by a potentially unstable character of dependence of the data we are interested in from these initial/boundary conditions.

More precisely, a mathematical description of the "scene" upon which develops kinematics and dynamics in these models is also represented by highly compressed mathematical images, only this time of geometric nature. Thus, the postulate that kinematics of a single massive point is represented by its position in an ideal Euclidean space represents one of the "laws" as well. To describe kinematics, one should amplify this "configuration space" and replace it by the "phase space" parametrizing positions and velocities, or, better, momenta. For one massive point it is a space of dimension *six*: this is the answer of mathematics to Zeno's "Achilles and the Turtle" paradox. For a planet system consisting of n planets (including Sun) the phase space has dimension $6n$.

For Einstein's equations of gravitation, the relevant picture is much more complicated: it involves configuration and phase spaces that have *infinite* dimension, and require quite a fair amount of mathematics for their exact description. Nevertheless, this part of our models is still clearly separated from the one that we refer to as the part of infinite Kolmogorov complexity, because mathematics developed a concise language for description of geometry.

One more lesson of our analysis is this: "laws" can be discovered and efficiently used only if and when we restrict our attention to definite domains, space–time scales, and kinds of matter and interactions. For example, there was no place for chemistry in the pictures above.

From macroworld to microworld: the Standard Model of elementary particles and interactions. From astronomy, we pass now to the deepest known level of microworld: theory of elementary particles and their interactions.

I will say a few words about the so-called Standard Model of the elementary particles and their interactions, that took its initial form in the 1970's as a theoretical construction in the framework of the Quantum Field Theory. The Standard Model got its first important experimental correlates with the discovery of quarks (components of nuclear "elementary" particles) and W and Z bosons, quanta of interactions. For a very rich and complex history of this stage of theoretical physics, stressing the role of experiments and experimenters, see the fascinating account [Zi] by Antonio Zichichi. The Standard Model recently reappeared on the first pages of the world press thanks to the renewed hopes that the last critically missing component of the Model, the Higgs boson, has finally been observed.

Somewhat paradoxically, one can say that mathematics of the Standard Model is firmly based on the same ancient archetypes of the human thought as that of Hipparchus and Ptolemy: symmetry and uniform movement along circles.

More precisely, the basic idea of symmetry of modern classical (as opposed to quantum) non-relativistic physics involves the symmetry group of rigid movements of the three-dimensional Euclidean space, that is combinations of parallel shifts and rotations around a point. The group of rotations is denoted $SO(3)$, and celestial spheres are the unique objects invariant with respect to rotations. Passing from Hipparchus and Ptolemy to modernity includes two decisive steps: adding shifts (Earth, and then Sun, cease being centers of the Universe), and, crucially, understanding the new meta-law of physics: *symmetry* must govern *laws of physics themselves* rather than objects/processes etc. that these laws are supposed to govern (such as Solar System).

When we pass now to the quantum mechanics, and further to the Quantum Field Theory (not involving gravitation), the group of $SO(3)$ (together with shifts) should be extended, in particular, by several copies of such groups as $SU(2)$ and $SU(3)$ describing rotations in the *internal degrees of freedom* of elementary particles, such as spin, color etc. The basic "law" that should be invariant with respect to this big group, is encoded in the Lagrangian density: it is a "mathematical formula" that is considerably longer than everything we get exposed to in our high school and even college courses.

Finally, the Ptolemy celestial movements, superpositions of rotations of rigid spheres, now transcend our space-time and happen in the infinite-dimensional Hilbert space of wave-functions: this is the image describing, say, a hydrogen atom in the paradigm of the first decades of the 20th century.

Information compression: second summary. I will use the examples above in order to justify the following viewpoint.

Scientific laws (at least those that are expressed by mathematical constructions) can be considered as *programs for computation*, whereas observations produce *inputs* to these programs.

Outputs of these computations serve first to check/establish a domain of applicability of our theories. We compare the predicted behavior of a system with observed one, we are happy when our predictions agree quantitatively and/or qualitatively with observable behavior, we fix the border signs signaling that at this point we went too far.

Afterwards, the outputs are used for practical/theoretical purposes, e.g. in engineering, weather predictions etc., but also to formulate the new challenges arising before the scientific thinking.

This comparison of scientific laws with programs is, of course, only a metaphor, but it will allow us to construct also a precise model of the kind of complexity, inherently associated with this metaphor of science: Kolmogorov complexity.

The next section is dedicated to the sketch of this notion in the framework of mathematics, again in its historical perspective.

14.3. Integers and their Kolmogorov complexity

Positional notations as programs. In this section, I will explain that the well known to the general public decimal notations of natural numbers are themselves programs.

What are they supposed to calculate?

Well, the actual *numbers* that are encoded by this notation, and are more adequately represented by, say, rows of strokes:

$$7: \quad |||||||, \qquad 13: \quad |||||||||||||, \quad \ldots \quad , 1984: \quad |||| \cdots ||||$$

Of course, in the last example it is unrealistic even to expect that if I type here 1984 strokes, an unsophisticated reader will be able to check that I am not mistaken. There will be simply too much strokes to count, whereas the *notation-program* "1984" contains only four signs chosen from the alphabet of ten signs. One can save on the size of alphabet, passing to the binary notation, then "1984" will be replaced by a longer program "11111000000". However, comparing the length of the program with the "size" of the number, i.e. the respective number of strokes, we see that decimal/binary notation gives an immense economy: the program length is approximately the logarithm of the number of strokes (in the base 10 or 2 respectively).

More generally, we can speak about "size", or "volume" of any finite text based upon a fixed finite alphabet.

The discovery of this logarithmic upper bound of the Kolmogorov complexity of *numbers* was a leap in the development of humanity on the scale of civilizations.

However, if one makes some slight additional conventions in the system of notation, it will turn out that *some* integers admit a much shorter notation. For example, let us allow ourselves to use the vertical dimension and write, e.g. $10^{10^{10}}$.

The logarithm of the last number is about 10^{10}, much larger than the length of the notation for which we used only 6 signs! And if we are unhappy about non-linear notation, we may add to the basic alphabet two brackets (,) and postulate that $a(b)$ means a^b. Then $10^{10^{10}}$ will be linearly written as $10(10(10))$ using only 10 signs, still much less than $10^{10} + 1$ decimal digits (of course, 10^{10} of them will be just zeroes).

Then, perhaps, *all* integers can be produced by notation/programs that are much shorter than logarithm of their size?

No! It turns out that absolute majority of numbers (or texts) *cannot* be significantly compressed, although an infinity of integers can be written in a much shorter way than it can be done in any chosen system of positional notation.

If we leave the domain of integers and leap, to, say, such a number as $\pi = 3.1415926\ldots$, it looks as if it had infinite complexity. However, this is not so. There exists a program that can take as input the (variable) place of a decimal digit (an integer) and give as output the respective digit. Such a program is itself a text in a chosen algorithmic language, and as such, it also has a complexity: its own Kolmogorov complexity. One agrees that this is the complexity of π.

A reader should be aware that I have left many subtle points of the definition of Kolmogorov complexity in shadow, in particular, the fact that its dependence of the chosen system of encoding and computation model can change it only by a bounded quantity etc. A reader who would like to see some more mathematics about this matter is referred to the relevant references.

Here I will mention two other remarkable facts related to the Kolmogorov complexity of numbers: one regarding its unexpected relation to the idea of *randomness*, and another one showing that some psychological data make explicit the role of this complexity in the cognitive activity of our mind.

Complexity and randomness. Consider arbitrarily long finite sequences of zeroes and ones, say, starting with one so that each such sequence could be interpreted as a binary notation of an integer.

There is an intuitive notion of "randomness " of such a sequence. In the contemporary technology "random" sequences of digits and similar random objects are used for encoding information, in order to make it inaccessible for third parties. In fact, a small distributed industry producing such random sequences (and, say, random big primes) has been created. A standard way to produce random objects is to leave mathematics and to recur to physics: from throwing a piece to registering white noise.

One remarkable property of Kolmogorov complexity is this: *those sequences of digits whose Kolmogorov complexity is approximately the same as their length, are random in any meaningful sense of the word.* In particular, they cannot be generated by a program essentially shorter than the sequence itself.

Complexity and human mind. In the history of humanity, discovery of laws of classical and quantum physics that represent incredible compression of complex information, stresses the role of Kolmogorov complexity, at least as a relevant metaphor for understanding the laws of cognition.

In his very informative book [De], Stanislas Dehaene considers certain experimental results about the statistics of appearance numerals and other names of numbers. cf. especially pp. 110–115, subsection "Why are some numerals more frequent than others?".

As mathematicians, let us consider the following abstract question: can one say anything non-obvious about possible probabilities distributions on the set of *all* natural numbers? More precisely, one such distribution is a sequence of non-negative real numbers $p_n, n = 1, 2, \ldots$ such that $\sum_n p_n = 1$. Of course, from the last formula it follows that p_n must tend to zero, when n tends to infinity; moreover p_n cannot tend to zero too slowly: for example, $p_n = n^{-1}$ will not do. But two different distributions can be widely incomparable.

Remarkably, it turns out that if we restrict our class of distributions only to *computable from below* ones, that is, those in which p_n can be computed as a function of n (in a certain precise sense), then it turns out that there is a distinguished and small subclass C of such distributions, that are in a sense *maximal* ones. Any member (p_n) of this class has the following unexpected property (see [Lev]):

the probability p_n of the number n, up to a bounded (from above and below) factor, equals the inverse of the exponentiated Kolmogorov complexity of n.

This statement needs additional qualifications: the most important one is that we need here *not* the original Kolmogorov complexity but the so called *prefix-free* version of it. We omit technical details, because they are not essential here. But the following properties of any distribution $(p_n) \in C$ are worth stressing in our context:

(i) Most of the numbers n, those that are Kolmogorov "maximally complex", appear with probability comparable with $n^{-1}(\log n)^{-1-\varepsilon}$, with a small ε: "most large numbers appear with frequency inverse to their size" (in fact, somewhat smaller one).

(ii) However, frequencies of those numbers that are Kolmogorov very simple, such as 10^3 (thousand), 10^6 (million), 10^9 (billion), produce sharp local peaks in the graph of (p_n).

The reader may compare these properties of the discussed class of distributions, which can be called *a priori distributions*, with the observed frequencies of numerals (number words) in printed and oral texts in various languages: cf. Dehaene, loc. cit., p. 111, Figure 4.4. To me, their qualitative agreement looks very convincing: brains and their societies do reproduce a priori probabilities.

Notice that those parts of the Dehaene and Mehler graphs in loc. cit. that refer to large numbers, are somewhat misleading: they might create an impression that frequencies of the numerals, say, between 10^6 and 10^9 smoothly interpolate between those of 10^6 and 10^9 themselves, whereas in fact they abruptly drop down.

Finally, I want to stress that the class of a priori probability distributions that we are considering here is *qualitatively distinct* from those that form now a common stock of sociological and sometimes scientific analysis: cf. a beautiful synopsis by Terence Tao in [Ta]. The appeal to the uncomputable degree of maximal compression is exactly what can make such a distribution an eye–opener. As I have written at the end of [Ma2]:

"One can argue that all cognitive activity of our civilization, based upon symbolic (in particular, mathematical) representations of reality, deals actually with the *initial Kolmogorov segments* of potentially infinite linguistic constructions, *always* replacing vast volumes of data by their compressed descriptions. This is especially visible in the outputs of the modern genome projects.

In this sense, such linguistic cognitive activity can be metaphorically compared to a gigantic pre-computation process, shell-sorting infinite worlds of expressions in their Kolmogorov order."

14.4.   New Cognitive Toolkits: WWW and Databases

"The End of Theory". In summer 2008, an issue of the "Wired Magazine" appeared. It's cover story ran: "The End of Theory: The Data Deluge Makes the Scientific Method Obsolete".

The message of this essay [An] written by the Editor-in-Chief Chris Anderson, was summarized in the following words:

"The new availability of huge amounts of data, along with statistical tools to crunch these numbers, offers a whole new way of understanding the world. Correlation supersedes causation, and science can advance even without coherent models, unified theories, or really any mechanical explanation at all. There's no reason to cling to our old ways. It's time to ask: What can science learn from Google?"

I will return to this rhetoric question at the end of this subsection. Right now I want only to stress that, as well as in the scientific models of the "bygone days", basic theory is unavoidable in this brave new Petabyte World: encoding and decoding data, search algorithms, and of course, computers themselves are just engineering embodiment of some very basic and very abstract notions of mathematics. The mathematical idea underlying the structure of modern computers is the Turing machine (or one of several other equivalent formulations of the concepts of computability). We know that the universal Turing machine has a very small Kolmogorov complexity, and therefore, using the basic metaphor of this talk, we can say that the bipartite structure of the classical scientific theories is reproduced at this historical stage.

Moreover, what Chris Anderson calls "the new availability of huge amounts of data" by itself is not very new: after spreading of printing, astronomic observatories, scientific laboratories, and statistical studies, the amount of data available to any visitor of a big public library was always huge, and studies of correlations proliferated for at least the last two centuries.

Charles Darwin himself collected the database of his observations, and the result of his pondering over it was the theory of evolution.

A representative recent example is the book [FlFoHaSCH], sensibly reviewed in [Gr].

Even if the sheer volume of data has by now grown by several orders of magnitude, this is not the gist of Anderson's rhetoric.

What Anderson actually wants to say is that human beings are now – happily! – free from thinking over these data. Allegedly, computers will take this burden upon themselves, and will provide us with correlations – replacing the old-fashioned "causations" (that I prefer to call scientific laws) – and expert guidance.

Leaving aside such questions as how "correlations" might possibly help us understand the structure of Universe or predict the Higgs boson, I would like to quote the precautionary tale from [Gr]:

"[...] in 2000 Peter C. Austin, a medical statistician at the University of Toronto, and his colleagues conducted a study of all 10,674,945 residents of Ontario aged between eighteen and one hundred. Residents were randomly assigned to different groups, in which they were classified according to their astrological signs. The research team then searched through more than two hundred of the most common diagnoses of hospitalisation until they identified two where patients under one astrological sign had a significantly higher probability of hospitalisation compared to those born under the remaining signs combined: Leos had a higher probability of gastrointestinal haemorrhage while Sagittarians had a higher probability of fracture of the upper arm compared to all other signs combined.

It is thus relatively easy to generate statistically significant but spurious correlations when examining a very large data set and a similarly large number of potential variables. Of course, there is no biological mechanism whereby Leos might be predisposed to intestinal bleeding or Sagittarians to bone fracture, but Austin notes, 'It is tempting to construct biologically plausible reasons for observed subgroup effects after having observed them.'

Such an exercise is termed 'data mining', and Austin warns, 'Our study therefore serves as a cautionary note regarding the interpretation of findings generated by data mining' [...]"

Therefore my answer to the Chris Anderson's rhetorics "What can science learn from Google?" is this:

"Think! Otherwise no Google will help you."

Topological analysis of data. Recently a very interesting and meaningful way of compressing information contained in large databases was suggested: see the survey [Ca] for main ideas and references.

Basically, the strategy described in [Ca] consists in encoding the data by a simplicial complex and subsequently passing, say, to its homology groups.

One version of encoding starts with *clustering*: imagining elements of a database as points say, in a metric space, one can choose a real parameter $\varepsilon > 0$ and then to consider subsets of points $\{x_0, x_1, \ldots, x_k\}$ such that the pairwise distances $d(x_i, x_j)$ are bounded by ε. All such subsets taken together have a natural structure of the simplicial complex, called *Vietoris–Rips* complex $VR(X, \varepsilon)$.

Since often there is no natural notion of distance d and/or no natural choice of parameter ε, one is bound to consider functorial maps between VR-complexes constructed for various values of ε. Then final topological invariants are declared to be (some versions of) *persistent* homology classes. Qualitatively speaking, persistent topological invariants should not depend on the indeterminacies of metric. To this last condition are often added problems of computational complexity, forcing the researchers to apply clustering to samples of data: subsets $Y \subset X$. The notion of persistency must be adapted to this additional complication.

A considerable part of work in this direction was motivated by neuroscience and attempts to imitate certain brain activities by computer programs: see [LePeMu], [SiMeIshCaSaRi], and further references in [Ca].

A related but different inspiration comes from postulating that patterns of neural spiking activity in certain domains of brain can and should be "decompiled" as referring to certain characteristics of *stimuli space* activating respective neurons: see [CuIt], [CuItVCYo], [Yo], and the survey [Ma5].

Cognitive data. It would be important to develop other possible applications of topological analysis of data, in particular, to the analysis of human languages, their semantics, syntaxes, history: see, for example, [PoGhGClLiDaMar].

Here I will briefly discuss the example of "semantic space". In most variations, one starts with the assumption that "the space of meanings" (say, of words in a language) is a certain set X. The next step consists in postulating additional structures (in Bourbaki's sense) on it.

The most straightforward assumption is that meanings form *subsets U_i* rather than points of X so that we can imagine them as *a covering* even before (or without) postulating a topology.

For example, Guiraud [Gui] suggests that subsets of meaning U_i have a natural embedding into affine spaces $\mathbf{R}^d$, whose axes are marked by "semes". Each seme axis corresponds to a semantic opposition (in the structuralist paradigm), such as "animate/inanimate", so that a pure "yes/no" picture would provide only an embedding into $\{-1, +1\}^d$ or else $\{0, 1\}^d$. A more realistic description of meanings would allow less localized positions on the seme's axes.

Discussing Zipf's Law, D. Manin in [Man] postulates furthermore that X is endowed with *a measure*, and that U_i are its measurable subsets. He uses this structure in order to provide a mechanism generating Zipf's Law.

On the other hand, in the generating model of Zipf's Law developed in [Ma3] (see also [Ma4] and [MaMar]) the key role is played by the Kolmogorov complexity of the hypothetical *neural encoding* of the semantic space rather than any specific structure of this space itself. It is implicitly suggested that such encodings are combinatorial objects, exactly as in stimuli spaces encodings considered in [Yo] and references therein. Therefore it would be extremely interesting to study neural encodings of human languages from the perspective of [CuIt] and [CuItVCYo].

Bibliography

[An] Ch. Anderson. The end of theory, *Wired*, 17.06, 2008.

[Ca] G. Carlsson. Topology and data, *Bull. Amer. Math. Soc.*, 46(2) (2009), 255–308.

[ChCoMar] A. H. Chamseddine, A. Connes, M. Marcolli. Gravity and the standard model with neutrino mixing, *Adv. Theor. Math. Phys.*, 11 (2007), 991-1089. arXiv:hep-th/0610241

[CuIt] C. Curto, V. Itskov. Cell groups reveal structure of stimulus space, *PLoS Comput. Biol.*, 4(10), (2008), 13 pp. (available online).

[CuItVCYo] C. Curto, V. Itskov, A. Veliz-Cuba, N. Youngs. The neural ring: An algebraic tool for analysing the intrinsic structure of neural codes, *Bull. Math. Biology*, 75(9), (2013), 1571-1611.

[De] S. Dehaene. *The Number Sense. How the Mind creates Mathematics,* Oxford UP, 1997.

[FlFoHaSCH] R. Floud, R. W. Fogel, B. Harris, Sok Chul Hong. *The Changing Body: Health, Nutrition and Human Development in the Western World Since 1700,* Cambridge UP, 2011.

[Gr] J. Groopman. The body and the human progress, *The New York Review of Books,* Oct. 27, 2011.

[Gui] P. Guiraud. The semic matrices of meaning, *Social Science Inform.* 7(2) (1968), pp. 131–139.

[LePeMu] A. B. Lee, K. S. Pedersen, D. Mumford. The non-linear statistics high–contrast patches in natural images, *Int. J. Comput. Vision,* 54(1–3) (2003), pp. 83–103.

[Lev] L. A. Levin. Various measures of complexity for finite objects (axiomatic description), *Soviet Math. Dokl.* 17(2) (1976), pp. 522–526.

[Ma1] Yu. Manin. *A Course of Mathematical Logic for Mathematicians,* 2nd Edition, with new chapters written by Yu. Manin and B. Zilber. Springer, 2010.

[Ma2] Yu. Manin. Renormalization and computation II: Time cut-off and the Halting Problem, *Math. Struct. Comp. Sci.,* 22 (2012), pp. 729–751. Preprint math.QA/0908.3430

[Ma3] Yu. Manin. Zipf's law and L. Levin's probability distributions, *Funct. Anal. Appl.,* 48(2) (2014), pp. 116–127. Preprint arXiv: 1301.0427

[Ma4] Yu. Manin. Complexity vs energy: theory of computation and theoretical physics, *J. Phys. Conf. Ser.* 532 (2014), 012018. Preprint arXiv:1302.6695

[Ma5] Yu. Manin. Neural codes and homotopy types: mathematical models of place field recognition, *Moscow Math. J.* (to appear). Preprint arXiv:1501.00897

[MaMar] Yu. Manin, M. Marcolli. Kolmogorov complexity and the asymptotic bound for error–correcting codes, *J. Differential Geom.,* 97 (2014), pp. 91–108. Preprint arXiv:1203.0653

[Man] D. Yu. Manin. Zipf's law and avoidance of excessive synonymy, *Cognitive Sci.* 32 (2008), pp. 1075–1098. arXiv: 0710.0105 [cs.CL]

[Pa] D. Park. *The How and the Why. An Essay on the Origins and Development of Physical Theory,* Princeton UP, 1988.

[PoGhGClLiDaMar] A. Port, I. Gheorghiţa, D. Guth, J. M. Clark, Cr. Liang, Sh. Dasu, M. Marcolli, *Persistent topology of syntax.* Preprint arXiv:1507.05134

[SiMeIshCaSaRi] G. Singh, F. Memoli, T. Ishkhanov, G. Carlsson, G. Sapiro, D. Ringach. Topological structure of population activity in primary visual cortex, *J. Vision* 8 (2008), pp. 1–18.

[Ta] T. Tao. E pluribus unum: From complexity, universality, *Dædalus, J. AAAS*, (2012), pp. 23–34.

[Yo] N. E. Youngs. *The neural ring: using algebraic geometry to analyse neural rings.* arXiv:1409.2544 [q-bio.NC], 108 pp.

[Zi] A. Zichichi. *Subnuclear Physics. The first 50 years: Highlights from Erice to ELN.* World Scientific, 1999.

Chapter 15

Informational Perspective on QBism and the Origins of Life

Koichiro Matsuno
Nagaoka University of Technology
Nagaoka 940-2188, Japan

Abstract

One interpretation of quantum mechanics dubbed Quantum Bayesianism or QBism in short can be considered as a useful tool for approaching the origins of life as the genuine source matrix of complexity and information on the empirical ground. Any user of quantum mechanics that can assign a probability to whatever event other than itself within the framework of QBism is to occur with the conditional probability of duration approaching unity. Such a user occurring with the probability unity can be equated with the occurrence of the internal observer that can make itself durable. A physical means of making the internal user durable is through the preservation of its own class identity that can remain invariable while being subject to the constant exchange of component atomic elements. The emergence of a durable material organization upon exchanging individual component elements with another ones of the similar kinds can be taken to be an instance related to the origins of life. A concrete empirical case of a durable material organization is a reaction cycle in which each atomic component such as the carbon atom comes to experience the organizational whole from within through the constant replacement of the components. The source of complexity and information is found within the richness of counterfactual conditionals prepared and perceived by the user of quantum mechanics. Biological complexity is unique in appreciating the chemical affinity operating as crossing and integrating different tenses in a sharp contrast to the physical counterpart upon the physical affinity operating in tenseless time.

15.1. Introduction

One aspect that is certain with our endeavor for addressing the thorny issues of complexity and information is to make a dependable proposition in one form or another. In addition, any material phenomenon perceivable in the empirical world is supposed to be quantum-mechanical in its intrinsic makeup. Since quantum mechanics sets the stipulation of being probabilistic in regard to its measurement outcome as appealing to Born's probability rule, the proposition on the informational aspect of quantum-mechanical nature would turn out to be probabilistic accordingly.

Once the probabilistic nature of whatever observational proposition is taken for granted, its qualification would require further scrutiny on the identification of an object to which the value of the probability of occurrence is assigned. As facing this issue, Born's probability rule proposes that the length of the state vector or the amplitude of the wave function conceivable in the Hilbert space gives the probability amplitude specific to that state represented by the state function. To be sure, there has been no single observation demonstrating the violation of Born's rule empirically so far. Despite that, the objective nature of the state function remains to be equivocal.[1] The present convolution stems from the observation that the specification of a Hilbert space comes from the interplay between the two of the quantum-mechanical law of motion and the imposed boundary conditions. Although it remains methodologically indisputable, the Hilbert space would be forced to remain indefinite in its actual implication unless it is supplemented with the act of preparing the boundary conditions in a specific manner.

---

[1]A forerunner calling critical attention to the notion of state in quantum mechanics was Einstein, Podolsky and Rosen (1935, p. 778-9) as expressed in the following quote: "In quantum mechanics it is usually assumed that the wave function *does* contain a complete description of the physical reality of the system in the state to which it corresponds. At first sight this assumption is entirely reasonable, for the information obtainable from a wave function seems to correspond exactly to what can be measured without altering the state of the system. We shall show, however, that this assumption, together with the criterion of reality given above, leads to a contradiction."

One alternative for approaching the probabilistic nature of quantum mechanical phenomena without relying exclusively upon the state function in a Hilbert space would be to directly address a probabilistic proposition of an observational character. We shall focus upon the extent to which the probabilistic proposition could cope with quantum-mechanical phenomena without direct reference to the state description accepting the Hilbert space.

15.2. Probabilistic Proposition

One issue relevant to the probabilistic proposition is its logical character. For instance, let us imagine a simple proposition such as "Phenomena are probabilistic". If one tries to understand this proposition within the framework of first-order logic, quantification would apply only to the subject "Phenomena" covering the spectrum ranging over from a phenomenon to any phenomenon. No quantification would apply to the predicate "to be probabilistic". This form of first-order logic is certainly in conformity with the state description accepting a Hilbert space supplemented by Born's probability rule.

Once the amplitude of the state function appearing in the subject is specified, the probability for the state to occur is predicated to be in proportion to the amplitude squared. No further room of quantification is left for the predicate. The probability measured as the amplitude squared also applies to the linear superposition of the state functions if the state functions belong to the same Hilbert space. However, the linear superposition of the state functions and the resulting first-order logic of a probabilistic nature could not function properly if the state functions belong to different Hilbert spaces, that is to say, if the boundary conditions specifying each state function are different.

A conspicuous example pointing to a failure of first-order logic of a probabilistic nature is available from a well-known two-slit experiment. When an electron gun shooting at two slits cut on a thin plate, right and left in parallel, both of which are open, the electrons detected on the screen placed behind the plate with the two-slit inscribed demonstrate an interference pattern. In contrast, the pattern detected with only one of the two slits open demonstrates no such interference. This observation reveals that the interference pattern retrievable from the two-slit open definitely differs from the resultant of the patterns each of which is available only when one slit, either right or left, is open. The conclusion thus derived is that the probabilistic nature of quantum mechanical origin is highly context-dependent. This context dependence may invite the likelihood of quantification to be applied even to the predicate as appearing in a simple example of "Phenomena are probabilistic".

The irrevocable intrusion of quantification to be applied to the predicate makes its logic at least second-order. Second-order logic must be inescapable once it is admitted that the quantum phenomena in focus may admit the likelihood of changing the boundary conditions in movement.

A similar concern may also be applicable to another observation such as "Information is probabilistic". Needless to say, Shannon's information in terms of information bits is unfailingly for first-order logic as limiting quantification only to the subject "Information" with no further quantification applied to the predicate. Nonetheless, once one pays due attention to the fact that information to be received depends upon the contextual specification unique to each recipient, quantification to be applied to the predicate "to be probabilistic" would also become inevitable.

Then, a stressful situation comes up to the surface. On first look, a probabilistic proposition in second-order logic would seem self-defeating. While the multitude of each of the subject and the predicate to be quantified must be at most of countable infinity, the multitude of the consequential probabilistic proposition must be of uncountable infinity. This is simply because the composite ordinal products figured out of the two sources of independent countable elements are necessarily made to be uncountable thanks to the argument after Cantor diagonalization. Its inevitable consequence is that there should be no likelihood of assigning a non-negative value of probability to each of the resultant products whose multitude is of uncountable infinity.

Now, we may come to face two options to choose from. One would be to drastically abandon a probabilistic proposition altogether in the practice of empirical sciences.[2] One more alternative, which will be our choice in this article, may be to find a scheme for saving a probabilistic proposition at the expense of the notion called a state that is all-pervasive both in physical and informational sciences.

15.3. Conditional Probabilities: Revisited

One suggestion for saving a probabilistic proposition, while circum-venting the state description, in the practice of empirical sciences may come from probability theory in pure mathematics. Consider, for instance, a conditional probability $P(A|A)$ as implying the occurrence of event A under the prior condition that event A is to occur. Obviously, the equality $P(A|A)=1$ is no more than a mere tautology upon the premise that the multitude of distinguishable events conceivable is at most of countable infinity. Furthermore, the mathematician setting the conditions for distinguishing between the different countable events is also presumed to be present there.

Needless to say, there is no likelihood of gaining a de novo empirical implication from a mere tautology in pure mathematics. However, there should remain some room left for cultivating the potential empirical implication if both the specification of countable events and the role assumed by the mathematician can further be qualified from an empirical or naturalized perspective (Matsuno, 2014). If the two individual events A_1 and A_2 belong to the same class of event A while both A_1 and A_2

---

[2]The individual quantum processes can be seen as going beyond probabilistic predictions. This perspective may invite a wholesale renunciation of the probability assignment to the predicted outcome or event of an individual quantum experiment. This view is due originally to Bohr (1987, p. 34) as quoted: "It is most important to realize that the recourse to probability laws under such circumstances [atomic phenomena] is essentially different in aim from the familiar application of statistical considerations as practical means of accounting for the properties of mechanical systems of great structural complexity. In fact, in quantum physics we are presented not with intricacies of this kind, but with the inability of the classical frame of concepts to comprise the peculiar feature of indivisibility, or 'individuality,' characterizing the elementary processes." In contrast, the Bayesian scheme accepts probability assignment to each individual event of interest as a matter of course. If the Bayesian perspective can be saved in whatever sense as facing quantum phenomena, the nature of an adopted event would have to be scrutinized in a critical manner.

distinguish either one from the other individually with regard to their atomic components, the equality $P(A_2|A_1)=1$ as a concrete instance belonging to the equality $P(A|A)=1$ could gain a new empirical implication without offending the original mathematical tautology unnecessarily.

There may remain an empirical possibility for a material body supporting the occurrence of event A_1 to come up with another event A_2 belonging to the same class with probability unity in sequence. This is due to such an additional qualification that the preceding event A_1 may come to further assume the capacity of setting and detecting the conditions for guaranteeing the production of event A_2 by replacing some of the atomic components constituting event A_1 with another ones of the similar kinds. The preceding production sets the condition of the succeeding production of a similar nature to come with probability unity by the help of the replacement of the component elements. In short, the product sets the condition for the production of another product of the similar kind to come.

This distinction between the concrete individual events A_1 and A_2 belonging to the same class event of A goes beyond the scope of the competence specific to the mathematician. For the distinctive class events acceptable to probability theory in mathematics are set to be countable, while it remains to be seen whether the individual events that may appear as replacing their components could also be countable.

The mathematician can safely avoid such a danger of assigning a non-negative probability value to each member of the uncountable set constituting the concrete individual events. Instead, conditional probabilities depend upon the agent that sets and detects the conditions. The agent cannot be limited only to the mathematician. Even material bodies having the capacity of measurement can set and detect such conditions distinguishing between different individual events belonging to one and the same class event.

Accordingly, the new implication of the equality $P(A_2|A_1)=1$ is such that the probability of the occurrence of the individual event A_2 under the prior conditions of the occurrence of the individual event A_1 must be unity. The material body supporting event A_1 comes to assume the capacity of detecting the conditions for the production of event A_2 subsequently. It can safely avoid the danger of assigning a probability value to each of the uncountable individual events thanks to the participation of the agency of setting the conditions to be detected as such. What is more, event A_1 has the capacity of detecting the conditions for making A_2 out of A_1 as referring to the immediate surroundings at the same time. The distinction of event A_2 from event A_1 stems from replacing some of the atomic components constituting event A_1 by another new components of the similar kinds. Prerequisite to replacing some of the atomic components is the affinity of material origin for making the product belonging to the same class as the preceding product belongs to. What should be focused upon is the physical likelihood of harboring the occurrence of those material bodies maintaining themselves through the act of material exchange. This issue must totally be an empirical or experimental matter.

Event A_1 in the equality $P(A_2|A_1)=1$ assumes two roles. One is to detect the condition for the production of event A_2 belonging to the same class of A to which A_1 belongs also. One more role is to make the actual product A_2, which definitely differs from A_1 individually, while keeping both A_1 and A_2 belonging to the same class of A. Once the equality $P(A_2|A_1)=1$ is guaranteed as being accompanied by another event A_3 belonging to the same class event A subsequently, the equality $P(A_3|A_2)=1$ would naturally follow unless the conditions of the immediate surroundings are disturbed significantly in the process. The repetition of the cycle would remain robust insofar as event A_3 happens to belong to the same class A while distinguishing itself from either of the preceding A_1 and A_2 in regard to replacing their constituent elements individually. As repeating this cycle, the probability of duration of the class event A would asymptotically come to approach unity.

What is unique to the likelihood of the probability of duration approaching unity is the participation of an agential material body functioning as an internal observer being competent in distinguishing between the different individual events belonging to the same class event. The internal observer processes the exchange of atomic component elements while keeping the class identity of the material body which it is going to maintain intact. The difference between the internal observer of material origin and the mathematician is that the latter can remain indifferent to the occurrence of the exchange of the atomic component elements individually. The mathematician finds no need for distinguishing those individual material bodies insofar as they belong to one and the same class.

The internal observer comes to detect the conditions under which the product can maintain itself durable as constantly exchanging its constituent atomic elements. Rather, the durable product feasible upon the constant exchange of component elements on the individual basis is a naturalized way of observing the probabilistic tautology of the two events of preparing the conditions for making the product and its actual making on the class basis. The conditional probability of duration approaching unity is in fact a natural consequence of the likelihood of the durable material bodies that do not significantly disturb the environment they experience between before and after each act of exchanging the component elements. The internal observer assuming the first-person status that is constantly looking for the conditions for making itself durable, once succeeded, would not fail in keeping itself durable since then unless the external conditions may happen to turn out quite adversary in the process. This issue must totally be empirical, rather than merely being theoretical. Once the role of the internal observer is focused upon as facing quantum phenomena, this would be equivalent to appraising the user of quantum mechanics.

15.4. Quantum Mechanics and Its User

Of course, it goes without saying that the most obvious user of quantum mechanics is the physicist as an external observer. Consequential to adopting this standard methodology is the acceptance of the notion called a state that can stand alone without any intervention or help from the external observer. Nonetheless, this strategy may meet a difficulty in interpreting the empirical observation of quantum phenomena. The probabilistic nature of the measurement outcome may not necessarily guarantee the preservation of an invariant frequency distribution of the individual probabilistic events if the context for defining the probability distribution is also in movement as displayed in Wheeler's delayed-choice experiment. One likely countermeasure for coping with the present impasse as being faced with the lack of the dependable probability distribution must be the switching over of the role of the agency of measurement from the externalist to the internalist.

The internalist or the internal observer potentially ubiquitous in the material world is unique in the act of measurement in precipitating an individual event of concrete nature. Measurement is concrete in the effect in abstracting something concrete out of something else to be measured. For instance, the two-slit experiment in quantum mechanics is concrete enough in registering a single spot on the screen when it detects the arrival of an electron emitted from an electron gun. The quantum nature of an electron is preserved even if it is subject to an abstraction of measurement origin of whatever kind. Measurement dynamics is thus in the form of an indefinite sequence of the quantum act of concretizing the consequence of an abstraction from the preceding similar concretization. It is exclusively of quantum mechanical origin in letting both the antecedents and the consequents of the process of abstraction be the quantum act of concretization, while classical mechanics does not distinguish between the two processes of abstraction and concretization.

The successive reverberation between the abstraction and the concretization back and forth repeatedly markedly differs from the state dynamics in quantum mechanics. In fact, there is no recovery of the repeated concretization from the once completed abstraction within the framework of the state dynamics alone. The state dynamics is paraphrased at best in terms of the already abstracted state function sanctioned within the adopted methodology unless it is further assisted by the measurement with use of the apparatus prepared by the externalist.

It is the internal observer that is in charge of constantly updating the act of concretization as necessarily being mediated by the intervening act of abstraction. Accordingly, the internal observer as an agent is part of quantum mechanics within the framework of measurement dynamics. That comes to imply that the internal observer as the user of quantum mechanics is of quantum-mechanical origin at the same time. Quantum mechanics would then have to provide the internal observer with the necessary material resources for its own material makeup and the agential operation thereupon.

Measurement dynamics is more inclusive than state dynamics is, since both the antecedents and consequents of whatever dynamics are concrete and specific enough when they are measured. From this perspective, the state dynamics of quantum mechanics remains under-complete in leaving the consequents of the dynamics not specific enough compared to the actual measurement attempted by the externalist who can stand alone by declaration. In contrast, the measurement dynamics of quantum mechanics is required to furnish the internal observer with the necessary resources.

The act of measurement requires some resources for concretization, to be taken in from the outside for the sake of implementing its own task. Above all, the internal observer must be durable otherwise the likelihood for the durable sequence of the act of concretizing the consequence of an abstraction from the preceding concretization must be jeopardized. Suggestive to the possible occurrence of a durable observer of material origin as the user of quantum mechanics could be the internal observer that can set and detect the conditions for making itself durable. That is the case for the conditional probability of duration approaching unity. The user of quantum mechanics can extensively be naturalized beyond the extent to which the original Quantum Bayesianism or QBism has alluded (Mermin, 2014). The QBist as the durable internal observer lets the conditional probability of its own duration approach unity under the guise of the first-person or subjective probability, in sharp contrast to the third-person or objective probability addressing the durable invariant ensemble of probabilistic events.

The appraisal of QBism from the perspective of the internal observer or the internal user is within shedding light on the occurrence of an agent of material origin. The internal observer which holds its own conditional probability of duration less than unity cannot survive indefinitely in a durable manner since it could eventually be alternated by the one which maintains the greater conditional probability of duration. The surviving internal observer is the one that can identify the condition letting itself be durable.

The factor making the durable internal observer agential in the effect is in its faster competency of recruiting necessary resources prior to that the likely would-be contenders may come to intervene. What makes the resource intake agential is the quantum nature of each resource element which sets the condition of being indivisible as prohibiting the element from being further split into the smaller pieces so as to be shared among the contenders.

15.5. Facing up to the Reaction Cycle

One empirical support for the occurrence of the conditional probability approaching unity is a reaction cycle. Unique to the operation of a reaction cycle is the scheme of transforming the preceding reaction product in the downstream back into the succeeding initial reactant in the upstream again as reactively feeding upon the resources available from the immediate neighborhood outside. Insofar as the reaction product is of the same kind as the initial reactant only with the difference of some of the atomic components replaced by another ones of the similar kinds, the reaction product comes to detect the succeeding production condition of exactly the similar type as the preceding initial reactant did. Then, it could sustain the cycle of product-to-production-to-product indefinitely.

The chemical affinity acting between the reaction product turned into the succeeding initial reactant and the external resources available from the immediate neighborhood is due to the path-dependent nature of the very affinity. In other words, some of the component elements constituting the reaction product are the survivors from those already taken in the preceding cycles. Reaction cycle is unique in replacing all of the atomic components by new ones of the similar kinds in due course, while some of them can survives at least over one round of the cycle operation of chemical reactions. Otherwise, the cycle would have to lose its material identity referring to the cycle as it is as a concrete material object.

The affinity acting between the components carrying the path-dependent history in the cycle and the other ones found in the resources just recruited from the immediate neighborhood outside can stabilize the path-dependent history to be frozen in the cycle by repeating the cycle operation. The component elements surviving in a reaction cycle can leave behind the stabilized path-dependent histories even if those elements are constantly replaced by another ones of the similar kinds.[3]

---

[3] A reaction cycle upon the path-dependent chemical affinity of a historical nature is impredicative in the sense that the individual atomic elements constituting the cycle are

The component element pulled into the cycle is going to participate in the succeeding act of pulling in another component element into the cycle, thus letting the resulting affinity cross different tenses. That means that the activity of integrating both pulling in and being pulled in is required to cross different tenses. It exhibits a sharp contrast to physical affinity conceivable only in tenseless time, in which both pulling in and being pulled in are concurrent in the same present tense if both are conceived in common tenseless time.

The appearance of the chemical affinity latent in the reaction product that leaves behind the memory of the path-dependent history is of emergent character structurally.[4] For the circular pathway from the initial reactant going along with the available resources as a reaction partner via several steps of the reaction intermediaries to be followed in sequence up to the reaction product and eventually back to the initial again serves as an emergent cohesive factor of a structural nature. No such affinity could be conceivable unless a reaction cycle is likely.

The affinity acting between the reaction product and the external resources is thus both structural and functional as letting the functional affinity be dependent upon the specification of the structure engulfing the reaction pathway implementing the path-dependent history in a circular form. The operation of such a reaction cycle can be repeated and stabilized

---

constantly exchanged. The elements constituting the cycle as a set are impredicative due to the intervention of the act such that new individuals entering the cycle goes along with letting different individuals leave it, thus making the operation of the cycle non-computable on the individual base (Rosen, 1991). How the leaving individuals differ from the entering ones depends upon the entire historical development of the cycle. That is context-dependent. The chemical affinity supporting the cycle upon the path-dependent history is, however, immune to the impredicativity since it refers to the affinity acting between the incumbent elements surviving in the cycle, though only over a limited time interval, and new elements to be recruited from the immediate neighborhood outside.

[4]The memory of the path-dependent history is about the functional attribute of the durable now that the internal observer experiences. This is different from the temporal attribute of the specious present which the external observer like a philosopher can conceive of as referring to the short-term duration or the relation of experience to time, and time in the latter is already an abstract notion. The durable now to the internalist may be defunct once it would lose its tie to the historical origin, like a lost kite cut off of its yawn. The specious present to the philosopher, on the other hand, is claimed to remain steady once it is set up by the externalist as such.

in a durable manner insofar as the available resources are guaranteed in the neighborhood of the cycle. And yet the operation of the cycle is historical in that the individual atomic elements to be exchanged are distinguishable between themselves. The historical sequence of the exchange of the atomic elements could eventually be back-extrapolated into the historical origin of the cycle itself insofar as each individual element to be exchanged is focused upon in a mutually distinguishable manner by the internal observer.

What is more, the most dominant reaction cycle is the one that can be fastest in the resource intake among the possible contenders since there is no leftover to feed upon for the late comers. This is a simple demonstration of how the conditional probability of duration approaching unity could be implemented in the quantum-mechanical world. The underlying rule is the mutual exclusion of resource allocations. There is no likelihood for dividing those atoms found in the resources into the smaller pieces.

Duration of a reaction cycle goes along with the realization of the chemical affinity enabling the initial reactant to transform itself into the reaction product that is similar to the initial reactant in kind at the possible fastest rate. Accordingly, both preservation of the conditional probability of duration approaching unity and facilitation of the chemical affinity realizing the resource intake at the possible fastest rate are mutually supportive with each other. If the conditional probability of duration happens to be less than unity, the supporting reaction cycle may exhibit the capacity of adjusting the chemical affinity so as to raise the conditional probability toward unity. Likewise, if the chemical affinity is yet to attain the rate of the fastest resource intake, the accompanied conditional probability unity may assist in enhancing the resource intake rate.

A reaction cycle is unique in holding the class identity of the cycle through the constant alternation of the constituent elements carrying the individual identities belonging to the same kinds. When the updated initial reactant originated from the preceding reaction product extends the chemical affinity toward the component elements to be taken in from the available resources in the neighborhood, the supporting chemical affinity functions only between the individual elements in the resources and the different individuals already belonging to the cycle.

Needless to say, it would be inappropriate for us to conceive that the material constituent elements by themselves could perceive the cycle as such from within. Each constituent element experiences the cycle only through the chemical affinity acting between the constituent elements. When we say that the constituent elements experience the cycle, it is just about the specific chemical affinity acting between the constituent elements to be found inside the cycle and outside it.

When we refer to the constituent element surviving over one round of the cycle, that individual element is meant to leave behind the path-dependent history on how it has moved round the cycle in a concrete manner. In short, each individual element has the capacity of experiencing the totality from within. This observation comes to invite an inverted perspective toward the organizational whole. That is to say, the organizational whole would turn out to be what each constituent element experiences from within over the limited period from entering it through leaving there in due course.

The updated initial reactant feeding upon the external resources thus comes to embody the chemical affinity acting between the individual elements carrying the path-dependent histories of going round the cycle at least once and the de novo elements of the external origin. Henceforth, the constituent elements carrying the path-dependent history can be stabilized in the cycle as repeating the reaction cycle.

What is responsible for raising the reaction cycle is the likelihood for the occurrence of the path-dependent chemical affinity. More specifically, a reaction cycle is a material vehicle for stabilizing the path-dependent chemical affinity. The chemical affinity acting between the resource element from the outside and the memory element surviving in the cycle at least over the preceding one round of the cycle operation can transform the preceding resource element into the succeeding memory element, and repeats the cycle indefinitely.[5] The complexity of the reaction cycle

---

[5]Memory assumes an agency of reading and interpreting it as such. Moreover, that activity presumes the affinity of material origin toward the act of reading and interpreting the memory. The memory agency is originally embodied in the chemical affinity enabling a reaction cycle to carry the path-dependent history with regard to each participating atomic element. It would only be after the appearance of a molecular representation of the reaction

resides within the path-dependent history latent in the memory element which is not directly accessible to the external observer, while its stability rests upon the durable class identity of the reaction cycle which is accessible to the external observer.

The user of quantum mechanics as facing the occurrence of a reaction cycle thus assumes two roles. One is for processing the concrete material elements carrying their individual identities, and the other is for facing and addressing the complex organization carrying its class identity. The naturalized internal user of quantum mechanics is more versatile and competent compared with the external user identified as the physicist.

The external user cannot address both the content of the memory element holding its own individual identity and the class identity of the supporting reaction cycle at the same time. When one of the constituent elements of the reaction cycle is focused upon, the external user does not have any reliable means for distinguishing whether the identity of the focused element may be about the individual or about the supporting reaction cycle as a class property. The individual identity can be specified only at the expense of the class identity and vice versa. Likewise, the internal user cannot cope with both the individual and the class identity at the same time. Nonetheless, the internal user can have the privilege of leaving behind the consequent of processing the elements carrying their individual identities so as to let the external user observe and address the consequential class identity.

The internal user that is synonymous with the internal observer processes only those concrete particular individuals. A paradigmatic example of processing the concrete individuals is a reaction cycle. Of necessity to its operation is to implement the chemical affinity acting between the individual elements in the resources and another individual elements carrying the path-dependent history of survival residing in the cycle at least over one round of the cycle operation. The internal user can proceed without reference to what the external user being synonymous with the external observer could perceive even if it is legitimate from the externalist perspective. Put it differently, the class identity occurring with

---

cycle when the informational molecule such as an RNA molecule may happen to be conceivable and referable.

the conditional probability of duration approaching unity that can be explicit to the external user may remain indifferent or irrelevant to the internal user since the class property is not the concrete individual object directly maneuverable by the internal user. Despite that, what the internal user constructs in the end comes to conform to what the external user perceives from the externalist perspective.

Quantum mechanics is quite peculiar in supporting both the internal and the external user, while classical mechanics allows for only the external user being at home with the externalist perspective. This is because quantum mechanics is intrinsically inclusive of the dynamics of preparing and forming the boundary conditions themselves that are not directly maneuverable by the external user. In other words, the internal user can influence the boundary conditions applied to the quantum phenomena which the external user can identify as such. A most telling example of the boundary conditions being susceptible to the internal user or the internal observer is seen in the implementation of chemical affinity. For instance, setting the boundary conditions for the onset of sharing an orbital electron between a pair of reacting molecules is due to the measurement by the participating internal observers.

The chemical affinity acting between an arbitrary pair of reacting molecules depends upon the boundary conditions applied to both of them. In the natural setting, the actualization of chemical affinity could be apparent only after the event. What could have been going on before its fixation must be the competition among the reacting molecules involved in meeting the reaction partners. The chemical reaction to be actualized should be the one that could proceed at the possible fastest rate among the mutually exclusive contenders, for there would remain no resources left over to the slower contenders. The role of the external user is just like that of a watchdog overseeing what the internal user has accomplished so far.

15.6. Only the Internal User Alone

The internal user of quantum mechanics can construct a material organization that may look complex and informational to the external user even without recourse to the notion called complexity or information. This observation touches upon quite a subtle issue on the nature of the propositions amenable to the external user. For instance, the statement like "Information is meaningful or meaningless" that may be accessible to the external user remains undecidable in its implication. This is because the predicate "to be meaningful or meaningless" accepts its quantification as implying that the implication of the predicate is highly dependent upon the context in which it could appear. In addition, although Shannon's information bits are decidable as facing the uncertainty to objectively be quantified, the unqualified predicate appearing in "Information is meaningful or meaningless" may also admit its quantification distinguishing between the universal and the existential quantifier as much as the subject does. Consequently, the resulting proposition would end up with at least that of second-order logic allowing for quantification applied to both the subject and predicate. In most cases, second-order logic remains undecidable and then not computable compared to first-order logic because of the intervention of an unqualified nature of the predicate to further be quantified. The present malaise would raise a serious challenge for our endeavor of making the issues of complexity and information to be decidable or to comprehensively be grasped in a meaningful manner.

One breakthrough to be figured out to get out of the present impasse is to notice that second-order logic would apply only to the external user. The internal user is free from suffering such a charge since it can be decidable in fixing and modifying the boundary conditions within the framework of quantum mechanics of itself.[6]

The decidability latent in the internal user is undoubtedly of quantum-mechanical origin. As far as empirical observations are concerned, quantum phenomena are probabilistic while also being decidable. Even in the simple paradigmatic example of two-slit experiment in quantum

---

[6]Second-order logic is undecidable and remains under-complete by itself. However, every empirical phenomenon is decidable in the sense that every experience conceivable in the empirical domain is about the act of a concrete particular nature. This may suggest that empirical phenomena could have the capacity of making the underlying second-order logic decidable. At this point enters the significance of the phenomenon of information. The price to pay for the appraisal of information as an agency for making second-order logic decidable is to part with its long-held tradition of computability, since computable information is limited to first-order logic.

mechanics, a single electron emitted from an electron gun passes through the two slits in a comprehensive manner and registers only a single spot on the screen placed behind the thin plate in which two adjacent slits are cut in parallel and open. The external user can say that the spots on the screen are generated in a probabilistic manner but cannot be sure whether a single electron would register a single spot before the event. Similarly, the internal user may also admit that the production of the spots on the screen would be probabilistic. But, the internal user definitely differs from the external counterpart in confirming that a single electron is decidable in registering a single spot on the screen.

The decidability of the internal user would thus become most acute and pronounced when chemical reactions are addressed within the framework of quantum mechanics. Any pair of the reactants making a chemical compound together lets one party be the resource to the other one and vice versa for preparing the compound. What is more, resource intake of any sort is mutually exclusive in that once a reactant has been captured as a resource by another party to make a compound, no third party is allowed to share the same resource unless the preceding compound is broken. Each reactant as a quantum particle then guarantees the mutual exclusivity of resource allocation. What underlies resource intake on the mutually exclusive basis is the principle of first come, first served.

One positive implication latent in mutual exclusivity of resource allocation is found in its dynamic characteristic, though the exclusivity in and of itself sounds a bit negative. The dynamic characteristic is selective in actualizing the chemical affinity facilitating the resource intake at the possible fastest rate in the face of the multitude of counterfactual conditionals. The internal user is thus synthetically selective, while the external user is no more than being analytically selective. The internal user is positively opportunistic in its activity of resource intake. Although both the conditional probability of duration and the class identity could serve as useful analytical tools for deciphering what complexity and information are all about, it is the internal user that provides the external user with an interesting object full of complexity and information.

Only the internal user alone can be responsible for constructing the organization of interest in a bottom-up manner as leaving behind the external user as a mere bystander. Such a synthetic construction can proceed even without referring to the direct help of the externalist nature such as the one under the guise of the closure of efficient causation of Rosen (1991) or the relational totality of Maturana (2011). In contrast, however, the external user does require the internal user so as to take advantage of the decidable synthesis attributed to the internal user to make the underlying second-order logic decidable. That is to say, the internal user can provide the external user with the necessary boundary conditions of a concrete nature under which the external user can grasp how the quantum phenomena of interest could proceed probabilistically in a decidable manner. Here, the decidability is meant to be just about an evidence for making any proposition decipherable in terms of the accepted fundamental predicates.

Participation of the internal user within the framework of quantum mechanics can make the issue of information decidable. The superficial malaise surrounding information has been that it is undecidable. Information is certainly undecidable and equivocal insofar as it is approached with use of the proposition in logic alone. Information would have to follow second-order logic unless it is further qualified. The standard practice appealing to the hypothetico-deductive scheme does not apply to the endeavor for making second-order logic decidable. This is because the hypothetico-deductive scheme takes it for granted that the scheme itself is justifiable without presenting the supporting evidence. The set of basic predicates employed for an arbitrary scheme of hypothetico-deduction does not allow for their further quantification on the methodological ground alone.

It is not the hypothetico-deductive scheme itself which can make the very scheme decidable and workable. While the hypothetico-deductive scheme has been quite effective in the practice of physical sciences, this versatile effectiveness of the scheme does not apply to the issue of information. The malaise of lacking the decidability is already latent even in the early phase of the development of quantum mechanics as revealed in the context-dependent nature of probabilities. Strangely enough, however, quantum mechanics has lived with the endogenous capacity of varying the context or the boundary conditions under which the specification of being probabilistic can be made variable even in the process, from the very beginning.

Problematic to addressing the issue of information in an unequivocal manner must be how one can come up with a dependable set of the irreducible fundamental predicates. Even if the initial proposition is framed in the mold of second-order logic going along with an equivocal variety and implication of the predicates, the chances of letting it to be transformed into that of first-order logic may be envisaged once the set of the irreducible predicates happens to be available. This irreducibility of the foundational predicates markedly differs from the standard scheme of hypothetico-deduction as accepted and practiced in the paradigm of computability, in the latter of which the set of the predicates is simply a matter of choice on the part of the practitioner. As a matter of fact, complete lossless integration of information as expected to proceed in the brain is non-computable because of the difficulty in finding a right set of basic predicates (Maguire *et al.*, 2014). Although it may be possible to imagine the computability of information within the framework of first-order logic, the inevitable quantification of the predicates may make the underlying logic higher than the first-order.

Once information or the material activity of informing something of something else is naturalized, the reliable reference must be the material support for guaranteeing the activity. That is the durable internal user of quantum mechanics. The internal user detecting the conditions of making itself durable and practicing its durability in the actual setting turns out to be a reliable reference for analyzing the underlying informational process in the eyes of the beholder, that is, the external user. As referring to the durable class identity of the internal user, the external user can take the internal observer as a foundational predicate for deciphering the underlying informational process.

Then, the issue would be reduced to how could the internal user be figured out and guaranteed in the material world. This must be totally empirical in seeking the decidability of material origin. A most conspicuous case of the emergence of such an internal user could be associated with the origins of life at least on our Earth.

15.7. Toward the Origins of Life

One likely pathway approaching toward the origins of life could be to examine the experimental likelihood of constructing a reaction cycle in an abiotic manner in the laboratory. A case in point could be an onset of the citric acid cycle without assuming the full-blown biology. The underlying issue must be how to reach biology as starting from chemistry.

Although the citric acid cycle operating inside the mitochondria is ubiquitous in the biological world (Buchanan *et al.*, 2000), one relevant issue is whether the reaction cycle could run even in the absence of all of the enzymes of biological origin including a lot of dehydrogenases, synthases and synthetases. One related experiment is to circulate the mixture only of all of the major carboxylic acid molecules constituting the cycle even including pyruvate as the carbon and energy sources in a flow reactor simulating a hydrothermal circulation of seawater near a hot vent on the primitive ocean floor. We could observe that the two carbon atoms in the form of the acetyl group released from a pyruvate molecule enter into the cycle and that they form a citrate molecule as synthetically reacting with an oxaloacetate molecule already present in the cycle. The two carbon atoms pulled into the cycle survived there at least over one round of the cycle operation of reaction (Matsuno, 2012).

An experimental demonstration of the abiotic genesis of the citric acid cycle would suggest the likelihood of a durable internal user of quantum mechanics since each chemical reaction appearing in the cycle is of quantum-mechanical origin. The two carbon atoms of the acetyl-group origin entering into the cycle as participating in the vehicle of a citrate molecule as their derivative product of the synthetic reaction with an oxaloacetate can survive in the cycle until finishing the first round of the cycle. This means that the carbon atoms leave behind the path-dependent history of the survival of the preceding one round of the reaction cycle.

The oxaloacetate as the end-product of the first round will then turn out to be another oxaloacetate as the updated initial reactant going to react with another acetyl group available in the immediate neighborhood outside. Once the synthetic reaction of making another citrate out of the updated oxaloacetate and another acetyl group is completed, the second round of the cycle will start. This sequence of going round the cycle could be repeated indefinitely unless it is severely interrupted otherwise externally. Instrumental to the lasting operation of the reaction cycle is the chemical affinity acting between the oxaloacetate molecule possessing the two carbon atoms carrying the path-dependent history of the survival of the preceding one round of the cycle and the additional two carbon atoms in the acetyl group to be found in the immediate neighborhood outside.[7]

Once the likelihood of a reaction cycle is confirmed on the empirical or the experimental basis without assuming the apparent contribution from the full-blown biology, we may be able to expect to approach the pathway toward the origins of life more closely. A key issue at this point is the transference of the information on the makeup of a functional organization such as a reaction cycle into a single molecule. In the case of the citric acid cycle, the intake of the two carbon atoms of the acetyl-group origin into the cycle takes place with the aid of the chemical affinity acting between an oxaloacetate molecule in the cycle and the acetyl group available in the immediate outside neighborhood of the cycle.

Furthermore the oxaloacetate molecule can incorporate into itself the two carbon atoms which carry the path-dependent history of how each of the two experiences the reaction pathway step by step until completing one round of the cycle. This is equivalent to saying that the oxaloacetate molecule carries the memory of each reaction step constituting the whole

---

[7]The indefinite operation of a reaction cycle may look a form of self-reference. However, it is free from suffering the malaise imputed to self-reference. The oxaloacetate molecule referred to by the acetyl group entering into the citric acid cycle constantly exchanges the constituent carbon atoms with different individuals of the similar kind. Consequently, that updated oxaloacetate molecule prevents itself from being associated with an invariable individual self of a definite nature even if it may be referred to by the same name of oxaloacetate molecule belonging to the same invariable class category. Such an association of the individual with the class could be simply a category mistake. Despite that, the predicate for qualifying a quantum particle is multifarious in its implication. Each carbon atom participating in the operation of the citric acid cycle is qualitatively malleable enough to accommodate itself with a wide variety of chemical affinity even including the one being susceptible to the path-dependent histories while leaving its irreducible individuality as a quantum intact. Information is just a factor for transforming the universal quantifier applied to the predicate, rather than to the subject, into the existential quantifier. Empirical phenomena of a quantum origin are intrinsically competent in making second-order logic decidable.

reaction cycle. For each surviving carbon atom to be found in the oxaloacetate as the reaction product from the preceding one round of the cycle has experienced the whole cycle from within. That carbon atom experiencing the preceding one round of the cycle participates in the succeeding act of pulling in another carbon atom from the outside as crossing different tenses. What can be revealed at this point is that the reaction product of a reaction cycle which can exhibit a chemical affinity toward the outside of the cycle so as to recruit the necessary resources can maintain the memory of how the reaction cycle operates at least over the preceding one round of the cycle. At this point, it should be noted that it is the reaction cycle itself that can read and interpret the memory as such. The consequence of reading and interpreting the memory is seen in the implementation of the chemical affinity having a historical path-dependent nature.

Of course, it remains hard for the external user of quantum mechanics to decipher the memory of the cycle operation of each reaction stored in an oxaloacetate molecule in the citric acid cycle as it is. Rather, it is the internal user of quantum mechanics that can read the memory stored in the oxaloacetate molecule as in the form of the path-dependent history of how each carbon atom entering the cycle moves around the cycle until it finally leaves the cycle. Each step-by-step transit of the entering carbon atom from the outside follows the chemical reasons in the cycle.

Release of the carbon atom from the citric acid cycle is made possible only from the carboxyl group $-COO-$, and the carboxyl group is further required to be attached to the functional group functioning as an acceptor of the donated electron in order to make it easier to transform the carboxyl group into the outgoing carbon dioxide molecule through oxidation. In addition, each of the entering two carbon atoms in the form of acetyl group $-CO-CH_3$ is required to be transformed into the carboxyl group $-COO-$ beforehand. The path-dependent history that each entering carbon atom carries is thus full of detailed chemistry.[8] The internal user can provide

---

[8]In particular, the reaction pathway of an oxidative decarboxylation of isocitrate toward alpha-ketoglutarate in the operation of the citric acid cycle lets one of the three carboxyl groups in the molecule appearing as a reaction intermediary have a carbonyl group beta to it. The carbonyl group serves as an electron-withdrawing group acting as an agent

the external user with the organizational information latent in the reaction cycle in focus under the guise of the reaction product that can exhibit the chemical affinity to resources to be taken in.

The citric acid cycle is a cycle of carboxylic acid molecules. Likewise, it would also be conceivable to imagine a putative RNA-cycle and a protein-cycle in the prebiotic phase in addition to the DNA-protein cycle that is ubiquitous in the biological world. The common denominator is the occurrence of a reaction cycle. This observation may provide the origins of life with an inverted perspective such that what should be focused upon is not the informational molecules, but is rather the informational reaction cycles. The informational decidability is sought in the reaction cycles themselves, rather than in the reacting molecules in isolation. The reacting molecules can be informational only in the sense of a representation of the supporting reaction cycles. This change of the perspective may be relevant even in theory alone.

Once the issue of the origins of life is grasped within the framework of quantum mechanics, it would become inevitable to distinguish the external user from the internal user. Although any theory in quantum mechanics can easily be associated with the practice by the external user, it would raise a serious drawback if the issue of information is focused upon. Addressing the issue of information would have to end up with being equivocal if second-order logic intrinsic to quantum mechanics is left unattended.

Quantum mechanics in theory alone is probabilistic and undecidable. However, once it is approached empirically, quantum mechanics can be competent enough to figure out a way of empirical qualification to make it decidable as getting rid of the tenacious undecidable nature exclusively of a theoretical origin. This is to call our attention to the internal user that is decidable in and of itself, and is in essence equivalent to appraising the occurrence of a reaction cycle in the empirical world. The internal user makes itself decidable through the constant act of actualizing the factual as facing a multitude of the counterfactual conditionals. The naturalized

---

of oxidative decarboxylation of the carboxyl group adjacent to it. This is due to a strong electronegativity of an oxygen atom of the carbonyl group.

guidelines for fixing the factual could be the principle of first come, first served on the ground of the history-dependent affinity acting between the elements constituting an organization and another elements to be found in the external resources nearby.

The history-dependent affinity is accessible only at the durable now distinguishing itself from preceding historical events, rather than at the present moment in tenseless time as practiced in physics. The present tense in tenseless time may allow us to address the presence of an invariable object in a tenseless manner in the sense that it can invariably be approached in whichever tense out of the past, present and future tense. In other words, the present tense in tenseless time could be taken to exhibit an intimate affinity both to the past and the future tense interchangeably only on the methodological ground without taking any trouble to provide a supporting empirical evidence. In physics observing tenseless time, there is no likelihood of complexity and organization to be established as crossing and integrating different tenses.

In contrast, the occurrence of the chemical affinity leaving behind the path-dependent history takes it a serious matter to figure out the empirical underpinning for guaranteeing the scheme of referring to the past in the present. The likelihood of referring to the past that is adjacent to the present assumes an intrinsic affinity between the two tenses. Biology takes it a serious issue to figure out the empirical underpinning for guaranteeing the scheme of crossing and integrating the past and the present tense at the durable now. That is an issue of the durable now from the historical and evolutionary perspective.

The informational implication of the appearance of a durable reaction cycle in evolution may set a historical watershed for letting first-order logic be resurrected even in the theoretical practice of quantum mechanics. Crucial at this point is that the internal user of quantum mechanics happens to provide the external user with the dependable identity of the class property occurring with the probability unity under the condition of letting the internal user be durable. Then, the external user takes the durable class identity to be a foundational predicate to decipher the supporting evolutionary process, of course, to a certain limited extent. The material vehicle upholding the foundational predicate workable in the resurrected first-order logic toward the external user must be the informational molecule such as a DNA or RNA as a reliable representation of the information to be latent in the durable reaction cycle.

15.8. Concluding Remarks

Practical effectiveness of the state description in quantum mechanics has been undeniable and unbeatable. Nonetheless, we are required to have second thoughts to the time-honored practice of accepting the state description once the issue of complexity and information appearing in the empirical world happens to be scrutinized in a serious manner. The notion called a state has been about something that can be supposed to stand alone by itself by definition. Once the state is accepted as a basic factor for specifying the descriptive predicate of quantum phenomena, the resulting proposition would have to be forced to follow first-order logic in the sense that the predicate is not subject to any further quantification.

In this regard, the empirical practice of quantum mechanics still remains ambivalent in the good sense of the word. While the theory of quantum mechanics being faithful to the notion of state may be asked to follow first-order logic, the empirical qualification of quantum mechanics suggests a testimony to the contrary as revealed in John Wheeler's aphorism as saying "No phenomenon is a real phenomenon until it is an observed phenomenon". Measurement is prior to making the quantum phenomena decidable, instead of merely being a subsidiary means of confirming the decidable theoretical predictions to be contrived otherwise. In addition, no theoretical prediction to be confirmed or refuted could be conceivable unless the notion of state that can stand alone by itself is accepted.

Information turns the situation totally upside down. Gregory Bateson's aphorism referring to information as "difference making a difference" reminds us that information is intrinsically undecidable in climbing up the ladder of a difference making the "difference making a difference" ad infinitum. Theory alone cannot make information decidable. Rather, it is information that makes a phenomenon decidable thanks to the participation of the internal observer. Quantum mechanics can certainly take advantage of such a qualifying capacity of information of empirical origin. Information makes quantum mechanics decidable. Information is about the act of making whatever issue concrete enough while being lined with a lot of counterfactual conditionals. One necessary price to pay for seeking the decidable capacity within information is the appraisal of the internal user of quantum mechanics in place of the longstanding notion of a state that could be claimed to stand alone of itself by the external user.

The conditional probability of duration is to the internal user of quantum mechanics what Born's probability rule is to the external user of quantum mechanics.

Bibliography

Bohr, N., 1987. *The Philosophical Writings of Niels Bohr*, 3 vols., Ox Bow Press, Woodbridge CT, U.S.A.

Buchanan, B.B., Gruissem, W., and Jones, R.L., 2000. *Biochemistry & Molecular Biology of Plants*, 1st ed. American Society of Plant Physiologists, Rockville MD, U.S.A.

Einstein, A., Podolsky, B., and Rosen, N., 1935. Can quantum-mechanical description of physical reality be considered complete? *Phys. Rev.* **47**, 777-781.

Maguire, P., Moser, P., Maguire, R., and Griffith, V., 2014. Is consciousness computable? Quantifying integrated information using algorithmic information theory. *arXiv:* 1405.0126v1 [cs.IT].

Matsuno, K., 2012. Chemical evolution as a concrete scheme for naturalizing the relative-state of quantum mechanics. *BioSystems* **109**, 159–168. doi:10.1016/j.biosystems.2012.04.002.

Matsuno, K., 2014. Self-identities and durability of biosystems via their abstracting capacity. *BioSystems* **120**, 31-34. doi:10.1016/j.biosystems.2014.04.006.

Matsuno, K., 2015. On the physics of the emergence of sensorimotor control in the absence of the brain. *Prog. Biophys. Mol. Biol.* **119**, 313-323. doi:10.1016/j.pbiomolbio.2015.08.004

Maturana, H., 2011. Twenty years after — preface to the second edition of origins and implications of autopoiesis (Paucar-Caceres, A., and Harnden, R., trans.). *Construct. Found.* **6**, 293-306. www.univie.ac.at/constructivism/journal/6/3/293.

Mermin, D., 2014. Physics: QBism puts scientist back into science. *Nature* **507**, 421-423. doi:10.1038/507421a.

Rosen, R., 1991. *Life Itself: a Comprehensive Inquiry into the Nature, Origin, and Fabrication of Life*. Columbia University Press, New York, NY U.S.A.

Index

present tense, 377
principia, 150
principle of first come, 377
principle of first come, first served, 370
prior analytics, 135, 138–139
Prisoner's Dilemma, 189–190
probabilistic predictions, 357
probabilistic proposition, 355–357
probability, 17, 20, 22, 26, 28, 30, 353
    p. distribution, 22, 26, 28
    p. mass function, 22
probability amplitude, 354
probability assignment, 357
probability laws, 357
probability of duration, 359
probability theory, 357–358
probability unity, 358
problem, 17, 20, 29, 31
process, 54–55, 57, 59, 63, 68, 71, 74, 76, 78, 83, 85, 90–91, 96
    Planckian, 53–54, 68, 74, 80
    random, 77, 80, 83, 90
property, 130
protein-cycle, 376
protein-length, 70, 97
    7-mer, 66, 68, 71, 78
pyruvate, 373
Pythagoras, 264

Q

QBism, 353, 362
QBist, 362
quanta, 59, 84, 87
quantifier, 369
quantization, 73, 75, 77, 85, 87
quantum Bayesianism, 353, 362
quantum mechanics, 60, 84, 86–87, 353–354, 361
quantum of action, 72, 84
quantum particle, 374
quantum phenomena, 360
quantum physics, 357
quantum randomness, 250, 266, 269, 271

quantum-mechanical law of motion, 354
qubit, xv, 250, 271–272

R

random, 17, 20, 22, 27, 32
    sequence, 18–19, 21, 23, 30
randomness, 20, 32, 49
Rate Amplification through the Substrate-Enhanced Reaction (*see also* RASER), 76
Ray Solomonoff, 157
reaction cycle, 353, 363–364, 366–367, 372–375, 377–378
reaction pathway, 364, 375
reaction product, 363–365, 374–375
reasoning, 20
reductionism, 198
reductionist methodology of science, 158
relational totality, 371
relative uncomputability, 6, 12
res extensa, 252, 259, 271
resonance, 53, 66, 70, 81, 96
resource element, 366
resource intake, 365, 370
result, 18, 20, 29
RNA, 66–67, 378
RNA levels, 67
    in breast tissues, 66–67
RNA molecule, 367
RNA-cycle, 376
rule, 23

S

saving the appearances, 146
scale, 178
second-order logic, 356, 369–371, 374, 376
selection, 54, 69–70, 72, 82–83, 86, 90
    goal-directed, 54, 82
selective manifestation of information, 120
selective-structure duality, 145
self-organization, 91, 97